When Nationalism Began to Hate

When Nationalism Began to Hate

Imagining Modern Politics in Nineteenth-Century Poland

BRIAN PORTER

New York   Oxford

Oxford University Press

2000

Oxford University Press

Oxford   New York
Athens   Auckland   Bangkok   Bogotá   Buenos Aires   Calcutta
Cape Town   Chennai   Dar es Salaam   Delhi   Florence   Hong Kong   Istanbul
Karachi   Kuala Lumpur   Madrid   Melbourne   Mexico City   Mumbai
Nairobi   Paris   São Paulo   Singapore   Taipei   Tokyo   Toronto   Warsaw

and associated companies in
Berlin   Ibadan

Published by Oxford University Press
198 Madison Avenue, New York, New York 10016

Oxford is a registered trademark of Oxford University Press

Library of Congress Cataloging-in-Publication Data
Porter, Brian (Brian A.)
When nationalism began to hate : imagining modern politics in
nineteenth-century Poland / Brian Porter.
p.   cm.
Includes bibliographical references and index.
ISBN 0–19–513146–0
1. Nationalism—Poland—History—19th century.   2. Poland—
Politics and government—1795–1918.   3. Anti-Semitism—Poland.
I. Title.   II. Title: Imagining modern politics in nineteenth-
century Poland.
DK4349.3.P67   2000
320.54'09'034—dc21   99–20039

9 8 7 6 5 4 3 2 1

Printed in the United States of America
on acid-free paper

To Susana, Sofia, and Alexandra

Acknowledgments

Perhaps the most satisfying part of completing this book is the opportunity it provides to thank those I am fortunate enough to consider mentors and friends. Special recognition must go to David McDonald, who shepherded this work through its incarnation as a doctoral dissertation at the University of Wisconsin. The help of Lawrence Dickey and Alfred Senn must also be singled out, along with that of all the others in Madison who provided me with such an excellent graduate education. If they find it hard to recognize the book now, any improvement is due mainly to the helpful criticism I have received in more recent years from Stanislaus Blejwas, Robert Blobaum, Jane Burbank, Prasenjit Duara, Todd Endelman, Thomas Green, Raymond Grew, William Hagen, Janine Holc, Jerzy Jedlicki, Michael Kennedy, Padraic Kenney, Valerie Kivelson, Ezra Mendelsohn, Norman Naimark, Bill Rosenberg, Rebecca Scott, Keely Stauter-Halsted, Andrzej Walicki, Larry Wolff, and Ernie Young. Several groups deserve collective thanks for listening to presentations related to this work and for providing me with invaluable feedback: the University of Michigan's Center for Russian and East European Studies, the junior faculty reading group of Michigan's history department, the members of Jerzy Jedlicki's colloquium at the Polish Academy of Sciences, and my own students from History 652. I also wish to express my gratitude to the editors of the *Journal of Modern History*, the *American Historical Review*, *Studia Polityczne*, and *Slavic Review* for publishing articles derived from this project. Finally, I could never have completed this book were it not for financial assistance from the Fulbright Fellowship, the International Research and Exchange Board, the Faculty Recognition Fund of the University of Michigan, and the Joint Committee on Eastern Europe of the American Council of Learned Societies and the Social Science Research Council.

Three wonderful women entered my life while I worked on this project: my wife Susana and my daughters Sofia and Alexandra. For guaranteeing that Polish history will always be the *second* most important thing in my life, I am eternally grateful to my family. With all my love, I dedicate this volume to them.

June 1999   B. P.
Ann Arbor, Michigan

Contents

When Nationalism Began to Hate

Introduction

During the late nineteenth century (so the story goes) Poland entered the modern world. As this happened, an appropriately modern form of nationalism emerged, one that allowed all Poles to identify with "their" nation. The old forms of elite political culture became irrelevant as various mass movements burst onto the public stage and the vectors of power shifted toward "the people." Now workers and peasants would be players in the political game and the domination of the nobility and the intelligentsia would come to an end. According to the historian Anna Żarnowska, this process reached its climax during the 1905 Revolution: "The most essential element introduced by the Revolution to the political culture of society in the Polish Kingdom was the democratization of political life, a dramatic expansion of the circle of people not only hungry for political knowledge but also actively involved in political life. [The Revolution also brought about] the active inclusion of the 'common man,' not only in collective political protest but also in the creation of institutions and political organizations."[1] Even the definition of the nation would have to change in this new world, and Poland would be reimagined as a broadly based cultural community encompassing all those who spoke Polish. The old, restrictive conception of the nation (with membership limited to the nobility and the intelligentsia) had been challenged throughout the nineteenth century; now it would be consigned irrevocably to the archives. The new, more "democratic" Polish nation was firmly established. As Andrzej Walicki put it, "the 'nation of the people' . . . was the beginning of something radically new—of the *modern* Polish nation, as a body embracing all strata of the Polish-speaking population."[2]

For the student of nationalism, this story will be familiar. The adjective "modern" is attached to "nationalism" with such regularity that we have come to take this linkage for granted, to assume that the nation is primarily a means of establishing collective identity in the era of mass politics and that modernity necessarily works through the political form of the nation-state. Scholars then worry about how and when "modern nationalism" was born and how this form of identity structures social relations today. It is usually taken for granted that nationalism serves to draw boundaries around human communities, to impose some degree of homogeneity within the nation, and to define those outside as alien. Julie Skurski reflects a common view when she argues that "representations of national belonging weave together images that promise collective unity as well as collective exclusions."[3] If the nation is necessarily rooted in modernity, and if modernity is distinguished by the rise of mass participatory politics, then the nation provides a common bond for these new communities of political actors and allows or compels people to imagine new and higher walls between "us" (who must be in some way alike, who must share an identity) and "them."[4]

Some scholars have gone a step further, suggesting that nationalism necessarily moved from the benign delineation of cultural communities to more violent forms of imposed exclusion. For example, Peter Pulzer believes that "nationalism degenerates, like the larger Romantic movement of which it was a part, first into irresponsibility, then into nihilism. . . . Though often inspired in its first stage by the urge to emancipate, it finds its logical conclusion in a paroxysm of destructiveness."[5] In Central and Eastern Europe this "degeneration" of nationalism is typically associated with the rise of modern anti-Semitism. Many scholars presume that as nationalism was transformed from a narrow conspiracy of idealistic elites into a mass movement, it inevitably became mired in popular xenophobia and had to reconfigure its rhetoric accordingly. Hillel Kieval, for example, suggests that nationalists in late nineteenth-century Prague abandoned liberal tolerance as they adapted to the changed electoral landscape of modern politics.[6] Many authors have in essence equated mass nationalism with hatred, assuming that when one tries to appeal to a broad public, long-standing popular animosities will overwhelm all but the most dedicated multiculturalists. Ezra Mendelsohn argues that "the triumph of unbridled Polish nationalism was bound to be accompanied by anti-Semitism, given the legacy of Polish–Jewish relations and the supreme Polish nationalist doctrine of 'Poland for the Poles.'"[7] Here Polish–Jewish hostility appears as a constant force which any mass nationalist movement must take into account.

In hindsight, it is easy to assume that within each nationalism there exists some force driving toward an exclusionary and disciplinary logic. The concept of the nation itself seems to push particular individuals or groups—either political dissidents or ethnic minorities—into the status of "outsider." But as self-evident as this development may seem, it was not always true, nor did it inevitably become true. It cannot be denied that nationalism entered the twentieth century as an ideology of violence and hatred, and that even its more innocent forms now tend to enforce cultural homogeneity and suppress difference. Clearly, nationalism today is a means to establish and reinforce collective identity, to designate what "we" are like and how we differ from "them," and to specify what political consequences should flow from these distinctions. But while it may appear that drawing lines around collective identities and defining relations of authority are inherent and predictable functions of nationalism, the Polish case demonstrates the complexity of this process. As we will see in chapter 1, the nation *became* an enclosed space, but it was not always held within such rigid boundaries. For the first half of the nineteenth century, to speak of national liberation for Poland was to imagine a chiliastic moment of emancipation for all humanity—"for our freedom and yours," as a slogan of the day put it. Polish patriots of that era were *not* fighting for a "Poland for the Poles," and ethnicity was *not* the prism through which they perceived their world. Although they were concerned with issues of language and culture, they employed a definition of the nation that permitted (and often explicitly mandated) that Ukrainians, Lithuanians, and even Jews be accepted as Poles. By the twentieth century, Polish intellectuals had developed ideologies of both social discipline and ethnic hatred, but in order to do so, they had to reconfigure the very concept of the nation. Before the nation could oppress or exclude, those who talked about Poland had to place this concept within a framework that allowed them to talk about both *authority* and *cultural identity.* Neither discipline nor exclusion was definitionally linked to the idea of the nation, nor did nationalism inevitably "degenerate" toward authoritarianism. Only after decades of contestation could the nation become a vehicle for the exertion of social control and the establishment of mutually antagonistic identities. Only with time would nationalism begin to hate.

This book explores how writers, artists, political activists, philosophers, poets, journalists, military officers, and others in nineteenth-century Poland used the term "nation." It traces the development of this concept up to the moment when nationalism became a mass movement, arguing that it became an ideology of hatred in conjunction with—*but not simply because of*—its reconfiguration as a vehicle for popular politics. We should take care not to blur the distinction between two important questions: (1) how did millions of people come to accept some form of national identity, making this one of the defining elements of nineteenth- and twentieth-century politics; and (2) what sort of conceptual universe did these people enter when they chose to talk about the nation? As Josep Llobera has argued, scholars too often conflate the origins of *mass* nationalism with the origins of nationalism in general.[8] The rhetoric of Polish nationalism existed long before the emergence of a mass national movement in the early twentieth century—just as the idea of "France" predated 1789— but in both cases "the nation" was discussed only within a relatively narrow social circle. The new voices employing the term "nation" at the turn of the century could (and did) stretch the boundaries of patriotic vocabularies in many directions, but they could not pretend that those boundaries did not exist. To speak the language of nationalism, one had to accept some established conventions and definitions and choose from a limited repertoire of worldviews. Once a worker or peasant became "national," there were limits to what he or she could imagine, to what could be said, and to what had to remain unspoken. These boundaries were always changing—and after the turn of the century the new peasant patriots would change them even more—but the configuration of the nationalist discourse at the moment it was deployed within the arena of mass politics would have profound consequences.

It follows that no explanation of nationalism can be reduced to a discussion of social structures or changes in social relations, as many scholars have claimed.[9] It is undeniably true, as Robert Blobaum has argued, that in 1905 "politics ceased to be the preserve of a gentry and intelligentsia elite" and that the historian (even the his-

torian of political thought) must show an appreciation for the social realm and for
the voices of subalterns.[10] But this does not mean that we ought to invert the arrows
of causation and look for the sources of ideology within "the people" or within abstract social forces. Instead, we must focus on the dialogical nature of political rhetoric
and explore the ways in which elites imposed (or attempted to impose) vocabularies of order and social discipline on a vox populi that never ceased to talk back.[11]
Chatterjee speaks of a "coming together of two domains of politics" (the elite and
the popular) and recognizes that "the language of nationalism underwent a quite radical transformation of meaning in the peasant domain of politics." Elite nationalism,
he concludes, was never able to "absorb and appropriate its other within a single
homogeneous unity."[12] But the methodological consequence of this observation (as
Chatterjee's own scholarly practice demonstrates) is not to abandon the study of elite
discourse, or to describe well-formulated ideologies as if they were mere reactions
to (or worse, reflections of) popular desires. Nor should we allow ourselves to imagine a clear dichotomy between the "ideologies" of intellectuals and the "practices"
of the masses. Instead, we need to read the intelligentsia's texts with an eye toward
their struggle against the heterogeneity of social reality, a reality with its own well-
formulated worldviews, its own discursive practices, and even its own distinctive
ideologies. In fact, we are really dealing with more than two domains: there is too
much variety within each of Chatterjee's categories to sustain such a crisp distinction. It might be better to describe the intelligentsia's search for coherence and singularity, set against a world of irreducible multiplicity. More than twenty years ago
Theodore Zeldin directed our attention to the "makers of myths" who strive to "master variety and make it uniform," and since that time we have grown accustomed to
considering how discursive formations structure and limit the very choices we perceive, how the plurality of social existence can be disciplined in ways that limit the
expression of "popular aspirations."[13] In this book I attempt to penetrate the world
of those who talked about Poland, defined what Poland was, and (in a sense) "created" modern Poland. My objects of inquiry are the discursive frameworks that were
available in 1905, within which "the masses" would henceforth articulate their desires (often in idiosyncratic ways) and talk about what it meant to be Polish, and with
which the elites could attempt (with only limited success) to impose social discipline.
I set the stage for twentieth-century politics by explaining how it became possible
for the concept of the nation to serve as a means of defining identities in the modern
world and by elaborating what it meant for the nation to become popular at that particular moment. I turn a critical eye on the problem first posed by Hans Kohn so long
ago: how was the "idea of nationalism" reconfigured as Poland moved into the "age
of nationalism"?

    Poland, of course, was not invented or imagined ex nihilo by a small group of
intellectuals; it had an undeniable cultural foundation. In the realm of the quotidian,
some conception of what Stephanie Platz calls the "ethnonation" existed long before
the term "nation" came to have meaning within the framework of modern politics.[14]
That is, people spoke Polish and were aware that this language differed from German, Ukrainian, and Yiddish; people cooked their barszcz in a particular way and
recognized that other people made borshch or borscht using slightly different recipes;

people celebrated weddings, funerals, and religious holidays with distinctive rituals and realized that those in the next village or province did not share these customs. Moreover, people configured (and still configure) highly elaborated identities around these everyday cultural practices. But it must not be taken for granted that any of this necessarily led to, or even had anything to do with, the development of the concept of "nation." It is essential to distinguish between an enacted Polishness (understood as a cluster of cultural practices) and the idea of the Polish nation. The latter had specific (albeit contested) meanings within a recognized sphere of elite politics, while the former served to define social relations on local and personal levels, regardless of how or even whether it was explicitly labeled and discussed. Often such identities *were* explicit, ensuring that the intelligentsia's vision of the nation would encounter other, equally well-developed depictions of social relations. We are dealing with a clash of alternative worlds, not a clear-cut confrontation between ideas and reality, ideologies and practices. However articulated, though, this enacted and locally formalized Polishness was not necessarily linked to a politicized concept of the Polish nation.

As I argue in chapter 1, during the early nineteenth century the "national cause" was often discussed without any reference to the ethnonation. In subsequent chapters I show how these two domains came together during the 1870s, 1880s, and 1890s—how it came to be taken as self-evident that "the nation" was coterminous with a sociological formation of "Poles" who possessed identifiable characteristics and enacted their everyday Polishness in a particular way. There was nothing inherent within the concept of "the Polish nation" ensuring that this expression would eventually delineate a concretely defined social group, or even that it would come to serve primarily as a tool for demarcating "us" and "them." In fact, the opposite is true: the early nineteenth-century definition of the nation in Poland specifically rejected any dependency on sociology, concentrating instead on the realm of the "national spirit" and the "national ideal." Instead of developing from the sociocultural to the political, Polish nationalism began as a politicized ideology and was only gradually linked to the quotidian domain of Polishness. Andrzej Nowak has observed a striking gap between the private talk of Poles in the 1820s and 1830s (in which one could easily express antipathy toward all things Russian) and the nationalist discourse of the day (in which such sentiments were virtually unspeakable).[15] How one felt about one's own identity and how one perceived the differences between one's own group and the surrounding "others" had little connection to the rhetoric of nationalism. For this link to be established, the whole discourse of the nation would have to be reformulated. In the 1840s and 1850s, to fight for the nation was to fight for universalist (and abstract) ideals of freedom and justice; by 1900, to fight for the nation was to struggle against concrete enemies and (to facilitate this struggle) to build ideological and cultural unity within the nation. As the nation became sociological, and thus more tightly linked to the everyday enactment of Polishness and the ethnolinguistic study of Polish society, so did it come to serve as a means to talk about social discipline and international struggle.

By casting a light on the intelligentsia's struggle to construct modern ways of being national, I hope to interrogate more deeply the accepted narrative of Poland's political modernization. Political culture was indeed becoming more inclusive and participatory as the Revolution of 1905 approached, and mass politics did indeed explode onto the scene during that momentous year. But these developments were accompanied by a crucial transformation in political rhetoric—not in the direction of popular empowerment, as is so often implied, but toward the ordering and disciplining of these newly mobilized "masses" by a self-proclaimed elite. At the center of this process stood the concept of the nation, which was transformed so that it could sustain, rather than subvert, hierarchy and organization. Meanwhile the rhetoric of nationalism also became a site for talking about difference and exclusion, and eventually about hatred and struggle. We cannot explain these developments simply by referring to Poland's modernization or to the rise of mass politics, because this new way of talking about the nation also structured the way Polish intellectuals imagined their position in historical time, and the way they defined modernity itself.

It has become common to highlight the imagined quality of the nation, to unpack the ways in which ideas of community are constructed, imposed, and enforced, but even as scholars chip away at the presumed solidity of the nation's sociological or ethnographic foundations, many continue to accept well-established stories about the nation's movement through historical time. It is widely assumed that *with time* the ideology of nationalism must necessarily move in a certain direction and that theorists of the nation must contend with the movement of time toward modernity. That is, we accept that the definition of the nation is mutable but we cling to the idea that as it changes it must adapt to the demands of modernization, to the changing conditions of a world moving along an overarching timeline. Even Benedict Anderson's provocative and influential discussion of temporality still posits a single style of national time ("secular, serial time") and contrasts it with a premodern, prenational way of perceiving one's relationship to the past and the future.[16] Prasenjit Duara goes a step further, emphasizing "how historical actors mobilize particular representations of nation or community against other representations and, while doing so, appropriate dispersed meanings and pasts as their own."[17] Building on this approach, I argue that perceptions of historical time—the way people conceptualize history and prophecy, the means by which they plot their lives vis-à-vis the past and the future—structure and limit how the nation can be imagined. Instead of describing the nation as something that changes over time, or something generated by the movement of social formations through time, I show how, in the Polish case, both nationalism and the historiosophy of the nation were contested and variable, and how the latter conditioned the former. The march of historical time was not just the background to the development of "modern" nationalism; instead, the way in which modernity itself was perceived and positioned in time shaped how people talked about the nation.

Following Brian C. J. Singer, I explore the nation as a chronotope, as something which, in its many forms, is linked to variety of temporal visions.[18] If we approach nationalism in this way, we gain new insights into the process by which the nation became a space within which people could talk about ethnic animosity and the enforcement of cultural and political cohesion; we can see more clearly how the concept of the nation contributed to the ordering and structuring of political modernity.

As is explained in chapters 2 and 3, Polish liberals of the 1860s and 1870s developed a sociological and ethnographic definition of the nation, in sharp contrast to what they considered to be the abstractions of romantic idealism. Their nation would be a community of Polish speakers, inhabiting a specific territory and cultivating certain customs and norms. This new way of talking about the nation, described at the time as a "modern" approach to Polishness, did not necessarily lead to exclusionary identities or disciplinary politics, because these tendencies were held in check by a vision of progressive time. Even as writers in the 1870s solidified the nation in social space, they emphasized the mutability of nearly all the characteristics they cited as markers of national belonging. Everything social was advancing through time toward a liberal utopia, they believed, and thus few exclusions or inclusions could be permanent or inevitable.

Chapters 4, 5, and 6 show how the ensuing debates over the nature of historical time led Polish intellectuals to rethink the construction of political power. Socialists, liberals, and even some populists sustained a commitment to a progressive future, and this allowed them to accept a greater degree of ideological diversity and social conflict in the national present. Poland ought to be united, they argued, but such cohesion need not exist today because it was promised by a vision of the future. A number of disillusioned populists, however, were less sanguine as they looked at the present and dreamed of the nation to come. These young authors, who would later become the leaders of the radical right nationalist movement, soon abandoned their faith in historical time; as a result, they were driven to an agenda of enforcing national unity, discipline, and obedience. If the future could not be counted on to bring Poles together, then the nationally conscious elite would have to compel such unity today.

Finally, chapters 7 and 8 trace the impact of various historiosophies on the reconfiguration of social space, on the ways in which "Poles" were defined vis-à-vis a variety of "others" (above all, the Jews). Again, I argue that those intellectuals (mainly socialists) who managed to retain their faith in historical change could also imagine a world in which the boundaries between ethnic groups were porous and not necessarily of critical importance. Those who renounced their trust in time, however, perceived a world populated by mutually hostile and competing communities surrounded by high walls of inclusion and exclusion. The way people positioned themselves in historical time, therefore, enabled—perhaps, on one level, caused—the development of exclusionary and disciplinary forms of nationalism. The locating and relocating of the nation within time, and eventually (fatally) outside of time, made it possible for nationalism to begin to hate.

National Democracy

Our story will ultimately lead us to a movement known as National Democracy. When the resurrected Polish state held elections for a constitutional assembly in January, 1919, the National Democrats emerged as the largest political party. The group's strength would ebb and flow during the interwar years but the Endecja (as it was commonly called) remained one of Poland's most powerful political forces.[19] A few citations from the movement's leader, Roman Dmowski, will indicate what sort of organization this was.

> The only salvation for us is to stop being an incoherent, loose mob, and to change into a strongly organized, disciplined army.[20]

> The state, if it is healthy and based on a strong foundation, will always assimilate foreign tribes politically and culturally, whether through violence or not. . . . The state will always and everywhere, more or less consciously, aspire to create cultural unity.[21]

> In relations with other nations there is neither right nor wrong, there is only strength and weakness.[22]

> The Jewish population is undeniably a parasite on the social body of whatever country it inhabits.[23]

I will analyze these passages later, but for now they should suffice as a summary of National Democracy's main tenets. The movement created a new form of Polish nationalism, one that embraced anti-Semitism, chauvinism, and authoritarianism. This book will trace the origins of National Democratic thought and explain how it became possible to articulate these ideas within the framework of Polish nationalism. But this study will offer far more than just another intellectual genealogy of the radical right. By placing the darker side of the Endecja at the center of my analysis, I problematize something that is all too often underemphasized by historians of Polish nationalism: the link between the construction of modernity, the exertion of authority, and the establishment of exclusionary boundaries around the nation. By integrating these developments into the wider history of Polish political culture, we will be forced to challenge some of the most cherished narratives of Polish historiography and rethink the very nature of Poland's modernity.

Most Polish historians today are highly critical of the memory of National Democracy. However, the interpretive frameworks used to analyze the Polish radical right often make it difficult to focus on the darker aspects of the movement's rhetoric and to position the Endecja adequately within the broader history of Polish nationalism. The most common approach has been to insert the National Democrats into a timeless (or perhaps merely endless) debate between "realism" and "idealism" in Polish intellectual life.[24] According to this story, since the eighteenth century the Poles have been divided between the advocates of "realism" and the proponents of "idealism." The latter have embraced maximalist agendas of national independence and/or social justice, and in doing so they have pushed Polish political thought beyond the realm of the feasible. In chasing after dreams, the argument goes, this sort of patriotism does more harm than good because it accomplishes nothing (by definition) while provoking retribution from Poland's enemies. In contrast, the "realistic" school has been willing to challenge the cherished dreams of the idealists and work for what can actually be achieved in any given situation. Within this dichotomy, the

National Democrats are firmly in the camp of the realists. Barbara Toruńczyk, for example, has argued that the elastic political methods and the attainable goals of the Endeks distinguished them from their contemporaries, so much so that "realism in politics . . . is conceivable in Poland only on the basis of an in-depth consideration of the political teaching of National Democracy."[25] This approach is defended as a "sober" or "objective" way to analyze the historical contribution of National Democracy, with appropriate scholarly remove from divisive polemics about anti-Semitism or right-wing politics.[26] For those interested primarily in the tactics employed by Polish political activists in their quest for national independence, it makes sense to focus on the programatic flexibility of the Endecja and to praise them for their willingness to work within the existing political, military, and diplomatic circumstances. For those authors in communist Poland who looked for tactical models in their national past, the National Democrats seemed more responsible and reasonable than the advocates of armed insurrection. When we find serious and respected scholars writing in such measured tones about the "realism" of the early Endecja, we must place their position in the context of a debate in the 1960s, 1970s, and 1980s between those who struggled for a relaxation of the authoritarianism of the Polish People's Republic and those who insisted on an absolute negation of communism and an eventual overthrow of Soviet domination. Seen in this light, it is certainly unfair to accuse such authors of rehabilitating National Democracy; their repudiation of the movement's anti-Semitism is emphatic and their evocation of Dmowski relates purely to his tactical restraint. Moreover, all the scholars cited above stress that the early Endecja (from which they attempt to salvage some wisdom) differed significantly from the savage movement of the interwar years, which they unequivocally condemn.[27]

Nonetheless, this tendency to downplay the unpleasant or embarrassing aspects of early National Democracy has shaped the scholarship on this topic by delineating the sorts of questions that can appropriately be asked. For American scholars a comparison between German National Socialism and Polish National Democracy might seem quite natural, but most Polish historians would resist any such parallel. As a result, the literature on National Democracy has differed sharply from comparable histories of fascism, National Socialism, or the *Action Française*. It has become common to observe the existence, around the turn of the century, of a style of thought (a "fascist ideology," as Zeev Sternhell has labeled it) that united diverse movements behind a shared antiliberal nationalism and an "antimaterialist revision of Marxism."[28] The specialist will (justifiably) wish to emphasize the many ideological, social, and political differences between these movements and to distinguish between their early manifestations in the nineteenth century and their final articulations in the 1920s and 1930s, but all such radical right ideologies force us to pose a similar question: what went wrong? How could "modern" and "civilized" Europe produce such brutal, authoritarian political movements? Such issues are traditional starting points for students of the European radical right, but they are almost entirely missing from discussions of National Democracy.

Since the viciousness of the Endecja is rarely problematized, and sometimes not even emphasized, it becomes possible to incorporate the Polish radical right within a well-established narrative about the transformation of Polish political culture at the

turn of the century. Many authors have argued that the National Democratic movement, much as its name might suggest, was both popular and democratic, devoted to
the mobilization of the peasant masses into a modern political force. Such interpretations are merely tendentious when they come from the Endecja's apologists, so we
might be tempted to dismiss assertions by the movement's official historian, Stanisław
Kozicki, that "the modern national movement in Poland [the Endecja] . . . was the
herald of a new period—a new Poland, in which leadership would pass to the hands
of the people."[29] But we cannot escape this argument so easily, because even authors
who could never be described as sympathetic to the Endecja have placed the movement, alongside the Polish Socialist Party (the PPS), within a tale of modernization
and democratization. For example, Andrzej Walicki writes that "the PPS (despite all
its romantic and socialist illusions) and the Endeks (despite all the nasty features of
their ideology) greatly contributed to the shaping of a modernized Polish nation."[30]
The term "modernity" was central to the Endecja's self-image, and it continues to
influence how scholars describe the movement. Dmowski entitled his programatic
book *The Thoughts of a Modern Pole*, and the historian Teodor Mistewicz (among
others) has dubbed the Endecja's ideology "modern nationalism."[31] Most historians
would accept this description of the Endecja's place in Polish history: the movement
may have had its faults, but it must nonetheless be given credit for participating in
the momentous transformation of Polish politics leading up to 1905, when we can at
last observe the long-awaited entrance of "the people" or the masses onto the public
stage. But this view raises a curious paradox that is all too often unexamined (and
frequently not even perceived as a paradox): how could a right-wing organization
devoted to concepts like authority, organization, and discipline be simultaneously
democratic and popular? Many scholars have simply posed this as an unresolved
irony, a curious disjuncture between the broad base of National Democracy and its
authoritarian leadership.[32] Others have suggested that the Endecja changed, evolving from democratic roots but somehow degenerating toward the right after completing the historic task of popularizing political life.[33] Finally, some have argued
that the National Democrats were always hostile to democracy but cynically exploited
the rhetoric of the left in order to gain support.[34]

   The ideology of the National Democrats did, of course, change over time, and
there was doubtlessly a good deal of cynicism in some of the movement's pronounce-
ments. But I argue that it is more productive to see the early, populist writing of
the National Democrats as part of the same ideological totality that includes the
authoritarianism of the movement's later years. This approach will force us to challenge the common view that democracy and pluralism were somehow linked to what
we call "modernity," and that fin de siècle politics (in contrast to the authoritarianism
of the interwar years) was all about expanding the base of political life. Many historians would agree with Stephen Kern's description of a "general cultural reorientation" from 1880 to 1914 "that was essentially pluralistic and democratic."[35] Even
those who locate the origins of fascism in the 1890s describe the progenitors of the
radical right as rebels against rationalism, materialism, democracy, and modernity
in general.[36] There certainly was a revolt against modernity, which this book will
explore in depth. However, it was not necessarily antirational, antimaterialist, or even

antidemocratic in any global sense. Instead it was a revolt against one, crucial aspect of the modernist project: the belief in progressive historical time, in the movement of humanity toward a predetermined future of equality and justice. The future founders of the Polish radical right turned away from capital-H History (i.e., history as a means of interpreting the past so as to predict the future) even as they continued to tout the slogans of "reason," "science," and "democracy." They would eventually repudiate these expressions but (as I show in chapters 6 and 8) their move to do so was in no sense antimodern. This book will demonstrate that authority, modernity, and democratic rhetoric were inextricably intertwined; following Anthony Giddens, I want to explore how "totalitarian possibilities are contained within the institutional parameters of modernity rather than being foreclosed by them."[37] It was not mere cynicism that led people like Roman Dmowski, Jan Popławski, and Zygmunt Balicki to "turn to the people" in the 1880s, nor were they abandoning their youthful ideals when they moved to the right in the 1890s. The rhetoric of democracy contained ample spaces for the exertion of authority, for the "colonization" of the the people by the intelligentsia (to borrow an expression from Katherine Verdery).[38] In recent years scholars from many disciplines have demonstrated how the narratives of modernity impose silences that conceal the workings of power in the age of "democracy." In turn-of-the-century Poland, where the edifice of modernity was only then being constructed (on shaky foundations), the Endecja did not honor all of those silences, thus exposing more blatantly the sites within democracy where authority could emerge. This book, then, will explore the troublesome bond between authority and popular politics, casting the former as an *aspect,* rather than a *negation,* of the latter.

Notes on Terminology

To write about the issues explored in this book is to enter a terminological minefield, because the term "nationalism" is used differently by Polish and English speakers. Although for us the word is both broadly applied and vaguely defined, in Poland its meaning is precise: "*nacjonalizm*" is a chauvinistic, xenophobic, and aggressive ideology of the extreme right. For more benign phenomena the Poles have alternative labels: *narodowcy* (nationalists), *ruch narodowy* (the national movement), and above all *patriotyzm*. This value-laden distinction seems to be derived from nineteenth-century French usage and first appeared in Polish among émigrés in Paris during the 1880s. Today "nationalism" is unambiguously an expression of opprobrium, so to speak (in Polish) of a nationalist tradition that extends across the entire nineteenth century and includes such diverse figures as Staszic, Mickiewicz, and Dmowski is either absurd or incendiary. Nonetheless, and with all due apologies, I have decided not to bow to Polish sensitivities on this point, because it is my contention that there are important linkages—even though there is no necessary teleological progression—between the "good" romantics and the "bad" Endecja.[39] With this in mind, the term "nationalism" will be used loosely in this book to refer to any conceptual or discursive framework that prioritizes something called "the nation." Following Prasenjit Duara, I argue that nationalism "marks the site where different representations of the nation contest and negotiate with each other."[40] Since the meaning of "the nation"—its contents, its boundaries, its position in historical time, its political function, and its destiny—is always contested, no more precise (or less circular) definition is possible. This approach presumes variety and resists the homogenizing effects of a more precise denotation. Moreover, it allows us to analyze the variety of ways people have constructed their own narratives of national history, instead of forcing us to fit the words and deeds of historical figures into abstract categories like "modern nationalism," "cultural nationalism," "religious nationalism," "integral nationalism," "romantic nationalism," and so on. All these terms and expressions, as Gauri Viswanathan points out, "assume a seamless unity of aspirations, goals and agendas, a selection and filtering that irons out the contradictions embedded in the construction of national identity from the fragments of religious, racial, cultural and other forms of self-identification."[41] This book will resist the assumption that there exists a (singular) history of nationalism that can be abstracted from local particularities and counterhegemonic (or even idiosyncratic) usages. Instead, I begin with the assumption that this flexible term has served different purposes for different people in different contexts and that all attempts to define what a nation *is* (as if it had the same ontological status as a physical object) only reinforce unproductive homogenizing impulses. While recognizing that people have come to talk about the nation, feel for the nation, even kill and die for the nation, I make no presumption that there is a single, identifiable object at the other end of their imaginings (at least not one that can be explored without a careful consideration of the act of imagining itself). The nation indeed does exist in some sense—it is not constructed arbitrarily, in the absence of some social foundation—but the *meaning* of the nation is indeterminate, variable, and always disputed.

Another problematic term is the Polish word *lud*. This is generally translated as "the people," but as late as the 1880s there were some doubts among Poles regarding the distinction between the words *naród* (nation) and *lud*. I cannot offer a single translation for *lud* here, since the changing meaning of the word will be one of the topics of this book. Moreover, *lud* is grammatically singular, while the English word "people" is plural. This difference not only makes translating difficult but suggests some important conceptual problems for the English-language reader. The fact that we *must* make the word plural allows for a greater plurality within "the people," while Poles are more likely to speak of the *lud* as both semantically and grammatically unified and undifferentiated. With this in mind, I use the Polish term directly (with singular verbs) when this sense of organic homogeneity is important.

Finally, a less theoretically loaded problem: the terms "Endecja" and "National Democracy" are somewhat anachronistic for much of the period examined in this book: the latter came into use gradually around the turn of the century and the nickname dates from a later period. More precise would be "The All-Poland Camp" (*Obóz Wszechpolski*) or "The National League." For the sake of simplicity and easy identification, however, I have chosen to commit the minor temporal sin of using "Endecja" prematurely. In general I have tried to keep such Polish terms to a minimum, although it has proven necessary to use a few tongue-twisting polonisms for the sake of precision and simplicity. To the American or English reader I can only offer apologies and pronunciation guides (in the notes).

1

The Nation as Action

Before we begin the quest for the origins of the exclusionary rhetoric and authoritarian politics of "modern" nationalism, we must survey a very different style of thought: Polish romanticism. In this chapter we will explore the discursive framework that delineated conversations about the nation for most of the first half of the nineteenth century. Until the very end of the century, the "Polish question" concerned only a minority of those we might categorize as Polish, with few peasants demonstrating any interest in independence. The national lexicon described in this chapter, therefore, was restricted to a relatively small group of people. But herein lies the fundamental paradox of nineteenth-century Polish nationalism: at a time when the number of people professing Polish patriotism remained small, the rhetoric they used facilitated discussions of radical egalitarian social change and revolutionary disruption. Only at the end of the century, when a genuine mass movement at last began to emerge, did nationalism become authoritarian. The style of national thought described in this chapter was not linked to the enforcement of social discipline; quite the contrary, it was by definition a challenge to existing networks of power. It could almost be said that to be a Pole one had to be a revolutionary, because the very essence of the nation was conceptually located in the insurrectionary act (a fact that plagued conservative patriots). The greatest irony— perhaps the greatest tragedy—is that the process of popularizing the nation later in the century would entail the repudiation of this early version of Polish nationalism. Or perhaps the divergence between the scope of the national movement and the disciplinary force of the national discourse is not really paradoxical at all: as I argue later in this volume, only when Polish intellectuals were forced to confront the gap between their imagined nation and the actual peasants and workers did they feel the need to formulate ideologies of discipline and order. During the early decades of the nineteenth century the Polish national movement operated on a different plane and could easily incorporate revolutionary rhetoric.

Not only were the Polish nationalists of the early nineteenth century linked to radical politics, but they imagined a community with remarkably fluid boundaries. The most striking aspect of the nationalism of the day was that it did not necessarily entail the description (or creation) of an ethnically and culturally homogeneous social collective. The Polish patriot of the early nineteenth century *enacted* the nation rather than *embodying* it. As patriotic Polish intellectuals tried to cope with the loss of statehood after the third partition in 1795, they took comfort in the belief that Poland was more than just a place on the map of Europe; they removed their nation from the material world in which tyrants could destroy and oppress, and they relocated it onto a transcendent, spiritual plane. Poland was no longer a mere community for them but a "national essence," defined by the moral principles it was said to represent. By reconceptualizing the nation as a spirit or an ideal, these Poles could sustain their national identity without depending upon the immediate reestablishment of the state. At the same time, they utilized the teleological historiosophies so popular in the early nineteenth century to give this nation an exalted mission of salvation for all humanity, making national resurrection both morally and historically inevitable.

They would not, however, allow destiny to imply passivity: Polish nationalists remained committed to a philosophy of *action* that could justify the continued pursuit of independence. In fact, their very definition of the nation was dynamic, rooted in the patriotic *act* or *deed* rather than in any static conception of identity or belonging. "Poland" was understood to be a historical actor, a collective but nonetheless coherent entity, not merely an assemblage of individuals demarcated by certain observable characteristics. One *participated* in the nation by striving to realize its principles and fulfill its historical mission, and the nation thrived when enough people acted in its name.

Obviously there existed a population of individuals who spoke Polish and performed cultural rituals that distinguished them as a separate ethnic community; this fact was obvious but irrelevant, and few writers in the 1830s or 1840s felt a need to discuss the cultural boundedness of Poland. As a result, patriotic intellectuals up to the mid-nineteenth century could easily imagine cultural diversity within the nation, because for them the quotidian expression of ethnicity was of secondary importance. Of course, this also meant that they could easily imagine a Poland that extended to the prepartition boundaries, far into what we today call Lithuania, Belarus, and Ukraine. Later many non-Poles in Eastern Europe would understandably perceive the expansive (not to say expansionist) concept of Poland as a challenge to their own national aspirations, so we must be careful not to rest too comfortably on a simplistic formula of inclusive = good, exclusive = bad. By the early twentieth century few Ukrainians wanted to be included in any sort of Poland, but like it or not, many of them eventually were: only about two thirds of the inhabitants of interwar Poland were ethnolinguistically Polish. The Lithuanians, Belorussians, Ukrainians, Poles, Jews, and Germans did not live in homogeneous blocs with clearly defined ethnonational boundaries, and because of these complex patterns of cohabitation, it is hard to imagine how any twentieth-century Poland (or Ukraine, or Lithuania, or Belarus) could have been ethnically "pure." Given this situation, it is worth asking how it came to pass that the multicultural Polish state of the early twentieth century was no longer accompanied by a multicultural vision of the Polish nation.

To understand the concept of the enacted nation, we must begin by challenging our tendency to see all nations as embodied social collectives. George Mosse exemplifies a common oversimplification when he writes:

> The belief in the existence of a "national character" was present from the beginning of modern nationhood. Romanticism, with its emphasis on organic development, on the totality of life, was at the root of this search. It meant that regardless of the unity in diversity advocated by some nationalisms, cohesion and uniformity were always potentially present. The foundation upon which national character was built did not differ greatly from nation to nation: a certain morality, comportment and appearance were crucial, usually linking the nation with the moral attitudes of the newly triumphant middle classes.[1]

Patrick Michel argues along similar lines, suggesting that romantic nationalism was merely "the alibi of a search for identity that ought to involve the universal in order to be legitimate."[2] At least in the case of Poland (where there was no "triumphant middle class"), such interpretations of romanticism fail to do justice to the thinkers of the early nineteenth century. Among Poles, the idea of an observable and definable "national character" was called into question by a vision of the nation rooted in the *deed*, the act that would help bring about a new age of freedom for both individuals and nations. To imagine the "cohesion and uniformity" Mosse describes, or the "identity" that Michel prioritizes, the idealistic nationalism of the 1830s and 1840s had to be thoroughly taken apart—it did not inevitably or naturally develop into exclusionary depictions of national culture, nor did it necessarily enforce the bourgeois norms Mosse found in Germany. In this sense, "the foundation upon which national character was built" did indeed "differ greatly from nation to nation." In Poland the rhetoric of nationalism did not initially serve to impose cultural uniformity or social discipline, because the definition of the nation did not (yet) contain the spaces within which one could talk about exclusion or authority.

The Christ of Nations

Although Poland was removed from the map of Europe by the partitioning powers in 1795, the "Polish question" remained an important political issue and most intellectuals refused to accept the finality of the third partition. Napoleon's advance into Central and Eastern Europe gave many Poles hope that their state would be resurrected, but even the disappointing French-sponsored Duchy of Warsaw proved short-lived, and after 1815 the bulk of the old Polish Republic was within the boundaries of the Russian Empire. More precisely, the Congress of Vienna created a new Kingdom of Poland, a geographical space with an elegant name but only limited autonomy. Although the Kingdom enjoyed a constitution that preserved both the *sejm* (the parliament) and an autonomous Polish administration, the crown of Poland was granted to the Romanov family. Both Alexander I and Nicholas I recognized the incongruity of creating a constitutional monarchy within an autocratic empire, and both violated

that constitution with increasing regularity. After fifteen years of accumulated grievances, the Kingdom exploded with the November Uprising of 1830–1831. The
insurrection was soon defeated, and what autonomy the Kingdom had enjoyed was
eliminated: the constitution was nullified, the *sejm* was abolished, the army was dis-
banded, the *złoty* was replaced by the *ruble*, and many elements of Russian law were
introduced. In 1832 Nicholas I issued the Organic Statute to replace the old constitution of the Kingdom, but even the weak guarantees of this document were never respected. Much of the political and cultural elite felt compelled to leave Poland, but
both émigré communities abroad and conspiracy movements at home tried to sustain the ambitions of 1830 by analyzing what had gone wrong and by planning for
the next revolt.

Throughout these tumultuous events Polish intellectuals grappled with the difficulty of talking about a nation that no longer had a state. This rhetorical challenge
was a vital corollary to the political and military struggle: before one could act on
behalf of the nation, one had to imagine it in a new way and place it within a worldview
that granted efficacy to such actions. During the first few decades after the partitions
the need to address this rhetorical problem was mitigated by the optimism with which
people greeted the Duchy and the Kingdom. As disillusionment and dissatisfaction
grew, however, so did the desire to come up with a new definition of "the nation,"
one that would serve Polish intellectuals as they faced new—indeed unprecedented—
circumstances. We can trace the roots of this redefinition as far back as the summer
of 1797, when a writer named Józef Wybicki wrote the lyrics to a march—or more
precisely, a mazurka—for Jan Henryk Dąbrowski's "Polish Legion" in France. This
popular song, which was adopted in the twentieth century as Poland's national anthem, demonstrated that Wybicki's nation was caught in a world of violence and
contestation.[3]

> Poland has not yet died,
> As long as we live.
> What foreign force has taken
> We will reconquer by the sword!

The first sentence was crucial: as long as Poles were alive, Poland would continue to
exist. The nation was no longer equated with a state but was instead contained within
all those who called themselves Polish. Statehood had been taken from this nation
by foreigners, but this was simply a problem of military force and could therefore
easily be remedied (by force). On the other hand, even though the nation resided in
the hearts of those who lived as Poles, neither they nor their nation were complete as
long as they remained in the emigration. This way of conceptualizing the nation made
political existence unnecessary for survival but, conversely, it posited the restoration of the nation-state as a basic imperative. This style of reasoning worked both
ways: it allowed people to see themselves as Poles even when there was no Poland
on the map, and then it turned this argument around so as to inspire (or justify) their
efforts to redraw that map. The refrain of Wybicki's mazurka declared:

> March, march, Dąbrowski,
> From the Italian to the Polish lands.
> Under your leadership,
> We will join with the nation.

Here the nation was less a community than it was a goal. Living in Italy (the legion was based in Lombardy at that moment) had separated these soldiers from Wybicki's Poland, and they needed to return to East Central Europe in order to "join with the nation" once again. A later verse proclaimed, "We will cross the Vistula, we will cross the Varta; we will be Poles." The future tense is significant: the essence of the Polish nation could be realized only when the émigrés returned to their homeland and liberated their country from its enslavement. The nation of Wybicki was closely—indeed, definitionally—linked to the concept of *action*.[4]

Wybicki had introduced a crucial innovation into the discussion of nationalism in Poland: a distinction between the ideal nation that dwelt within each Pole and the real nation that remained along the Vistula. The former could never pass away as long as patriotic Poles sustained its existence, Wybicki believed, but only a restoration of the state and a physical return could make manifest this ideal Poland. To be a Pole, therefore, meant to retain the nation in one's heart and to fight for independence; it implied both a sense of identity and a plan of action. But this optimistic duality, which assumed that the "inner" Poland would find an expression in the "real" fatherland in the near future, had to be reconfigured as hopes for independence receded. As early as the 1830s, Polish authors began to plug Wybicki's dichotomy into a vocabulary of romantic idealism, which both elevated the nation into the realm of "the spirit" and transformed the goal of statehood into a more grandiose ethical principle. On the one hand, the nation no longer required a state in any conceptual or definitional sense, because political form was merely the means by which the nation could most effectively act in the world. Not wanting their sense of identity to rise and fall with the disappointments of the Napoleonic interlude or the 1830 Uprising, Polish intellectuals removed their nation from the material world. On the other hand, they did not depoliticize their image of Poland, and they certainly did not weaken the imperative to act. Quite the contrary, the national will became more important than ever as it drove Poland into an eternal struggle between good and evil. "Crossing the Vistula" (i.e., regaining statehood) was important—indeed, vital—but for most Polish intellectuals it was no longer enough: the "true" Pole became a champion of "justice" and "freedom" for all mankind.

To understand what the romantic nation was, we must first consider what it was not. Above all, it had no clear ethnographic content. This is both the most important aspect of Polish romantic nationalism and the most difficult to grasp for those accustomed to linking the origins of ethnography to romanticism. Language and folk culture were important for some Polish romantics, but for none of them did these factors *define* the nation. When they talked about things such as language, their categories were fluid, and the link between ethnicity and the nation was always uncertain. In one extreme case from 1834 an émigré named Piotr Semenenko composed an essay entitled "On Nationality," in which he argued that despite Poland's past as a noble republic, it could serve as a model for the democratic nation of the future. To demonstrate the bond between nation and people, he predicted, the reborn Poland would adopt that quintessentially peasant language, Ruthenian (Ukrainian), as its national tongue. For Semeneńko there was no paradox in this imagery, because a large share of the peasants in prepartition Poland had in fact spoken Ukrainian.[5] In 1830 a contributor to *Gazeta Polska* named J. J. Rusin offered a less provocative version of this idea in an article entitled "On the Songs of the Polish People," in which he described as "Polish" any folk song historically tied to the old Poland, regardless of the language in which it was sung.[6] Joachim Lelewel, one of the most influential patriotic writers of the era (and its leading historian), instructed his countrymen not to "differentiate the sons of Poland, whether they speak the Ruthenian, Polish, or Lithuanian language."[7]

If the nation was not an ethnolinguistic group and if it was not equivalent to the state, then what was it? In fact it was no longer a mere "thing"—it was no longer perceived by national activists, philosophers, and poets as a purely material or social object. Instead the nation was an ideal, a principle that gave meaning to history. The nation might be manifest in a specific population with identifiable characteristics, but neither that social group nor those traits fully expressed the true nation. Poland, which was said to exist in the hearts of all Poles, embodied an ethical principle and acted as a motive force in history. Conceptually, the nation was placed within a realm in which ethnic identity was of secondary importance and even, for some, irrelevant. Insofar as this style of national imagining was exclusionary, it isolated only those who were identified with the forces of evil, oppression, and tyranny (that is, those who loyally served the partitioning powers and, more broadly, the ancien régime of East Central Europe). It did not push anyone outside of its ranks solely on the basis of language, cultural practices, religion, or ethnicity.

The literary critic Maurycy Mochnacki (1803–1834) was one of the most important philosophers of this new nation. In his short life Mochnacki propagated a definition of the nation that deemphasized the empirical in favor of the spiritual and moral.[8] Mochnacki first articulated this in a short article in 1827 entitled "Is It Appropriate to Consider Translations from Foreign Languages Harmful for Polish Literature?" Although he believed that translations were in fact dangerous (because they discouraged original composition in the Polish language), he defined the nation in a way that distinguished it from linguistic, ethnic, and geographical categories. "The essence of the nation," he wrote, "is not a collection of people living on a territory defined by certain borders, but rather the collection of their own ideas, feelings, and thoughts. Those ideas, feelings, and thoughts must necessarily result from history, religion, legislation, traditions, etc."[9] In this article Mochnacki disassociated the nation from any "collection of people," suggesting that "Poland" signified something more profound than a mere sociological category. He granted conceptual primacy to "ideas, feelings and thoughts," even though he continued to derive these from externally discernible factors like history and religion. Three years later, in a more widely publicized volume entitled *On Polish Literature in the Nineteenth Century*, Mochnacki took this reasoning a step further. The wording was similar, but he further subordinated the empirical aspects of the nation.

One man, when he begins to think, moves toward a realization of himself, and in the same way an entire nation, in its thoughts, must have a self-recognition of its being [*uznawanie się w swoim jestestwie*]. Just as the thoughts of one person contain within them, so to speak, the essence of his essence, so all thoughts gathered together into a whole represent the essence of a nation. More precisely, the nation is not a collection of people living on a territory defined by certain borders. Rather, the essence of a nation is the collection of all concepts and feelings regarding religion, political institutions, legislation, [and] customs. [The national essence] even has a tight bond with geographical location, climate and other factors of empirical existence.[10]

Mochnacki continued to recognize these "factors of empirical existence," but he carefully distinguished them from the nation *as such.* The "concepts and feelings" of the national "essence" were tied to the material world, but they were no longer entirely dependent upon that world. Earthly history itself, for Mochnacki, was nothing but "the dream of the people, a shadow of their being," a reflection of developments in the realm of ideals.[11] The nation existed in that higher realm, and even though it possessed a physical manifestation here on earth, the representation should never be confused with the "national being."

With this conception of the nation, Mochnacki was able to preserve his identity as a Pole. If the nation resided on the plane of ideas and feelings, then the lack of material form—that is, statehood—did not threaten its continued existence. Mochnacki believed that after the partitions "the land was divided, but only the land: what constituted the essence of the nation was preserved. The nation lost its political existence as a result of the impotence of its old government, but it did not lose its societal bond; it did not lose its social being, which was considerably strengthened, which aspired to even greater perfection."[12] The distinction between a geopolitical Poland and an ideal Poland—the "national spirit"—was the foundation of early nineteenth-century nationalism. Wybicki had suggested this dichotomy and Mochnacki had given it a more complex form by placing it within the already well-developed framework of romantic idealism. On one level this more enduring Poland was a sociological concept—a *społeczny związek* (societal bond), in Mochnacki's terminology. As in Wybicki's poem, Poland existed because *Poles* existed, whatever their political fate. But this vision of the nation functioned on a deeper level as well: Poland was fundamentally the representation of a moral principle. The nation arose from the ideas, feelings, and thoughts of the Poles, but it also possessed a coherent existence (Mochnacki's "social being") which transcended this disparate conglomeration and which was moving toward the realization of an inner telos, toward "greater perfection." Apart from any individual Pole, the nation was the representation of a universal ideal, which others would identify more precisely as freedom, justice, or brotherhood.[13]

A few years before the uprising, in 1828, Mochnacki composed an open letter to the Polish Senate that received widespread attention and approval in Warsaw. The fatherland was not a territorial unit, Mochnacki repeated, nor anything physical at all. Rather it was "the great idea of political independence and the hope that someday, under the leadership and help of God, we will join in one indivisible whole, that we will be the fortress of Europe, an affliction on our evil neighbors and the chosen people of Slavdom. *Only these ideas, Senators, constitute Poland today.*"[14] Poland was not merely fighting for freedom, it was a representation of the principle of freedom. True Poles, Mochnacki believed, had to be virtuous citizens fighting for the ideal of independence on behalf of all Europe as well as for their own liberation. If all nations were fully aware of their own essence, he argued, they could live in harmony within the greater collective of humanity, to which all belonged.[15] Even as the nation came to occupy the central place in Polish intellectual life, the universalist concept of "humanity" retained its rhetorical potency. As the authors of a revolutionary manifesto put it in 1835, "the existence of a nation is determined by the role it has in aspiring toward the goals of all humanity."[16] Polish troops could (and did) fight for France, Hungary, or the United States as well as for Poland, and for "the rights of man" as well as for "the nation."

Meanwhile, and more important, the romantic nationalists defined their enemy as tyranny rather than as Russia—or, if the enemy was Russia, it was so because the tsarist regime had come to embody tyranny in the world, just as the Poles represented freedom. International hatred, the romantics believed, was the fruit of oppression, which prevented people from realizing their essential brotherhood. If evil could be defeated, then all people would be free to embrace their own national identity within an international framework. The rhetoric of the rebellion of 1830 demonstrated how widespread and influential this faith was. During the revolt Polish intellectuals insisted that they were fighting against evil itself, not merely against the Russians. Indeed, the most prominent slogan of the uprising was "for our freedom and yours" (usually written in Russian and Polish for added emphasis), as Poles proclaimed that they were struggling for the liberty of Russia and Poland alike. The *sejm* (the national assembly) issued a proclamation at the height of the conflict, declaring that the Poles "were not inspired by any national hatred toward the Russians, a great tribe [*szczep*] of the Slavic family [*ród*], just like ourselves." The newspaper *Nowa Polska* asserted simply, "We love the Russian people."[17] The crucial distinction here was between the virtuous people and the oppressive Tsar. If Poland could defeat the latter, the rebels argued, then the former would be liberated. This was not (or at least not only) a tactical prediction that liberalization in the Russian Empire would lead to Polish independence, nor that the establishment of a constitutional regime in Warsaw would inspire similar changes in Petersburg. The argument was extended much further, as the rebellion was transformed into a metaphor for the struggle against tyrannical rule everywhere. As Jan Olrych Szaniecki, a contributor to the appropriately named *Dziennik Powszechny* (Universal Daily), wrote in 1831: "Our revolution ought to be a revolution of nations. All of Europe, the entire world ought to support it. And they will support it, if we conduct it not only according to our own needs and interests but [according to the needs of] all people. . . . Nations of the entire world! See how holy is our cause! Support it for your own good!"[18] As the historian Andrzej Nowak has written, "one gets the impression that on the day after the outbreak of the uprising, there was a general desire not to have any enemies."[19]

From right to left, from philosophical essays to popular battle songs, Poles insisted in 1830 that they were fighting not for themselves but for "justice" and for the

welfare of all humanity. Even as some Poles began to question the idea that a virtuous but oppressed Russian people stood behind the evil Russian Tsar (and the conduct of the Russian soldiers during the uprising did challenge this belief), they still
imagined that the Russo-Polish conflict was a metaphor for (or manifestation of) a
much larger struggle between the "Polish idea of freedom" and the "Russian idea of
despotism." Obviously not every Polish intellectual or patriotic activist accepted the
idealism described above with equal enthusiasm and conviction. Moreover, there was
space within this framework for many diverse political positions and strategic arguments: romanticism was neither monolithic nor unchallenged, and the brief survey
offered in this chapter necessarily abstracts from the complexities of the day. Nonetheless, these concepts, slogans, and metaphors provided an effective solution to the
doubts and disappointments of 1830, and idealism retained a general appeal until the
next uprising (in 1863).

This worldview gave Polish nationalists a way to conceive of a nation without a
state and it gave them a reason to hope for national rebirth. Perhaps even more important, it helped them justify a program of national action even at those moments
when there seemed to be little chance that Poland could regain its independence. As
Poles spoke the vocabulary of idealism, the concept of "the deed" (*czyn*) became an
integral part of their definition of the nation: to be a Pole, one had to join in the enactment of the nation's historical mission, one had to both recognize and contribute
to the fulfillment of the nation's destiny. The actions of any Pole who was truly conscious of his or her Polishness were supposed to be imbued with an awareness of the
greater historical meaning of the national cause.

In 1838 a young philosopher named August Cieszkowski (1814–1894) wrote a
small book which could serve as the manifesto of Polish romanticism: *A Prologue to
a Historiosophy* (published first in German as *Prolegomena zur Historiosophie* and
later translated into Polish).[20] The term "historiosophy"—which refers to the interpretation of time in a way that inscribes the past with meaning and offers predictions
for the future—was of fundamental importance to Polish intellectuals in the 1830s
and 1840s. Cieszkowski was inspired by Hegel (he wrote the first draft of his *Prologue* while studying at the University of Berlin, where Hegel's legacy was still
strong), but he also wanted to transcend what he perceived as the limitations of the
master. Like Hegel, Cieszkowski saw history moving forward in a dialectical process toward a state of absolute self-awareness. But this Polish philosopher went a
step further, arguing that Hegel had given insufficient attention to the future, to the
further development of humanity beyond the state it had reached in the early nineteenth century. That future (which Cieszkowski believed could be foreseen by means
of "speculative philosophy") would be the age of "the deed."[21] For the romantics, a
deed was more than just an assertion of human volition: it had to be infused with
self-awareness and with an understanding of one's place in time, one's role in the
construction of the future. The coming third stage of history (Cieszkowski's vision,
like so many others of the day, was trinitarian) would be an "objective, essential realization of the perceived truth." That is, in the future, humanity would make manifest in the social world the understanding that had been articulated by Hegel and other
philosophers in the realm of abstract thought. Cieszkowski hoped to inaugurate a new

discipline that he called "the philosophy of practice," which would facilitate the "development of truth in concrete action."[22]

Although the details of Cieszkowski's vision would be contested, nearly every philosopher, poet, journalist, and political activist of the 1830s and 1840s held a similarly diachronic view of the world, and within the nationalist framework it was virtually unimaginable (or at least unspeakable, which may amount to the same thing) that social institutions and behavior might be locked into unchanging laws. It was inconceivable that history might be meaningless or that humanity might be destined only for more of what had already been experienced. History *had* to have a design; progress *had* to be assured; the future *had* to be different (and better). We can understand the rhetoric of Polish nationalism only if we recognize the impact of this prophetic sensibility. Polishness was something one acted out in historical time, not something one merely embodied in social space, and nations were transcendent spirits with clearly defined missions to be realized over time. We should not place questions of cultural or ethnic identity at the center of our inquiry, at least not until the end of the century; instead we should explore the ways Polish patriots positioned themselves along a continuum of progress. To cite Cieszkowski once more, the nationality of a given population "is *not* just a product of their thought, it does not just rest in their consciousness; rather, [nationality] truly *is,* it lives in the political organism, it is a *deed.*"[23]

The philosopher Józef Gołuchowski gave a public lecture in January 1831 in which he established the relationship between the nation-as-identity and the nation-as-historical-actor.

> Nations can be considered in two ways: first physically, as a collection of individuals autonomously directing their lives; second morally, as a collection of individuals tightly bound with each other in a certain whole. . . . And what is that force, that cement bonding people into a nation? It is the national spirit. It is some kind of moral force, some kind of soul which does not lend itself to description and which can only be perceived by those who remain in this force, who are received into it and are driven by it.[24]

Gołuchowski contrasted the physical, the individual, and the autonomous on the one side, with the moral, the collective, and the dependent on the other. The true national essence, he believed, rested with the latter, and an empirical conception of the nation would reveal only its superficial and static characteristics, overlooking its dynamic "soul." People did not simply constitute the nation: they were received into it and subsequently driven by it. This was a diachronic worldview, based on the belief that our individual and collective existence depended upon our relationship to a common history and, more important, a prophesied future. As Mochnacki put it, movement was the very foundation of existence: everything "was becoming," and nothing simply "was."[25] The romantics believed that individuals gained meaning and identity by participating in the national will, by working toward the nation's goals, not just by exemplifying its language, its religion, and its folkways.

The poet Juliusz Słowacki (1809–1849) went even further with this reasoning. Things such as custom, language, history, and tradition had little to do with Słowacki's nation; for him, the material world was an embodiment of the more essential realm of the "spirit," and the national "idea" generated the external expressions of ethnicity and culture. "Just as the Word—that is, the Spirit having to reveal itself in visible form—was created before the world," he wrote, "so the beginning of every nation was preceded by the creation of an idea, which later people could realize, crystallize, create in a certain form. From such an idea emerged a certain aggregate form—and that became a nationality."[26] The idea preceded the national culture; the idea was the historical force, while the traditions and institutions of the nation were merely the means for that idea to realize itself. Moreover, Słowacki argued, when a given cultural collective was no longer suitable for the realization of the idea, the national principle migrated, as a soul would move from one body to another in its quest for perfection (Słowacki, like many of his contemporaries, believed in reincarnation). As an example of this form of national palingenesis, Słowacki claimed that the idea of spiritual freedom had once resided in Novgorod and Pskov (Russian city-states legendary for their supposedly democratic institutions), until those polities were subjugated by Moscow in 1478 and 1510. After this, "the people of Novgorod and Pskov escaped from the enslaved bodies and became Poles."[27] The cultural forms of any given community were only of transient significance. Much more important was "the idea."

In an apparent contrast to this view, the philosopher Karol Libelt (1807–1875) gave a great deal of attention to the material factors that Słowacki considered so unimportant.[28] No other nationalist of the time was so eager to emphasize the communal bonds of language and ethnicity, but even Libelt, in the end, felt compelled to recognize that only through action could the nation be fully realized. Libelt attributed great importance to the "corporeal side" of each nation, which was rooted in the land and which expressed itself through language and culture. But even Libelt positioned his "nationality" within a historiosophical framework. "Nations are not toys of fate," he wrote. "Each one has a certain calling, a certain mission which it took from God, and to fulfill [this mission] is the goal of its existence." To find space for both the enduring cultural community and the dynamic historical actor, Libelt distinguished between nation and nationality. The latter was an ethnolinguistic group, but it was also the source of a spirit that joined with the body (the land) to produce the complete nation. Once integration was achieved between body and spirit (land and nationality), the resulting nation would be infused with a divinely inspired idea or mission. At this point Libelt introduced a concept that had to penetrate virtually any discussion of the nation in the nineteenth century: statehood. The state, he argued, consisted of "the union of the corporal and spiritual fatherland into the life of the fatherland; the fusion and shaping of all the activities of the national body and soul into a single living, acting nation. The life of the nation: this is the fullest description of the state." A nation might be able to exist for a time without a state (any Pole had to believe this), but it could not complete its mission, it could not ultimately sustain its "life" without that vital bond between spirit and body. To secure that bond and sustain the life of the nation, Libelt concluded, Poles had to *act*. Only if Poland aroused itself to act in defense of its existence, he wrote, could it "really call itself a nation." Even Libelt, then, despite all the emphasis he gave to nationality, fell back in the end to the idea that the nation could *really* exist only through its deeds. "Poland," discussed in this way, did not contain spaces for talking comfortably about cultural identity, understood as a static concept of being or belonging. The nation's very existence was *dynamic*. One did not simply *belong* to the Polish national community, one *participated* in Poland's national mission. Even for Libelt, the synchronic features of nationality acquired life only through action.

A more serious challenge to the idea of a transcendent (and thus multicultural) Poland came from further on the left, when the term *naród* (the nation) was combined with the equally important expression, *lud* (the people). The word *lud* was hardly new, but its central importance in Polish political vocabulary emerged only after the November Uprising.[29] Before 1830 (and afterwards in the work of Mickiewicz and a few others) the term was defined expansively to include the entire population—the human incarnation of the national spirit. Some on the left, however, began in the 1830s to question whether exploiters and oppressors deserved to be considered part of the "Polish people." Jan Janowski, for example, divided the nation into the cosmopolitan nobility and the truly Polish *lud*. This approach in turn drew him toward an uncomfortably exclusive definition of Poland. Concluding that those who were turning their back on the national mission were also those most likely to embrace a cosmopolitan culture, Janowski decided that the fatherland should be defined as "a place of birth and residence of free people, with boundaries defined not by force but by nature itself, by linguistic identity and by custom."[30] For Janowski the turn to ethnicity was an easy way to exile from his nation the rich and powerful, those who had been alienated from "the people" by an international and elitist high culture. It would be many years, however, before others would follow Janowski's shift from the patriotic deed toward ethnographic national space.

Most others on the left continued to describe a world of national missions and national ideals; their Poland was still primarily an ethical concept and their political agenda was still driven by a universalist moral vision. Even as they tried to embody the nation in the *lud*, they were reluctant to accept a purely ethnolinguistic metric. In 1835 Tadeusz Krępowicki argued that the peasants would rise on behalf of Poland, regardless of where they lived or what language they spoke, as long as the national cause was linked to an agenda of emancipation. "There is no Lithuania!" he cried. "There is no Ruthenia! There is no Mazovia, Wielkopolska, or Małopolska. . . . There is only one Poland."[31] As we will see, the tendency to position the nation within a historiosophical vision made it possible to retain spaces for both cultural diversity and radical politics, even as ethnography grew in importance. Only when all eschatological hopes were abandoned could "the nation" really sustain sharp ethnolinguistic boundaries.

The nation, then, was defined by action. But action to what end? The restoration of the prepartition map of Eastern Europe was a self-evident objective for any early nineteenth-century Polish patriot, but once the nation was inserted into the broad historiosophical framework described above, statehood was no longer enough. For

Słowacki, Libelt, and (until the last few years of his life) Mochnacki, Polish independence was not just a geopolitical objective, but part of a broader mission of salvation for all humanity. During and after the November Uprising of 1830 there emerged in Poland a rhetorical framework that historians have labeled "messianism."[32] This style of nationalist thought gave Polish intellectuals a vocabulary with which to talk about their nation as they tried to cope with the failure of 1830. The struggle for Poland, already joined with the welfare of all humanity, was further justified through use of a heterodox religious terminology: the quest for independence became a divine imperative and Poland became the "Christ of Nations." Kazimierz Brodziński, a prominent literary critic and poet, was one of the first to put the messianic metaphor into play. On May 3, 1831, in a speech in honor of the anniversary of the Polish Constitution of 1791, Brodziński restated—to an enthusiastic response—the idea that the national struggle was part of a wider cause. He declared that "every nation ought to be a part of the whole and circle around it as the planets around their focal point." This message of international brotherhood was a divine truth, Brodziński argued, and Poland was blessed as the first nation to become aware of God's plan. He extended his astronomical metaphor to label Poland "the Copernicus of the moral world." Just as the great Polish astronomer had discovered that the planets orbit around the sun, so did Poland embody the revelation that all nations revolve around the central values of humanity and justice. Because his compatriots realized this fundamental truth, Brodziński believed, they were able to synthesize their love of the fatherland with a devotion to humanity as a whole. Brodziński concluded his speech by proclaiming that if Poland was victorious in its struggle, it would bring freedom to all nations. If it failed (as must have seemed likely at that time), "our ashes will be sacred, [and] the cross raised above them will be the object of pilgrimages by [all] peoples, to the tomb of that nation [which was] the student of Christ."[33] From Copernicus to Jesus: Poland became a disciple of Christ, and one of the most powerful metaphors in Polish nationalist rhetoric was formulated.

Brodziński may have introduced the messianic metaphor, but it was propagated and elaborated primarily by the poet Adam Mickiewicz (1798–1855). It is impossible to overstate the importance of this author, whose poetry could (and still can) be recited from memory by almost every educated Pole. After the failure of the 1830 uprising, thousands of Poles—mostly noble officers, but a handful of foot soldiers as well—were forced to leave their homeland and emigrate to the West. Most of them found refuge in France, where a thriving émigré community of political activists survived for decades. Their publications were filled with doubts about their future and with mutual recriminations for their defeat. Into this environment came a small volume, published anonymously with the author's own funds: Mickiewicz's *The Books of the Polish Nation and the Polish Pilgrimage*. The purpose of the tract was to inspire the émigrés with hope for the future and to advance an idiosyncratic political and moral vision. Although the details of Mickiewicz's utopian program were generally ignored, his language shaped the way an entire generation talked about the nation.

The style of this text evoked the Bible, as Mickiewicz blended the language of a sermon with that of a revolutionary tract. He started with Genesis: "In the beginning there was faith in one God and there was Freedom on earth. There were no laws, only the will of God, and there were no masters or slaves, only the patriarchs and their children." This primitive (and gendered) equality did not last, however, and soon humanity divided itself into exploiters and the exploited. It was therefore necessary for Christ to come to earth in order to bring mankind a message of brotherhood, equality, and freedom. According to Mickiewicz, this message was soon repudiated by evil monarchs who substituted false idols for the one true God and His message. Amid widespread corruption and injustice stood Poland, the one nation that did not "bow before the new idol." Mickiewicz reconfigured the history of prepartition Poland into a morality tale of brotherhood and harmony, declaring that the "knights" of Poland had always been free and equal and that "in the end Poland said, Whosoever comes to me will be free and equal, for I am Freedom." Just as Christ was killed for his message, an evil trinity of oppressive monarchs destroyed Poland because they feared the freedom it embodied. But this apparent death was not the end, "for the Polish nation did not die. Its body lay in the grave and its soul had gone from the earth, that is, from public life, into purgatory, that is, into the domestic life of [those nations] suffering from slavery. . . . And on the third day the soul will return to the body and the nation will rise again and free all the peoples of Europe from slavery."[34] Mickiewicz later distanced himself from the idea that Poland would serve as a collective savior; instead he came to believe that an individual messiah would work *through* the nation in order to bring the New Age to the rest of humanity.[35] But whether the nation was the agent for eschatological transformation or the vehicle for a personal messiah, the link between the nation and a dynamic vision of historical time, culminating in a utopia of peace and brotherhood, was well established.

Mickiewicz's writing became enormously popular and *The Books of the Polish Nation* was soon established as the bible of the Polish emigration.[36] This text was so successful that even those who opposed Mickiewicz's vague political program came to employ his messianic metaphors. As Andrzej Walicki has written, messianism "was a condensed, augmented expression of hope in an approaching total regeneration of humanity—a hope which to one degree or another, in a more or less rationalized form, the entire émigré community shared."[37] We find the following passage, for example, in the 1834 manifesto of a radical group of émigrés in London: "The French Revolution of the last century was the John the Baptist of the new faith, but until now Christ has not appeared. . . . This Christ will not be an individual man but some great nation which, having assimilated everything truly good in the achievements of all its predecessors and having created from this an ordered whole, will bring to humanity a new social faith."[38] These metaphors helped the romantic nationalists reconceptualize the nation as a bifurcated entity, which (like Christ) possessed both a spiritual and an earthly existence. The nation could thus be divorced from the state, as had in fact occurred, and continue to thrive. The messianic metaphor placed Poland within the divine plan of salvation, imbuing nationalist rhetoric with a teleological dynamic that guaranteed both the establishment of universal justice and the resurrection of the nation. The result was a faith in national rebirth that was simultaneously political and religious (albeit heretical by Rome's standards, because it promised an earthly, social incarnation of the divine).[39]

The romantic Poland, then, was to be the "Christ of nations," or at the very least it was to be the vehicle through which individual Poles were to pursue truth, justice, brotherhood, or some other universal goal. But herein lies the great irony of romantic nationalism: *conceptually* the idea of the nation had been opened up as never before and linked to ambitious, even utopian visions of social equity and spiritual salvation, while *in practice* the discourse of the nation remained limited to a narrow intelligentsia. The complex and abstract rhetoric of romantic nationalism limited the audience for patriotic propaganda; this was not an appeal likely to resonate among illiterate peasants, particularly since the specific social content of these calls for liberation remained vague. Precisely because of this tension, the socially restricted base of the national movement was a source of great discomfort and debate throughout the early and mid-nineteenth century. One of the driving imperatives of the national movement was to broaden its foundation, expanding ethnically and socially the circle of those who spoke the language of nationalism. This goal opened the door to two striking developments: the infusion of revolutionary content into the nationalist agenda, and an unprecedented demonstration of Polish-Jewish amity.

The Revolutionary Nation

After the November Uprising of 1830 it became increasingly difficult to discuss traditional forms of authority, hierarchy, and power within a nationalist framework. The image of Poland as an incarnation of justice, freedom, and brotherhood easily assumed revolutionary overtones, and a style of rhetoric emerged that made it difficult to defend relations of power within the nation. When the nation became a deed, it became, almost by definition, revolutionary. Power itself had not been obscured from the nationalist view: quite the contrary, the unsettling of preexisting systems of authority became the very raison d'être of Polish nationalism, allowing Marx to declare in 1848 that "[Poland's] liberation has become a matter of honor for all the democrats of Europe."[40] If the Polish cause could be praised by someone like Karl Marx, then conservatives, not surprisingly, grew increasingly uncomfortable with patriotic slogans. The assertion by the revolutionary nationalist Henryk Kamieński that "he who wants an independent Poland must want a people's war and thus a social revolution," would be echoed by a wide variety of publicists (sometimes with confident anticipation, sometimes with dismay).[41] The networks of authority had not necessarily been weakened in Poland (although some had, for a variety of reasons), but "the nation" could no longer serve as a rhetorical space within which one could advocate the enforcement of existing structures of power and discipline.

The left found "the nation" to be a useful term in the 1830s and 1840s, as exemplified in the writings of the Polish Democratic Society (or TDP, from its Polish initials), the largest radical émigré organization of the time. Polish independence, the TDP declared, could not be separated from democracy, and Poland's mission could be fulfilled only if both were obtained. The Democrats of the TDP did not subordinate their nationalism to a political agenda; rather they configured the idea of a national mission so that Poland became "the eternal representation of democratic ideas."[42] They believed that Europe was preparing for a great war between the forces of "freedom, equality, and brotherhood" on the one side and "despotism and shackled slavery" on the other.[43] In this struggle the Polish nation (as the eternal representation of freedom) had to stand with the forces of justice. The link between democracy and the nation was conceptual rather than logical: the TDP offered no specific mechanism through which Polish resurrection would initiate the New Age; rather they declared that this had to be the case because Poland *was* liberty. Jan Janowski (a co-founder of the TDP and an author of its manifesto) went so far as to write that one could forfeit one's national membership and "place oneself outside the boundaries of society" if one violated the principles of "the rights of man." If one repudiated the revolutionary agenda, one could no longer perform the requisite act of patriotic rebellion—and only through the deed did one establish a bond with the nation.[44] In 1846 a 25-year-old radical named Edward Dembowski tried to give nationalist meaning to a peasant jacquerie in Galicia (the Austrian partition of Poland) by arguing that the nobility was not really Polish. They had oppressed the people and persecuted those who tried to act; in doing so they had forfeited their right to call themselves Poles.[45]

Although the concept of the nation gradually became the property of the left after the 1830s, it had earlier been highly contested terrain. On the one hand, nationalism had been used by the left since at least 1789 to justify revolution: the will of the nation was set in opposition to the oppressive rule of monarchs, and those acting through the nation were presumed to possess the power to shape their own lives. At the same time, counterrevolutionaries like Edmund Burke and Joseph de Maistre employed similar terms while denying the power of human volition. Their nation was a historical constant of cultural and political traditions, and willful action could not change it. In principle, then, nationalism could represent either popular sovereignty or its negation, either revolution or reaction. After 1830, however, the idea of Poland became so wedded to a program of action and a dynamic historiosophy that both the left and the right had to contend with the consequences of a nation that was seen to possess its own revolutionary will, or at least its own progressive trajectory. W. A. Djakow's study of Russian police and court records demonstrates that Polish activists were growing ever more radical in the 1830s and 1840s, and moderate (let alone conservative) social positions were becoming increasingly rare.[46] If conservatives continued to feel "Polish," they found it increasingly difficult after 1830 to speak within the framework of nationalism; they may have retained some sort of Polish identity, but they lacked a vocabulary with which to talk about it in the public realm.[47]

Wybicki may have thought that it was enough for a group of patriotic soldiers to "cross the Vistula" in order to restore Polish independence, but by 1831 it was clear that this was not the case. There was a growing consensus among patriotic intellectuals that traditional diplomatic and military tactics were inadequate for the needs of the national struggle, and some patriots began arguing that a truly popular uprising might succeed where conventional warfare had failed. As Polish intellectuals "went to the people" in an effort to gain support for the national cause, they simultaneously struggled to redefine the nation so as to establish some conceptual space for the peasants. This was a daunting project, because it entailed far more than a mere assertion that the fatherland encompassed all social classes. During the insurrection of 1830 most "Poles" had remained apathetic toward the national struggle, and for many decades afterwards the efforts of intellectuals to generate popular enthusiasm for their cause were sporadic and ineffectual. The challenge, then, was to imagine a popular Polish nationalism that did not exist—or rather did not *yet* exist: in the end Polish romantic nationalists could cope with the gap between their expansive national desires and the narrow social range of their patriotic rhetoric because they were able to believe in the future. They could envision a national spirit transcending any "collection of people," moving through time toward both a restoration of independence and an expansion of the number of those willing to fight for Poland's rebirth. The social content of the national idea was destined to change, they believed, and the historiosophies they constructed in the 1830s and 1840s would promise such a transformation.

Not surprisingly, this situation created some dilemmas for traditional conservative patriots. These were illustrated during the November Uprising, when the Poles were unable to convince the Catholic Church to support their struggle against the Tsar. The rhetoric of the nation (in Italy as well as in Poland) had already become so infused with socially and politically disruptive content that the Vatican came to see the Orthodox Tsar as less of a threat than a Catholic (but revolutionary) Poland would be. Within Poland most of the bishops came to the same conclusion, and they denounced the national struggle even before the Pope issued the 1832 encyclical *Cum Primum* (which chastised the Poles for their attempt to "disturb the peace of the Kingdom," "overturn the order of society," and upset "the authorities established by God"). Few Poles in 1830 characterized the uprising in terms of a religious conflict between Orthodoxy and Catholicism, and for the rest of the century the relationship between the institutional Church and the national movement would remain tense.[48]

After the uprising of 1830, conservatives began to drift away from the national movement. By mid-century few on the right were interested in talking about "the nation," which came to be seen as a dangerous term signifying disruption, disorder, and even revolution. In the emigration a cluster of nobles gathered around the man many considered their uncrowned king, a scion of a once powerful aristocratic family, Adam Czartoryski. But this group, fearing the prospect of social unrest, restricted themselves to pointless diplomatic maneuvering among the European powers. They hoped that Poland might be restored in the name of legitimacy, on the basis of a negotiated settlement that would avoid the dangers of another rebellion. Within Poland itself many nobles may have shared the hopes of the Czartoryski circle, but since they could do little to further such a cause, they retreated to apolitical (and sometimes loyalist) lives.[49] Not only were the conservatives uncomfortable with the politics of the patriotic activists, but they found it difficult to speak the language of national romanticism. They might appreciate some of the poetry of Mickiewicz or Słowacki, but they soon discovered the disruptive force of the progressive historiosophies to which the concept of the nation had been so firmly linked.

Mochnacki was one of the first to attempt to construct a bridge between the traditional elites and the perceived democratic imperatives of Polish nationalism. He wanted to find a way to reconcile "revolution" and "restoration," but it seemed that there was no way to do so without resorting to a dynamic vision of historical time— and this was precisely what troubled most conservatives. During the November Uprising Mochnacki was widely regarded as a revolutionary, and his writings from the time justify this reputation. In February 1831 he argued that Poland had lost its independence, "because with us a minority, not a majority, has always constituted the nation." The social, cultural, and economic exploitation of the peasants, Mochnacki believed, prevented them from developing any loyalty to a nation. This situation would have to change. Mochnacki implored his countrymen to recognize that "the final moment is here, so stop persisting in that perverse reasoning, according to which an insurrection alone will save the country. A social revolution is necessary."[50]

After the defeat of the uprising, however, Mochnacki swung rapidly to the right, surprising and alienating his previous allies. Only seven months after penning his last cry for a social revolution, he declared that it was "obvious and doubtless" that "we rose up in the name of the eternal Poland! Our cause is restoration!" In one of the most curious political reversals of the day, he proclaimed that the revolt had really been an attempt to rebuild "the ancient monarchy of Bolesław or the Jagiellonians" rather than an effort to implement the "utopias of sophist theoreticians." Mochnacki had come to the conclusion that "now the only thing that matters is that we exist," so it was premature to worry about the social or economic forms of the future Polish state.[51]

Two days after publishing this startling self-renunciation, he attempted to clarify his position, revealing in the process how hard it was for a patriotic insurgent of the romantic era to become a conservative. In an essay entitled "Restoration and Revolution" Mochnacki repeated his thesis that Poland had to regain its independence before anyone could even talk about social reform. On the other hand, he still believed that Poland could never successfully rebel against Russia unless the nobility "called on the help of the people," which was possible only if the patriots "acted in the spirit of the people," with a "liberal imagination" and "revolutionary means." So, he concluded, the conservative nationalists had to embrace "the great idea of revolution, without which we will not save the monarchy . . . !"[52]

Mochnacki could not extricate the idea of radical social change from the patriotic discourse. The best he could do was to argue that social liberation had to come after independence, although this reasoning led him in circles, since he could not imagine a successful revolt without mass participation. Mochnacki's problem was that he was not merely arguing for a tactical recruitment of popular support for the national cause: he believed that such support was necessary if Poland was ever to become a nation in the fullest sense of the word (as he defined it). As we saw earlier, Mochnacki's nation was more than just a social category, more than just a "collection of people." Existence, therefore, did not depend upon Poland's "material form" or class structure. However, Mochnacki's nation also existed *in historical time,* within a diachronic framework that positioned a democratic nation at the end of Poland's march through a progressive narrative. For Mochnacki, "to be a nation"—to fully make manifest the national idea—required that Poland realize its inner need to express itself across all social classes and break down the barriers separating the powerful from the disenfranchised. But since this was a vision of the future, Mochnacki could also hope for another, more mundane form of national existence in the present: a restoration of the prepartition state. This progressive historiosophy helped Mochnacki integrate revolution and restoration, but it did not allow him to construct a compelling conservative stance. He seemed to be quibbling over timing, suggesting alternative chronologies without really weakening his original conviction that a People's Poland lay in the future. It was little comfort to a serf-owning aristocrat to say that the ancient monarchy had to be restored, only to supervise the transition of Poland toward less exclusive, more democratic form. Mochnacki's contemporaries, whether on the left or the right, were unable to square the circle of this reasoning, and in the last few years of his short life he was politically isolated.

At least two prominent conservatives, Henryk Rzewuski and Zygmunt Krasiński, employed some of the rhetoric of romantic nationalism. Both, however, eventually learned how difficult it had become to be a nationalist on the right. The former remained a consistent reactionary by effectively dehistoricizing national idealism, but in the process he abandoned the national cause altogether. The latter tried to sustain both a dynamic vision of historical time and a conservative political and social stance, only to have his work suppressed as "unchristian."

Count Henryk Rzewuski (1791–1866) has been justifiably dubbed the "Polish de Maistre."[53] He was an unapologetic reactionary, longing for a society in which a hereditary aristocracy ruled over an obedient peasantry, in which education was limited to instruction in religion and practical skills, and in which nothing of substance ever changed. He had no tolerance for any of the cultural, political, or social developments of the nineteenth century (or the eighteenth, for that matter), and he gained some fame writing historical novels glorifying the imagined golden age of the Polish "noble Republic."[54] His main work of nonfiction was *Wędrówki umysłowe* (*Intellectual Wanderings*, 1851), much of which was directly plagiarized from de Maistre. Rzewuski's writing on the nation employed the vocabulary used by the romantic nationalists, up to a point. His Poland, like that of Mochnacki and Mickiewicz, was more than just an aggregation of its constituent parts. "The nation is not only a collection of individuals living on some land," he wrote, employing a familiar formula, "because a collection is not yet a union of separate pieces into one discrete body."[55] But at this point Rzewuski's scheme veered sharply away from the accepted rhetoric of patriotism, because his Poland had no role in any progressive mission of salvation. Instead it was a static representation of an unchanging principle. "Every nation is the manifestation of some moral idea," he wrote, "to which its existence is bound. It lives as long as it represents [this idea]—if it stops practically expressing it, it must die, because it is not in its power to change its calling, since the moral idea is given by God."[56] Rzewuski's "moral idea" expressed itself *over* time but not *through* time; it was the manifestation of an unchanging divine law but it was not part of any historiosophical design. It could not be, because for Rzewuski the basic norms of a society, along with its hierarchies of authority, should never change. If they did, God would punish the nation in question, and this was precisely what happened to Poland. For Rzewuski it was impossible to intervene willfully in history so as to regain independence, and history itself held no promises of any sort of social or national redemption. God's verdict had been issued; now the Poles must obey the divinely ordained authority of the Tsar. Not surprisingly, Rzewuski was a lonely figure on the Polish intellectual scene.[57]

In contrast to Rzewuski, Zygmunt Krasiński (1813–1859) tried to remain a conservative while also embracing the historiosophical visions of his contemporaries, but even he was never entirely sure that doing so was possible. Krasiński is recognized today as one of the great Polish poets of the romantic era (along with Mickiewicz and Słowacki), but he was also a self-described conservative, praising the Catholic Church (the actually existing, institutionalized Church, not an idealized Christianity) and defending the authority of the nobility (the real aristocracy, not some sort of reformed meritocracy). But as much as Krasiński was drawn toward piety and tradition, he was also devoted to his nation and he could not reconcile himself to the loss of independence. Like Mochnacki, he had to imagine some sort of historical transformation, because as things stood, it was hard to see how Poland might return to the map of Europe. He thus accepted social and political change; he came to assume that "life" entailed "constant progress for all eternity." To find a theology of change within a conservative framework, he turned to a belief that was popular at the time: reincarnation.

For Krasiński, the idea that souls incarnated themselves in ever more perfect forms justified the existing social hierarchies: an aristocrat did not enjoy power and wealth by an accident of birth, because only noble souls would locate themselves within noble bodies. To position the nation within his scheme, Krasiński argued that the process of birth and rebirth did more than perfect individual souls; it moved humanity toward the creation of a true Kingdom of God on Earth. Employing a familiar romantic argument, Krasiński assigned nations the key role in constructing the collective utopia. "Just as humanity aspires to eternal life," he wrote, "so nations aspire to humanity." Krasiński realized that he was skirting the edges of heresy and he feared the condemnation of the Church. Upon his death in 1859 he bequeathed his theological–historiosophical work to two close friends—both of whom were priests—with a mandate to determine whether or not it should be posthumously released. The two suppressed the work, recognizing it as "unchristian both in its first principles and in its final conclusions."[58] Krasiński had attempted to distinguish his worldview from the pantheism and evolutionary spiritualism so characteristic of the early nineteenth-century left, but most scholars agree that he had to split some theological hairs to do so.[59] His belief in reincarnation was only a manifestation of a deeper transgression: an acceptance of *meaningful historical change.* A Catholic (and a conservative) was supposed to recognize that all transformations in social practices and political institutions were superficial and unimportant when set against the immutability of moral laws and spiritual existence (as, for example, had another Polish romantic, Cyprian Norwid).[60] God, the soul, good, and evil were all supposed to be constants, but Krasiński described humanity's progress toward what he called *boskość* (divinity). Krasiński's faith in history was far-reaching, encompassing both the spiritual and the social realms. To sustain his hopes for Poland's resurrection, he accepted the romantic faith in historical time and, in doing so, he embraced a teleology that prophesied social salvation as well as spiritual and national salvation. Krasiński wanted to be a conservative but he ended up with a historiosophy that made it difficult to conserve much of anything.

To say that it was hard to sustain a conservative stance within the nationalist framework is not to imply that it was impossible to talk about order or power altogether. There was little about Juliusz Słowacki, for example, that could be called conservative, but authority did play an important role in his writing. Although he declared that the idea of Poland was "spiritual freedom," this stance did not make him a democrat. He believed that the Polish idea of freedom was merely the means of creating a hierarchical world "in which higher souls would not serve lower ones," and he praised the fact that in the prepartition Polish state "no one would have thought about taking a drunken peasant . . . and placing him alongside a beautiful and noble knight." The purpose of freedom in Słowacki's ideal Poland was to ensure that "a soul growing in beauty would have no obstacles," and this entailed "a true hierarchy on earth according to service and spiritual strength."[61] Nonetheless, even as Słowacki repudiated egalitarian democracy, he was equally fervent in his rejection of all traditional forms of hierarchy. He demanded that all social and political systems allow for unlimited flexibility and mobility, so that the "great soul" could rise to the top and lead the community into the future. His vision of progressive time was the keystone that held this worldview together: the purpose of all existence was progress, the advancement of the Spirit toward its (re)unification with the divine.[62] But Słowacki would not equate the spiritually advanced with the socially or economically privileged; he would not allow his belief in reincarnation to become a justification for any stabilized (not to mention existing) forms of hierarchy or power. Quite the contrary, he insisted that greatness could come from any source, particularly the peasant masses. So, despite his principled opposition to egalitarianism, Słowacki in practice endorsed the social and political agenda of the radical left, hoping to break down existing forms of discipline and restraint in order to liberate the spiritual potential of the masses. He was driven, like so many of the others we will examine in this book, by a belief in historical time, in the need for humanity to move toward spiritual perfection. Even a potentially conservative and antiegalitarian doctrine like individual reincarnation became, in Słowacki's hands, a justification for revolutionary populism. He could imagine authority, but he could never stabilize this into a *system* of conservatism.

This sincere belief both in historical time and, more specifically, in an eschatological prophesy of dramatic change was so strong among the Polish romantics that even those who remained liberal in their political practice often advanced historical visions that presumed a future of radical social transformation. Perhaps the best example is August Cieszkowski, who could hardly be described as a revolutionary. Cieszkowski was a landowner and he participated in the leading political, social, and economic institutions of his day. From 1848 to 1870 he served as a delegate to the Prussian assembly, acting after 1860 as chair of the "Polish circle." He was one of the first to advocate "organic work," a plan to serve the Polish cause within the sociopolitical status quo (an approach we will explore in the next chapter), and he spoke of his desire for a "moral government" that would guide his countrymen toward practical engagement with their circumstances, away from the dangers of revolution. In *De la patrie et de l'aristocratie moderne* (Paris, 1844) Cieszkowski complained about any conception of democracy that placed numbers above quality, and he longed for the time when the "principle of organization" would arise to counter the "principle of equality."[63] But authority, in Cieszkowski's world, was always unstable. His liberalism was distinguished from the disciplinary preaching of a Malthus by his belief in historical time. Even as he called for a new "aristocracy" and defended "tradition," he added that "tradition is not shaped with one blow in an eternal form; it is ceaselessly shaping itself, it is transforming itself in the process of taking shape; it is progressing forward in accordance with the level of its development."[64] The philosophical principle behind this argument was elaborated in Cieszkowski's *Prologue to a Historiosophy*: "The famous and respected saying of Hegel, that everything rational is real and everything real is rational, requires a correction, in that both the rational and the real are only the results of development. In other words, at certain stages of the spirit, reason corresponds to reality, only to later outstrip each other dialectically; thus there arises in history epochs of dissonance. Reality is constantly *accommodating* itself to reason." The process of accommodation ensured that social forms were never fixed, that hierarchies were never to be taken for granted, that obedience could never be given without qualification, that social discipline would always contain within itself the dialectical seeds of creative disorder.

While claiming that socialism was an unrealistic dream for the moment, Cieszkowski also noted that it was possible for such a utopia "to have enormous meaning for the future."[65] This ambivalence toward the radical left was typical of Cieszkowski, who opposed the "terror" of revolution but argued that even such uncontrolled progress was better than stagnation or reaction.[66] He was unable to stabilize a liberal social order, let alone a conservative one, because he was convinced that all social and economic forms were transitory. A conservative would argue that certain hierarchies were naturally or divinely established; a liberal would respond that traditional networks of power were arbitrary but that certain economic "laws" (and thus certain forms of economic authority and property ownership) were natural and eternal. Cieszkowski, on the other hand, located all social practices and even all aspects of human personality within a diachronic framework, evolving toward a utopian "age of the Holy Spirit." This view is most striking in his *Ojcze Nasz* (Our Father), a lengthy meditation on the Lord's Prayer in which Cieszkowski criticized those who imagine anything to be constant.

> If the universe was dead, then the *here* and *there* would also be eternally engraved, immobile; the one world could never become the other, nor could the other become the first. And the miserable worlds would be eternally miserable, condemned, while the others would be eternally perfect and happy. But this universe is *alive*, so it has its own movement within itself, just like everything that is alive. So, by its immanent dialectic [the universe] transforms its constituent worlds; the state of reality is changed into the ideal and vice versa. . . . From this moment we will no longer consider heaven to be some sort of nonterrestrial sanctuary, nor earth as some sort of mundane sanctuary, and as a result the world will no longer be godless for us and God [will no longer be] transcendent [*bezświatowy*]. . . . This will be the ascension of earth and, correspondingly, the arrival of the Kingdom of Heaven on earth.

Cieszkowski envisioned a world marked by eternal harmony, a world without exploitation, poverty, suffering, misery, or injustice. While meditating on the prayer to "give us this day our daily bread," he praised Fourier for articulating one of the basic principles of the coming utopia: "that every member of society, without qualification and without exception . . . would have a permanent and unfailing guarantee of the means for survival, in accordance with individual needs and the level of their education." This guaranteed minimum would not be basic subsistence but would be enough to ensure that one could participate in society and work toward the fulfillment of one's potential. In *Du crédit et de la circulation* (Paris, 1839) he argued vigorously against the idea of *laissez passer,* offering instead the slogan *aidez á faire et developpez.*[67] Liberals assumed that humanity had a single, unchanging nature, Cieszkowski complained, when in fact almost anything—even the structures of human motivation—could and would change. "Everything will become new," he wrote, "just as with the coming of Christ the form of the world was entirely renewed."[68]

Cieszkowski defies all our ideological labels, because the sincerity of his historical vision allowed him to adopt a variety of political stances while never accepting any principle that fell short of his ideal as a permanent law of nature. It is no coincidence that Zygmunt Krasiński's path toward his "unchristian" heterodoxy began with a reading of *A Prologue to a Historiosophy.*[69] Cieszkowski was the most sophisticated of the romantic philosophers of history, but in most important aspects he was typical. Like his contemporaries, he saw the nation's salvation within a diachronic framework, and this belief drew him inexorably toward the left.

Jewish Poles

Romantic nationalism, as we have just seen, destabilized traditional networks of authority and challenged the very idea of a lasting system of power. Similarly (and for many of the same reasons) it undermined the rigid boundaries that separated the ethnic and religious communities of Eastern Europe. Polish nationalism in the period from 1830 to 1863 became more inclusive than it ever had been before and perhaps ever would be again. The most striking example can be seen in the unparalleled openness Polish nationalists showed toward the Jews around mid-century. As long as romantic idealism retained its power, it was difficult to enunciate openly one's judeophobia. This is not to say that all animosity faded away (it certainly did not), but to speak about hatred or exclusion forced one to step to the very edge of nationalist discourse. One could still be a judeophobe, but it was becoming increasingly difficult to be a judeophobic nationalist. Hatred was exiled, at least temporarily, from the rhetoric of nationalism and was relegated to other, less potent spaces.[70]

A certain tension between nationalism and judeophobia first emerged at the time of the third partition, in 1795. The brief Russo-Polish war preceding the final dismemberment of Poland (the so-called "Kościuszko Insurrection") was accompanied by a novel development: the creation of a Jewish-Polish legion. The legacy of the Polish Enlightenment was not necessarily favorable to the Jews, but Tadeusz Kościuszko's slogans of emancipation and independence attracted sufficient support, at least among polonized Jews, to justify the formation of a special Jewish military unit. Not only did about 500 Jews volunteer for the legion, but most of them lost their lives fighting for the Polish cause.[71] After these events we see the introduction of a new expression: "Poles of the Faith of Moses" (*Polacy wyznania mojżeszowego*). This suggests a strikingly new conception of Polishness: it became possible to construct such a formulation only when "Poland" came to signify something more than the narrowly defined noble community of the First Republic.[72] This term reflects a new conception of Jewishness as well, because to fit within this phrase, Jews had to relegate their distinctive identity to the private realm. Public spaces were reserved for "Poles," while "Jews" (and "Christians") were exiled to the world of "faith." This was undoubtedly a dramatic development, but it was necessarily limited to the tiny constituency of the assimilated (and, from the other side, to the small community of secular Enlightenment thinkers). Almost by definition, neither a Hasidic or Mitnagdic Jew, nor a traditional Catholic, could ever accept the requisite alienation of the secular and spiritual realms. All this suggested a new inclusiveness, but there were still too many strings attached.

During the first decades of the nineteenth century "equal rights" were often discussed, but few Poles were willing to follow this line of thought all the way to Jewish emancipation. The minister of the interior in Napoleon's Duchy of Warsaw, Jan Luszczewski, demonstrated how the vocabulary of equality could coexist with discrimination: "Everyone receives a fair share of rights and liberties," he wrote, "according to the age, civilization, customs, and even the religion that he brings into society. Nobody is likely to deny the Jews the right to civil freedom and equality before the law, but everybody must admit that these rights may be restricted by police regulations. . . . [Jews can be denied civic freedoms] because of the lower level of culture this people has in our country, compared with the West European states."[73] The ambivalence suggested by this passage was reflected in legal practice. Warsaw declared its public parks open to everyone as long as they wore "European dress," and the finer parts of town were closed off to Jews unless the individuals in question could demonstrate a "Polish" lifestyle.[74] In other words, Jews could be accepted as Poles, but only if they appeared to be Polish.

None of this should be surprising; such an approach was common throughout Europe at the time.[75] But this vocabulary was limited, and it was still very hard to talk about "Jewish Poles." To attach the adjective "Jewish" to the noun "Pole" implies that the former can serve as a subset of the latter. For this to work, only one of these terms can be defined as a culturally bounded community; otherwise the linkage creates an oxymoron. Before 1830 it was still generally accepted that Poland was delineated in this way; a concession might be made for religion (allowing the "Pole of the Faith of Moses"), but the specificity of this expression implied that faith would be stripped of broader cultural meaning. Even as the transcendent definition of the nation described above was taking hold among Polish intellectuals, a culturally limited approach to Polishness held on longest in discussions of the "Jewish question." As long as this was the case, the only path to Polish–Jewish amity was to limit the concept of "Jewish," devaluing (or even erasing) the Yiddish language and the traditions of the community. This made the emotional and cultural cost of entry into the

Polish community too high for most Jews. Before more Jews could be drawn to the idea of the "Jewish Pole," the noun in this phrase would have to become more expansive, so that the adjective could retain its cultural singularity.

During the November Uprising of 1830 it became clear how limited the offer of admission into "Poland" was. Faced with the urban unrest that accompanied the rebellion, the elites of Warsaw formed a National Guard, financed entirely by their own contributions, to establish "order" in the city. This conservative institution was highly prestigious, and several of Warsaw's wealthiest Jews wanted to join. After some initial hesitation the Guard was opened to the most distinguished Jews, with the proviso that they shave their beards. Poorer Jews (and those unwilling to shave) were allowed to join a less distinguished Urban Guard.[76] This story reveals the degree to which the idea of Polishness was still bounded, but it also suggests some of the tensions that were soon to emerge. The judeophobes who wanted to keep the Jews out of the struggle for Polish independence altogether were challenged, because the nationalism of 1830 was already too intertwined with a revolutionary message of justice, freedom, and inclusivity. It was hard to defend discrimination while fighting under the banner of "for our freedom and yours"; it was hard to extend an open hand to the enemy (the Russians) while refusing the outstretched arms of Warsaw's own Jews. The exclusion of Jews from the Polish community was becoming rhetorically difficult, even if it was still taking place.

In the decades after 1830 the Polish press (particularly in the emigration) debated the so-called Jewish question with renewed vigor. Many believed that the hesitance in welcoming the Jews into the rebellion contributed to Poland's defeat. The old arguments were repeated, but the terrain had shifted significantly. The principle of inclusivity described above was so well established that few could deny the *possibility* that Jews could join the nation. Even overtly judeophobic essays began with the presumption that Jews *could* be Poles. "Show that you really are Poles," declared an editorial in the periodical *Nowa Polska* in 1835. "Throw off your Jewish nature, stop being a separate nation which loves its customs, has its hopes and is awaiting liberation and days of supremacy. . . . The dissolution of the Israelite population as a nation, the changing of its inner, spiritual nature are conditions necessary for its political emancipation."[77] But this sort of argument was already old; similar citations could be found from the eighteenth century.[78] The only novelty was the pervasiveness of this attitude, or at least this rhetoric. By the 1850s, however, we can find Poles willing to accept Jews as compatriots without any presumption of cultural assimilation. The idea of the transcendent Polish nation had pushed ethnicity so far into the background that it became possible to imagine cultural diversity within the national community.

To explore how this happened, we must jump ahead of our story to glance momentarily at the next major Polish revolt, the January Insurrection of 1863.[79] When several patriotic demonstrators were killed by the police in early 1861, a period of national mourning was proclaimed by Catholic, Protestant, and Jewish leaders alike. In an unprecedented move, Jewish representatives attended Catholic commemorative masses in several cities, and Catholics in turn participated in comparable services at a number of synagogues.[80] On April 8, 1861, another demonstration ended in violence, and this time several Jews were discovered among the dead. The Polish response, across the political spectrum, was stunning. Adam Czartoryski, the leading aristocrat in the emigration, proclaimed, "Today the Polish Jews, united with us by the enormous sufferings and tortures inflicted by the same hand, have ceased to be a nation within the nation and, having recognized as their mother this motherland which has fed them for such a long time, have rendered it great services."[81] A similar assessment came from some nationalists inside the Kingdom when they petitioned the Council of State that "in accordance with the general wish of the nation, [you] decree full equality before the law for the Jews, as our brothers and the sons of one Fatherland."[82] The language of the left was even more enthusiastic. A manifesto released by the revolutionary underground inserted the Jews into the familiar Polish teleology: "Another visible grace of Providence for Poland, which is only now being redeemed from the sins of captivity, is the union, sealed by the joint martyrdom of Poland's Christian and Israelite sons: these arks of a funeral covenant were borne on the shoulders of both Levites and Christians to the fraternal cemetery and thus to a joint resurrection. Since this day there have no longer been two population groups on the common soil of oppression, but one nation."[83]

All of these citations, from opposite political camps, reflect the new vision of the nation that had finally taken root. A proclamation of the uprising's National Government, dated June 22, 1863, announced that the leaders of the revolt "recognize no differences between faiths. Henceforth in the Polish lands it will not be asked whether one is a 'Jew' or a 'Christian' because the name 'Pole' alone will suffice."[84] These were not proposals for Polish–Jewish cooperation or understanding: these were assertions that there was only one nation, with a common teleological history, to which both groups belonged. More precisely, there was now only one nation within which Jews and Christians alike *participated*. In all these citations membership in the nation required *action*, not cultural change. It no longer mattered what the Jews were *like*—it was what they had *done* that counted. As a character in Józef Ignacy Kraszewski's novel *Żyd* put it, "be our brothers, but brothers in spirit rather than in word; brothers in deed rather than in appearance."[85] Once again Poland was embodied in the deed, and cultural characteristics were relegated to the margins. As the unrest in Poland escalated and more Jews died—several hundred were killed in the fighting and at least twenty were hanged—the image of the Jewish Pole gained currency.[86]

The Jews of Warsaw responded with enthusiasm to this new conceptualization of "Poland." One of the city's leading rabbis, Izaak Kramsztyk, had been delivering his sermons in Polish since 1852. In 1861, right after the violent demonstration mentioned above, he declared, "There, where the heart feels tenderness, where love unites couples, where we heard for the first time the sweet, babbling expressions, 'father, mother'—there, brothers, there is the country which we ought to love. So let us unite in love for the country and for the remainder of our brothers of different faiths; let us go forward with them on the path of enlightenment and civilization, on the path of science and tolerance."[87] As is suggested in this passage, the first Jews to respond to the changed Polish rhetoric were those already favorably inclined to assimilate. In July 1861 a new periodical appeared: *Jutrzenka—Tygodnik dla Izraelitów Polskich* (The Dawn—A Weekly for Polish Israelites). As the title reveals, this was a Jewish magazine written in the Polish language, an almost unprecedented novelty.[88] The introductory editorial in the first issue, written by an assimilated (polonized) Jew named Daniel Neufeld, explored the new inclusiveness by deploying such loaded terms as "fatherland," "compatriots," and above all, "us."

> The Israelites constitute among us almost one eighth of the population, yet regarding religious and family life they are practically unknown to their compatriots of other faiths; thus the warped images of them, thus the misunderstandings—temporary of course, but always painful for both sides (which really ought not to be [separate] sides) and harmful for the community. . . . Appearing in the Polish language, *Jutrzenka* will influence the spread of the language of the fatherland among all strata of the Israelite population.[89]

The paper was assimilationist and reformist—the fact that it was written in Polish demonstrated this—but it also emphasized the need to respect religious diversity. Neufeld published translations of Hebrew texts and strove to explain Jewish traditions to a Polish audience. It was as if the willingness of Poles in 1861 to accept the Jews *as Jews* created a space within which at least some Jews were comfortable identifying themselves as Poles without feeling defensive about charges that they were abandoning their heritage. Kramsztyk could now cry with enthusiasm, "The children of one land are brothers."[90] Perhaps the great irony of tolerance was that it furthered the cause of assimilation and facilitated the appearance of new periodicals like *Jutrzenka.* The Polish press responded with enthusiasm to this new paper, and it seemed possible that the ancient wall between Pole and Jew was finally cracking. The editors even received a letter from a Warsaw priest, Father F. Mikulski, with his "wish that differences of faith will no longer divide the sons of one land. . . . Love, brotherhood, can only bring together the sons of one God."[91] A new nation seemed to be emerging, one that contained room for plurality. Appropriately, one of the strongest Jewish supporters of the Polish cause during the 1863 Uprising was Warsaw's leading Orthodox rabbi, Baer Meisels—otherwise no friend of the progressive Jews who frequented Kramsztyk's synagogue.[92]

Did all this imply that judeophobia was fading from Polish culture? Not at all. But it did signal that judeophobes had to find places outside the nationalist discourse within which to talk about their hatreds. One such place was the Church, where the Archbishop of Warsaw, Zygmunt Feliński, typified the attitude of the Catholic hierarchy. For Feliński, the philo-Semitism of the nationalist underground was one of the reasons for collaborating with the Russians. His image of the Jews belonged to a world that nearly all Polish nationalists had abandoned, at least temporarily. "Jews have been sent to Poland by God," he wrote "to be a gutter into which, in the era of the stock exchange, trade, and swindle, carries away all the dirt which should not soil Polish hands."[93] Feliński found a small audience among the most conservative aristocrats, but his voice was relegated to the margins of public life, and his pro-Russian, judeophobic diatribes were widely scorned. For decades after this the most vitriolic judeophobia would be similarly linked with collaborationist politics and calls for Russo-Polish unity against the "Jewish menace."[94]

The nationalism of the mid-nineteenth century—the nationalism of Mochnacki and Mickiewicz—had thus opened up new spaces for inclusivity and diversity. We should not make too much of this, because Poland did not suddenly become a multicultural utopia. My claim here is more modest: as long as the nation was perceived in terms of the revolutionary and patriotic act, all conceptual frontiers had to remain permeable. Soon, however, the moment of national action would arrive, with the largest rebellion in the history of partitioned Poland, the January Uprising of 1863. Then the world described in this chapter would begin to unravel.

2

The Social Nation

In 1863 the call for action was heeded. Aided by the atmosphere of reform in the tsarist empire during the early 1860s, patriotic activists in Warsaw began a campaign of public demonstrations on behalf of the Polish cause. Each time the Russians tried to suppress these protests, the movement only grew. For decades nationalists had claimed that only through "the deed" would Poland be made manifest, that only "national action" would advance them toward the promised land of peace, brotherhood, justice, and (not least) independence. Now the ultimate opportunity to act had arrived, and in early 1863 hundreds of thousands of Poles took up arms against the Russian occupation. The so-called January Uprising brought unprecedented violence and mobilized more Poles than any previous display of patriotism. The revolt was fought as a guerrilla war and was accompanied by all the violence and destruction we have come to expect from such conflicts. But it was all in vain: by mid-1864 the Russians had captured the last of the rebellion's leaders, and a dark period of military occupation and martial law began. What 1848 had been for most of Europe, 1863 was for the Poles. The moment of national salvation seemed to have arrived, but in the end the dream turned out to be as distant as ever. Not only did thousands lose their lives, but the defeat seemed to negate the ideals, beliefs, and hopes that had sustained so many for so long. To make matters worse, out of the ashes arose not a Phoenix, but something distressingly mundane: liberalism.

Liberalism played a central role in the intellectual life of the Russian partition of Poland for only a brief moment (from the late 1860s to the mid-1880s), but during this period the very definition of the nation was reformulated to accommodate the needs of an era in which revolt no longer seemed possible. Polish liberalism was part of a broad intellectual and cultural trend—this was an era when the ideas of writers such as John Stuart Mill and Herbert Spencer were transforming the intellectual landscape all over Europe—but in Poland liberalism was also a specific response to the failure of 1863. The Polish liberals (more commonly known, for reasons I explain later, as the "Warsaw positivists") did not just talk about laissez-faire economics, bourgeois values, anticlericalism, and modernization; above all they gave Polish intellectuals a new way to talk about the nation and to imagine its future. The positivists took Poland out of the political framework—out of the realm of open contestation and action—and recast it within a *social* mode of thought. The nation-as-public-actor described in the last chapter became the nation-as-social-collective. When the positivists discussed the nation, they addressed issues of structure and identity; agency and will were deemphasized and eventually delegitimized. The nation became a "society," not a "cause," and the language used to talk about it was that of science rather than poetry. The nation that had once acted in history became a community, subject to the laws of nature.

Before 1863 there was little space within the framework of Polish nationalism to talk about either ethnic identity or social discipline and authority. The nation was an act, not a static social object; that is, it expressed its being through the deeds of revolutionary patriots and did not merely exist as a sociological category. For the nation to exclude and oppress, it had to be embodied (so that walls could be constructed around it) and it had to be inserted into a framework that allowed for the exertion of discipline. The positivists would perform both these maneuvers as they attempted to reassemble the world that had been shattered in 1863. In this way liberalism helped set the stage for the chauvinism and authoritarianism that would come later. This is not to blame the liberals for the sins of the extreme right; rather, it is to point out that liberalism, for all its talk of "freedom," contained within itself the seeds of its own negation. Our discussion of Warsaw positivism, however, will also show that the reconfiguration of social space (the delineation of the nation as an ethnolinguistic community instead of a transcendent collective actor) was not enough to unleash the full disciplinary power of "modern" nationalism. This move had to be accompanied by an abandonment of historical time, and that would not come until later.

Positivism

The story of Polish positivism begins in 1866 with a struggling young journalist named Adam Wiślicki (1836–1913).[1] For four years he had been trying to find a place for himself in the intellectual life of Warsaw, but he remained isolated. Not only was he a liberal in the conservative world of the legal (i.e., censored) press, but he was an opponent of violence at a time when it seemed that all his peers had taken up arms. In January 1866, as Poles were still adjusting to the new conditions of the post-uprising world, Wiślicki carved out his own space amid the rubble by founding a magazine called *Przegląd Tygodniowy* (The Weekly Review). In the first issue he declared enigmatically, "I am founding a new publication because I see a position that has not yet been occupied."[2] He did not give that position a name, but it was soon obvious that he was trying to establish an organ for a nascent Polish liberalism. Within a few months he had composed articles praising industrialization, modernization, secularism, and women's rights. In September he introduced to his Polish readers the enormously popular English liberal Samuel Smiles, and early the next year he published his own translation of Smiles' most famous book, *Self Help*.[3] "Work, learn, save!" Wiślicki proclaimed, as he urged his compatriots to embrace entrepreneurial values.[4]

Despite all these familiar arguments, *Przegląd Tygodniowy* was not the mouth-piece of a rising business class. In fact the paper was not anyone's mouthpiece in the 1860s: it had few readers or advertisers and was constantly on the edge of bankruptcy. Wiślicki's dream was to *create* a bourgeoisie—and thus an audience—where one did not exist.[5] Faced with declining circulation and unable to afford any of the noted publicists of the day, he decided to fill the pages of his modest paper with the writing of recent university graduates, making a virtue out of a necessity by advertising *Przegląd Tygodniowy* as the voice of a new generation. He drew his staff primarily from the *Szkoła Główna Warszawska* (The Warsaw Main School), a university formed in 1862 in a failed attempt to appease the restless youth of Warsaw. This institution never gained much respect among the Poles. The professors signed a loyalty oath rather than face the closure of the academy in 1863, and the atmosphere on campus was widely perceived to be loyalist.[6] Moreover, conditions at the *Szkoła* were poor: the library was woefully inadequate, the professors were poorly qualified (with salaries half that of their Russian counterparts), and the facilities were dreadful. This hardly seems like the environment from which the leading minds of late nineteenth-century Poland would emerge, but during its few years of existence the *Szkoła* produced a cadre of alumni who were soon to transform Polish intellectual life: the so-called *młoda prasa* (the young press).

The early contributors to *Przegląd Tygodniowy* included Jan Baudouin de Courtenay (1845–1929), Walery Przyborowski (1845–1913), Feliks Bogacki (1847–1916), Piotr Chmielowski (1848–1904), Józef Kotarbiński (1849–1928), Aleksander Świętochowski (1849–1938), Julian Ochorowicz (1850–1917), Adolf Dygasiński (1839–1902), and Bolesław Limanowski (1835–1935). This partial list illustrates the most important feature of *Przegląd Tygodniowy*: most of these authors were born between 1845 and 1850 and were therefore in their early twenties when they joined the paper. The "elders" of *Przegląd Tygodniowy*—Dygasiński, Limanowski, and Wiślicki himself—were only about ten years older. These ambitious, articulate young intellectuals had a lot in common.[7] None of them was tied to the old aristocracy: most of their parents were either merchants or professionals, and the few nobles among them were from poor, landless families. Also they came of age during and after 1863 and saw their lives disrupted by a revolt they were too young to join or, at the time, fully understand. These were people with little allegiance to either the old noble elites of Poland or the radical nationalists. They would turn against both.

Hoping someone would write something outrageous enough to bring attention to his paper, Wiślicki exerted little editorial control over his young charges.[8] He was not disappointed: in 1871 Aleksander Świętochowski turned the paper around with a blistering assault on the entire older generation. Both Świętochowski and his friend Piotr Chmielowski later described an article from that year, "We and You," as the manifesto of their generation, and subsequent historians have identified this as a turn-ing point in the development of Warsaw positivism.[9] "We" were the young, with no time to worry about the past; "you" were the old guard, desperately holding on to antiquated principles. "The old ones," he wrote, "instead of retreating from a field upon which they can no longer accomplish anything, stand on it stubbornly, delaying the progress of convictions."[10] Thanks to Świętochowski's vitriolic prose, the conservatives finally noticed *Przegląd Tygodniowy*. The "debate" that followed degenerated into an exchange of insults, but Wiślicki was satisfied: his circulation doubled the following year.[11]

Świętochowski later characterized the emerging ideological divide in Warsaw with typical invective. On the one side, he wrote, stood "the slavery of thought, self-praise, the degradation of others, error, lies, hypocrisy, [and] ultramontanism." Opposing these principles were "the freedom of conviction, justice, science, tolerance, and truth."[12] From this list of terms, the most important might seem to be the least emotionally charged: science. The members of the *młoda prasa* proclaimed themselves to be "positivists," and when in 1872 some of them founded a new magazine called *Niwa* (The Field), they adorned the masthead with the revealing slogan "Knowledge Is Power." Their science, however, was distinctly liberal. The hostile eye of Teodor Jeske-Choiński, a leading conservative critic of the positivists, was in this case perceptive:

> If our positivists had been a scientific school . . . only supporting the hard
> sciences, it would be possible to forgive them for their excessive trust in the
> witness of the senses. But they wanted to reform views on the corporeal world
> and [the world] beyond the grave, on feelings, dreams, aspirations, work
> practices; in a word, they wanted to turn man inside out, give him another soul,
> another heart, blood, instincts; they were not scientists, but in the first place
> publicists, teachers of society.[13]

The positivists did indeed want to give their fellow Poles "another soul, heart, blood, and instincts"; they wanted to replace what they saw as the characteristics of the old Poland—traditionalism, particularism, chauvinism, mysticism, and obscurantism—with the traits of the modern and scientific individual. The new Pole would bring the nation out of the backwardness of the Russian Empire into the modern world of Europe by shifting the nation's attention to problems of administration, management, economics, education, and industry. For the positivists, science was to be the new national agenda—a means of negating both the "national action" of the romantics and the conservatism of the legal Warsaw press.

The label "positivism" was actually attached to the *młoda prasa* by some conservative opponents before the positivists themselves knew what it meant. Not surprisingly, then, the relationship between these Poles and their supposed Western models would always be problematic. Chmielowski admitted that he and his friends accepted the label "positivist" after being so tagged by an opponent, because it sounded fashionable and because they could think of nothing better to call themselves.[14] Much of what they initially knew about West European positivism came through the prism of conservative professors hostile to new trends in philosophy and science.[15] Świętochowski tried to put the best face on his youthful ignorance: "We called ourselves positivists before we were familiar with positivist literature. This was indeed the case, but this fact brings honor, not insult. It demonstrates that this was an indigenous movement, that the flood of ideas arose from local ground and did not flow from abroad."[16] We must therefore be careful when we use the term "positivism." To the Western reader the label might evoke images of Comte's religion of the *Grande Être,* with its hierarchical secular priesthood, its managed economy, and its boundless faith in science. The Warsaw positivists, however, were not Comtean; in fact, none of them read Comte or even his popularizer, Émile Littré, until several years later, at which time they firmly rejected the Frenchman's religiosity and mysticism.[17]

Instead of Comte, British liberals such as John Stuart Mill and Herbert Spencer stood at the center of the *młoda prasa*'s pantheon.[18] The Poles found in these authors a combination of liberalism and science that served them well. Świętochowski read a translation of *On Liberty* while still in secondary school, and for the rest of his life he declared himself to be Mill's disciple. He included Mill on his list of the great minds of history, along with Copernicus, Kepler, Newton, Voltaire, and Darwin.[19] The positivist philosopher Władysław Kozłowski credited Mill with turning his attention to the "objective world," away from the abstractions of "metaphysics" and "Kantian reason."[20] But Mill, for all his prestige, could not compete with the amazing popularity of Herbert Spencer in post-1863 Warsaw. The novelist Bolesław Prus was probably not exaggerating when he pointed to the second volume of *Principles of Sociology* as the source for his own "first principles."[21] Kozłowski echoed the opinion of most of his colleagues when he described Spencer as "one of the most powerful thinkers; a philosopher who amazes [us] as much by the enormity of his knowledge [and] the depth and originality of his ideas, as by the precision of his proof and the clarity of his presentation."[22] Beginning in 1872 *Przegląd Tygodniowy* printed several articles about Spencer's thought, including a systematic five-part outline of his ideas, and between 1878 and 1884 *Ateneum* (a respected positivist monthly) published an irregular series by Kozłowski summarizing Spencer's work. These interpretive essays were important, because with a few minor exceptions Spencer's writing was not translated into Polish until 1884. Before then the Spencer so many Poles exalted was primarily a creation of Świętochowski and Kozłowski.[23]

Another Englishman, Charles Darwin, is mentioned in the secondary literature alongside Mill and Spencer, but his relationship to the positivists is more problematic. Even in the 1860s his name was a symbol—an ideal for the liberal positivists and an expletive for the conservatives. *The Origin of Species* was translated in 1873 (by a former student of the *Szkoła Główna,* Adolf Dygasiński), but there is little evidence that many people actually read it. "Darwin" became a sort of mantra, a name to be repeated rather than a thinker whose ideas one should engage. A critic for *Przegląd Tygodniowy* even invoked Darwin, with amusing but typical misunderstanding, in a fashion review: the English master has taught us, this author proclaimed, that women's clothing should be more comfortable so as to advance the positive evolution of the species.[24] Chmielowski admitted that even as the publicists of *Przegląd Tygodniowy* defended Darwin against conservative Catholic critics, they had not yet read his work. Darwinism, he wrote, "was a question that caused a lot of noise, brought forth hysterical brochures, aroused a terrible uproar on the pages of the conservative press, but for the time being could not become a general slogan—because not only its opponents, but even its adherents did not have a clear conception of it. To understand [Darwin], a well-founded knowledge of the natural sciences was required, and at that time most of its advocates were counted among philologists and lawyers."[25] Whether or not Darwin was indeed this difficult to understand, it is certainly true that the positivists only adopted his name as a slogan. The meaning of that slogan was evident in Świętochowski's 1882 eulogy: "Darwin has died. This means as much as the death of Aristotle, Copernicus, or Kant. . . . All the sciences should gather together and weep over his coffin, for he gave all of them new life. . . . For the conservatives, Darwin was perhaps the most threatening sage in history; no one in our century has gained so many scientific victories, no one has brought about so many intellectual revolutions."[26] Świętochowski pitted "science" against "the conservatives" and described the former as the cause of a revolution that was both epistemological and political.

"Science" signified to the positivists a monistic philosophy, based upon laws of universal applicability. As one of the earliest expositions of positivist thought in Poland put it, "thanks to the positivist method, the physical world is tied to the social world; the unity dissolved by the centuries is returned. Just as those two worlds belong to each other, so must the sciences occupied with them belong to each other, [and] stand as one science."[27] This scientific (or scientistic) optimism became quite popular in Warsaw in the early 1870s, but "science" was not merely a way to obtain knowledge: it was a foundation upon which one could build a better world. Ochorowicz was searching for the "basic laws that ought to guide our actions," and the editors of Niwa declared that "the most magnificent product of science is the cleansing, elevating, and ennobling of ideals, along with the provision of the means to realize them."[28] Prus was perhaps the most devoted to this "practical positivism," arguing that people would never be able to improve their lives or their societies if they did not first gain an understanding of the natural and social sciences.[29] The "laws of development" sought by the positivists turned out to be quintessentially liberal: they discussed issues like women's rights, Jewish emancipation and assimilation, the role of the Church, and the virtues and vices of industrial development. On this level their arguments were familiar and could be heard in London, Paris, or Berlin as well as Warsaw. In Poland, however, the debates were more than a translation of well-established polemics, because the entire discussion was superimposed upon a dispute about the nature and direction of the national cause. The positivists were not just trying to bring liberalism to Poland; they were trying to create a *national* liberalism that would make sense in the atmosphere of defeat and despair after 1863.

Work, Work, and Work

From the earliest days of *Przegląd Tygodniowy,* Wiślicki tried to direct his countrymen away from the "grand ambitions" and "adventuresome conspiracies" of the past. He wanted to shift their attention away from "high politics" (the "abstract" problems of international diplomacy or the conflicts of ruling elites), toward "small politics" (the newest methods of raising sheep, spreading literacy, financing higher education, and building railroads). As he put it in 1871, "Small politics is internal work; it is a small seed, but a fertile one. High politics is a roar of meaningless clichés, clichés without end."[30] Świętochowski echoed this argument in 1872: "Only a madman would lie in a dirty peasant hut and dream of crystal palaces. Let society, rather than complain about obstacles, work wherever it has an open field."[31] The "dream" became a common positivist trope, allowing them to contrast productive "work" with all sorts of lofty ambitions—most important those of the romantic nationalists. Świętochowski even argued that romanticism, despite its doctrine of action, was in fact a justification for passivity. In his most scathing satire of national messianism, he came as close as he ever would to attacking Mickiewicz directly.

> Songs praising our greatness and deriding the pettiness of the Germans, the
> English, the Americans, the French, the Italians, etc. sound most beautiful to our
> ears. The first do not have enough faith, the second feeling, others higher
> pleasures, others finally morality. We and only we are the embodiment of all
> virtue, according to this theory. . . . If our professorial researchers do not know
> what the Germans have done in their science for the last half century . . . that
> does not matter. For we, as the chosen people, take our knowledge through the
> medium of inspiration directly from heaven. . . . Possessing such a privilege, we
> base our political, social, and intellectual careers upon it. We do not die, because
> we sleep and dream.[32]

Not only was Świętochowski lampooning the national stereotypes and biblical imagery of the romantics, but he even dared to parody Józef Wybicki's famous lyric, "Poland has not yet died." For the romantics, to dream was to envision the ideal, so as to fight for its realization; for Świętochowski, to dream was to sleep and to ignore the necessity of science and hard work. As he put it in another article, "In a word, every individual ought to know precisely how far the bounds of possibility extend. . . . We make thousands of errors not knowing what can be freely done. . . . The strong soul easily shakes off the most painful impression, soberly looks around at his circumstances, seizes upon all his advantages, and with the force of energy throws himself *to work* with a full awareness of its burdens." Instead of wasting lives in a futile uprising, Świętochowski argued, Poles should determine precisely what they could do under the existing circumstances and "exploit that situation as far as possible for the common good." Now that the rebellion had failed, the true hero would no longer be the warrior—the man of action—but instead "the one who, in the moments of both exaltation and peace, refuses to abandon [his] duties concerning the general welfare."[33] Elsewhere an anonymous contributor to *Przegląd Tygodniowy* contrasted the worthless "sacrifice" with the productive work that arose from one's "duty" to advance "the common good."[34] In a particularly controversial article (and a particularly long sentence) from 1887, Bolesław Prus instructed the young to remember:

> that great ideas are made up of the simplest ideas and only he who does not place
> before himself projects exceeding his strength may be great; that the greatest
> social reform is the perfection of the individual and that only he who manages to
> perfect himself may think about [social reform]; that the greatest work is

precisely the fulfillment of those obligations that seem to us to be every-day,
shallow, and at times even unpleasant; that the greatest undertaking is to restrain
one's imagination and succumb to the yoke not of personal feelings and impulses
but of the interests of the whole; that wanting to know the interests of the whole,
it is necessary to carefully study it for many years; that wanting to be ever more
perfect, it is necessary to shape one's muscles, reason, and character; that,
finally, it is necessary to shun clichés and count on facts.[35]

Prus was inundated with letters protesting this thesis. The young need ideals to inspire them, many of his readers argued; they could not be satisfied with such mundane tasks. If the young took his advice, they would become passive. Prus responded
that "there are intermediate times between the idyll and the battle, when it is not
possible to either live with a smile, or die with honor, only work, work, and work."[36]
There was no room for the Christ of Nations in the world of the positivists. There
were no miracles, no moments of salvation, no revolutions, no sudden resurrections.
Instead of Mickiewicz, we find Mill; instead of the visionary, we find the realist;
instead of national action, we find work.

All this implied more than just a change of tactics: this was a reformulation of
the entire discursive framework within which the positivists could talk about the
nation, and a dramatic shift in the imagined consequences of Polish nationalism. For
Poland to be a space for work and duty rather than for action and sacrifice, the positivists had to reconsider the very definition of the nation. In doing so, they transformed it into something that could be worked upon—into an empirically identifiable *society*. Prus put it this way:

> [The romantic nationalists] do not *really* love our landscapes and they have
> contempt for the peasants, the craftsmen, the merchants. . . . This means that
> these people do not love the *real* country and society in which we live and which
> constitute the real human fatherland, but are in love with some sort of mental
> construct built from distant memories and vague desires. For that *unreal* country
> and society they are indeed prepared for sacrifices and exertions, which,
> however, do not bring the least benefit to the *real* land and its inhabitants.[37]

This "real land," this "real country and society," constituted the positivist nation. It
was supposed to be concrete, visible, tangible—the stuff of science, not the stuff of
poetry. "Poland" was now a community of Poles, not a transcendent "national spirit"
or "essence" moving through and driving history. The authors who first introduced
this vision of Poland into the nationalist discourse did not articulate precisely who
these "real Poles" were or what standards one could employ to delineate this new
community. They talked about things like language, folk practices, history, and traditions, but the censorship of the post-1863 era made it difficult to confront this
issue directly.[38] Nonetheless, it was clear that the positivists were striking at the very
definition of the nation: for the romantics, the nation was made manifest through the
patriotic act; now the nation was a sociological formation, a community stripped of
independent volition.

Work, then, was not just an alternative form of national action, but a repudiation of action altogether and a concomitant redefinition of the nation itself. On the most basic level this shift reflected a departure from the world of "will" and the construction of a new world of "science" and "law." The positivists removed their nation from the realm of active contestation, stripped it of will, and took from it the power to shape history. "Naturally," Świętochowski proclaimed in 1872, *"will is only another manifestation of a general process that takes its beginning from reason and feeling."* He relied heavily on citations from Spencer to demonstrate that the very concept of an autonomous subject—"the free will of a certain 'I'"—was not a viable category for those who understood the modern science of psychology.[39] Władysław Kozłowski, Spencer's leading disciple in Poland, further negated the power of independent volition in a series of articles from 1886 entitled "Determinism and Free Will." The idea of autonomous volition, Kozłowski wrote, was a mere "doctrine" that had "absolutely no meaning in real life." Even thoughts and feelings were no more than "a reflection of external forces, their passive echo."[40] Another (anonymous) author in *Przegląd Tygodniowy* located these external forces in the social collective: "the community [*ogół*] strongly influences the individual—and in contrast the individual's power of action upon the community is reduced to very narrow boundaries and depends upon circumstances. The more a man is above his epoch, the less he will be understood and the less influence he will have on his contemporaries."[41]

There was, then, a strong tendency among these Warsaw writers to negate free will in favor of a scientistic determinism.[42] Having subjected the individual to such powerful social forces, however, the positivists had to configure this argument so as to make it possible to "work" (even if one could no longer "act"). To justify his call for work, Świętochowski attempted to reintegrate some form of self-determined activity within his tightly bounded universe of science. "Everyone is the blacksmith of his own fate," he declared, "[and] that maxim is just as valuable in social life as in individual life. Let us not search, therefore, for any dreamed-of friend or savior, but place all our trust in our own strength; let us not consider ourselves a chosen nation, the happiness of which is the obligation of all others, but [instead let us see ourselves as a nation] destined for the hard and difficult conditions of existence." But to become the blacksmith of one's own fate did not suggest any course of political action. Quite the contrary: Świętochowski instructed his countrymen to turn away from grand hopes, to turn away from "politicizing" (*politykowanie*) and to begin "conducting a policy [based upon] the interests of our society, a policy that is open, pure, [and] feasible within the bounds of the currently existing laws."[43] Elsewhere he warned, "When the community falls because of the ruinous negligence, laziness, and backwardness of its members, no complaints about hurt feelings will manage to ward off its dissolution. Happiness and prosperity must be constructed. Every phenomenon has its natural source and its natural consequences and no force will change the logic of events."[44] There was room in this argument for work—for the "construction" of "happiness and prosperity"—but there was no space for the sort of political action that stood at the center of Mickiewicz's world. Work was part of a *social process:* one could construct the tools, apply the basic force of labor, and the "logic of events" (the laws of nature) would do the rest, for better or worse. Work was thus contrasted with willful action, but it was also an alternative to passivity.

For the positivists, the difference between action and work paralleled that between politics and economics, between the insurgent and the entrepreneur, and above all between the "ideal" and the "real." One engaged in willful acts when one stepped beyond the realm of the "real" (defined as the political status quo) and pursued an agenda of revolutionary change. At the same time, if one remained "passive," one was equally guilty of "ruinous negligence." Into the gap between passivity and revolution, the positivists inserted liberalism—the "small politics" of Wiślicki, the "work, work, work" of Prus. Their critique of free will was not just a philosophical argument: it was part of a quintessentially liberal shift away from the political realm, toward the "private" world of work. The positivists still imagined liberal *social* change, but they limited their agenda to that which could be achieved within the boundaries of the existing political structures and property relations. In Western Europe such a shift to the private ensured that the state would not restrict the activities of the individual entrepreneur; in the Russian Empire, where a bourgeoisie (as commonly understood) hardly existed and where the state was most emphatically *not* the organ of any "public," this rhetorical move had profoundly different consequences. In this context, to repudiate collective action could not lead to the consolidation of liberal individualism, but could only reinforce the autocracy. The potentially subversive force of nationalism was suppressed as the positivists deprived both individuals and communities of the power to strive for change. The disavowal of "great ideals" was not a mere turn toward practicality, but a rejection of any active program of substantive political transformation. Not all nationalists before 1863 were revolutionaries, but the discourse of nationalism had contained abundant spaces within which one could talk about radical change. As was discussed in the previous chapter, many Polish intellectuals had struggled with the revolutionary implications of national idealism; now the positivists—though liberals all—were going to have to struggle with the conservative implications of "work."

Authority and the Social Organism

Decades later, at a student reunion for the Lublin secondary school at which Prus, Ochorowicz, and Świętochowski had studied, a speaker claimed that the positivists had introduced the idea of "organic work." He described the after-school discussion groups of the 1860s:

> in which they talked about how to organize the social order so as to extricate themselves from the disaster that had been caused by the defeated uprising. As is known, they criticized the political leadership for starting the uprising in the wrong way and at the wrong time, [and argued that] the disaster was caused by our national romanticism, of which we had to be cured, creating a different social order. The result of the deliberations among the young people of those days was the rise of the idea of organic work—work at the foundations and later positivism.[45]

This speaker was recounting an already familiar narrative, but one containing a significant misrepresentation: the idea of organic work did not emerge from these discussions among the youthful positivists-to-be, because conservatives had been advocating the same agenda for several years. This brings us to a complex set of tensions within Warsaw positivism. The positivists wanted simultaneously to advance "scientific" liberalism and to repudiate the nationalist activism of 1863, but to accomplish the latter they had to occupy the same position that the conservatives then held. Even before the 1860s much of the landed nobility, frightened by nationalism's revolutionary content, had abandoned both the language and the agenda of the romantics, turning instead to a more "sober" vocabulary and a less assertive patriotism. When Wiślicki and his contributors tried to depoliticize the nation and remove it from the world of contestation and volition, they found themselves alongside their ideological adversaries.[46] The positivists were to learn that their creative assimilation of the right's terminology was not without consequences. There were several holes through which conservative principles of stability, hierarchy, and discipline penetrated the allegedly transformative, progressive liberalism of the *młoda prasa*.

Many Polish conservatives remained within the patriotic tradition even after the defeat of 1830, but it became increasingly difficult for them to do so after 1846, when a nationalist conspiracy in Galicia helped spark a violent peasant jacquerie. Two years later the events of 1848 demonstrated to nobles throughout the region the dangers of patriotic rhetoric. At the time of the November Uprising it had been possible to imagine a national war of liberation without significant consequences for the social order, but this was no longer conceivable after the tumultuous 1840s. Since the Habsburg Empire experienced the most turbulence in those years, the Austrian partition—Galicia—became the bastion of a new sort of Polish conservatism, one that dramatically reconfigured the relationship between nation and state. As early as 1846 a Galician named Antoni Helcel argued that a nation did not need a state to exist: all that was necessary was a language, an educational system, a religion, a set of traditions and laws, and some hereditary institutions. If the Poles could sustain these attributes, they could thrive within the boundaries of the Habsburg Empire. Put differently, if the established Polish elites could rule through traditional institutions, thus preserving their language, customs, and privileges, then the nation could survive.[47]

This approach spread rapidly, and by the time the Habsburg Empire redefined itself in the 1860s, the Polish elites were rhetorically prepared to take their place within the new order. From the October Diploma of 1860 (which granted greater authority to the Galician *sejm*) to the polonization of the administration and the courts in 1869, noble conservatives in Kraków and Lwów worked with their counterparts in Vienna to construct both a new system of administration and a new concept of nationhood. Agenor Gołuchowski, governor of Galicia intermittently since 1849 and Imperial Minister of State in 1860, was the main architect of the former. The latter was developed primarily by a group of writers known as the *Stańczycy:* Ludwik Wodzicki (1834–1894), Józef Szujski (1835–1883), Stanisław Koźmian (1836–1922), and Stanisław Tarnowski (1837–1917).[48] These men—contemporaries of Wiślicki—were able to establish such authority over Galician intellectual life that few challenged their dominance for the remainder of the century. In 1866 these four founded a magazine called *Przegląd Polski*, which became Kraków's leading periodical. They had a ready audience, as was demonstrated that same year when the Galician *sejm* passed the following resolution addressed to the emperor: "Without fear of denying our national thought, with faith in the mission of Austria and with trust in the decisiveness of the changes which Your royal word declared to be an unchanging goal, from the depth of our hearts we proclaim that we stand and wish to stand with You, Your Majesty."[49]

A brochure published by Szujski in 1867 entitled "Several Truths from Our History" was hailed as the program of *Przegląd Polski* and the *Stańczycy*.[50] Szujski's view of history was peculiar for a conservative: he argued that one should not idealize the Polish past, because it did not deserve such respect. The partitions were not just the result of external aggression, he wrote, but the product of profound internal weakness. Szujski considered it his duty to propagate "those great truths, that if the nation as a state fell, it was from its own guilt, [and] if it rises, it will be from its own work, its own reason, its own spirit."[51] The political institutions of Poland led to the nation's dissolution, according to Szujski, because they did not emphasize order, discipline, obedience, hierarchy, and faith, and a true conservative should have nothing to do with these aspects of the national tradition. Szujski argued that at the time of the partitions, "the old Republic died, it died forever . . . and it will never arise such as it was then! . . . The Republic died, I say, and new times began."[52] The *Stańczycy* could show such contempt for the national past because they distinguished the state and its institutions from the traditions that were to be sustained. Koźmian believed that "tradition and history are inseparable from the national existence; they are the foundation and the soul of custom and civilization," but he also recognized that to preserve what was truly important, it was sometimes necessary to be selective. "Separating national existence from independence and state form," he wrote, "[we] made possible [the nation's] preservation and eased its development."[53] In other words, the *Stańczycy* discovered a usable set of national traditions that did not depend upon the restoration of the Polish state.

There were those who disagreed with the *Stańczycy*, and they were usually allowed to publish their views, but the majority of the reading public in Kraków and Lwów remained loyal to *Przegląd Polski* and to the Habsburgs. The circumstances in Galicia, however, were unique: in this impoverished, agrarian backwater student activism was minimal and the conservative nobility faced few challenges. In the very different social and political environments of the other two partitions, the message of the *Stańczycy* was far less persuasive. Nonetheless Szujski and his colleagues had some counterparts elsewhere. In the Prussian partition Hipolit Cegielski and August Cieszkowski became prominent advocates of what they called "organic work" as early as the 1840s. Since national revolt could so easily lead to social revolution, they argued, Poles should instead work for economic prosperity. From the emigration Cyprian Norwid developed an even more consistently conservative and Catholic vision of work, arguing that gradual material progress should be pursued without any reference to the metaphysical goals of the idealists or to the revolutionary objectives of the nationalists. In the Kingdom Prince Andrzej Zamoyski founded the Agricultural Society in 1858, with the goal of developing the rural economy while maintaining traditional rural hierarchies.[54]

Others, therefore, had employed the idea of organic work (as opposed to revolt) before the positivists came on the scene. Not surprisingly, *Przegląd Tygodniowy*'s critique of the national movement was familiar: both the liberals and the conservatives of the 1860s criticized the "dreams" of romanticism and both offered the alternative of work.[55] The positivists, however, wanted to detach this argument from the conservatives and appropriate it for their own needs. Where the conservatives placed "tradition," the positivists offered "progress" and "science"; while the conservatives advocated conciliation and cooperation in order to save the status quo, the positivists hoped to utilize the same means to create a new, modern Poland. As the editors of *Niwa* put it, they wanted to liberate the slogan of organic work from the "backwardness" and "darkness" with which it had been associated.[56] On at least one level they were successful: to this day many Poles use the term "positivism" loosely to describe anyone who places quiet work above violent revolt.[57] A more careful reading of the positivist press, however, leads one to wonder who was appropriating whom. By using the language of science and work to describe the nation, the positivists were opening new possibilities within the nationalist discourse to talk about hierarchy and authority, turning "Poland" into a site for discipline and control. The Warsaw positivists were sincere liberals, but this very fact forces us to reconsider the role of liberal thought in preindustrial and industrializing societies. What may appear (and claim) to be progressive, emancipatory, and "modern" may turn out to be deeply implicated in networks of power, both old and new.

The most corrosive point of tension in positivist rhetoric came from a Spencerian metaphor: "the social organism." The idea that society was analogous to a living being had a long history, stretching back at least to the Middle Ages. More recently, conservatives like Joseph de Maistre and Edmund Burke had argued that each social "organ"—from the "mind" (the aristocracy) to the "muscles" (the peasants)—had specific tasks assigned by God or Nature. The social order thus became, for these authors, as immutable as one's bodily form.[58] Liberals, most notably Herbert Spencer, co-opted this metaphor, giving it new meaning by pairing it with the concept of evolution. What had been static and unchanging was subjected to "scientific laws" that mandated gradual but inexorable transformation.[59] The liberal use of the organic metaphor thus facilitated a delicate balance between progress and the status quo, between the subversion and the justification of existing social hierarchies. Because society was organic, its stratification was "natural," but like all aspects of nature, these structures would change with time. This tension contributed to liberalism's infamous Janus face: for ancien régime elites it was a revolutionary ideology, but for radical egalitarians it was only a more subtle form of reaction.

When Prus talked about the nation, he enthusiastically embraced the organic metaphor. He wrote in 1882, "Every type of living organism possesses its own laws of development . . . nations are also living organisms, thus they are also subject to certain unyielding laws." As he explored this trope, Prus encountered its conservative ramifications. "Just as in plant and animal organisms," he wrote, "so in a social [organism] we see a division of labor between various organs, mutually supporting each other. . . ."[60] The class structure of Polish society was thus cast as a benign system of mutual support—precisely the imagery the nobility had once used in referring to serfdom. The positivists remained embedded in this sort of reasoning, even as they tried to talk about making the nation more inclusive and less hierarchical. For Prus, the most important aspect of "work" was popular education, which would help "elevate the will of the masses, today powerless and dreaming."[61] The evocation of popular will, however, could not be allowed to imply independent popular action; instead, the positivists wanted to "elevate" the peasants while simultaneously binding them to the social organism.

The very slogan "work at the foundations"—the positivists' own spin on "organic work"—came from a discussion of "the peasant question" in which the ambiguous intersection between inclusivity and hierarchy was particularly evident. In 1873 Świętochowski and his lesser known colleague Leopold Mikulski co-authored a series of programatic essays entitled "Work at the Foundations." They began with a seemingly radical declaration of equality: "Science does not know better and worse varieties of occupation and neither does it classify human blood according to [hereditary status]; it knows only man, and in the name of natural rights it demands for him social rights."[62] Immediately, however, Świętochowski and Mikulski pulled back and returned agency to the elites. The goal was to integrate the peasants into the nation, but this should not be understood as a call for popular sovereignty: "In this matter the whole weight of duty must be laid on the enlightened element, that is, on the landed citizens. Their task is as follows: for the good of the community, for the peasants as well as for themselves, [the nobles] ought to use all legal means to exert influence on the affairs of the people and their development, establishing between themselves a bond of tight union. . . . Naturally, we are speaking here above all of moral influence and not authority."[63] Świętochowski and Mikulski wanted it both ways: they wanted to challenge the old aristocracy with a message of social equality, anticlericalism, and liberal economic reforms, but they did not want to grant autonomous volition to "the people." They rejected authority, but they insisted on "moral influence."

To sustain this tenuous argument, the positivists cast themselves as educators who would train the peasants in the doctrines of work, so that direct authority would no longer be necessary. Once the peasants understood their duty—once they saw the world as the positivists did and behaved appropriately—then strict external controls would be superfluous. In other words, the goal was to get the peasants to internalize the discipline of the "modern" world, as defined by the liberal intelligentsia. Popular education was vital to this project, but it was conceivable only under the tutelage of the "enlightened" elements of society. "Just as the blind cannot judge colors," Świętochowski and Mikulski wrote, "so those without education cannot evaluate its benefits."[64] These authors were confident that a "mature" peasant would "willingly submit to the authority of his benefactor," who in turn would use his wealth to protect and guide his charges. Such obedience was only natural, because the peasant would certainly trust his "more cultivated and more talented" landlord rather than another "dark simpleton" like himself.[65] The intelligentsia had to retain control of this pedagogical project, Świętochowski and Mikulski continued, because otherwise it might be diverted from its sober goals and moved outside "the law." "From all this it follows that our society, not from some romantic sentiment 'for the people,' but for our own well-reasoned interests, ought to take part in popular education from those foundations and with those methods that lie within the bounds of the laws applying to our country."[66] Despite all the talk of inclusion, they still equated the intelligentsia with "society" and set "the people" aside as an object to be worked upon, to be elevated.

The national inclusivity that would supposedly result from this program was thus guaranteed to preserve social distance and distinction. "We want the community to gather together into one body," Świętochowski and Mikulski wrote, "the members of which, though formed differently, would be related [*pokrewne*] and mutually helpful." Of course, they quickly added, this did not imply that they wanted to "thrust the *obywatel* into the peasant hut, or the peasant into the salon."[67] The bond of nationality would not be allowed to imply a union of equals—only of "related" people with "different forms." The very terminology used here speaks volumes. *Obywatel* means "citizen" in modern Polish, but well into the nineteenth century the label was applied only to members of the landed nobility, thus reflecting the idea that only nobles were truly part of "Poland." By 1873 (when these essays were written) more modern definitions of *obywatelstwo* (citizenship) had been in circulation for quite some time, so Świętochowski's deployment of this archaic usage stands out, highlighting his desire to reassure an audience worried about its social status. Liberalism was not, after all, going to generate any confusion of social roles or any significant challenge to the authority of the "citizens."

The positivists made the nation concrete—they turned it into an ethnolinguistic community rather than an ideal or a spirit—and in doing so they both blunted the revolutionary implications of nationalism and set the stage for solidifying cultural boundaries that had heretofore remained ambiguous and porous. But the *młoda prasa* had not yet imagined the nation of the twentieth-century radical right, and positivism had not generated the unqualified forms of authority and exclusion that would mark later visions of "modern Poland." Nor did Warsaw liberalism set in motion an inevitable process that would ultimately lead to an unmitigated preoccupation with social discipline. The die was not yet cast, because, as we will see in the next chapter, the positivists still believed in historical time.

3

The Struggle for Survival

The rhetoric of "science" and "work" allowed the positivists to shift attention away from the violence of 1863, but not without a price. Not only had they opened gaps through which hierarchy and authority could penetrate the discourse of patriotism, but by describing the nation as a "society" rather than a "cause," by transforming Poland from a historical actor into an ethnolinguistic community subject to the laws of nature, they had called into question the bond between nation and state, between patriotism and the quest for independence. Most Poles, including most of the positivists, were still drawn to the famous lyric, "Poland has not yet died, as long as we still live," but talk of the social organism and the struggle for survival raised the possibility that Poland might die. If one could no longer fight for national liberation, what did it mean to "build" for the nation in a Spencerian world? Could the positivist program possibly lead to independence? The opponents of Warsaw liberalism would claim that it could not, that there was no meaningful difference between work and collaboration. Scholars have been less judgmental, but there is a general consensus that however patriotic the positivists may have been, they considered political independence to be of secondary importance—desirable perhaps, but not necessary.[1] In this chapter I argue that the authors at *Przegląd Tygodniowy* were, in fact, able to remain within a patriotic tradition by creatively interpreting a liberal teleology in a way that allowed them to sustain their desire for, and belief in, Polish statehood. This rhetorical maneuver was possible because the English liberals who were so admired in Warsaw were translated and appropriated in innovative ways and utilized creatively to solve some distinctly Polish problems. By exploring the intersection of liberalism and nationalism in Poland, we can see how a political space (the state) could be retained within a worldview that rejected political action.

Most scholars seem to agree that a political goal—the quest for independence—has been a necessary part of every nationalist program. Elie Kedourie's definition, now more than thirty years old, remains widely accepted: a nationalist doctrine "holds that humanity is naturally divided into nations, that nations are known by certain characteristics which can be ascertained, and that the only legitimate type of government is national self-government."[2] Even those who have recognized that there are many different styles of nationalism have still focused on competing visions of the ideal nation-state.[3] This concentration on political aspirations is often heuristically useful, insofar as it helps us distinguish between "modern" nationalism and other forms of "ethnic" identity. However, for this very reason it compels us to over-emphasize the link between the concept of the nation and the construction of modernity, and to imagine a *single* narrative of nationalism and nation building, a single historical trajectory from "premodern" forms of identity to the triumph of the nation-state. Doing so narrows our vision, obscuring the diverse ways in which "the nation" has been employed in a variety of discursive frameworks, for a variety of purposes. Brian Singer has written, "Only where power is explicitly identified with the mass of citizens in their union can one properly speak of a nation," yet this statement ignores the fact that people have spoken of the nation in many other ways.[4] Specifically, it makes it difficult to interpret those who repudiate or downplay the quest for political independence while still placing something called the nation at the center of their rhetoric. If such individuals are discussed, they are typically relegated to a "preparatory" or "preliminary" stage of a nationalist movement; they are the ones who are said to lay the cultural foundation for those who will ultimately create the nation-state.[5]

An examination of the Polish case will allow us to link a group of seemingly apolitical intellectuals to a broader nationalist framework in a less teleological manner. The Warsaw positivists did indeed say that the nation could exist without political form (without a state) and thrive without openly pursuing independence, but a simplistic political/apolitical, state/culture dichotomy conceals more than it reveals. Liberalism came to Poland as a solution to a paradox: how to dream of independence while insisting that states did not matter and that political action (as the romantics had understood this expression) was futile. The positivists resolved this dilemma by creatively configuring Poland's position within historical time. They did *not* imagine, as some accounts would have it, that in the absence of political action they had to limit themselves to the propagation of national culture, thus laying the foundation for a future nation-state. Instead they applied the principles of liberal political economy to the "national question" in an idiosyncratic way, allowing them to locate the nation at the end of a progressive narrative driven by socioeconomic development, secularization, and liberal economics. The positivists were able to combine the new vocabulary of liberal scientism with the old dreams of Polish independence because they were able to rely on their own vision of history, inspired by the mechanics of political economy. As we will see in the next chapter, the eventual collapse of the positivists' diachronic perspective would lead to a fundamental reconceptualization of what it meant to be Polish and what political implications followed from "the Polish question." But as long as the positivist worldview was sustained, it was possible for Poles to imagine that they were embedded in progressive historical time and that the future would bring them independence in a liberal utopia, even without "the deed."

Fitting the positivists into our story demonstrates that there were many ways to imagine the nation's past and to foresee its future.

Working for Independence

Conservatives regularly accused the positivists of being "antinational" and "cosmopolitan," with an imported ideology that negated Polish tradition. A pseudonymous author from Warsaw, writing in the Lwów paper *Gazeta Narodowa* in 1872, attacked the liberals for denigrating "the church, the entire national past, tradition." In their alleged devotion to science, he complained, they constantly belittled their homeland, trying to undermine its customs, its institutions, its distinctive past.[6] The socialist author Bolesław Limanowski rose to the defense of the positivists in a letter to the editor, but he was fighting an uphill battle.[7] Both scientism and liberalism were universalistic worldviews, cosmopolitan doctrines virtually by definition. As Władysław Kozłowski put it, "There are no exclusively national laws; there are only human, universal laws, because there is only one reality."[8] Aleksander Świętochowski complained about the "cult of particularism" and rejected all arguments based merely on the alleged Polishness of some idea or custom.[9] The *młoda prasa* did not perceive any uniquely Polish problems; instead they saw human problems that happened to afflict the Poles. But despite their rejection of particularism, the positivists wanted to sustain their Polish identity and their bond with Polish history. Prus acknowledged that his ideas were often borrowed from English, French, or German authors, but he added that "every discovery, every novelty taken from foreigners must be reworked, digested, in a word—polonized."[10] In his memoirs, Świętochowski admitted that he had been selective in his appropriations from the Polish past, but he insisted that he had always respected the power of national history.[11] Kozłowski even argued that the very empiricism upon which positivism was based compelled him to take national traditions seriously. "Positivism does not in any way threaten nationality," he wrote, "because, based on experience, it must recognize [nationality] as a fact of historical life."[12]

To sustain both their universalism and their national credentials, the positivists developed a distinction between patriotism and chauvinism. In an 1880 text entitled *Patriotyzm i kosmopolityzm*, Eliza Orzeszkowa argued that patriotism was a natural and praiseworthy affinity for one's community; unfortunately, hatred against other communities was all too often associated with patriotism, at which point it degenerated into chauvinism. The task of "scientific" and "progressive" Poles, she concluded, was to respect nationality while simultaneously propagating an appreciation for diversity, purging all remnants of national exclusivity and animosity from the national organism.[13] Prus similarly acknowledged that patriotism could be a good thing, as long as it was stripped of its "harsh and even wild characteristics." He warned his readers that "hatred, just like a fever or typhus, once contracted, comes to dominate the entire organism. Start to hate your political enemies and you finish [by hating] your compatriots, your family, even yourself."[14]

This distinction between good and bad forms of national sentiment is familiar; even today Poles differentiate between *nacjonalizm* (bad) and *patriotyzm* (good). For the positivists, however, this involved much more than just a critique of hatred, because it was linked to a rhetorical maneuver of fundamental importance: a shift away from "tradition" toward "history." Świętochowski wrote in 1872, "The concept of tradition is for many a vague concept, imprecisely defined, a will-of-the-wisp flying around one's head rather than a real truth based on facts."[15] Later that year he was even more emphatic: "The urn of the past is filled with the ashes of death and not the juice of life. We do not gain nourishment from that which is tainted by death, but from that which creates strength."[16] For all his rhetorical intensity, however, Świętochowski still insisted that he had a deep respect for history. To sustain this claim, he introduced a terminological distinction between the power of history and the "empty sounds" of tradition. Civilized nations, he wrote:

> have history, but not tradition. The difference between these two concepts is as great as, for example, the difference between scientific truth and superstition. The foundation in the development of a society aware of its goals and knowing its path can only be history. . . . History is the path along which thousands have passed; every newly arriving generation ought to recognize the entire course of the path and stand in the place where they last stopped, and then proceed further along the highway of science and of life.

History might be located in the past, but it was directed toward the future. Recognizing the importance of historical time did not imply, for the positivists, a desire to preserve any national customs, norms, or institutions. Quite the contrary, history demanded that one participate in the grand march of progress. "Every present is the result of a past," wrote Świętochowski, "but never the past itself. . . . In a word, the *past* is the *foundation* and the *present* is the *principle* of our activities. The more we study history, the more we understand the present and the more we recognize the conditions and needs of the moment, the more we obtain a measure for action and a guide for progress. The past, therefore, will give us no ideals, models, or principles—it only places us in a given position."[17] The positivists preserved tradition but desanctified it. The past was not to be respected under all circumstances; it was to be appropriated if useful and to be abandoned if not. In contrast, "history" was a *dynamic* concept, linked to a vision of movement through time. As Kozłowski put it, Poles needed to "stop regarding tradition as the ark of the covenant," but instead approach the past as "the support for further national exertions, as the foundation of national life." Otherwise, he concluded, they would be condemned to "stagnation and backwardness."[18] The positivist philosopher and editor Julian Ochorowicz claimed to take a more moderate stance than the polemical Świętochowski, but in fact he remained within the same diachronic framework. "All previous ideals must be valued," he wrote, "so that they may become the foundation for further combinations; no one, therefore, lest they suffer the punishment of isolation, may break with the course to date of either universal or national history. . . . Only by understanding how it was and how it is may we know how it ought to be."[19] Ochorowicz, like Świętochowski, appreciated the past, but *only* insofar as it contributed to the building of the future. For the *młoda prasa,* the past was just tradition, but history was the foundation for prophecy.

The positivists' commitment to their redefined notion of history was not just a way to escape the charge that they had repudiated the nation's traditions. More fundamentally, their diachronic worldview allowed them to answer a disturbing question: how could Poland's future be imagined by those who ruled out the possibility of another uprising? How could the injustices of the world be remedied if one could only "work," but not "act"? Above all, how could Poland regain its independence? The positivists were able to respond to these challenges by resorting to a liberal historiosophy that promised victory in the struggle for survival to those who were most "civilized" and "advanced," rather than to those with the most military might. By placing their faith in the forces of history, they could remain hopeful for the nation's future even as they tried to deprive the nation of the power to willfully "act."

Józef Hłasko summarized the views of most of the *młoda prasa*'s critics when he complained that the positivists had "tried to convince themselves that independence was not an essential condition for national development."[20] Liberalism, with its emphasis on the private over the political, was considered by many to be incapable of supporting the quest for Polish statehood. Before the *młoda prasa* came along, one of Poland's few liberal publicists, Józef Supiński (1804–1893), arrived at precisely this conclusion.[21] He argued that the state and the nation were two different things and that the latter did not require the former to survive. Supiński's libertarian antipathy to strong government was so great that he repudiated all politics; he even preferred the expression "social economy" over the usual "political economy." The state, he argued, might be needed to control the "animal" nature of mankind, but with progress our "human" side would take over and replace authority and violence with "exchange."[22] So as to retain some sort of patriotic identity despite his aversion for politics, Supiński disassociated the nation from the state.

> The nation and the state are two different entities; their social organisms were
> formed along separate paths. . . . The growth of social forces in the nation
> revives its internal movement and freedom; the growth of state power leads to
> centralization and autocracy. The organic bonds of the nation are its history, its
> *literary* language, its customs, its temperament and aspirations, which permeate
> it through long centuries and successive generations. The state is bound together
> by commands, along with the officials and the army standing guard over [these
> commands]. . . . While nations are natural creations, existing according to eternal
> laws, . . . the state often appears suddenly, after successful wars. . . .[23]

Supiński believed that the nation was manifest in its "nationality," not its political life. The former was defined according to language, territory, religion, history, customs, and clothing (he considered fashion extremely important in defining one's individuality). A "living nation," Supiński believed, could easily cultivate these things on its own, without the assistance of any state apparatus. He regretted the fact that "uniting the state and the nation is the ideal toward which the contemporary world is working," because he dreamed of a future in which people could live "without fear, supervision, glory, poetry, or slavery," and above all without states. Replacing the

fractured world of autonomous statehood, he hoped, would be a cosmopolitan regime of work and knowledge.[24]

Like Supiński, the Warsaw liberals made a distinction between state and nation.
Prus first approached this issue when he considered the possibility that the national
organism might someday die. In 1872 he concluded that "a nation, like every living
organism, arises and develops in a certain space and time, passes through an epoch
of childhood and maturity, states of wakefulness and sleep, health and sickness. It
changes its form and constituent parts, and finally—thanks to its own weakness and
external circumstances—it dies."[25] This was a logical and well-established extra-
polation from the organic metaphor, but it was certainly a distressing thought for a
Pole. Later Prus backed away from the consequences of this reasoning, arguing that
"social organisms are probably the longest lasting of all those that the earth has seen.
We do not know if they can die or not, although they frequently transform themselves. . . . The great collapses of the ancient states were basically only transformations, in which the ruling class and its language died; the national material, however,
exists to this very day, in new forms."[26] In this loaded passage Prus confronted a great
point of crisis in the positivist worldview, only to retreat by suggesting a distinction
between the "ruling class" and the "national material." Elsewhere he clarified this
argument by drawing upon the liberal dichotomy between state and nation.

> In our times much is said about nations, but—how unusual!—definitions of the
> nation are often exceedingly unsteady and superficial. In my opinion 'the nation
> is a social organism and at the same time a variety of the human species. It is an
> organism insofar as it possesses the most important social organs. It is a variety
> [of the human species] because people of the same nationality possess common
> moral and certainly anatomical and physiological traits that distinguish them
> from others.' . . . The clearest form of social organization is the state, which very
> often is a collection of several or more nations.

The Polish national organism, in this model, could survive even if it had to do so
within the Russian Empire. By employing (once again) the organic metaphor, Prus
was able both to naturalize the nation and to marginalize the state. He clarified (or
perhaps muddled) his definition with yet more metaphors, explaining that the skele-
ton of the *state* was its territory and infrastructure, while the nourishment of the *nation*
was trade. In other words (and in good liberal fashion) Prus suggested that the nation
could survive without a state as long as it enjoyed the benefits of a robust economy.
The positivists often urged the Poles to cultivate their economic links with the remainder of the empire and to view the Russians as customers rather than oppressors.
This approach gave them access to a liberal vocabulary of economic development,
but it offered no justification for Polish independence. Not surprisingly, because of
this essay Prus was often singled out for criticism by more "patriotic" opponents. If
we read further in Prus' essay, we see that he allowed himself a way to escape the
charge that he had surrendered the goal of independence: in the aesopian language
required of the censored press, he argued that each nation eventually needed a territory of its own if it was to preserve all its "organs."[27] But this slippery argument hardly

satisfied his critics. Prus did indeed come perilously close to Supiński's liberal rejection of statehood, in exchange for a "nationality" distinguished by its ethnicity and sustained by its economy.

Świętochowski approached the same perilous rhetorical cliff in the early 1880s. This was a difficult time to be a liberal in the Russian Empire and an even harder time to be a Pole. The reformist agenda of Alexander II, which had barely survived the 1870s, collapsed entirely when the Tsar was assassinated in 1881. His successor, Alexander III, reversed many of his father's measures and took an even harder line against the Poles. Just then Świętochowski had to confront simultaneous crises in his personal life (his son died) and in his public life (he was struggling to find an audience for his new weekly, *Prawda* [The Truth], in a climate hardly auspicious for a liberal journal). Against this backdrop, Świętochowski wrote two provocative articles: "I Think, Therefore I Am," and "Political Directions."[28] These essays convinced some contemporaries that the author had abandoned the national cause. "Political Directions" was the more controversial, because it appeared in a volume of essays dedicated to the novelist Zygmunt Miłkowski, an officer in the 1863 rebellion and a well-known author of romantic, patriotic novels (under the pseudonym T. T. Jeż). Here Świętochowski declared that the nation was a social collective with no political consequences: "From the liberal position, the mere loss of our own political institutions does not seem to us to be a misfortune at all. The happiness of a community, according to us, is not unconditionally dependent upon its political strength and autonomy, but on the possibilities of participating in universal civilization and advancing our own."[29] The international order, he continued, was based on the law of the jungle, and there was no use pretending that this was not the case. Poles had to recognize that their state had been subjugated and had to cultivate material progress without resorting to pointless conspiracies.

Not unreasonably, most people understood this essay to be a repudiation of the very idea of independence. Both his enemies and friends reacted with horror, and Jeż took offense that such an essay could be published in a volume dedicated to him. Świętochowski himself later claimed that he had been misunderstood.[30] He may have been right: if we place this article in the context of his other writing from the same time, we find that his argument was more subtle than it seems. In "I Think, Therefore I Am," which was published several months earlier, he again seemed to turn away from any political agenda: "As is known, a political map is not an ethnographic map. . . . State independence is, so to speak, a title, a tool which one can lose without losing the real characteristics of one's essence. A king deprived of his throne ceases only to be a king, not a man; similarly, a nation deprived of its political independence ceases only to be a state, but not a nation." The only true measures of national existence, Świętochowski continued, were "civilization" and "thought," and the appropriate slogan for the Poles ought to be, "I think, therefore I am." This does indeed seem to be evidence of a thorough depoliticization, but as we read further we realize that Świętochowski's move to distinguish between the terms "state" and "nation" did not mean that he had severed all ties between them. Quite the contrary: he insisted that although the nation was not *defined* by the state, it was nonetheless compelled to regain its independence. Compounding metaphor upon metaphor (a style of writing made necessary by the censors), he stressed that he did "not deny that a person with a revolver in his pocket is safer from violence than one with understanding in his head; this does not mean, however, that those who are deprived of a revolver feel that they are deprived of life. *Yes, a plant needs a certain atmosphere, a certain warmth and moisture; but that atmosphere, that warmth and that moisture do not constitute its essence.*"[31] If the state was to the nation as moisture and air were to plants, then one could hardly claim that Świętochowski had denigrated the value of independence; he had only rejected the *definitional* link between Poland and its government. This was nothing new: he was just reiterating Wybicki's verse, "Poland has not yet died, as long as we still live," while jettisoning the poet's call to battle.

Later that summer of 1881 Świętochowski made his commitment to statehood as explicit as possible in the censored press when he tried to distinguish between his position and that of the Galician *Stańczycy,* who were openly and enthusiastically loyal to the Habsburg Empire. In Świętochowski's view, they wanted Poles "to reject the hope as well as the desire to obtain an independent existence." Świętochowski could not accept this idea. "These political moralists," he wrote, "believe that with people, just as with vessels, one can pour out some feelings, convictions, aspirations and pour in some others from one day to the next." This was both impossible and inappropriate. Emphasizing a curious terminological distinction, Świętochowski wrote that Poles should not surrender their "*dreams,* because those are beneficial and inspirational, but [only their] *illusions,* which are harmful and murderous." To stop dreaming, he concluded, would lead to abdication.[32]

The "dream" of independence remained a powerful presence, and the positivists were sensitive to the charge that they were not committed to this goal. But their problem was not simply one of censorship: their own scientistic rhetoric posed an even greater challenge, because the denial of the "national will" and the call to "work" made it difficult to imagine *how* they might win back their independence. How could Poland recover its state without any action? The positivists may have retained the goal, but they had deprived themselves of any obvious means of liberation. The solution to this dilemma would be found, once again, within the framework of liberalism. Specifically, by appealing to a liberal teleology that linked socioeconomic progress with prosperity and power, the positivists were able to imagine a world in which independence would be the result of a scientific and historical *process*, not the result of willful *action*. The key to this scheme was one of the *młoda prasa*'s favorite terms: evolution.

The Survival of the Fittest

When one spoke of evolution in the 1860s, one could not avoid the work of Herbert Spencer, a towering figure in European intellectual life at the time and the exponent of a complex historiosophy that linked liberal ideals with "scientific laws" about evolution. The Warsaw positivists, moreover, made no attempt to avoid Spencer: he may not have been the most prestigious liberal of the nineteenth century, but after reading the Warsaw press one would be forgiven for thinking that he was.[33] Spencer's work offered the positivists just the blend of science and liberalism they wanted, and by evoking his prestigious name they could easily justify their turn away from insurrection to "work." Unfortunately, he also passed along some unpleasant expressions such as "the struggle for survival." Most English liberals, comfortable within the British Empire, tended to describe big nations as definitionally more progressive than small ones and thus to justify conquest and empire. As Spencer put it, "The forces which are working out the great scheme of perfect happiness, taking no account of incidental suffering, exterminate such sections of mankind as stand in their way, with the same sternness that they exterminate beasts of prey and herds of useless ruminants. . . . What are the prerequisites to a conquering race? Numerical strength, or an improved system of warfare, both of which are indications of advancement."[34] Many contemporaries thought that this argument justified violence and brutality, and both Spencer's name and the term "Social Darwinism" came to suggest an amoral acceptance of the law of the jungle.[35] Spencer himself declared that "by force alone were small nomadic hordes welded into large tribes; by force alone were large tribes welded into small nations; by force alone have small nations been welded into large nations."[36]

It might be argued that these selective citations present a caricature: Spencer was a committed pacifist and much of his work can be read as a critique of militarism. He could not accommodate a bloody vision of struggle in perpetuity, so he saved himself by positing a moment after which violence would fade from the human condition, made unnecessary by a higher stage of moral development.[37] Nonetheless, even as Spencer proposed a better future for humanity, he never really abandoned his equation between competition, size, and progress. "After this stage has been reached," he wrote, "the purifying process, continuing still an important one, remains to be carried on by industrial war—by a competition of societies during which the best, physically, emotionally, and intellectually, spread most and leave the least capable to disappear gradually, from failing to leave a sufficiently numerous posterity."[38] Spencer perceived the market as "industrial war," a more civilized version of the violence and brutality of an earlier age. More important, the result was the same whether the means was actual war or just industrial conflict: the "purifying process" that destroys "inferior races," still defined (albeit no longer exclusively) as the physically weak and demographically smaller.

The Poles understood how dangerous such arguments could be. Świętochowski briefly endorsed a Spencerian vision of struggle, but he soon backed away. "Every nation that does not die, but lives and progresses, must be aggressive," he wrote in 1881, "if not by arms, then with civilization. . . . [Fate] has opened before us a wide field for industrial-mercantile conquest, which we have not yet sufficiently taken advantage of."[39] Within two years, however, Świętochowski would claim that terms like "conquest" and "aggression" had no place in the vocabulary of a good liberal. Writing against the backdrop of the *Kulturkampf,* Świętochowski complained that German liberals understood "freedom" to mean only the "unlimited domination of force—any kind of force. . . . Who would have predicted that the term liberalism would eventually serve to hide the most disgraceful violence?"

Large capital, large nations, large civilizations, according to [the German liberals], ought to absorb small ones with impunity. . . . That the poor, the weak, the uneducated also want to live—this does not concern them and does not even awaken their compassion. . . . They do not see in [smaller societies] anything other than vanishing species. That is the blindness of brutal snobbery, the adornment of the most base instincts with scientific truths, of dishonor with the appearance of fairness.[40]

It was easy enough to blame the Germans for this "distortion," but unfortunately the Poles' beloved Spencer said more or less the same thing. So, to both retain a Spencerian historiosophy and avoid the conclusion that might makes right, the Poles had to translate and appropriate their English mentor creatively and selectively. They found three ways to both exalt Spencer and condemn the partitions of Poland. The first was the easiest and most obvious, but the least common: to accept the general thrust of the Spencerian worldview but to argue explicitly against his emphasis on struggle. Prus, for example, evoked Spencer as the inspiration for his own "first principles," but then went on to question a central aspect of the master's argument. "There exists today a fashionable theory of 'the struggle for existence,'" he wrote, "according to which everyone ought to quarrel with everyone else. Even though the struggle for existence is a very widespread and necessary fact of nature, to elevate it to the height of an exclusive principle is simply stupid." In fact, Prus continued, nature was *not* governed by struggle, but by the principle of mutual support and cooperation. Development comes most quickly when organisms collaborate, when they exchange services so as to work together for a better future. Prus stayed comfortably within the liberal tradition by referring to the market as the zone for collaboration and progress, but he abandoned the idea of conflict so central in Spencer's work. "The only good, although not always easy policy is the universal application of the principle of exchanging services both internally and externally," he wrote. "Our national life will only flow normally when we become a useful, necessary member of civilization, when we manage to give nothing for free and demand nothing for free."[41] Again the nationalist message entered in aesopian terms: if Poland became "useful," then national life would flow normally. If Poles could offer something to universal progress, their demands (i.e., independence) would be met.

However consistent such arguments might have been for a patriotic Pole, few liberals were willing to confront Spencer directly. An alternative solution was to recast the Englishman in their own image, softening his edges with some selective and creative translating. The Poles did not actually have to misrepresent Spencer; given the diversity and sheer quantity of his writing, they merely had to be careful *which* Spencer they read. In other words, they had to pay attention to Spencer's distaste for militarism but avert their eyes from his glorification of conquest; they had to concentrate on his End of History without talking much about how he got there. The Spencer who emerged from the pages of the positivist press, then, was a much nicer Spencer than most of his English readers knew. Kozłowski directed his Polish audience's attention away from the image of the strong conquering the weak, of small nations being submerged into large ones. His Spencer was the philosopher of *The Data of Ethics* and *First Principles*; even when Kozłowski turned to questions of social evolution, he chose not to discuss the more dangerous *Social Statics* or *The Study of Sociology*.[42] Kozłowski's Spencer was the advocate of altruism and social harmony, not the prophet of the war of all against all. According to Kozłowski, Spencer believed:

> life in general is a struggle for existence, first of all a struggle with the forces of nature and then with competitors for those same rewards. Among this general struggle of individuals against individuals and races against races, all efforts aimed at extending the life of the individual and preserving the species would appear pointless. They achieve positive results only when individuals stop harming each other and hindering each other in their efforts, and moreover through mutual agreement and collaboration begin to help each other.[43]

This reading allowed Kozłowski to argue that with time conflict itself would cease. When this happened, the strongest (Kozłowski mentions the Germans directly, but any reference to the Russians had to remain implicit) would no longer dominate the earth. Programs of denationalization, in which rulers placed strength above law, were just perversions of the true doctrine of "realism."[44] Kozłowski believed that those who constructed the most balanced, harmonious society, and those who grasped "progress" most fully, would receive their just rewards.

> In the relations of both social life and international affairs, egoism depends upon altruism. Therefore, to the degree that humanity develops, the dependence of egoistic interests on altruism becomes tighter and stronger. Societies bound by political and trade relations are dependent upon each other's strength and wealth. The impoverishment of one, lowering its productivity and purchasing power, would impact negatively on the interests of all the others.[45]

The premise here was taken directly from *Data of Ethics* (or perhaps *Principles of Psychology*), but the conclusion contradicted Spencer's warning from *The Study of Sociology* that even after violence has been superseded, the "purifying process" would continue by other means. Spencer's struggle for survival, in Kozłowski's hands, became the foundation for international cooperation and harmony. In order to place the Spencer of "altruism" on an international plane, one had to avoid the Spencer of "industrial war."

In an 1881 book by the novelist Eliza Orzeszkowa entitled *Patriotism and Cosmopolitanism* we find an even gentler Spencer. Orzeszkowa offered pages of selective citations, transforming Spencer into an advocate of love and peace. Violence and strength, according to her Spencer, were detriments to human progress, not instruments of evolution. She described as "false patriotism" all national sentiments based on international hatred or national self-exaltation, offering two full pages of citations from Spencer to demonstrate that hatred was a dangerous force in society and had to be supplanted by love. Insofar as Orzeszkowa retained the struggle for survival at all, she relegated it to a "distant, dark past" (recall that Spencer had located peace in a *future* industrial society). Nations were formed not by conquest, according to Orzeszkowa, but through a recognition of certain common traits such as language, mutual sympathy, and physical or psychological similarities. Only in passing did Orzeszkowa mention that the communities thus formed might engage in "defense or acquisition." War played only an indirect role in her scheme, as one of the many threats such "natural" communities would face.[46]

But none of this really addressed the central problem. To critique or soften the idea of struggle might imply that the Russian and German conquest of Poland had been wrong, but what could one do about it? "Action," traditionally understood, had already been precluded. "Work" remained, but how could this overcome force? Spencer offered no help here: for him, violence had to be met with violence, and industry could take over only *after* war had been transcended on all sides.[47] The solution to this dilemma necessitated a very different approach than those developed by Kozłowski and Orzeszkowa, one that concentrated on a different sort of liberal teleology. Liberalism was not merely a recipe for economic practice, but a promise that if such policies were adopted, a new era of universal prosperity and harmony would arrive. Evolution, when discussed as a social concept (and even, for some, as a biological concept) slid into a related term: "progress." Both implied not only movement, but direction, and the concept of evolution reinforced the utopian dreams of liberal political economy. Spencer himself occasionally cast aside his sober and scholarly tone to proclaim the immanent dawn of a new age, but on this issue he was not the primary guru of the Warsaw positivists. Spencer was a sociologist rather than a historian, and he did not have much to say about the movement of states or nations through historical time. One of his contemporaries, however, had prioritized these matters: Henry Thomas Buckle. Few thinkers enjoyed such prominence in their own day and such oblivion afterwards as Buckle, but although his fame in his native land proved temporary, it continued to grow in Eastern Europe.[48] His only book, the incomplete *History of Civilization in England* (1856–1861), was translated into Polish in 1862.[49] The positivists eagerly embraced Buckle's ideas and, thanks to their efforts, he became one of the most popular foreign writers in Poland by the 1870s. Buckle made his first appearance in *Przegląd Tygodniowy* in 1868, when an essayist positioned him alongside Darwin as one of the great scientific pioneers of the century.[50] Walery Przyborowski even believed that the positivist movement had its source in Buckle's work. Another positivist wrote later that Buckle was "untouchable . . . for some time he was *sacrosanctus* for us." Young people in Warsaw were so enthusiastic about this book that one poor student, who could not afford to buy his own copy of Buckle's *History,* transcribed the entire text by hand.[51]

Buckle's fame in Poland did not reflect an appreciation of his unqualified support for laissez-faire, or even his anticlericalism. Rather, the Poles liked Buckle because he offered them a "scientific" vision of history in which the best educated and the most liberal, rather than the strongest, would be victorious. Above all, for Buckle victory meant *independence*. Buckle based his work on the same naturalistic monism that characterized all the positivists, and he employed the same style of argumentation. However, he differed from Spencer in two ways. First, he shifted the focus of analysis from society to history, and in so doing he made "the nation" his prin-

ciple actor. That is, he moved from Spencer's grand vision, mapped out chronologi-
cally and spatially over all of human existence, to a tighter focus on documented
European history. Even more important, he reconceptualized the engine of progress,
negating the power of violence in favor of intellectual development. Buckle therefore demonstrated how the language of scientism could be used to describe a world
of culture rather than of conquest.

Like Spencer, Buckle constructed a teleology ending in a liberal utopia. He
envisioned a future world of free thought and democracy, and he defined progress
as the antithesis of both "superstitious" religion and conservative politics.[52] Both
Spencer and Buckle employed the idea of evolution, but where the former placed
"struggle," the latter inserted "doubt." "Until doubt began," he wrote, "progress
was impossible."[53] Buckle made thought dependent upon material forces, but in
turn he made historical progress dependent upon ideas. He was thus able to condemn the violence and conquest that his more famous colleague had been forced
to accommodate. Great changes in government, Buckle argued, were brought about
"not by any external event, nor by a sudden insurrection of the people, but by the
unaided action of moral force—the silent, though overwhelming, pressure of public opinion."[54] In shifting the focus from violence to ideas, Buckle found a way to
retain his respect for the small, militarily weak, but civilized community, and he
negated the force of conquest.

> The foreign spoiler works mischief; he cannot cause shame. With nations, as
> with individuals, none are dishonored if they are true to themselves. . . . And,
> even in a material point of view, such losses [those caused by pillage] are sure to
> be retrieved, if the people who incur them are inured to those habits of self-
> government, and to that feeling of self-reliance, which are the spring and the
> source of all real greatness. With the aid of these, every damage may be repaired
> and every evil remedied. Without them, the slightest blow may be fatal.[55]

Buckle therefore represented an alternative to the brutality implied by "the struggle
for survival," and this was precisely how he was appropriated by his Polish readers.
Władysław Zawadzki, in the introduction to his own translation of *The History of Civilization,* regretted Buckle's "Protestant" worldview (i.e., his anticlericalism) but was
convinced that the book's argument about evolution made it a masterpiece. According
to Zawadzki, Buckle believed that "the essential condition of civilization is *knowledge.*
. . . Knowledge and civilization are nearly synonymous. The progress of knowledge is
the only condition for the progress of humanity." For Zawadzki, Buckle articulated a
vision of the future in which the most intelligent, rather than the mightiest, would pre-
vail.[56] Zawadzki's translation quickly came to the attention of Adam Wiślicki, who
gave the book an enthusiastic review in *Przegląd Tygodniowy.* His reading of Buckle
placed an unusually strong emphasis on intelligence, going so far as to suggest that
it provided a solution to the implications of natural law itself. "The progress of civilization is the result of a reduction of the influence of the laws of nature and an increase in the influence of intellectual laws," Wiślicki wrote. "Since the measure of
civilization is the triumph of the spirit over the external world, intellectual laws are

more important than the laws of nature for the progress of humanity. The study of the laws of European history merges with the study of the laws of human thought." Buckle, this review concluded, offered an explanation of how "intellectual progress" and "virtuous acts negate the self-defeating acts of warriors, and evil decreases."[57]

Bolesław Limanowski, writing for *Przegląd Tygodniowy* in 1869, drew similar conclusions from Buckle's work. Buckle has taught us, Limanowski wrote, that progress was "drawn from spring of knowledge," and that one could find the cure to society's ills if one simply studied. "Woe to the blind!" Limanowski proclaimed. "In the struggle with those who see clearly, he will always fall. . . . The more fierce the struggle, the wider the field on which it is conducted, the more alert must be one's consciousness. And this draws its strength from the treasury of knowledge that humanity has gathered over many centuries of historical work."[58] The editors of *Niwa,* another positivist journal, took the same approach. "Buckle asserts," they wrote in 1874, "that in human history it is mainly and predominantly the intellect which develops. . . . The ideal of society ought to be only (or primarily) the increase of education and intellectual development." *Niwa* then used this idea to redefine the concept of "force," which became for them the "harmonious union of physical force and mental-moral force, which in turn must necessarily be based on justice."[59]

Charles Darwin was read in a similar manner by some Polish liberals, who deemphasized the struggle for survival and stressed the superiority of mind over strength. The translator of *Origin of Species*, a biologist named Ludwik Masłowski, wrote:

> Man, therefore, just like every other species, struggles for survival with his
> neighbors, and based on that struggle weak and incapable individuals vanish
> from the world's horizon, as a result of which the human race achieves ever
> more perfection. Among people, just as among the rest of the animal world, that
> struggle was based in the beginning on direct conflict and on the attainment of a
> piece of nourishment. However, from the moment society arose . . . that struggle
> took on a totally different form. From the stage of physical struggle it was
> transformed into psychic conflict, into intellectual competition. The victor was
> not the person with the strongest teeth or the most powerful upper body; instead,
> the person with the most developed mind and the most highly perfected nerves
> obtained the laurel wreath.[60]

As soon as history began, as soon as men moved beyond the stage of animal existence with the development of "society," then the primacy of physical struggle was transcended. The moment that Spencer placed in the future, Masłowski's Darwin transposed to the distant, prehistoric past.

This temporal aspect was crucial, because without it Poles could not sustain both the dream of independence and a belief in the efficacy of work. Buckle was clearly more useful here than was Darwin, because many were not able to follow Masłowski's optimistic interpretations. More common was the reading of Józef Nusbaum, a noted biologist who also translated some of Darwin's work. In an 1885 letter to Wiślicki, which the editor published in *Przegląd Tygodniowy*, Nusbaum linked Spencer and

Darwin by claiming that both agreed that the laws of evolution would change only in the distant future.

> *Currently*, among people as well [as animals], not always the most talented and the most moral have better living standards. No biologist who believes in the natural law of the struggle for survival would assert . . . that the manifestations of the struggle for survival will remain unchanged. The same natural law of evolution which once, through natural selection, sustained the lives of individuals having stronger muscles, claws and teeth, and which currently [sustains] the most clever and shrewd, might *in the distant future,* with the continuing progress of the human spirit and with changes in social relations, guarantee a better existence to the most intelligent and moral individuals.[61]

If the weak but intelligent were going to trust the Spencerian or (for some) Darwinian natural law of evolution for their salvation, they would have to wait until some future age. There was still a note of optimism in Nusbaum's voice, but he demanded some patience of his readers. In contrast, Buckle allowed them to embrace scientific laws now, and to base their hopes for national redemption upon these laws.

Świętochowski demonstrated his Bucklean reading of evolution in an important series of essays from 1882, provocatively entitled "The Struggle for Existence." Directly contradicting Spencer's implication that numerical strength was a mark of progress, Świętochowski used the rhetoric of science and nature to deemphasize physical strength.

> If every species searched for and did not find a means to defend its existence, there would exist only lions, tigers, and elephants among animals and strong, huge states among people. . . . It is a fatal error in our political-social reasoning to compare our own society with others [and] explain its victory only [by referring to] physical superiority, to numbers and armies. If the strongest state possessed only many armed people, it would quickly succumb to complete destruction. No Krupp could make such armaments as would kill Copernicus and no Moltke could vanquish Mickiewicz or Matejko.

These concluding references were transparent: the German armaments manufacturer and the German general were placed against a Polish scholar, poet, and painter. Military might was contrasted with artistic and scientific talent; strength was said to be inferior to intellect; the large conquering nation was located beneath the small conquered nation. To cultivate all these qualities, Świętochowski continued, required work, which "constituted the primary force in the struggle for existence" and "determined the fate of nations."[62]

This was the central message of Warsaw positivism, the point where liberal scientism and nationalism intersected. Repeatedly *Prawda*, *Niwa*, and *Przegląd Tygodniowy* stressed that the mind was stronger than brute force and that victory in the struggle for survival would come to the most civilized and intelligent, not to the one with the greatest army. This was not capitulation in the quest for independence, but a quintessentially liberal way of continuing that battle by other means. The key to this argument was the positivists' vision of history, as demonstrated by the very title of an 1882 series in *Prawda*: "An Attempt at a New Historiosophy." The author, Ignacy Radliński, not only allowed the "intelligent" nation to survive, but actually declared that it enjoyed primacy over other nations. He embraced the concept of struggle, which "just lies in the nature of things," but he believed that only primitive nations substituted strength for the more potent assets of law and work.[63] Radliński's commitment to statehood was clear: he described it as the principle means of regulating the struggle for survival so as to ensure that it did not degenerate into mere violence. For a state to serve as an instrument of progress in this way, Radliński continued, it had to evolve from "the correct development of history" and be a "faithful reflection of the nation." If it was the product of "a social catastrophe, usually a fatal war," then it necessarily "originated from outside, and as something imposed, was alien to society. In this case, instead of regulating relations and returning harmony, it itself becomes an expression of the struggle for existence, it itself violates that harmony, upsets order and negates progress."[64] Radliński closed by plugging the idea of work into his historiosophy: "If the key to happiness is in anyone's hands, that key can only be work. Work carried mankind above the world from which he originated; work created culture, changed and adapted nature itself to its needs; with work [mankind] broadens its knowledge, ennobles itself, elevates future generations."[65]

Here was the entire argument of the Warsaw positivists summarized in a few sentences. The purpose of work was to advance knowledge and further progress, and this task was in turn placed within a "new historiosophy" that promised victory in the struggle for survival to those who followed such a program. The Russian and German Empires no longer enjoyed any primacy in this scheme—as they did in Spencer's equation between size and progress—because few would argue that Russia or Germany was among Europe's more "progressive" nations. The Poles, moreover, had long thought of themselves as a more developed, more "European" counterpart to the "backward," autocratic, "Asiatic" Russians. (The deployment of orientalist categories had long been a feature of Polish political rhetoric, although obviously Germany's inconvenient geographical position to the west of Poland had to be passed over in silence.) If Buckle was right, then the Poles needed only to cultivate and demonstrate their superiority in order to negate the effects of the partitions. They need not think of themselves as one of the small nations destined for absorption into a larger neighbor; if they could only loosen the shackles of conservatism and superstition, their cultural preeminence would solve all their problems and "every damage could be repaired, every evil remedied." In other words, they could use a Bucklean teleology to recast themselves, the conquered nation, as the "European" power destined to rise above the "Asiatic" Russians (and, though this was unclear, the "Teutonic" Germans). Moreover, they could describe liberalism as the ideal national program. The romantic nationalists based Poland's claim to greatness on its status as victim, as an emblem of freedom, suffering at the hands of evil neighbors (but destined to vanquish the forces of tyranny at some future moment of revolution). For the positivists, on the other hand, Poland's superiority arose from its cultural and economic proximity to "the West," understood here as the "civilized" and "modern" world (i.e., France and England, but not Germany). Poland was no longer the martyr or even the missionary; it was now (liberal) "Europe" confronting the (autocratic and conservative) "East." And surely, they reasoned, Europe could not be colonized by Asia and civilization could not remain subordinated to the uncivilized. Within this frame of mind, even though the nation's present might be work, its future would certainly be the state.

As we will see in the next chapter, this trust in historical progress would soon erode, leading to a crisis of identity and purpose for Polish nationalists of all stripes. The one thing the positivists shared with their romantic predecessors was a faith in historical time. Even though Świętochowski's vision of the future had little in common with Mickiewicz's, they both believed that Poland was moving forward, toward a world in which the social and political problems of the nineteenth century would be resolved. This belief allowed romantics and positivists alike to remain optimistic in the face of repeated political failure and persistent social injustice. It also permitted the *młoda prasa* to use phrases like "the struggle for survival" while repudiating most forms of political (not to mention military) contestation, and to rhetorically reinforce social hierarchies while still talking about "freedom" and even "equality." They did not need to plan another rebellion, because history would bring independence if Poland accepted the "principles of political economy." Similarly, they did not need to propose radical measures for social change, because historical progress would lead to a liberal utopia in which everyone shared the status of "citizen." In both cases, historical time stood between the positivists and an ideology of international struggle and domestic authoritarianism. Only a thorough dehistoricization of Polish political thought would remove these firewalls, which had heretofore guarded against the penetration of exclusion and social discipline into the discourse of nationalism. Unfortunately, just such an assault on historical time was about to take place.

4

The Return to Action

In 1878 a tsarist official in Warsaw described the Polish Kingdom as "the most peaceful part" of an empire that was otherwise "undermined by nihilism."[1] At a time when the likes of Mikhail Bakunin, Nikolai Chernyshevsky, Petr Lavrov, and Nikolai Mikhailovsky were inspiring hundreds of young Russian intellectuals to "go to the people" and work for social change, and at a time when political assassinations threatened to undermine the stability of the autocracy, Poland looked like a refuge of quiescence. The positivist program of "work at the foundations" appeared to enjoy wide acceptance, and the cloud of 1863 continued to hang over the Kingdom, bringing passivity if not loyalty. A decade later this had all changed and Poland was once again the center of the storm. In 1890 a poet named Franciszek Nowicki wrote, "Tomorrow is ours—for we are the young / The night must grow pale and the old must die."[2] By then the positivists, known in their day as "the young press," had become the old ones, struggling against an assertive challenge from a new generation of Polish intellectuals. Those born in the 1860s and 1870s dethroned the positivists, repudiating the agenda of "work" and the antipolitics of liberalism. They turned away from a world they considered prosaic and sterile, calling for a reclamation of "great ideals" and a return to action. The historian Bohdan Cywiński coined a name for this generation with the title of his 1971 book, *Rodowody niepokornych* (The Genealogy of the Defiant).[3] The *niepokorni*—the defiant ones—reclaimed the term that the positivists had tried so hard to suppress: *czyn* (the deed, the act). This return to action was accompanied by new forms of political culture, as the mass movement replaced the conspiracy in the political imagination (if not yet in fact) and as the agitator replaced the both the soldier-poet of 1863 and the entrepreneur-journalist of the 1870s.

But the rhetoric of positivism proved to be more resilient than the tactics of the positivists. The defining paradox of the Polish fin de siècle would be the amalgamation of "great ideals" and "science," the politics of Mickiewicz and the language of

Świętochowski. From this creative but tense intersection would emerge Poland's multiple modernities. The liberal tradition that is so often presumed to define modern political culture—the rhetoric of democracy, free markets, and a Habermasian public sphere—did indeed set the foundation for this new world, but the liberals at *Przegląd Tygodniowy* and *Prawda* were unable to realize their own imagined future. Instead they bequeathed a language of modernity to the *niepokorni*, who in turn gave political expression to the changing social and economic practices of the 1890s. These younger intellectuals and political activists reconfigured positivism so that it could fit within an agenda of action. In doing so, they devised their own "modern" ways to talk about mass politics and to discipline the newly mobilized "people."

In this chapter we will survey the world of the *niepokorni*, exploring the complex position they occupied between the Russian revolutionary movement, the Polish positivists, and the memory of 1863. Like their Russian contemporaries, they wanted to *act* against the injustices they perceived (both national and social) and they wanted to do so in a way that seemed "modern" and "scientific." But their science no longer promised a liberal utopia; indeed, the *niepokorni* came to see *all* the historical prophecies of previous generations as unrealistic and, more important, as deterministic restraints on individual volition. In the chapters that follow we will examine how this generation of Polish intellectuals struggled with the difficulties of being patriotic activists in an age haunted by the twin specters of Herbert Spencer and Karl Marx, of "science" and "revolution." The most important dilemma they encountered, as we will see, was the challenge of coping with "modernity" without the solace of historical time.

The Intelligentsia's World

The world of the Polish intellectual was changing rapidly and profoundly in the late nineteenth century. How those changes would be described and organized was open for contestation, but everyone—conservative or radical, young or old—perceived the emergence of something new. The conservative publicist Teodor Jeske-Choiński captured a nearly universal feeling when he wrote in 1893, "The civilized world is once again approaching a crossroads, which frightens us with the puzzle of unknown directions. Everything that was, everything to which today's adult generation devoted itself, is beginning to fade away, to flow into the blue fog of the past. No one can clearly see what will be."[4] This uncertainty was not, of course, unique to Poland: throughout Europe social and economic developments were accompanied by a reconfiguration of the nineteenth century's norms. In the Kingdom of Poland, however, the Russian presence inflected this process of cultural, political, and social flux by juxtaposing familiar stories of industrialization, dislocation, and political mobilization onto a regime of occupation and denationalization.

At the root of the cultural turmoil of the late nineteenth century was a demographic explosion (spurred by advances in medicine, sanitation, and diet), which increased the number of Polish speakers from 10 million in 1870 to 17 million in 1900. Connected to this growth, industrialization and urbanization were transforming the Polish landscape. Between 1863 and 1879, industrial production in the Kingdom increased by about 240 percent (a 15 percent annual rate of growth), but that was only the beginning: after the establishment of protective tariffs by the Russian Empire in 1877, Polish industry truly took off. Pushed by rural overpopulation and pulled by the promise of factory jobs, the cities of Russian Poland experienced some of the fastest rates of growth in all of Europe. Warsaw expanded from 222,900 inhabitants in 1864 to 383,000 in 1882, 456,000 in 1890, and more than 700,000 at the turn of the century. The small town of Łódź grew into a major textile production center, and the population increased from 40,000 in 1864 to 687,000 in 1914. Whereas in 1872 the proportion of urban to rural inhabitants of the Kingdom was 16:84, in 1910 it was 24:76. The cities became vast concentrations of migrants, cut off from their traditional village world but not yet embedded in a new set of cultural practices. In 1882 only 52 percent of the inhabitants of Warsaw had been born in the city, and registered permanent residents made up only 58 percent of the total. We might characterize this phenomenon as a transition from a rural peasantry to an urban work force, but such a comforting, forward-looking depiction of events cannot capture the pervasive sense of flux, uncertainty, and rootlessness.[5]

By the 1890s the image of Poland as an illiterate, rural backwater was no longer entirely accurate. The cultural historian Roman Zimand has argued that the last decades of the nineteenth century saw the emergence of the "intelligent mob": a growing audience of literate craftsmen, merchants, and even workers who regularly read newspapers and periodicals, albeit not always the same ones as the intelligentsia.[6] The literacy rate in Warsaw was high by regional standards: in 1883 57 percent of the permanent male residents and more than 70 percent of all migrants could read, while 10 percent of all migrant males had completed secondary school. The Poles were ill-served by an inadequate system of russified government schools (which enrolled only about 25 percent of the school-age children in Warsaw), but an extensive network of informal (usually illegal) elementary literacy programs helped to compensate—enough to reduce the illiteracy rate in Warsaw to only 30 percent by 1914.[7] Along with the rising ability to read came a market for reading material. By the 1890s per capita production of printed material in the Kingdom was the same as in Germany, and the periodical press was expanding rapidly. In 1864 there were only 20 periodicals published in the Kingdom; only two decades later there were 80 titles, and by 1904 there were 140. In 1900 Warsaw alone had 10 dailies, 52 weeklies, 22 monthlies, and 2 annuals. The cumulative single-issue print run for all Warsaw papers in 1896 was 55,730, and this number increased nearly threefold by 1904. The popular daily *Kurier Warszawski* had a daily readership of 25,000 in 1896, and *Goniec*, founded in 1903 as a mass-audience daily, expanded rapidly to 60,000 subscribers.[8]

But this "intelligent mob" was an urban phenomenon, and it gradually vanished from view the further east or south one traveled, into the sparsely inhabited, overwhelmingly agrarian regions of Polesia, Volhynia, Podolia, or East Galicia. Despite all the dramatic statistics cited above, life had changed little for most Poles. The peasants were still largely dependent upon a narrow elite of landowners, and the illiteracy rate in the countryside remained at about 70–80 percent. As late as 1904 Konrad Proszyński, a famous pedagogue and the author of a popular elementary grammar, was able to distribute only 13,000 copies of his peasant newspaper, *Gazeta Świąteczna.*[9] This growing disparity between rural and urban spaces would haunt fin de siècle Polish intellectuals as they tried to make sense of a world that was either transforming or not, depending on which part of that world one looked at. Poland's modernity would emerge under the shadow of this typically East European duality.

As Polish intellectuals struggled to make sense of these conflicting visions of urbanization and rural stagnation, they also had to cope with their own personal impoverishment. Whereas most Polish writers and political activists of the early nineteenth century came from noble families with independent financial means, by the 1880s the intelligentsia was a economically diverse group, most of whom had to make a living from whatever professional skills they possessed. Unfortunately, few opportunities were available. Even regular work as a journalist did not yet pay well enough to keep someone securely out of poverty; indeed, it was only in the last decades of the nineteenth century that the practice of paying writers for their contributions became widespread. Most of those who tried to earn their living from the pen were constantly on the edge of poverty, and few amassed any savings. The novelist Stefan Żeromski described going for weeks without a proper meal, and the wife of Jan Popławski, a prominent journalist and political activist, complained that she lacked the money to buy shoes for her children.[10] The chances were little better for those who pursued other professional careers. The state bureaucracy in the Kingdom was open to Poles only on the lowest level, and Warsaw had far more doctors and lawyers than could possibly find employment.[11] This situation led many intellectuals to look for personal fulfillment outside of their own lives, because professional success seemed to be a chimera not worth chasing. As the historian Lesław Sadowski has put it, these young men (and eventually a handful of women), "who did not have any certainty about tomorrow [and] who did not know what they would eat the next day, demanded great ideas capable of veiling the burdensome, tiring apparel of the Polish intellectual." As a result, the old self-definition of the intelligentsia as the guiding elite of the nation did not seem to make much sense: "in the confrontation with reality not only was the concept of the 'spiritual aristocracy' revealed as a fiction, but so was the concept assigning the intelligentsia a place in the middle class. Awakening from the beautiful dream of their social mission as spokesmen of progress, the intelligentsia stood quite simply before the specter of hunger."[12]

We thus see the conjuncture of two forces: an urban population in a state of cultural and social dislocation and an impoverished, frustrated Polish intelligentsia. The latter would turn to the former for salvation, but the link between the *niepokorni* and "the people" would always be problematic. Competing groups of intellectuals would have to define both "the people" and "the nation" before they could conceptualize or give meaning to any form of mass politics. As Prasenjit Duara has put it (in a different context), "the people would have to be created to serve as the people. . . . The nation had already emerged in the name of the people, but the people who mandated the nation would have to be remade to serve as their own sovereign. It was no longer a question of reawakening the nation and the people, but rather, making them from scratch."[13] Were it not for the demographic, social, and economic changes described above, political mobilization would have been impossible, but the intellectuals did not merely articulate the voices of the workers and peasants in an unmediated fashion. Instead, they carefully selected which voices they wanted to hear and crafted new discursive frameworks within which they could make sense of what was said.

This was happening all over the Russian Empire. Moscow and St. Petersburg, although in many ways less "modern" than Warsaw, were experiencing many of the same transformations, and the Russian intelligentsia was responding in similar ways. The Poles, however, had to face some unique challenges. While everyone in the empire had to contend with a state apparatus that was infamously arbitrary, things were particularly bad in the Kingdom. The position of the Vistula Provinces on the borderlands of the empire allowed the officials stationed there wide-ranging autonomy, which most of them exploited to its fullest extent. In fact these officials developed such an imperious attitude that they gained a reputation throughout the state bureaucracy as little despots.[14] But the Poles had to cope with more than just the stereotypical inefficiencies and inequities of the tsarist administration: they were also confronted with an often brutal campaign of forced denationalization. Even the loyalist editor Erazm Pilz criticized the russified educational system for creating a generation of dangerously volatile youth. "*That kind* of school," he wrote, "must produce *that kind* of youth. Schools which have not a scholarly but a political task must arouse in the minds of their students not scholarly, but political passions."[15] To the chagrin of the Russians, that was precisely what happened.

Russification did not come at once after 1863, because even many tsarist officials doubted its effectiveness and resisted its implementation. Ultimately, though, the skeptics were defeated: in 1866 Russian was made the mandatory language of instruction for history and geography in both state and private secondary schools; in 1867 this rule was extended to all subjects except religion and Polish language classes. A year later all these rules were applied to village elementary schools. The final blow came in 1885, when all subjects except religion (but including Polish language and literature) had to be taught in Russian in all schools, at all grade levels. By this time it was illegal to speak Polish on school grounds, even outside the classroom. One student later recalled that some of his teachers responded to this law by switching to Latin for their personal conversations.[16] Polish-language reading material grew scarce for the students. They were not allowed to own any books not assigned in class, and after 1887 they were even prohibited from using the already heavily censored public libraries.[17] Not surprisingly, education in general stagnated. While the number of schools in the Russian Empire increased 300 percent from 1880 to 1900, the Kingdom's school system grew by only 60 percent (barely keeping up with the population increase).

Educational denationalization could be brutal or subtle, but Polish students resented it in any form. It became common to beat students or lock them up in schoolhouse detention rooms for actively resisting the encroachment of russification. Ludwik Krzywicki recalled how one student was randomly selected for a beating (to set an example) when his whole class protested the cancellation of their Polish language class in 1874. On the other hand, Krzywicki also remembered that the librarian of his secondary school was a good-hearted Russian who refrained from stocking anti-Polish literature and was generally friendly to the Polish students. But he was merely a more clever russifier: to spread the use of his language, he obtained copies of all the most popular literature from Western Europe, but only in Russian translation. According to Krzywicki, this more casual approach was the exception. "In a word," he concluded, "the teachers were people called to their position in order to torment children."[18] Roman Dmowski was likewise convinced that his teachers "did not care about supplying the pupils with knowledge, but only about russifying them. . . . They hoped their students would not know too much."[19]

Denationalization continued at the Kingdom's only institution of higher education, Warsaw University (the russified successor to the *Szkoła Główna*). A former student characterized the university as "a tool for aggressive russifying activities, an institution designated for the inoculation against 'knowledge,' for bureaucratic censorship and certification."[20] In the words of the novelist Eliza Orzeszkowa, Warsaw University was a "sad parody" of an academic institution.[21] The historian Szymon Askenazy, who had studied law there, complained in 1905 that the school had declined so much that its degrees could no longer be recognized in good conscience as a mark of academic certification.[22] Those Russians who could not qualify for admission to any other school in the empire were allowed to enroll in Warsaw University, and soon they made up one third of the student body.[23] One of the most revealing descriptions of the school comes from a Russian, the historian Nikolai Ivanovich Kareev, who taught there from 1879 to 1885. He was suspicious from the start, when he obtained a full professorship in Warsaw immediately after receiving his degree, whereas at any other institution he would have been only a docent, with half the pay. Kareev hoped to demonstrate his friendliness toward the Poles, but he quickly learned that most of the faculty and administration were opposed to his conciliatory attitude. Kareev wrote that A. L. Apukhtin, the curator of education for the Kingdom, "arrived in Warsaw full of some sort of elemental hatred toward the Poles." Apukhtin admitted when they first met that he was not interested in Kareev's scholarship as long as he had "a Russian soul." Apukhtin was so hated that when he died in 1897 a commemorative coin was issued by some Polish nationalists with the inscription, "eternal damnation to his name, eternal disgrace to his shameful activities in the Polish Kingdom."[24] The atmosphere in Warsaw was such that even Kareev, for all his reputation as a polonophile, had few contacts with Poles outside of those he met in the course of academic business (Świętochowski was his only Polish friend). When finally a position in the history department at St. Petersburg University opened up, Kareev gratefully returned to Russia. Summarizing his experiences, Kareev wrote:

> I was always an opponent of any national exclusiveness and the sowing of discord between nations, an opponent of all kinds of insipid patriotism, chauvinism, etc. . . . Such an attitude determined my political behavior in Warsaw. Meanwhile, I saw that the Russians in Warsaw did not do anything other than oppress the Poles in every way. Their lack of culture defamed the name of [all] Russians, and I could not be indifferent to the honor of [our] name while I remained abroad [i.e., in Warsaw].[25]

Kareev's testimony was not exaggerated. In 1897 the Russian professors at the University of Warsaw demonstrated their hostility toward the Poles by composing an official letter from the faculty on the occasion of the erection of a new statue in Vilnius to General Mikhail "The Hangman" Muravev. As governor of the Vilnius region after 1863, Muravev had earned his nickname by brutally suppressing the Poles. Under his rule, Poles were prohibited from purchasing land, and any property they currently held was subject to a special 10 percent land tax (reduced to 5 percent in 1869). The Polish language was prohibited in all public places, Polish newspapers were banned, Polish libraries were closed, and even Polish shop signs were removed.[26] Despite (or more likely because of) Muravev's bad reputation in Warsaw, the university faculty sent a letter reading, "With all our soul we join in the current festivities surrounding the initial construction of a monument to a great statesman of Russia, M. Muravev, who saved the North-West region from Polish-Catholic slavery and affirmed the truth that this region was and is purely Russian." As one student dryly wrote, "in these conditions there was no chance of creating even polite relations between the youth and the faculty."[27]

Despite the mediocrity of the Warsaw University, the symbolic importance of the city grew for the Polish intelligentsia during the last decades of the nineteenth century. As russification made everything Polish dangerous, and thus alluring, the old capital became the most potent metaphor of all, drawing Polish writers, artists, and political activists from all over the Russian Empire. Ninety-five percent of all Polish periodicals published in the Russian Empire between 1864 and 1904 originated in Warsaw, even if distributed elsewhere.[28] As a result, many young Poles from Kiev, Minsk, and Vilnius made their way to Warsaw University, disregarding the scholarly reputation of the institution. One Kievian Pole related his excitement as he prepared for his first trip to the Kingdom in 1878:

> For a long time I could not sleep, dreaming of that beautiful, magical, yet so intangible "fatherland," about which at that time so much was said and [about which] such beautiful [songs] were sung. Those songs and those collections of "the loveliest poetry" . . . all that came from Warsaw. My mind, therefore, and my heart were brought up on the cult of Warsaw, which in my imagination went alongside "the fatherland." . . . At that time, real pilgrimages of Polish socialists from Moscow, Petersburg, Kiev, Podolia, and Lithuania to Warsaw took place. It was known that in Warsaw the "work" for which Polish socialists, scattered to all corners of Tsardom, had already been preparing for several years, was beginning.[29]

There was a powerful sense in the late 1870s, and particularly in the 1880s, that something was about to happen in Warsaw. The influence of positivism was starting to wane and the *niepokorni* were about to return to a program of "action."

Russian Examples

When Polish political activity revived in the 1880s, some examples were readily available: throughout the quiet 1870s the "roots of revolution" (to borrow Franco

Venturi's expression) were sprouting to the east. As we saw in the last chapter, the positivists treated Russia as an oriental power that was temporarily imposing political tyranny on Poland but that would somehow retreat to its own "Asian" spaces as soon as the Poles reclaimed their "European" heritage. The *niepokorni* would challenge these orientalist prejudices, and for a while the voices of the Russian radical intelligentsia were heard loudly in Warsaw.

From a Russian perspective, the January Uprising was but one chapter in the history of a turbulent era of social and political transformation. When Tsar Alexander II took the throne in 1855, he let it be known that he intended to modernize the administration of the empire, transform the army into an institution both more humane and more effective, reform the notoriously corrupt judicial system, and above all, liberate the serfs. He aroused great hopes among intellectuals, only to bring even greater disillusionment. On February 27, 1861, deadly force was used to break up a patriotic demonstration in Warsaw, and on March 3 (February 19 old style) the Tsar signed an emancipation decree that deeply disappointed reformist intellectuals and peasants alike.[30] Throughout 1861 there were numerous local peasant rebellions throughout the empire, accompanied by student demonstrations in Moscow and St. Petersburg. The peasants were forcibly suppressed, and restrictive laws regulating student activities were issued. By 1862 a tense calm obtained in the countryside, and many of the major universities had been temporarily closed. The émigré Nikolai Ogarev issued a defiant call:

> Let them close the universities; this will not make genuine learning perish. Let
> the young men of the universities scatter through the provinces. Any man worthy
> of anything will carry learning with him wherever he goes. Not government
> learning, whose aim is tuition; but vital learning, whose purpose is the education
> of the people. . . . Take advantage of this; do not go to the universities. Let them
> close; university youth spread throughout Russia will act as a unifying agent
> between the various classes. To become a free man it is essential to go to the
> people.[31]

Ogarev's summons to go to the people, to actively engage the peasant masses in a struggle for revolutionary change, did not provoke an immediate response, but throughout the 1860s dissatisfaction and frustration grew among the Russian intelligentsia. In contrast to the Poles, who were silenced by the crushing defeat of the January Uprising, the Russian opposition was suppressed in the early 1860s but not vanquished. The literary critic Nikolai Dobrolyubov captured the mood when he wrote in 1859, "What has our society done in the last twenty to thirty years? Until now— nothing. . . . It has prepared itself for action and done nothing. After the stage in which given ideas are *recognized*, there must come the moment when they are *realized*. Action must follow meditation and talk."[32]

Such action would indeed come: by the 1870s there seemed to be a widespread feeling among young, educated Russians that the existing social order was unbearable and that it was necessary to do something about it. Their anger stemmed from a combination of moral outrage at the poverty and powerlessness of the vast majority of the Russian population and a feeling of guilt for their own comparative wealth and privilege. Above all, they wanted to close the vast cultural and conceptual gap that existed between their Europeanized world and the seemingly impenetrable, alien universe of the peasantry. Mikhail Bakunin, writing from the emigration, perceived this desire when he called the young people of Russia to action: "Go to the people: there is your way, your life, your learning. . . . Young men of education must become not the people's benefactors, not its dictators and guides, but merely a lever for the people to free itself, the unifier of the people's own energies and forces. To gain the ability and right to serve the cause, youth must submerge itself and drown in the people."[33] The key term here was "the people" (народ—a troublesome "false friend" for Slavs because the term translates into Polish as *lud*, while the Polish word *naród* corresponds to the Russian нация). The tactical and ideological debates among Russian intellectuals in the 1860s and 1870s revolved around one central question: how best to serve—and eventually combine forces with—the people.[34]

One Russian student later recalled the atmosphere of those years.

The problem was raised in a ruthlessly categorical and extremely partial form: learning or work? I.e., was it necessary to devote ourselves, even if only temporarily, to our studies, so as to obtain diplomas and then live the life of the privileged professions of the intelligentsia; or should we remember our duty to the people, recall that all our learning had been acquired only by means provided by the people, who work like condemned men and are always hungry? Should we not rather, we students, give up our privileged position, give up scholarship and devote ourselves to learning a craft, so as to take part as simple artisans or laborers in the life of the people, and merge with it?[35]

This is precisely what a few thousand of them did—or tried to do—in 1873 and 1874, when students from all the major universities of the empire spread out in an uncoordinated rush to the countryside. They accomplished almost nothing. The peasants were suspicious of the young intellectuals with their unfamiliar words and their obscure motives, and many villagers summoned the police to deal with these strange outsiders. By the end of the "mad summer" of 1874 (as some contemporaries called it), between 2,000 and 4,000 individuals had "gone to the people," and several hundred were arrested as a consequence.[36]

These experiences did not lead to widespread disillusionment or resignation: instead, they inspired the formation of more tightly organized conspiratorial groups that combined the evangelical zeal of the "to the people" movement with a more specific political agenda aimed at the overthrow of the autocracy. In 1876 a group called *Zemlia i Volia* (Land and Freedom) was formed, dedicated, as they put it, to both "agitation" and "the disorganization of the state." In January 1878 a revolutionary shot the governor of St. Petersburg, in February a conspiratorial group in Kiev tried to murder the vice-prosecutor of the city, and in May they succeeded in assassinating a high-ranking police officer. In August *Zemlia i Volia* brought the violence directly to the inner circle of the autocracy by killing the head of the infamous Third Section (the political police). But this wave of political terrorism was short-lived. In

1879 *Zemlia i Volia* split into two parallel organizations: those opposed to the campaign of assassinations formed a small group called The Black Partition (*Cherny Peredel*), while those supporting the use of violence created The People's Will (*Narodnaia Volia*). On March 13, 1881, a member of the latter group tossed a bomb into the Tsar's carriage, killing both himself and the monarch. In the reprisals that followed, the members of *Narodnaia Volia* were hunted down and the organization soon collapsed. This blow would prove decisive, at least in the short term. Not only did most educated Russians turn against the revolutionaries after the assassination, but Alexander II was succeeded by the unapologetically reactionary and authoritarian Alexander III. Those few members of *Narodnaia Volia* who remained free after 1881 either fled abroad or were frightened into passivity. The resulting change in the political landscape was striking, and memoirists have described the decade of the 1880s as "the calm."[37] The turmoil of the 1870s, however, had lasted long enough to present an example of revolutionary action to a new generation of Poles, and just as things began to grow quiet in Moscow and St. Petersburg, Warsaw started to heat up once again. The Kingdom's own *niepokorni* (the defiant ones) were coming of age.

The Spirit of Protest against Everything Vile

One of those who survived the Kingdom's russified schools during the 1880s wrote later that he had been deprived of the happy memories that most children enjoyed but that he had no regrets. "In our memories of youth play the echoes of battle trumpets, which aroused us to a struggle for knowledge, for civil and human rights, for the rights of the nation, for the rights of the people, for their education and consciousness-raising, for the emancipation and the future of humanity, for the triumph of the free spirit and free thought, for the ideals of truth and goodness, for the victory of altruism and brotherhood over force, exploitation, and oppression!" He described Warsaw University as a place of great oppression, but he nonetheless cherished his days there. "That was life! . . . The collective spirit of the youth of Warsaw University created a sort of great, free Republic of ideas, in which were expressed the life of the soul, the life of the mind, and social action."[38] This last phrase, "social action" (*czyn społeczny*), would come to define the *niepokorni*, a generation characterized by the literary historian Stanisław Pigoń as "the first that emancipated itself from the atmosphere of panic after the disaster [i.e., 1863] . . . the first that, looking around at the terrible consequences of the disaster, began to think realistically about opposing the enemy and about salvation."[39]

For the positivists 1863 had been the defining memory of their youth, but by the late 1870s a generation of intellectuals too young to remember "the disaster" had come of age. Someone who was under ten years old in 1863 did not experience the uprising in the same way as someone who was twenty, or even fifteen. Ludwik Krzywicki (who was four at the time of the revolt) described his peers: "They came into the world after the events of 1863, [and] the more removed from personal recollections of that date, the more rebelliously they stood against the common sense of the older generation."[40] Stanisław Kozicki (not born until 1876), believed that positivism "was in accordance with the feelings and the atmosphere of the generation that remembered the uprising. . . . But it did not correspond to either the intellectual tendencies or the feelings of the generation that was born in the 1860s and entered [adult] life in the 1880s."[41] For university students in the 1880s, the January Uprising was as much a historical event as was the eighteenth-century collapse of the Polish Republic; it was not a living memory, not part of their own experiences. They did not perceive russification as a response to 1863, because most of them had never known anything else. They did not witness the despair of the defeat; they knew only the heroic war stories and patriotic songs of their fathers. Moreover, they grew up hearing about revolutionary action in St. Petersburg, Moscow, and Kiev, and (with the Russian language skills they had been forced to acquire) they read the clandestine brochures of groups like *Zemlia i Volia.* As a result, they had little patience for the sermons of *Prawda* or *Przegląd Tygodniowy.* A teacher named Helena Radlińska later recalled that she and her peers believed that only by breaking the law were they "really doing something."[42] At the same time, however, they found it impossible to escape fully the shadow of positivism. The vocabulary of science lost none of its allure, and even the idea of organic work could remain in play, if appropriately reconceptualized so as to accommodate "great ideals." Those born after 1863 did not really reject positivism: they *reconstructed* the positivists so that they could more easily attack what they saw as the passivity of liberalism while simultaneously appropriating the language of science.

As early as 1875 there were signs that positivism's program of organic work would be opposed by a younger generation and that the revolutionary unrest in Russia would spread to the Kingdom. In that year a few recent graduates of Warsaw University formed an ephemeral illegal group called The Society for National Education, which was based on the conviction that one could not bring "enlightenment" to the peasants within the confines of Russian law.[43] The students of the late 1870s and early 1880s shared with the positivists the desire to educate (themselves above all), but their experiences in secondary school and at Warsaw University impelled them to take their pedagogy underground. The first "flying university" appeared in 1875 and was well developed by the mid-1880s. This was an illegal but well-structured program offered to university-age students (men and women) who wished to avoid the restrictions of the official curriculum. Some of the leading intellectuals of Warsaw lectured in crowded student apartments, gave tests, issued grades, and even granted diplomas. Students could choose a degree program lasting several years, taking up to eleven hours a week of lectures. Several hundred young men and women a year took part at the university's peak, and during two decades of illegal education more than 5,000 individuals were involved.[44]

A more serious challenge to the positivist program was the emergence of explicitly political activism. A number of Poles participated in the Russian revolutionary movement of the 1870s, and Polish students at Russian universities helped bring dissent back to the Kingdom. More than 2,000 Poles attended the empire's institutions of higher learning in the 1870s, constituting nearly a quarter of the students at some schools (even though Poles made up barely 6 percent of the total population). In fact, Polish enrollment was so disproportionate that a *numerus clausus* was established, limiting them to 20 percent of any student body.[45] Ironically, at these Russian institutions polonophobia was much less pronounced than at Warsaw University, where denationalization was such a central commitment. In fact, many Russian students, particularly those involved with the revolutionary movement, supported Polish independence and admired the Poles' insurrectionary traditions. It was no surprise, then, when a number of Poles were found among the members of *Zemlia i Volia* and *Narodnaia Volia.* Polish socialism, in fact, had its roots in Russia. The first Polish socialist "circles" were formed in Petersburg in 1874, amid the excitement of the "to the people" movement, and an informal network linked Polish radicals from all the Russian universities before any attempt was made to spread the movement to Warsaw.[46]

Only in 1876 did socialist circles appear in the Kingdom, and even then the instigator was a young Polish student from the Petersburg Technical Institute, Ludwik Waryński.[47] By mid-1878 he had established a loose network of revolutionary cells with about 300 members, but at the end of that summer the police uncovered his nascent organization and he was forced to flee the country. A local group led by a Warsaw University student named Adam Szymański tried to provide a "patriotic" alternative to Waryński's "Russian" (or, more euphemistically, "international") socialism, but this effort attracted only a handful of participants and was uncovered by the police almost immediately.[48] During these years tsarist officials in Warsaw complained that the virus of revolution was spreading from Russia to an otherwise pacified Poland. "Tied to the Russian socialists by a unity of doctrine and lineage," wrote the chief prosecutor of Warsaw in a report from December 1878, "the members of the Warsaw circles must have been, and indeed were, in close contact with the Russian revolutionary circles. Those circles consider the Warsaw movement to be one of the manifestations of Russian socialism and they are extremely interested in it."[49] Viacheslav Plehve, then a police official in the Kingdom (and later the minister of the interior), reported in 1879 that virtually all the revolutionary agitation in the Kingdom came from Poles who had studied in Russian universities.[50] Waryński returned to the Kingdom in 1881, and this time he was able to create a more substantial group, called the Social Revolutionary Party "Proletariat" (often called The First Proletariat or The Great Proletariat, to distinguish it from later groups of the same name). Once again the police were able to break up Waryński's group; he was arrested in September 1883 and within a few years the besieged remnants of the First Proletariat had vanished. Four members of the party were hanged (the first political executions in the Kingdom since the 1863 Uprising) and Waryński himself died in prison in 1889.

Although the spark came from the east, it soon burned independently in the Kingdom. Despite the quick demise of all the groups formed in the 1870s, Ludwik Krzywicki, a student at that time, recalled these years as a turning point: the arrests and trials of these first activists, he claimed, inspired his classmates to further illegality.[51] What the Russians saw as the culmination of a revolutionary movement born of the frustrated hopes of the late 1850s the Poles perceived as a return to action after the post-uprising quiescence. The jailed revolutionaries who were mourned in St. Petersburg and Moscow as victims of a lost cause were idolized in Warsaw as martyrs to a struggle that was only just beginning. The atmosphere on the campus of Warsaw University grew more and more radical in the early 1880s, in part thanks to a student activist named Stanisław Krusiński. He organized a small display of defiance in 1881, when a Russian student named Ostrovidov denounced some of his Polish colleagues for singing patriotic songs and later (as Professor Kareev put it) "was stupid enough to brag about his offense." Denunciation was considered unethical by both Russian and Polish students, so Krusiński mounted a campaign to force Ostrovidov to leave the university. A group of students (Krzywicki estimated the number at 10 to 15 percent of the student body) gathered in the university auditorium to demand Ostrovidov's departure. To everyone's surprise, they prevailed.[52]

Krusiński struck again in 1883. A young Russian student in Warsaw, Evgeny Zhukovich, had been complaining about the anti-Polish brutality he witnessed in the Kingdom's educational system, and he had written letters to a variety of state officials complaining about Apukhtin (the curator of education). His missives went unanswered, so he arranged a meeting with the curator himself. Once in his office, Zhukovich slapped Apukhtin on the face and was promptly expelled from the university. Krusiński exploited this opportunity by organizing a demonstration in support of Zhukovich, in which hundreds of students (ironically, mainly the Poles) participated. Unfortunately, the only immediate result was that Krusiński and 93 other student activists (10 percent of the student body) shared Zhukovich's fate.[53] Krzywicki, who had participated in these protests, had to escape to Galicia to avoid arrest, and when he returned in 1886 he did not recognize Warsaw. "Everywhere I encountered illegal work," he wrote, "and moreover, people looked upon the consequences of their actions in case they were discovered with complete peace. . . . The apathy that one could feel so strongly at every step before my entry to the university, and the fear accompanying it, had weakened considerably." Krzywicki calculated that one third of those who graduated from secondary school with him in 1878 spent some time in jail for political offenses, or were forced to flee abroad.[54] Incarceration became a mark of honor rather than a threat: as Helena Radlińska put it, arrest "brought jealousy that someone else was distinguished, that we were not yet worthy."[55]

"1886 was the moment when that powerlessness into which Polish society fell after the 1863 uprising was overcome," recalled Zygmunt Wasilewski.[56] That year marked the founding of two weekly magazines: *Głos* (The Voice) and *Przegląd Społeczny* (The Social Review). Together these two publications provided the restless Polish youth with a forum and an alternative to the now well-established positivist press. The leading editors at *Głos*, Jan Ludwik Popławski and Józef Potocki, had been writing for Świętochowski's *Prawda*, but they wanted to create an alternative weekly that would provide a broad forum for the still ill-defined radicalism of their peers.[57] They succeeded. As the historian Janina Żurawicka put it, "There is no author of a memoir, a monograph, or even a work of *belles-lettres* regarding the end of the nineteenth century who . . . passes over the activities of the people tied to *Głos*."[58] Some memoirists and scholars would later characterize *Głos* as populist and anti-Marxist, but this description is not quite accurate. Feliks Perl (himself a socialist) was closer to the mark when he described *Głos* as "the organ of that section of the intellectual proletariat which, having an acute national sense and socialist sympathies, searched for national rebirth along the road to the peasantry."[59] The rhetorical mélange of this passage is symptomatic. A member of the editorial board, Józef Hłasko, put it well when he called *Głos* "the laboratory of new thinking in Poland. . . . Among the authors who began their careers in the period from 1887 to 1894 in Warsaw, there were hardly any who did not write for *Głos* or were not on its editorial board."[60] *Głos* was neither nationalist, socialist, nor populist: it was all of these things.

Alongside *Głos* stood a monthly with an almost identical profile called *Przegląd Społeczny*, founded in Galicia at the same time. *Przegląd Społeczny* was edited by Bolesław Wysłouch and included contributions by such diverse individuals as Zygmunt Balicki, Edward Przewóski, Bolesław Limanowski, Zygmunt Miłkowski, Ivan Franko, and even "Jerzy Plechanów" (a.k.a. Georgii Plekhanov). This was not as much a Galician version of *Głos* as it was an open window for the Warsaw *niepokorni*, who could send their writings to Wysłouch anonymously to escape the Russian censors. *Przegląd Społeczny* folded after two years and its importance to Galicia's history is limited. However, because it allowed the *głosowcy* (as those affiliated with *Głos* were known) to write somewhat more freely, it provides us with some insight into their views.[61]

Głos and *Przegląd Społeczny* propagated a cautious populism and a vague socialism, but they simultaneously tried to rekindle the national ambitions of 1863. The concrete link between the *głosowcy* and the legacy of the January Uprising was the Polish League, formed in Zurich in 1887 by the novelist and insurgent Zygmunt Miłkowski (a.k.a. T. T. Jeż).[62] This organization remained tiny: its Galician and Poznanian branches never got off the ground and in the Kingdom it had only a handful of members. The League's importance, however, did not lie in its own activities but in the bond it established with young people in the Kingdom via its student branch, the *Związek Młodzieży Polskiej* (Union of Polish Youth), popularly known as Zet. The initial meeting of Zet included delegates from every partition and the emigration, and branches were soon founded in 24 cities (with the largest in Warsaw). Zet was small at first, with barely 100 members, but it planted seeds wherever there were Polish students, and it gave the émigré insurgents access to some younger activists.[63]

Głos, Przegląd Społeczny, Zet, and the Polish League repudiated positivism and organic work, but the positivism they rejected seemed to have little in common with what Świętochowski, Prus, or Wiślicki actually believed. The *niepokorni* created their own vision of positivism to serve their polemical needs, inventing their opponents in order to better define themselves. Zygmunt Wasilewski demonstrated how positivism was reconfigured by the *niepokorni*:

> Social thought deprived of all soaring ideas, oppressed, closed in the boundaries
> of strict legality, searching for an escape for itself (mechanically rather than from
> a great program), began to work on the means of saving its material existence.
> . . . The program of organic work, formulated vaguely on the political side,
> extinguished the sun so as to avoid recognition and lost itself in the twilight.
> Historians see in that era a sort of sickness, derived from the denial of romanticism and great politics. The idea of an independent Poland was extinguished, so
> as to take it from the country's attention, so that children would forget about it,

so that finally there would be peace. In essence, however, it was extinguished because eyes that had cried for too long and that were afraid could no longer look at it. Organic work, as we see from recent tradition, went astray. In the twilight it took the means for the goal; it declared that work for material well-being was heroism, whereas in the normal world it is the duty of the day, subordinated under greater tasks.[64]

Wasilewski began this loaded passage by associating the positivists with the pursuit of material gains. The critics of the *młoda prasa*—first the conservatives, then the *niepokorni*—had long considered liberalism an apology for capitalism and greed, and positivism merely a local version of laissez-faire. The program of organic work, the critics alleged, only provided a justification for the exploitation of the poor, allowing people to feel good as they enriched themselves. Many agreed when Tomasz Ruskiewicz charged the positivists with making Polish society materialistic, when Popławski declared that organic work was nothing more than the a "gospel of egoism and apathy," or when Perl, Potocki, and many others described positivism as a bourgeois ideology.[65] If liberalism promised only material wealth, then the *niepokorni* were convinced that it was not adequate for the 1880s. Popławski described a new idealism within the "younger generation" and declared that "this feeling—slandered, disbelieved, fettered in the shackles of 'sober practicality'—does not find nourishment in that wealthy pantry, which has been filled to overflowing in recent years with products of economic virtue."[66] Paweł Czarnecki recalled that his peers had abandoned positivism because "confining oneself to material profit led to egoism [and] the forgetting of national concerns."[67]

These attacks were unfair and inaccurate (if that matters). The positivists were indeed liberals, but they were never apologists for laissez-faire economics; in this respect they were more akin to the so-called new liberals in Britain.[68] The positivist monthly *Ateneum* complained that only bad faith could explain the attempts to equate organic work with the ruthless pursuit of personal wealth.[69] Świętochowski recognized that some people had misused and misunderstood his ideas, but he insisted that he had no love of capitalist individualism and would tolerate no such elevation of material welfare above the good of the community.[70] *Przegląd Tygodniowy*, *Prawda*, and *Ateneum* went so far as to open their pages to those who would be most likely to attack laissez-faire from a "social" perspective: the *niepokorni* themselves.[71] Popławski, for example, used the pages of *Prawda* to announce the death of "the ruthless, metaphysical system of the Manchester school" and proclaim the birth of the "realistic school" of socialism. Although he was later to blame the positivists for propagating egoism, he recognized in this article that "the theory of evolution and positivist philosophy" had itself undermined laissez-faire economics.[72]

Popławski may have been willing to give the positivists some credit, but Krzywicki was not. In April of the same year he mounted an attack on Bolesław Prus, setting off a round of polemics that would last into the summer.[73] Krzywicki went right to the heart of Prus' rhetoric, attacking the supposedly scientific nature of positivism. When Prus claimed to be objective, Krzywicki complained, he was in fact only making deductions from the status quo and projecting them into the future. In this way he ended up with a profoundly conservative argument and was unable to conceive of meaningful social reform. "In his objectivism Mr. A. G. [Aleksander Głowacki—Prus' real name] does not go beyond the differentiation of existing social institutions and looks upon social phenomena as an 'impartial observer,'" Krzywicki wrote. "For our part, we are human beings; in our veins flows blood which curdles at the sight of poverty and darkness. . . . Therefore we cannot, like Mr. A. G., be 'impartial observers' . . . we cannot be satisfied with the understanding of laws, that is, with the formulation of existing relations and the observation of their metamorphosis." But Krzywicki was not really attacking the concept of objective science. Instead he was accusing Prus of hypocrisy: "his objectivism and 'impartial observation' are masks, under which, in the name of science, he follows Malthus, Bastiat, Spencer, and others who defend a social order based on free competition."[74]

Prus responded with anger. He not only defended the value of a scientific approach to the study of society, but (more important) he rejected Krzywicki's characterization of positivism. "On what foundation," he asked, "can the respected author charge me with masking the desire to defend castes, exploitation, poverty, darkness, the shattering of societies into atoms struggling amongst themselves? Can one reconcile my alleged faith in the immutability of today's forms with the principle of 'development'? Can one reconcile darkness with the aspiration to 'perfection,' poverty with 'happiness,' and exploitation with 'utility'?" Prus went on to refute each of Krzywicki's accusations, but his response could be summed up in one sentence: "As I am alive, I never said that."[75]

This exchange sparked a huge debate in the Warsaw press, but quickly the theme shifted to an attack on Krzywicki for espousing an orthodox Marxism that was allegedly inappropriate for a peasant society like Poland's. Krzywicki had many defenders, and the polemics continued for several months.[76] In the course of this exchange from the spring and summer of 1883, we see positivism left behind as the debate between Marxism and populism moved to center stage. The *niepokorni* took their arguments into the twentieth century, while the positivists were left complaining, "I never said that." Popławski, writing in 1886, astutely perceived what had happened.

> It is a very characteristic phenomenon that the policy of organic work, which
> was supposed to constitute such a decisive turn in the history of our nation, has
> abdicated almost without resistance. . . . What is more, the apostles of that
> principle often stand against its consequences: the collapse of public morality,
> apathy, bourgeois egoism, intellectual superficiality, etc. . . . "We did not say
> that, we understood this or that differently"; this is their only argument.[77]

As far as Świętochowski and Prus were concerned, it was a perfectly adequate argument, but by the mid-1880s it was no longer effective. The positivists did not refute the assertion that liberal political economy led to suffering and exploitation—indeed, they had been making the same claim for years. The *niepokorni*, however, equated organic work and laissez-faire and tied capitalism to both. No matter how hard the positivists tried to define the meaning of their own texts, they were stripped of the power to do so.

Why was it so important for the *niepokorni* to insist that the positivists were apologists for capitalism? The debate seemed to be about the virtues and vices of liberal economics—and on one level it was—but more deeply this was an argument about the *consequences* of positivism, and of science itself. While the *młoda prasa* insisted that they could be liberals without embracing the doctrines of political economy, the *niepokorni* declared that they could not, that one followed from the other. The positivists believed that their socioeconomic "laws" allowed for "development," for the unfolding of a world of social justice and harmony. Their subtle but crucial distinction between work and action was based on the conviction that the former could lead to (lawful) change, while the latter was a futile attempt to manage and direct progress. Both convictions, as was explained in the last chapter, rested on a "scientific" but still teleological vision of history. The *niepokorni*, on the other hand, claimed that positivism virtually required one to believe that "the economic order was unchanging" (as Popławski put it) and not subject to "interventions." In other words, positivism's historiosophy denied the *niepokorni* an opportunity to willfully, actively change the world. Prus missed the point when he evoked the concept of development as a means to resolve social injustice. The *niepokorni* were not interested in patiently "working" within the laws of progress and waiting for time and history to take their course. Like so many of their peers all over fin de siècle Europe, they wanted to intervene in the world and make their own futures. This is what lay at the heart of this curious argument in the Polish press over liberal political economy, which was really a debate about the possibility of applying *will* to the problems of the world. It was a struggle between capital-H History and the deed.

This wasn't just an argument between liberals devoted to "science" and radicals committed to "action." The context was more complex, involving fissures *within* the revolutionary left, not just in Poland but throughout the Russian Empire. Just as the return to action had its origins in Russia, so did the debate about history and volition. The revolutionaries of *Zemlia i Volia* and *Narodnaia Volia* had difficulty coping with the idea of historical progress. They had to configure their own historiosophies so that they could be both socialists and Russians, so that they could both accept European ("universal") progress and deal with the idiosyncrasies of an agrarian society. Dmitrii Pisarev, for example, attempted to combine revolutionary goals with an uncompromising devotion to science. In an odd echo of the Warsaw positivists, Pisarev argued in the late 1850s that work (not revolutionary action) was certain to bring about the golden age, because the forces of history would ensure its coming. He was so confident that progress was moving in his direction—toward the elimination of all "exploiters"—that he felt no need to actively *do* anything to bring about change. Indeed, he considered it impossible to willfully intervene in history. "I see in life only a process," he wrote, "and I eliminate purpose and ideal."[78]

This faith in science was common among Russian intellectuals in the 1860s and 1870s, but so was a concern about the way history seemed to be moving. As early as 1857 Nikolai Chernyshevsky articulated the ambivalence shared by many of his peers. "There is no doubt about the eventual success of the [revolutionary] cause," he wrote, "because historical necessity imposes it. But it is terrible to think how much time and effort it will require, how much suffering and loss it has already cost and how much more it will cost. . . . We must not lose the example of the West. . . . We still have time to profit from this lesson. Now, while we are still only foreseeing these changes, we must prepare for events and control their development."[79] The historiosophy of revolutionary socialism prophesied that European capitalism would generate the seeds of its own destruction, but only after it had driven millions into desperate poverty. Chernyshevsky looked into this future from a Russian perspective and saw a painful road that led from the country's agrarian economy, through capitalism and private property, and only then to the promised land. He could not abide the thought of such a long journey, so he came up with an alternative narrative. According to Chernyshevsky, Russia's communal, agrarian social structure, though precapitalist, had more in common with the future golden age than it did with Europe's present (just as the Hegelian thesis shared much with the ultimate synthesis). Perhaps, then, Russia could bypass the intermediate stage of industry and urbanization and move directly from the primitive commune to the socialist commune. Scientific history might have a preordained narrative, Chernyshevsky believed, but humans could use their free will to intervene in that story, hurry it along, and skim over its more unpleasant chapters.[80]

Even this optimistic vision, however, was set against a scientistic philosophy that left only limited space for human action and will. Chernyshevsky did indeed want to "control the development" of Russia, but like Pisarev (and like the Warsaw positivists), he had to fit this desire within a fundamentally deterministic worldview that dictated the form and direction (albeit not the speed) of progress. One could "work" within history, but one could not step entirely outside its boundaries. Many populists followed this model, not quite repudiating the idea of historical destiny but insisting that they could learn from the past in order to move more quickly into the future.[81] Others were more consequential in asserting their own free will. A manifesto from 1861 complained about those who wanted "to turn Russia into an England and feed us on the experiences of England. . . . We are a backward people and in this lies our salvation. We must thank fate that we have not lived the life of Europe. Its misfortunes and its situation without any way of escape are a lesson for us. We do not want its proletariat, its aristocracy, its governmental principles, its imperial power. . . . We have no political past. We are not bound by any tradition. . . . That is why, unlike Western Europe, we are not afraid of the future. That is why we move boldly forward to the revolution, why we long for it. . . . Without faith there is no salvation, and we have great faith in our strength."[82] For these revolutionaries, the force of will was more powerful than any economic laws—particularly in Russia, a land without a "past" (because the past was still present) and thus a country free from the tyranny of prophetic history. Writing in 1870, Nikolai Mikhailovsky was even more eloquent in his repudiation of determinism: "Man can say: yes, nature is merciless toward me, it knows no distinction, with respect to rights, between me and a sparrow. But I myself shall also be merciless to it and by my own blood and toil subdue it; compel it to serve me, wipe out evil and create good. I am not the goal of nature and nature has no other goals. But I have goals and I shall attain them."[83]

This desire to act—to intervene willfully in history and subdue nature—was what had drawn so many young Poles to the Russian revolutionary movement and what had motivated Ludwik Krzywicki's attack on Bolesław Prus in 1883. Helena Cey-singerówna recalled her frustrations as a young woman: "Who can forget those times, when for a person with a fiery heart, with a craving for social action, there was nothing, nothing to do?"[84] By the late 1880s this was no longer the case: in 1888 the novelist Stefan Żeromski could write in his diary, "Patriotic action is coming alive, even in the souls of the weakest. . . . Action! That is the only answer for everything."[85] This concept of "action" should not be understood superficially, as a mere desire to "do something" (although certainly the *niepokorni* had their share of youthful energy and impatience). More profoundly, the call to action implied a conviction that autonomous volition was the source of social change. The positivists had argued that change was part of history and that people neither should nor could direct this process. One could work *within* history, but one could never lead it. Against this positivist historiosophy, the *niepokorni* offered the "great ideals" that would liberate the forms of action closed off by Świętochowski and his colleagues. Against history (as a means of subordinating individuals to a deterministic narrative of progress) the *niepokorni* offered idealism (as an assertion of will). They did not narrate yet another vision of the future, within which their activities would produce clear and inevitable results. Instead they exalted the ideals that could motivate one to intervene in the world and *create* the future. The entire temporality of their worldview shifted: the positivists could not sustain their arguments without a vision of the future, while the *niepokorni* needed only a great ideal in the present.

Roman Dmowski described these developments as a move away from positivism toward "politics," but he was not referring to public engagement with or within state institutions.[86] That sort of politics was unimaginable for a Pole in the Russian Empire, where even the *zemstvos* (the tightly restricted institutions of local self-government created by Alexander II) were withheld from the Kingdom and the Western Territories (today's Ukraine, Belarus, and Lithuania). Nor was "politics" a codeword for revolutionary activities directed at overthrowing the state (as it was for *Narodnaia Volia*). Many of the *niepokorni* dreamed of such an opportunity, but the "return to politics" signified a much deeper transformation of the attitudes and the imaginary horizons of these young intellectuals. To be political meant, for them, to enter a world in which active subjects could create their own futures, whereas to be scientific implied that one was constrained by nature. A political mode of thought allowed (indeed, compelled) one to agitate, to revolt, to compete, to organize, and *to act*, while a scientific mode only had limited spaces, circumscribed by social or historical laws, within which one could work. The latter approach, wrote the socialist A. Zakrzewski, paralyzed people by preaching that "human suffering and despair" was the result of some immutable natural law.[87]

Przegląd Społeczny employed a revealing phrase when it declared its determination to resolve "the negative sides of reality."[88] Insofar as science had value for the *niepokorni*, it was as a source of knowledge that could facilitate willful intervention in human affairs. As Potocki put it, one could appreciate science only if one had "an awareness of how the laws of development and social life allow man to direct social laws and foresee the results of his actions."[89] While the positivists felt constrained to obey social laws and work within them, the *niepokorni* believed that they could direct them. Jan Stecki, later an important National Democratic activist, mounted an assault on the antipolitics of science in a three-part essay in *Głos* entitled "The Laws of Nature and Their Value for History." Stecki attacked the prevailing "fetishism" of science and bemoaned the retreat of all "feelings and ideals . . . before the victorious invasion of sobriety." These charges were familiar, but Stecki exposed their real polemical force by explaining that science, if accepted uncritically, led to a "presumptive or overt declaration of faith in the power and permanence of social processes." Only if we grasped the potential of the ideal, he argued, could we escape the conservative implications of science. To accomplish this, we had to understand that scientific laws "exist only in the human mind and are not in any way an internal cause of phenomena, that they do not possess real existence." This was true even for something as seemingly objective as physics, Stecki contended, and it was particularly the case with sociological laws, which he believed could be changed at any moment by an act of human will. "Every great poetic work, every creation of genius is a new force shaping human history, . . . " he wrote. "As long as the science of society is not based on the most precise understanding of the much-maligned spirit, it will be sterile and mistaken."[90] Thanks to our independent volition, we could intervene in history and shatter the illusion of lawful progress. In a world of will there could be no master narrative of history. All that remained was the deed.

For Popławski even "truth" was inadequate if it was not combined with action. "The goal of theoretical research," he wrote, "is a discovery of the truth and nothing more; that means today that it aspires only to point out certain regularities in our common existence, and the consequences of the facts. . . . But alongside thought, there are also developments of life, real existence, neither thought nor its reflection. The goals [of life] are, furthermore, different. Theory aspires to knowledge; praxis is action. So, while for the former a concrete phenomenon is only material for a generalization, for the latter it is a goal." Science as such, he argued, possessed "nothing repulsive, nothing offending our moral feelings," but if one did not apply such scientific principles with care, one could easily go astray. "Theory in its judgments must be ruthless, inhuman, cruel, cold, because it is only a generalization from facts . . . [but] one must use an entirely different measure when evaluating practical judgments. Here the goal is not the most ruthless truth, but the most success possible for the community.[91] "Science" and "theory" were acceptable if they were merged with "practice," which implied that they be directed toward the welfare of the community. The socialist Stanisław Karpowicz, in the evocatively titled article, "Knowledge and Pessimism," tried to establish that understanding, if not driven by a social conscience and a desire to change the world, would degenerate into impotent abstractions. The only point of sociology, for Karpowicz, was to arrive at great ideals.

> We therefore analyze social phenomena, and from them we arrive at bold
> generalizations and principles that are today in contradiction with life, but which
> in the future are to be resolved, bringing universal harmony. The gap separating

life today from the ideal will in time disappear entirely. . . . An ideal, therefore, arrived at through skillfully conducted research, has the same relation to the existing forms of existence as does a certain future epoch to the current day. Understanding things in this way, what does it mean to live in accordance with ideals, to manifest ideas in action? It means to bring closer the moment of the ideal future, it means to introduce into life those forms of existence which most quickly and most effectively will lead us to the state of perfection.[92]

However often the *niepokorni* used the rhetoric of "science" or spoke of "the laws of nature," they always returned to "ideals" and "feelings," rejecting the "sobriety" of the positivists. As a speaker at an 1890 patriotic meeting in Geneva put it, "We need feelings! . . . We need revolutionary feelings, which would not bear oppression, which would live, and, like the hot blood of a healthy organism, would throb through the pulses of thousands."[93] Even the *niepokorni*'s most "scientific" socialists were unapologetic about the emotional side of their political philosophy, leading Józef Uziembło to suggest that they be labeled "the romantics of Marxism."[94] Krzywicki himself recognized that for his generation "socialism was a sort of religion: [they were] enthusiasts, who did not measure their goals according to their strength, but increased their strength in accordance with their goals. It was as if they had a fever, a fever of action, a powerful faith that the desired social kingdom was only a few years away." As Krzywicki began translating *Capital*, many of his friends tried to dissuade him from doing so. The great revolution, they argued, was going to arrive too soon for such academic work to have any importance.[95] Even Krzywicki himself (who was among the most "objective" Marxists of his generation) was proud of his "subjectivism," which entailed "introducing to sociology, alongside the *empirical* element, the *desirable* element." The excessive objectivity of scientific determinism, he argued, was a form of slavery, because it made it conceptually impossible to change anything that had received nature's stamp of approval.[96] Edward Przewóski believed that knowledge about "the causal order of things" ought to give intellectuals "the capacity to influence human life by exchanging causes according to desired results. Without this, sociology would not be a practical science, a science of social life. This is a determinism that includes human knowledge and will as one of the natural forces." Przewóski dreamed of "a science of human and social goals, *a science of ideals*, that can be embodied in individual and social life." This sort of science would not merely take "as its normative model that *which is*," but move on "to an understanding of that *which ought to be*."[97]

An editorialist in *Przegląd Społeczny,* while criticizing the positivists for "living from day to day, deprived of wider aspirations and submerged in concerns about the mere means of material existence," admitted that they were patriots of a sort. Unfortunately, "political sobriety" forced them to suppress their national feelings, and as a result "they lost the thread tying today's practical work with distant national goals."[98] In other words, the problem with organic work was not *what* was done, but *why*. Because the positivists accepted reality and stopped dreaming of radical systemic change, their "work" became literally pointless. But as Krzywicki put it, organic work could still be valuable, as long as it was supported by a great ideal.[99] The *niepokorni* did not really abandon organic work, no matter how vigorously they attacked positivism—they simply redefined it. Zygmunt Balicki wrote, "Our generation is doubtlessly on the right path: we have stopped looking for all sorts of political-supernatural forces, taking up instead organic-revolutionary work. It is organic (not in the trivial sense of that word), because it penetrates to the depths of the national character, to its instincts and organization, but it is at the same time revolutionary, because the unavoidable consequence of a change of instincts must be a change in the external form."[100]

The *niepokorni*'s approach to organic work emerged most clearly in the reaction to Prus' controversial 1887 essay calling for "work, work, work."[101] Popławski published his response in *Głos* in an essay appropriately titled "Great Ideals." "No one can deny," the younger man wrote, "the meaning of that ant-like economical work, but no one ought to forget that a society demonstrates its values only insofar as it warms and enlightens them with the rays of the sun from some sort of great idea." Popławski believed that even the most modest labor had to be driven by a lofty goal: "We do not know how to fulfill even small duties, because we are not invigorated by a great idea that would give those small ideas movement and cohesion, and that would be for them a storehouse of strength." Groups like the Polish League and Zet were not just revolutionary conspiracies: they accepted their "small duties," but invested them with "great ideas." At times the Polish League's texts could sound as strident as any manifesto from 1863: "Will we succumb to these crushing forces, and with only complaints on our mouths, without struggle or action, vanish from the face of the earth, losing one position after another? Or will we break with this policy of suicide, gather together . . . our strengths, and return to the courageous struggle for national existence!"[102] The statute of the League, however, clarified the consequences of such rhetoric: "Having in view revolutionary activity above all else, the Central Committee will not neglect the use of its influence to support the education of the people, the welfare of the disinherited classes and in general the development of national strength in its social and economic [aspects]."[103] Zygmunt Miłkowski, the founder of the League, typically combined insurrectionary rhetoric with strikingly modest proposals. In 1887 he insisted that "active defense . . . does not at all preclude either the heart or reason. . . . [It] does not consist of either insurrection, or the renunciation of insurrection." Almost any "reasonable" activity could qualify as action if it was motivated by patriotism.[104] Miłkowski's émigré paper, *Wolne Polskie Słowo* (The Free Polish Word), summarized this ambiguous break with the positivist tradition: "It has become a necessity to replace that slogan [organic work] with a new one; to break with the program of dependency and subordination does not mean to break with cultural-national work, and neither [does it imply] throwing ourselves at once into an armed uprising. It is only necessary to broaden the program of activities, enlighten the goals of society, hold aloft without fear our national aspirations at every opportunity, and instill them into the masses."[105]

This was a subtle and seemingly paradoxical argument, and many readers interpreted the evocation of the term "action" as a call to violence. Some anonymous conservatives from Kraków printed a response to Miłkowski in which the old soldier was criticized for not understanding the situation in Poland. Things were not really so bad, this brochure claimed, and any rash conspiracies would only endanger the rights and privileges Poles already enjoyed.[106] But this reply missed—or misrepresented—Miłkowski's point. Neither he nor the *niepokorni* were trying to provoke another revolt (at least not right away); they just wanted to infuse the positivists' agenda of organic work with idealist content. The "deed" was defined by the goal, not by what was done.

Popławski was not optimistic, let alone naïve, about the possibility of quickly restoring independence or inaugurating a new age of social justice. He placed himself among those "who do not expect at all that the wall will be broken in the near future. Instead, [we] know that it will be necessary to wait many years, but [we] also know that in order for that moment to come nearer it is necessary to bang one's head against the wall, even if it only cracks."[107] Popławski was not challenging the positivist assessment that another insurrection would fail; instead, he was proclaiming quixotically that one had to be driven by a great ideal—and act for its realization—even if one realized that the pursuit of this dream would bring only nominal gains at the cost of great personal sacrifice. Another contributor to *Głos* described "premature action" as "the *malum necessarium* that purchases a thousand other good acts," and an émigré paper proclaimed, "Down with superficial, bourgeois patriotism, which trembles at the thought of losses! Sacrifices without end, uncounted disasters—that is the only path which honest patriotism points out to every nation that wants to rise up, live, and have a future."[108] Others were more optimistic. The anonymous author of a letter to the editor of *Kurier Warszawski* rejected Prus' alleged quiescence with an Archimedean metaphor: "You might call it an illusion, but we want to push the mass of the earth from its old orbit onto a new track. We feel that we have enough strength for this; we believe that we will be able to accomplish it, if we only find that point of balance, that focal point toward which we have to aim our thoughts and our spirit. For us this is necessary for life; without it our real strengths will be wasted, will vanish in inactivity."[109]

Ultimately, though, it did not really matter whether the promised land seemed distant or far, attainable or inaccessible. A Polish socialist, remembering his youth in the 1880s, later wrote, "We were certain that on the ruins of the old world 'a new world would arise.' We did not take into account, therefore, either [our] enemies or their strengths and means; nor did we take into account our allies. We were raised up on the wings of dreams, higher and higher. We escaped from that filthy reality, in which the majority of the youth wallowed."[110] This belief in a "new world" had little in common with the liberal faith in "progress." This was not something that would evolve out of the status quo, nor something about which one could be logically or scientifically certain. Instead, it was something in which one had to *believe* and something that one had to actively *create*. It was not the end of history: it was an ideal that had to be envisioned, imagined, and then realized—whatever the means. "Nations in slavery only have a future before them," declared a speaker at a patriotic meeting in 1891, "when they think constantly about fighting their way out of slavery, [when they] believe in a better future and undertake every labor with faith, in the name of and for [that future]."[111] The *niepokorni* used the concept of "ideals" to access the world of action, where the earth itself could be moved "onto a new track" and the seemingly immutable powers of the status quo could be overthrown.

This was what action was all about. It was not a new means of projecting the future, not a new way to plot the attainment of independence or social justice. It was a more profound challenge to the very idea that there was a future for which one could simply wait (or work). It was a rebellion against the idea that history had a set path, determined by laws of political economy, Spencerian evolution, or Bucklean progress. It was, above all, a reassertion of *will*. A declaration issued on the occasion of a patriotic demonstration in 1891 proclaimed that "the immortal spirit of protest against everything that is vile has begun to arise once again."[112] The positivists had based their entire worldview on a vision of history, thus freeing themselves from the need to defy "reality" in the pursuit of their goals. The *niepokorni*, in contrast, declared that the space between the act and the result could be bridged only by "the spirit of protest against everything that is vile." This difference illuminates the debate with the positivists about liberal political economy. If the *niepokorni* could not believe in prophecy, they could perceive only positivism's most materialistic and impotent face. Once they stripped away liberalism's teleology, laissez-faire was all that remained.

The Politics of Mickiewicz

Poles and Russians alike were searching for great ideals, for a way to conceptualize and justify action. The Poles, however, took this quest in a slightly different direction. While the Russians were arguing about the fate of the peasant commune, the Poles were debating the future of the nation; while the Russians were worried about social injustice, the Poles also dreamed of independence. This distinction should not be drawn too sharply, because in both cases social change was imagined within a national context. Nevertheless, the russification campaign gave the Polish revolutionary movement a particular coloration. Few of those who were educated in the brutal environment of the Kingdom's schools could remain indifferent to national oppression, even if they chose to focus primarily on the proletariat or the peasantry. The Polish quest for ideals, then, almost always assumed patriotic overtones, and this in turn led the *niepokorni* back to the national idealism of the early nineteenth century. Specifically, the reclamation of "the deed" inspired a renewed interest in Poland's most famous romantic bard, Adam Mickiewicz.

Paweł Czarnecki described his generation's quest for great ideals as an attempt to recover "the politics of Mickiewicz"; Jan Kasprowicz wrote that he and his peers had been "living under the mark of Mickiewicz"; and an émigré newspaper observed in 1891 that "those coming on the scene at the present moment are the grandsons of Mickiewicz."[113] For the *niepokorni*, Mickiewicz provided a point of access to romantic patriotism and (above all) to "the deed." He symbolized for them a chiliastic moment of universal salvation, after which justice would reign in the world and Poland would regain its independence. Władysław Studnicki wrote that Mickiewicz "was the poet of the struggle against slavery and thus he saved us from the degradation of slavery. We honor our romantic in poetry because he was closely tied with irredentism in politics."[114] Czarnecki's "politics of Mickiewicz" was the politics of revolution and of a neoromantic dream of national salvation.

But returning to Mickiewicz was not going to be easy, because various opposing groups wanted to claim him as their own. Two events focused attention on the contested meaning of the poet's work: the transferal of his remains from Paris to the traditional royal crypt in Kraków in 1890, and the 1898 centenary of his birth. Bolesław Limanowski, a prominent socialist, tried to appropriate Mickiewicz for the left in a speech he gave at the poet's exhumation. "We call him our predecessor," Limanowski proclaimed, "because the great poet not only inflamed in our hearts a feeling of universal brotherhood, but at a key moment in history he openly stood under the socialist banner." Better yet, his socialism had room for patriotism, "condemning the egotistic isolation of nations but respecting the independence and autonomy of every one of them."[115] Ignacy Daszyński, the leader of the Galician socialists, published an article in the Paris magazine *Pobudka* entitled "Mickiewicz as a Revolutionary and a Socialist." The poet "strongly believed in the independence and the high calling of Poland," Daszyński wrote, but he also perceived the power of "the revolutionary forces that were to weaken the shackles of his own nation and lay the foundation under the building of international freedom."[116] For these socialists, Mickiewicz's message of national freedom was simultaneously an endorsement of revolutionary internationalism.

Not surprisingly, the conservatives in Kraków who had arranged the reinternment challenged this interpretation. As was discussed earlier, the elites of the Austrian partition had reached a rapprochement with Vienna in the 1860s, so the insurrectionary content of Mickiewicz's writing was embarrassing for them. Nonetheless, in deference to his position as the century's greatest Polish poet, they had sponsored his reburial in the crypt of the Polish monarchs, under the Wawel castle in Kraków. Bringing Mickiewicz back physically was easy enough, but incorporating his poetry into a loyalist Galician canon was more problematic. When his remains arrived in Kraków, the conservative professor Stanisław Tarnowski gave a welcoming speech that shifted attention away from the content of Mickiewicz's poetry, focusing instead on the symbolism of the reburial itself. "At least here," Tarnowski said, "on this part of the Polish land, thanks to the generosity of the Monarch, we are able to give the honor to the ashes of Adam Mickiewicz." Poles ought to be grateful to Franz Joseph, he argued, and not transform this solemn occasion into a vulgar political demonstration.[117] Włodzimierz Lewicki, a student who spoke at the same ceremony, gave an entirely different spin on the event. Mickiewicz, he said, wanted his countrymen

> to look for that national soul, that love and strength for sacrifice and devotion,
> which elsewhere today cannot often be found. . . . We, those who are faithful to
> the spirit of the immortal prophet, respecting that past, following its virtues,
> avoiding its mistakes, want to build a new national structure of glory and
> independence. . . . We go forward in the name of your slogans, our great poet,
> carrying high the banner of progress and brotherhood; we will tear down in our
> Fatherland the structure of egoism, darkness, and hierarchy, which is already
> falling, so as to build on its ruins a better future in the name of equality, freedom,
> and brotherhood.[118]

This controversy was repeated, with even greater intensity, when Mickiewicz symbolically came to Warsaw in 1898, in the form of a statue commemorating the centenary of his birth.[119] The idea for the monument came from the loyalist editor of a provincial paper, *Gazeta Radomska*, who wanted the event to be an affirmation of Polish sobriety: "As evidence of our gratitude we ought to celebrate that anniversary with all the seriousness that is appropriate for a nation that places healthy political sense above everything. We are dealing here with giving honor to our greatest genius, not with some sort of insipid demonstration."[120] Reassured by this attitude, Governor-General Imeretynsky granted permission to build the monument, but he was taken aback by the enthusiastic reaction of the Poles. Almost 80 percent of the donations raised to pay for the statue were of one ruble or less, and the 12,000 tickets to the ceremony sold out rapidly.[121] Fearing that this popular response might presage a mass demonstration, the loyalists tried to stage an event that would be devoid of patriotic implications, and *Kurier Codzienny* published an editorial appealing for calm.

> We cannot allow that anyone at any time could accuse us of not being a mature, prudent and peaceful society. It is our duty to unite, if necessary, in a common effort to ensure that no premature wild fancy or manifestation throws even the slightest shadow on the ceremony, which ought to remain a ceremony for a great poet. Mickiewicz was not some kind of famous hero or national leader for whom a loud ovation would be necessary. He was a prophet. And just as prophets dream their words quietly, so should their commemoration be quiet and profound.[122]

Several jokes circulated around Warsaw at the time regarding this attempt to create a national monument without any manifestation of national identity. One said that the initials "A.M." on the tickets to the unveiling did not stand for Adam Mickiewicz, but *ani mru mru* (not so much as a peep). Another quip explained that the poet's head would be screwed on so that it could be exchanged for Pushkin's when no one was looking.[123]

The National Democrats tried to work within the official restrictions surrounding the unveiling, staging legal plays and speeches in the hope of spreading "national consciousness" among the workers and peasants.[124] The socialists, in contrast, hoped to organize a major antigovernment demonstration. 2,200 copies of a collection of the poet's more revolutionary writings were distributed; 1,600 copies of a special Mickiewicz edition of the socialist paper, *Robotnik,* were published; and 12,000 copies of a proclamation calling for a disruption of the ceremony were printed. The declaration not only condemned the loyalist hopes for a calm public display, but tried to claim Mickiewicz for "the masses."

> The Mickiewicz ceremony cannot be peaceful. It must be antigovernment, just as the spirit of Mickiewicz was antigovernment. . . . Polish patriotism, if it is to lead to the independence of the nation, must be antigovernment [and] revolutionary; it must take its life-giving strength from the political consciousness of the broad masses. Those masses have begun to live, to grow, to become strong, and for

sincere Poles there is no need to look for any other leader. . . . The proletariat today constitutes the heart of the nation, it will be the leader of the national uprising and only in its ranks is there space for those who honestly love the idea of freedom.[125]

Unfortunately for the socialists, their efforts failed: only small clusters of workers gathered at the unveiling site, making little impression in the large crowd. The factory owners in Warsaw had moved payday to the time of the unveiling so as to keep people away from the demonstrations, and this tactic proved successful.[126]

Despite the efforts by Polish conservatives and Russian officials to co-opt Mickiewicz, for the *niepokorni* he represented the politics of "action," of rebellion against all forms of oppression (social and national). One of the most popular of Mickiewicz's poems among the youth was his "Song of the Philarets," one verse of which became a slogan: "Measure your strength according to your aims / Not your aims according to your strength" (*Mierz siłę na zamiary / Nie zamiar podług sił*).[127] Popławski convinced his colleagues at *Głos* to send a wreath with this inscription to Kraków during Mickiewicz's reinterment, because, he felt, these words best articulated the mindset of their generation.[128] The same passage was quoted in an 1891 handbill, which explained that "this slogan of our fathers, mocked and laughed at today, has, with all its rashness, more value than our 'organic work,' our 'passive resistance,' our ugly careerism."[129]

The return to action, then, was also a return to romanticism, and the new era would be defined by "the politics of Mickiewicz." This gave the Polish commitment to "will" a distinctive tone, with roots in the populist voluntarism of the Russian revolutionaries, but with equally strong ties to the patriotism of the 1830s and 1840s. To complicate matters further, the Mickiewicz revival took place in the shadow of Świętochowski and Prus. The *niepokorni* were not just antipositivist, they were *post*positivist. When they returned to romanticism, they did so in a world that had already been fundamentally transformed by the *młoda prasa*. No matter how vehemently the positivists were attacked, their rhetoric had penetrated Polish life and could not be exorcised. An anonymous author observed in 1899 that "today's young generation grew up after the great transition achieved by the natural sciences and positivism," and as a result they could not as easily be inspired with talk of "the Christlike sacrifice of Poland, the future epoch of the Holy Spirit and all that."[130] Krzywicki recalled that young people in the 1880s (such as himself) were

penetrated by a faith in the power of knowledge and a critical approach to everything that science did not support. . . . Already as upperclassmen in the *gimnazjum* we absorbed the articles of *Przegląd Tygodniowy* and later *Prawda*; we swore allegiance to Darwin and Herbert Spencer, who were then known more by name than from their works; we wrote reports about Büchner and Draper; we worked hard on Buckle. Naturally, this movement did not encompass the entire youth, but it was considerable enough in terms of numbers and respect that it set the tone for the young generation. Even those who never looked at the aforementioned authors, nor read the journals of militant positivism, would nonetheless mention some name or another to the leading figures of the class and defend, badly, their undigested views.[131]

For those raised in this environment, a mediated romanticism was needed, one that took "science" seriously even as it cherished "great ideals." Stanisław Wojciechowski recalled that in the 1880s "the mind was embraced by the cult of reason and science, Darwinism and materialism undermined faith, but the heart remained under the influence of the romantics, particularly Mickiewicz."[132]

For the novelist Stefan Żeromski, this created a sense of being pulled in two directions. "I stand at the crossroads of two worlds," he wrote in 1884. "Idealism and realism, poetry and science rule me in turn."[133] A month later he described his life as "a terribly uncritical mix" of philosophy, poetry, mathematics, and science.[134] In a passionate diary entry of November 1886, Żeromski articulated the crisis of his generation: "I am not a revolutionary, I am not an action [sic]. I am . . . a romantic in the hat of a positivist, I am a man from the last generation lost in today's generation, I am a step backwards, I am zero today, I am a little Hamlet [*hamletyk*], a Hamlet and once again a Hamlet. In the depth of my soul I compose odes to the moon, but I read Mill and shout at romanticism, even at feeling; I cry over Słowacki and cite the sentences of Comte. Our century creates such damned monstrosities."[135] At times Żeromski embraced his "eclecticism," consoling himself with the thought that his "poetic mind" was not rejecting the principles of science but "feeling them in its own way, giving rationalist theories symbolic meaning."[136] More often, though, he was tormented by the internal paralysis caused by the contradictions battling within him. "That Hamlet—will he die someday? No, he will live and in the furthest generations he will live. . . . I am not some kind of pessimist, but something worse: I am Hamlet. A pessimist knows that he can accomplish nothing and thus he does nothing. A Hamlet thinks he can accomplish a lot—and he does nothing."[137]

Żeromski's dilemma was widely shared by Polish intellectuals in the 1880s and 1890s, although most authors cast it in a more positive light. Hłasko wrote about his quest for "some sort of new synthesis, some sort of idea that would join the broken bonds of tradition with the new demands of life."[138] Radlińska recalled the pride she took as a young women in her ability to chose the best aspects of Poland's past without fully subscribing to any particular school of thought.[139] "We indeed belonged to a synthetic generation," Zygmunt Wasilewski boasted. "We had romanticism in our hearts and positivism in our heads. We demonstrated that we were not averse to the principle of 'measure your strengths by your goals,' but we treated it rationally, not emotionally."[140]

The *niepokorni* were indeed "romantics in positivist hats." They had returned autonomous, willful action to the national agenda and repudiated the optimistic historiosophy that had allowed the positivists to work and wait. They did not, however, restore the messianic visions of Mickiewicz, but only the "dreams" and "ideals" captured in the slogan "measure your strength by your goals." This was an entirely new conceptual framework, within which the act itself, if driven by a dream, had value. Such an approach allowed the *niepokorni* to employ the metaphors of science and even the practices of organic work, as long as the dream remained at the center of their worldview. But this dream no longer contained within itself the promise of fulfillment; this aspiration to social justice and national independence was a motive force, not a telos. In contrast to both the romantics and the positivists, the *niepokorni* did not place their trust in a vision of historical progress. Whatever one did, one had to believe that only action (whatever its form) could "push the earth on to a new track."

5

The *Lud*, the *Naród*, and Historical Time

The novelist Stefan Żeromski described the politically active students at Warsaw University as "an agglomeration of the most contradictory elements, as obstinately contradictory as you can only imagine."[1] Even as these "elements" argued with each other, however, they were perceived—and perceived themselves—to be united against enemies both "Polish" (loyalists, landed nobles, capitalists) and "foreign" (state officials). Feliks Perl described "a sense of unity," supported by "an almost religious faith that a social revolution, a universal social transformation would at once solve all problems, remove in one blow all exploitation and all oppression."[2] Similarly, Ludwik Krzywicki recalled how all the young intellectuals of his generation "abandoned the path of organic work; all of them recognized the need to struggle with the Tsar for political rights; all of them considered the *lud* [the people] to be the foundation of the future. . . . All differences within our group were brought together in our dreams about that struggle."[3] According to Stanisław Koszutski, a student at Warsaw University in 1890, everyone in those days seemed to be "populist-democratic, socialist, free-thinking or progressive," with only trivial differences between "national-socialists" and "international-socialists." Everyone was committed to "the emancipation of the people," and no one challenged the assumption that there was a link between social revolution and national emancipation.[4] As late as 1903 the conservative journalist Erazm Piltz could write about "our youth" and "our extremist parties" as a single theme, blurring the distinctions between socialists and nationalists.[5]

Even as the *niepokorni* began to coalesce into "patriots" and "socialists" (as the two factions were called at the time), these labels remained unclear and permeable. Władysław Studnicki, a socialist throughout the 1890s, joined the nationalist movement after the turn of the century but insisted that this change of allegiance entailed only a new "terminology and argumentation." As he put it, "that which I once called the proletariat, then called the people, I now call the nation. . . . The details of my views changed, but the spirit remained the same." This sort of openness to alternative ways of talking about the world, Studnicki believed, was typical of the "children of 1863."[6] They shared a commitment to a social and national revolution and argued merely about priorities and tactics. In 1901 Studnicki wrote a letter to a "patriotic" magazine in which he reiterated his belief that the nationalists and the socialists were virtually interchangeable. "If the Democratic-National party did not exist at all . . . then a considerable number of those who support that organization would support the Polish Socialist Party, since it would be the only antiloyalist organization. If there was no Polish Socialist Party, then many of those who work in the ranks of that party would give their strength to the service of the National League, as the only organization that wants to fight for a better tomorrow."[7] All the *niepokorni* were driven by the "spirit of protest against everything vile" and by the conviction that through an act of will they could "push the earth into a new orbit." Whatever their disagreements, they shared a desire to subvert the existing order, and they all believed that such subversion had to be aimed in two directions: against the "foreign" oppressors in St. Petersburg, Berlin, and Vienna and against the "social" oppressors in the manor houses and factories. To put this differently, they juxtaposed the parallel discourses of community and revolution, so that "we" were both the Poles and the oppressed, and "they" were both the Russians and the propertied classes. As long as this idea of dual revolution united the *niepokorni*, their common front was impervious to arguments about nationalism and internationalism.

Ultimately the *niepokorni* would split into the competing ideological camps of the twentieth century, but the patriots and the socialists were not, contrary to most accounts, driven apart by a dispute between the rival concepts of nation and class. Both these terms had contested meanings and both remained important to just about every Polish intellectual. Nearly all the *niepokorni* placed some vision of "Poland" at the center of their world and nearly all professed great concern for "the social question." In fact, the driving imperative for almost every young writer and political activist in the 1880s and 1890s was to link the *naród* (the nation) and the *lud* (the people) so as to sustain a commitment to both. Eventually, however, the patriots and the socialists would come up with different resolutions to this problem. At the heart of their dispute was a disagreement about the positioning of human communities in historical time—that is, about the relation of terms like "the nation" and "the people" to some narrative of historical progress. We saw in the last chapter that the *niepokorni* challenged positivism by rejecting the historiosophy of liberalism, turning instead to a philosophy of "action." In the 1890s some intellectuals pursued this abandonment of teleology toward some unsettling conclusions, causing others to fall back, so to speak, into dynamic historical time. Those who would eventually constitute the Polish Socialist Party would sustain the bond between social revolution and national independence by accepting that the nation was internally divided by antagonistic classes, while insisting that in time (after the revolution) the proletariat would co-opt and embody the nation. Conflict within Poland could be accepted in the present because national unity was promised by a vision of the future. In other words, the socialists came to rely on their prophetic imagination. The patriots, in contrast, defined both the *lud* and the *naród* as sociological collectives existing in the present, rather than as historical actors destined for realization in the future. The only way to equate the *lud* and *naród,* in this case, was to insist that members of the former *identify* with the latter. To talk about economic exploitation or social struggle would be seen as a threat to this identity and thus a threat to the nation. As I show in the coming chapters, the way one approached historical time—how one's historical narrative was constructed, or whether one even believed in historical dynamics—would determine how one talked about the nation. The way Poland was positioned in time would distinguish those who saw the nation as a site for social revolution from those who placed the nation within a discourse of order and discipline. Ultimately this fundamental difference between diachronic and synchronic time would separate those who could imagine diversity within the nation from those who could not.

The Reactionary Nation?

Ludwik Waryński's small socialist group of the late 1870s (described in the last chapter) was never very large, and it did not survive long enough to have a lasting impact on the Kingdom's workers.[8] Its message, however, resonated widely among the intelligentsia, inspiring some and unsettling many. The problem was not that Waryński was a socialist and a revolutionary. Quite the contrary: he provoked so much controversy precisely because he tried to *sever* the bond between revolution and the nation.[9] Waryński and his colleagues could not imagine diversity and conflict *within* communities, which they saw as organic wholes. Because they cast both nations and classes as synchronic sociological entities rather than as moral or political agents acting in history, they could not imagine that a worker or peasant could feel loyalty toward a nation that was dominated by an oppressive elite. In the resulting debate, the point of contestation was both the definition of the nation and the temporal framework within which one talked about society.

When Waryński composed the first draft program for his new movement in 1879, he reflexively (or tactically) echoed a well-established theme: "We have been drawn to the conviction that the triumph of the principles of socialism is a necessary condition for the successful future of the Polish people. . . . We also believe deeply that the Polish people, mobilized in the name of social-revolutionary principles, will demonstrate irrepressible strength and steadfast energy in the struggle with the partitioning governments, which have joined economic exploitation with unprecedented national oppression."[10] Here socialism was a means to serve the nation, and "the Polish people" was a revolutionary force—a familiar formula in the nineteenth century. This passage, however, was deleted in the published version of the program, which appeared in the first issue of Waryński's émigré organ, *Równość* (Equality). In place of the original reference to the nation, there was only a vague commitment to "full social equality of all citizens without regard to gender, race, or nationality." Poland, the program explained, was already becoming a part of the capitalist world, and as such it was linked to an international struggle that cut across national lines.[11]

Contemporaries—both socialists and nonsocialists—were disturbed by this document's lack of any reference to national independence, and their unease would only grow in the months to come. In the second issue of *Równość,* Kazimierz Dłuski provoked a storm of protest with an article called "Patriotism and Socialism." Since the partitions, Dłuski argued, the movement for national independence had been the product of a "privileged fragment of the whole nation." As such, it was "partial and narrow in its ideas, because it could not transcend the boundaries of the political interests of a privileged segment of the Polish nation." Dłuski concluded that "the idea of socialism is broader and greater than the idea of patriotism," so his party would seek "solidarity among socialists of all nations" rather than a "narrow" national struggle.[12] Instead of linking the Polish cause with a broadly democratic agenda, as had been common since at least the 1830s, Dłuski moved *Równość* onto new territory by cutting the link between socialism and patriotism. The nation could no longer be embodied in the people, because the workers, peasants, and nobility were all cast as distinct segments of the Polish nation. Dłuski and Waryński could no longer present the nation as an agent for progress; instead of a historical actor, they were describing a sociological formation which had become, for them, a site for oppression.

Równość and its successors, *Przedświt* (The Dawn) and *Walka Klas* (Class Struggle), mounted an undifferentiated attack on all manifestations of national sentiment. Their slogans were uncompromising:

The independence of the fatherland will not remove the slavery of labor.[13]

The *lud* does not have a fatherland, because Poland has expelled it; our *lud* has another fatherland, the international solidarity of the laboring masses.[14]

We have nothing in common with the program of "Polish independence."[15]

We have broken once and for all with patriotic programs; we want neither a noble nor a democratic Poland.[16]

This was a dramatic turn away from the traditions of the Polish left, and the members of Waryński's group knew it. As one of them put it, "the principles of contemporary socialism . . . were totally new for us, a phenomenon having practically nothing in common with the old revolutionary tradition."[17]

In 1880 the *Równość* group openly proclaimed its break with the past during a ceremony in Geneva commemorating the fiftieth anniversary of the November Uprising. To the surprise of many émigrés, Waryński and his colleagues organized the commemoration of this quintessentially national holiday and sent invitations to hundreds of Polish and European leftists (about 500 attended). The speeches delivered for the occasion provoked a scandal. Szymon Diksztajn opened the gathering by announcing that *Równość* had used the anniversary of 1830 as an excuse: "We have gathered together . . . not to celebrate the uprising of 29 November, . . . but to give honor to *our* ideas." When Waryński took the floor, he described the revolt as a thinly veiled attempt to restore old privileges and inequalities. "The Polish nobility did not want a revolution," he said, "but respect for their old privileges. Loyalty, fear of the revolution, hatred of any sort of social reform—that is what the main leaders of the uprising demonstrated."[18] Marx himself rebuked Waryński for this stance. The role played by Polish volunteers in virtually every upheaval since the late eighteenth century—from the American War for Independence to the Paris Commune—inspired Marx to cast Polish patriotism as a force for disorder, as a potential spark for revolution.[19] In return, many Poles had embraced the label "socialist," and even those who had reservations about Marxism were quick to call themselves democrats and were cautious in their polemics with those further to the left. It would be an exaggeration to say that the terms "Poland" and "socialism" were entirely congruous in the mid-nineteenth century, but most observers—from Metternich to Marx—believed that they were related.

Waryński, however, did not. He responded to Marx's criticism by arguing that "a movement summoned in the name of Poland *must*, in the current social conditions, be reactionary."[20] This "must" would be the fundamental point of contention among Polish leftists for decades to come. The *Równość* circle believed that any national movement *had* to be counterrevolutionary, because the very concept of the nation implied an imperative for social solidarity that negated the principle of class struggle. As they put it in their program of 1882:

> The summoning of all Poles to unity and to a common struggle against external oppressors has extinguished in our society class consciousness in general, and particularly the consciousness of the working class. It has not allowed them to understand the contradictions that really exist between the interests and aspirations of the exploited and the exploiters; instead, it has attempted to convince society that external pressure has artificially conjured up in us that contradiction and that it will collapse the moment "national independence" is regained. That same "independence" is put forth as a means of resolving all social dissatisfaction, and, evoking agreement and class unity, it turns the attention of the worker away from the real causes of his poverty and oppression.[21]

On a superficial level this was an assertion that "class" was real while "nation" was not. More deeply, though, this argument reflected a new way of conceptualizing social formations in general. Stanisław Mendelson once asked how the members of a society based on inequality—on "the existence of ruling and oppressed classes"—could be expected "to subordinate themselves to one interest, in the name of nationality."[22] This argument was based on the conviction that both nations and classes had to be enclosed social groups, something like the social organisms of Spencer's world, if they were to be considered real. If a social organism was defined by its mutually cooperating parts, then a socialist could not classify the nation, with its competing classes and interest groups, as such an organism. Several years later a socialist named Feliks Daszyński (the older brother of the interwar socialist leader) wrote that "society is not an organism. . . . Society is instead a collection of individuals, living in groups cooperating with each other or struggling according to certain laws, with the goal of this or that interest." The real social actors, enjoying a true organic wholeness, were classes: they *were* homogenous formations (by definition, for a Marxist) and they *did* have well-defined collective interests.[23] If one began with a presumption that humanity was divided into concrete social units, each with a single interest and an identifiable set of characteristics, one did indeed have to chose between nation and class.

But there were other ways of describing social organization. Many Polish intellectuals still wanted to use words like justice, equality, and revolution when they talked about the nation, and their standard-bearer was a very different sort of socialist: Bolesław Limanowski (1835–1935).[24] Limanowski grew up near Vitebsk as the son of a moderately wealthy landowner and attended both secondary school and a few years of university in Moscow. He was arrested for his patriotic activities in 1861 and was forced to watch the January Uprising from Siberian exile. He was allowed to settle in Warsaw after an amnesty in 1867, and he began contributing regularly to *Przegląd Tygodniowy*. The amorphous blend of left-liberalism and patriotism which Limanowski cultivated during these years gradually shifted toward a more firmly articulated socialism when he moved to Lwów, in Habsburg Galicia, in 1870. In 1878 he organized a secret "Worker-Socialist Committee" and published a widely read pamphlet entitled "Socialism as a Necessary Manifestation of Historical Development." After being expelled from Galicia in late 1878, he moved to Switzerland, where he became one of the most respected figures of the émigré community.

Limanowski was initially enthusiastic about the emergence of Waryński's group. When the younger man was forced to flee the Kingdom, he spent some time with Limanowski in Lwów, and the two eventually found themselves together in Swiss exile. Limanowski, however, was never a "scientific" socialist, and his unswerving commitment to an idealist conception of the national cause would soon drive him away from Waryński. The first issue of *Równość* carried an article by Limanowski, but his collaboration with the paper ended when Dłuski's "Patriotism and Socialism" appeared in issue two. Their relationship was severed permanently in 1881, when Limanowski published a small book called (not coincidentally) *Patriotism and Socialism*. He defined socialism here as "the aspiration to true, real equality between people," which necessitated the destruction of all forms of economic exploitation, including private property. This programatic objective, however, was the only point Limanowski shared with Waryński. The former's version of socialism penetrated to the etymological foundation of the term, with "social" standing as an antonym (and antidote) to "individual" and "egoistic." Economic inequality and exploitation were among the forces of disintegration and disunity, Limanowski believed, but so was class struggle. In fact, Limanowski dreamed of ending injustice precisely so as to resolve social conflict. He did not want to pursue conflict to its bitter denouement; he wanted to save society by identifying a point of "moral" or "sentimental" unity, based on justice. "True patriotism" and "honest socialism" were mutually reinforcing for Limanowski. Poland could be saved—from both partition and social implosion— only if it were rooted in equity and equality, and the people could prosper only if united by "a love of the nation."

Patriotism, Limanowski argued, was a "feeling of social unity that lies at the heart of every individual in a collective organism." The nation wasn't a mere sociological object that could be described with the scholarly tools of the demographer or the economist, but something that would be made—or better, *realized*—over time, by those who shared the patriotic sentiment. Children displayed only hints of the traits that would someday distinguish them as adults; similarly, nations-in-formation could not be judged according to their present social relations. The only way the nation could fulfill its inner need to manifest itself as a true community, Limanowski believed, was by establishing justice for all its members—in other words, by inaugurating a socialist order. His was a community that existed only *in time*, to be realized or made manifest only when people finally shed their egoism and accepted their social obligations.[25] A few years later, in a much publicized open letter to the liberal economist Władysław Wścieklica, Limanowski insisted that real patriotism virtually *required* one to be a socialist, if the former term was understood to signify "a love of the nation, its majority and not its minority, [and] a desire to emancipate it from slavery, the harshest form of which is undeniably economic." In this letter Limanowski argued that there was no difference between the positivists and the *Równość* circle: both, he believed, had given up the dream of elevating the national spirit to its highest form. "In the articles of Mr. Świętochowski and in the articles of Mr. Dłuski," Limanowski wrote, "there rules one and the same fundamental spirit."[26] This was not a mere rhetorical ploy: from Limanowski's point of view, both of them had abandoned the *ideal* of the nation (to be realized in the future) in exchange for a materialist, scientistic worldview focused on the present. This might seem paradoxical: after all, both liberalism and Marxism were eminently teleological. Both, however, described sociologically defined collective actors which already existed and which would evolve through history according to already established laws. Limanowski's historical agent, however, was a community that had not yet manifested itself in the social realm but that would create itself over time: the nation.

In 1881 Limanowski decided to counter the growing prestige of *Równość* by putting together his own émigré organization, *Lud Polski* (The Polish People).[27] The manifesto of this group described nineteenth-century Polish history as a series of failed attempts to both emancipate and create the nation. That is, Polish patriots were called upon to restore the Republic while simultaneously transforming that old state into a "true" nation, a "true" society. To do this they had to make the people *feel* a part of Poland, since this feeling was the glue that held nations together. This would create the necessary conditions for community—and for socialism—by establishing an equivalence between *lud* and *naród,* between people and nation. The manifesto proclaimed, "Everything for the people, through the people and in the name of the people. Let the people themselves take in their hands the banner of the movement, let them raise socialism to the height of the leading idea of national life."[28] Limanowski was willing to acknowledge that the nation was not truly popular in its current form, but he believed fervently in the People's Poland of the future. *Przedświt* noticed a curious error in Limanowski's auto-translations of the *Lud Polski* manifesto: both *naród* and *lud* appeared in French as *peuple* and in Russian as народ.[29] But this was not a careless mistake. Limanowski wanted the words to be synonymous, and he thought socialism would achieve this equivalence in a way no previous patriotic movement could.

Limanowski's vision of the nation depended on a historical narrative leading from the exclusive noble nation to the inclusive popular nation. Once embedded in this story, *naród* and *lud* became virtually synonymous *in time*. That is, whatever the imperfections in the actually existing Poland, the nation was driven to realize its own ideal form and become democratic and egalitarian. Limanowski's nation was *historical*, not sociological; it was a dynamic ideal and a force for human progress, not a mere community of interests or ethnolinguistic features. It was a "psychic organism," as he put it elsewhere, held together by "spiritual" rather than "corporeal" or "material" bonds—held together, ultimately, by a vision of the future. This imagery allowed Limanowski to bracket class struggle, allowing it to remain a social force without undermining the promise of national unity. He imagined an international proletariat fighting international capital in the material realm, while national identity was cultivated in the world of the spirit. These distinct spaces would merge in Limanowski's socialist future.

> In a highly developed social organism—in a nation—the national bonds are manifest in what we call *patriotism*. Wherever conscious life still finds itself on a low level of development, this is really an instinct of self-preservation, holding stubbornly to its faith, language, customs, traditions, even clothing. On a higher level of development it is joined with the awareness that independent existence is assured only through internal freedom. The highest manifestation [of patriotism] is the desire to lead other nations in the attainment of more perfect forms of the social system.

This creative historiosophy allowed Limanowski to reach his final synthesis between class struggle and national solidarity. "The working class, the most numerous and the most moral part of the nation, aspiring to the system that best corresponds to its needs, is indeed governed by its own interests, yet [it works] for the common good. Class struggle understood in this way is a progressive force in the development of social life. But woe to the nation if class patriotism takes precedence over national patriotism."[30] The last sentence is the punch line that gives meaning to Limanowski's entire corpus. National patriotism appears as a moral bond that can both facilitate and contain class struggle, giving meaning to social conflict within a progressive vision of history. However, if class is *only* a force for division, untempered by the "psychic" unity of the nation, it leads to social chaos, to struggle without meaning.

Born in 1835, Limanowski was much older than the *niepokorni* and thus was less drawn to the rhetoric of science or the sociology of Spencer. When he wrote about positivism, he had in mind the utopian visions of Auguste Comte—whom he compared to Mickiewicz—rather than the cold rationality of English liberalism.[31] When he argued with Waryński and Dłuski (who were, despite their politics, heirs to the positivists' scientism), Limanowski was setting his nation-in-time against their sociological community. The real divide in Polish intellectual life in the late 1870s and the 1880s was not among conservatives, liberals, and socialists, but between those who saw only a Polish ethnicity, fractured by internal divisions, and those who envisioned a dynamic Polish nation, acting in history. This is not to suggest that Waryński (or Świętochowski, for that matter) lacked a conception of historical time, since each had well-articulated visions of the future. However, they did not define social organisms in relation to their temporality. Classes and nations might evolve through time, but they had to exist in contemporary social space in order to be considered "real." Limanowski, in contrast, believed that the nation existed only in nascent form in the present and could not be perceived in its entirety. Unfortunately, the unwavering faith in the future that sustained this position was already fading among Polish intellectuals in the 1880s. In Warsaw the *niepokorni* were drawn to Limanowski's emphasis on "action" and "the nation," but they were locked within a postpositivist, scientistic universe, in which sociology was hindering the quest for "great ideals." Limanowski could, and did, inspire them, but he could not guide them into the new world.

Two Civilizations

Like Limanowski, most of the young intellectuals of the Kingdom wanted both revolution and the nation. The *niepokorni* could simultaneously believe in social division (be it of a populist or Marxist variety) and national unity, but only as long as they could link the *lud* and the *naród* in the future. Social space could be fragmented, as long as it was reunified in historical time. Unlike Limanowski, however, these young radicals were deeply embedded in a positivist (or postpositivist) worldview. They were simultaneously drawn to the social agenda of Russian populism, the ideals of Polish romantic patriotism, and (paradoxically but inexorably) the vocabulary of positivism. Limanowski's developmental narrative, which had described a national "consciousness" gradually expanding from the nobility to the peasantry, struck them as excessively abstract, insufficiently grounded in the "real world" of actually existing social formations. These "romantics in positivist hats" reconciled Limanowski's idealism with positivism's sociology by granting historical agency not to the idea of Poland, but to the empirically identifiable "Polish people"—to the nation's poor and oppressed. They embraced a revolutionary eschatology that promised the birth of a radically new, popular Poland, achieved by actively overthrowing the sources of power and exploitation within the nation.

Limanowski accepted class divisions within the nation, but he could not describe class struggle as the engine of history. As we have seen, he would not allow the cause of the proletariat—important though it was—to ever "take precedence over national patriotism." This might seem a strange argument for a socialist, but Limanowski squared the circle by casting the national ideal as the motive force in history. If the workers and peasants could not *fight* for power, then the elites had to be persuaded to surrender it peacefully. Patriotism would inspire them to do so.

> The patriots already understood that the nobility, without the aid of the people, is helpless, and without them will not attain national independence; they therefore tried to urge the landowners to win over the people, so that they could act together. The democrats went further: for them it was clear that the Polish nation is the Polish people [*lud*] and not the nobility, that the latter has no right to a separate, privileged existence, that it ought to join the people and merge with

them. . . . The people do not need to follow the more exalted classes, but those
classes, if they feel patriotism in themselves, ought to lay down their property on
the alter of the fatherland and, on their own, enter into the ranks of the working
people.[32]

Limanowski's vague moral imperative struck the *niepokorni* as hopelessly utopian
and unacceptably passive. As we saw in the last chapter, the Kingdom's young intellectuals were driven by an impatient desire to act; they did not want to put their faith
in an unfolding destiny, nor could they quietly wait for the nobility to recognize its
patriotic duty. They wanted to find an active force in history and join with it in the
struggle for a better future. They found what they were looking for in the *lud*.

In its first issue, *Głos* declared that its leading principle and guiding idea would
be "the subordination of the interests of all the separate strata [of society] to the interests of the *lud*."[33] This phrase did not imply a sublimation of social division within
an integral whole, because *Głos'* *lud* was a sociological formation, not a metaphor
for national unity or an ideal of social harmony. The wording of this slogan was subtly
altered in the paper's prospectus so as to clarify that *Głos'* goal was "to recognize
the *lud* as the main component of national society."[34] Here, as in most of the paper's
rhetoric, the *lud* was a component of a broader social whole, which was in turn divided by social conflict. The *głosowcy* were children of *Przegląd Tygodniowy* and
Prawda, whether they liked it or not, and they had no fluency in a language of idealism that might have allowed them to liberate the concept of the *lud* from sociology, that might have helped them imagine a *lud* that transcended the divisiveness of
the "real" social world. Moreover, as we saw in the last chapter, the *niepokorni*
modeled themselves initially on the Russian revolutionary groups of the 1870s, with
their commitment to "the people" and their sharp distinction between the privileged
elite and the suffering masses. Because of these overlapping links to the sociologically minded positivists on the one hand and the Russian populists on the other, the
głosowcy could only imagine a world of empirically delineated communities, and
within that framework they defined the *lud* as all the poor, all the exploited, all those
who were not members of the nobility or the bourgeoisie. The *głosowcy* were not
necessarily Marxists (though some of them were), but they did employ a rhetoric of
class struggle and they did see the nation as a zone of conflict, not as a harmonious
social organism. Their goal was to change this situation, to place the nation at the
service of the *lud* and to subordinate the old elites.

To understand the position of *Głos*, we must abstract from later debates among
populists, nationalists, and socialists and concentrate on the fundamental move that
distinguished this seminal publication. For all those at *Głos*, Poland was an internally divided space, filled with social struggle. Jan Ludwik Popławski, one of *Głos'*
editors, was adamant in his rejection of "those organizations of the working class
that . . . cross the boundaries of state and national differences," but even he insisted
that "artificial, superficial harmony always designates the domination of one class."[35]
This image of domination *within* the nation was the opening that allowed people like
Ludwik Krzywicki (a leading socialist and the translator of *Das Kapital*) to contribute regularly to *Głos*.[36] For the *głosowcy*, to act on behalf of the people implied fighting

against those who oppressed and exploited others. Individuals could disagree about what sort of revolution they wanted and about the relative transformative potential of workers and peasants, but all dreamed of a better future for the disempowered and victimized. They all agreed that the *lud* was *by definition* oppressed by a propertied elite. Indeed, a privileged other was essential for the delineation of the *lud* itself. The prospectus for *Głos* contrasted the "real interests of the *lud*" with an older national- ist agenda rooted in the interests of the nobility, and it announced that the paper would "decisively condemn" anyone who tried to "step forward in the name of our thousand- year culture and tradition" and co-opt or domesticate popular unrest. Those traditions, the prospectus claimed, were "foreign to the majority of the nation." The authors of this text insisted that the peasantry had "its own religion, its own morality, its own politics and its own science; in a word, its own culture, the constituent elements of which cannot be considered a lower form of development."[37] Popławski, repeating an argument that had long been standard fare for revolutionaries in the Russian Empire, wrote in the same issue that there were "two civilizations" in Europe, the privileged and the popular.[38] A few weeks later, responding to some letters complain- ing about this argument, the editors of *Głos* wrote, "The Polish peasant has preserved only one memory of the past: the memory of the wrongs done to him over the course of many centuries. All other traditions remain alien to him." The nation was not rooted in this past, scarred as it was by privilege; instead, the real Poland resided in "that million-man mass of peasants."[39] The editors made no effort to smooth over the gap between rich and poor in the name of national unity because, they believed, "the harmonic reconciliation of two such contradictory directions of thought is an absur- dity that one cannot even imagine. The only possible relationship here must be *sub- ordinating* one of these demands to the other."[40] Or, as Józef Potocki, another of *Głos'* co-editors, put it in 1887, "It is pointless to talk about the most general goals, about common aspirations: such goals and aspirations in this case do not exist. . . . That which would be desirable for the noble stratum would be frightful for the *lud*."[41]

None of this, though, was allowed to challenge the centrality of "the nation" to the *niepokorni*. Few who survived the russified school system of the 1880s and 1890s could remain entirely immune to patriotic sentiments. Not everyone defined the na- tion in the same way (as was to become evident by the late 1890s), but the term did occupy a similar position in almost everyone's rhetorical framework. The nation, however perceived, provided the *niepokorni* with the ultimate goal that "action" was to serve. Stefan Żeromski saw in the nation not merely a source of identity, but a means of salvation. "The only dream, the only joy which I still perceive on my path," he wrote in 1887, "is to die for the country."[42] Żeromski never actually placed him- self in a position to fulfill this dream, but many of his generation did abandon their personal lives and risk imprisonment or exile in the name of Poland. One young nobleman approached Żeromski in October 1888, pouring out his feelings in an emotional exchange. "I have arrived at the conviction," he said, "that I ought to join with you, show my solidarity with you, feel with you, go and, God willing, die! . . . I cannot live without action; [I cannot just] look at my cattle, sow and reap. I do not have any place to put my energy. Finally, I do not want to die stupid and peaceful in this moment of despair that has come over me. If you knew my life, you would recognize that I am right, that it is inhumanly hard for me. I prefer to die for a holy idea. I will be an example."[43] The nation appears here as a vessel for action, an escape from boredom, a means of venting long dormant frustrations. Like all the *niepokorni*, Żeromski needed "great ideas," and he rejected one after another until only the nation remained.

> That heart, that great unknown will no longer be god [sic], because I do not
> know him, not religion, because I despise it, not a future life, because I doubt [its
> existence]—it will be the collective soul, the visible god, the tangible religion
> and the life of centuries: the fatherland. . . . I still have that holiness, that beloved
> feeling, that feeling which you can never doubt, which can never deceive you
> and which your skepticism can never dream of. . . . Oh, who can manage to love
> God if they do not love their native land? And one must not love humanity,
> because that is far-fetched—one can only love Poles. So my humanity are the
> Poles, my universe is my land and my God is the fatherland and everything that
> is included in that expression.[44]

For Żeromski, therefore, the nation was the path by which he could return to the world of ideals and commitment, to the world of the romantics.

The *niepokorni* were certain that in their new world there would be *both* social justice *and* independence. This was accepted even by those who, like Żeromski, were initially uncomfortable with the idea of class struggle. Back in 1883 Żeromski had lamented in his diary, "We have spurned the people. Our ruin lies in our noble arrogance and pride." Poland could survive only if it gained popular support, he believed, so the national cause had to become the cause of social revolution.[45] On one level this was an old argument, heard throughout the nineteenth century whenever Polish nationalists realized that the nobility could not liberate the nation on its own. This well-established reasoning, however, still cast the peasants as a force to be won over to the "larger" cause of national independence. For Seweryn Czetweryński, the *lud* was little more than the means of grounding the desire "to act" in a social "reality."

> Whether on the social right or left, both those believing in socialism and the
> pioneers of the national idea . . . both one and the other wanted to act and to base
> their actions neither on a chimera nor on the current unreal foundations, but on a
> basis that sooner or later promised attainment of the goal. Both one and the other
> placed in the foreground the acquisition by the national cause of the numerous
> mass from which the Nation is made, for which the old soldiers fought and died
> without the aureole of victory and for which [the masses] themselves suffered,
> without an awareness of what they were suffering for, or why they suffered.[46]

Głos argued that this approach was insufficient. It was not enough to say that the victory of the national cause would improve the lives of all; it was not enough to win over the masses to the struggle for independence. The nation itself had to become popular and the voice of the *lud* had to become hegemonic (if I may use an anachronistic expression) before the allegiance of the people could be demanded or expected. And for this to happen, the people had to actively assert their own author-ity. The writers at *Głos* could accommodate social discord in the present because they imagined national unity in the future. Popławski addressed this issue directly in 1888:

> Our argumentation is designated only for those readers who, sharing our democratic principles in economic and social concerns, deceive themselves with the worn-out cliché that national concerns are greater than the concerns of the *lud*, since the latter is included within the former, as a part in a whole. . . . This is, in our opinion, one of the most harmful of social prejudices. Not *through the nation for the lud*, but *through the lud for the nation*; that is a short formula of the principles that we profess, that is the practical conclusion from the sociologi-cal principle we declared: "the subordination of the interests of all other strata to the interests of the *lud*."

The nation, Popławski wrote, was generally understood to be "a collection of all social strata, joined by a common descent, historical tradition, and political ties," but he felt this definition should not be allowed to obscure the fact that "in societies in which there is a class system, based on the real privileging of certain interests—that is, in contemporary civilized societies—all gains designated for the benefit of the whole in fact become the exclusive or primary property of the privileged strata."[47] The rich were siphoning off the wealth of the nation, and the people had to claim what was rightfully theirs. In this context, social revolution could only strengthen the national bond, because the overthrow of existing hierarchies would bring the national inter-est in line with the needs of the masses. This argument allowed the *głosowcy* to talk about both class struggle and national solidarity, without either concept undermin-ing the other.

Zygmunt Wasilewski's eloquence, when he described his turn to the people, was revealing: "The new national spirit was clothed in the body of fact—a new life; here the word became flesh."[48] The national spirit was the word and the people were the body; the nation was a transcendent "imponderable," and the people gave it shape. The form of the nation was physical, based on "fact," while the essence of the nation was an idea and a goal. Thus we have the central equation of the *niepokorni*'s world: the *lud* was to the *naród* as the real was to the ideal, and just as the ideal was incar-nated in the real, so was the nation embodied (literally) in the people.[49] To devote oneself to the people, then, was to devote oneself to the "real" nation, and to fight for the nation one had to base one's strength on the people. The argument worked both ways and ensured that there was no contradiction between a still vaguely defined commitment to the masses and a return to patriotic activism. At the same time, this formula allowed the *lud* to be located in the postpositivist world of empirically de-fined social communities that existed in the present, while simultaneously position-ing the nation in historical time, as an ideal to be made manifest in the future. The revolutionary potential of this reasoning—its ability to sustain unity among the *niepokorni*'s nationalists and internationalists—depended on a historiosophical tra-jectory that distinguished the "real" *lud* of the present from the harmonious national union to be realized after the revolution. In the late 1880s some would question this comforting telos, and in doing so they would drive a deep, permanent wedge into the midst of the Polish intelligentsia.

The Common Front

Through most of the 1880s and into the 1890s, the young intellectuals of the Kingdom were unusually unified. Their arguments were, quite literally, among friends. For example, Zygmunt Balicki, later the leading theoretician of the radical right, had a long history of socialist activism. He began his political career while a law student in Petersburg in the late 1870s by joining the Commune of Polish Socialists, a small group combining slogans of national solidarity, independence, and social revolution. When he returned to Poland in 1881, he formed another ephemeral, vaguely socialist circle called the Warsaw Commune. This group was broken up almost as soon as it was formed, and Balicki escaped abroad, eventually finding his way into Limanowski's circle in Geneva. Balicki was involved with Miłkowski's Polish League (described in the last chapter) from its inception, and in 1886 he returned to Warsaw in order to help organize the League's student branch, The Union of Polish Youth (Zet). Only in the 1890s would he begin his gradual drift away from socialism toward the extreme right.[50] Even in 1897 Balicki and the Galician socialist Ignacy Daszyński could appear on the same dais at a patriotic ceremony in Switzerland, arguing with some bitterness but still agreeing to cooperate on a day-to-day basis and still hoping that their partisan differences would not distract them from the common foe.[51] Roman Dmowski, the president of Zet from 1890 and a leading campus activist at Warsaw University, would eventually become one of the most outspoken opponents of socialism, but as late as 1893 he could still praise the way "the aspirations of the working class, just now entering the political scene, have found an expression in [socialism]."[52]

By 1900, in contrast, Popławski expressed his dismay that cooperation between the socialists and the nationalists had grown impossible. "Despite adorning themselves in patriotic colors," he wrote, "the socialist party is, in its aspirations [and] in the character of its activities, antinational. . . . Their patriotism is, so to speak, forced, resulting from theoretical convictions . . . but it lacks the voice of Polish blood."[53] Popławski was more polite than some of his colleagues. When some Polish and Russian socialists got together for an antitsarist demonstration in 1899, a nationalist proclamation insisted that Poles should avoid such "all-Russian" activities, and denounced those "inclined [to make] national concessions on behalf of cosmopolitan-humanitarian slogans." A pernicious minority, the proclamation charged, had "entered into an alliance with their Orthodox [*popowiczy* (sic)] brothers and with russified Jews, thanks to the clandestine support of the group of local professors famous for their hatred of Poland." The nationalists described the demonstrators as "100 baptized cosmopolitans and 300 *Moskale* and Jews allied with them."[54] Within a few years the Endecja was calling the PPS the "exploiters and oppressors of the working people" and even declaring that a Poland run by the socialists would be "worse than under the Muscovite government."[55] This animosity was returned in kind (albeit without the racial slurs). A socialist pamphlet from 1907 declared that the National

Democrats were dangerous "not because they are conservatives, but above all be-cause they are barbarians, dark people who lower the level of political education in the nation and create in their midst an instinct for blind obedience. [They are] the worst kind of demagogues."[56] By the time Zygmunt Balicki died in 1916, the social-ists could not even bring themselves to print a respectful eulogy. Balicki, they wrote, had been nothing more than "an ardent agent of Russian policy in Poland. . . . Through 36 years of taking part in Polish political life, he took on various forms, but regard-less of the colors in which he appeared . . . he brought to each the fundamental ele-ments of his nature, to each he injected the same moral poison."[57]

But it took many years to reach the point when such harsh rhetoric was possible, and in 1889 few would have foreseen such an irrevocable and bitter split between the two factions of the *niepokorni*. At that time the socialist Ludwik Krzywicki was still contributing to *Głos*, enjoying close personal ties with many members of the editorial board. Józef Hłasko (a wealthy patriot who both wrote for *Głos* and par-tially funded it) and Felicja Popławska (the wife of *Głos* editor Jan Ludwik Popławski) even served as the godparents of Krzywicki's son.[58] Already in the late 1880s, how-ever, this camaraderie was starting to crack. The issue that drove them apart, pre-dictably, was the definition of the *lud*. During the first three months of 1889 Krzywicki published a controversial series of essays in Świętochowski's *Prawda* entitled "Demo-cratic Illusions" (under the name of K. R. Żywicki, certainly the most obvious pseud-onym of the era), in which he rejected the idea that the *lud* was a broad assembly of all the oppressed, for whom there could be a single collective interest. As Krzywicki positioned the *lud* within his own vision of the future, he discovered that only some of them (the proletariat) had a role to play and that only they could enjoy the power of historical agency. Whereas the "democrats" (a reference to the *głosowcy*) wanted only to "satisfy the demands of the *lud*," Krzywicki based his hopes on the "stra-tum" which awaits a great future: the proletariat.[59] Because the workers alone could participate in the march of progress, the other "branch of the *lud*" (the peasantry) was doomed to an inevitable collapse. There was therefore no point in trying to im-prove the lot of the peasants, because doing this would only prolong their agony as history continued its march toward urbanization and industrialization.[60]

Although Krzywicki contributed several more articles to *Głos* throughout the sum-mer and fall of 1889, "Democratic Illusions" exposed irresolvable tensions. These exploded into the open after the appearance of another of Krzywicki's articles in *Prawda* the following February, this one arguing that factory reforms and measures to alleviate rural poverty were counterproductive, because they softened class tensions and unnatu-rally slowed historical progress.[61] This was the final straw for Krzywicki's soon-to-be-former colleagues at *Głos*. J. H. Siemieniecki retorted, "We do not believe that a tem-porary improvement of the fate of any part of the working *lud* can hinder the realization of a better future for all of society." He suggested that Krzywicki was not genuinely concerned about the fate of the oppressed, because anyone "who wants above all to bring about the happiness of humanity will always support all reform that brings relief to current suffering, making possible the development and autonomy of the working masses."[62] Krzywicki responded by agreeing that "humanitarian feelings are neces-sary, but no less necessary is a 'doctrine,' . . . so as not to go astray, but to go along a more certain path toward greater prosperity." Because Siemieniecki had no such doctrine, Krzywicki continued, he fell victim to a utopia that would "temporarily increase prosperity, when more fundamental improvements are possible."[63] The debate grew increasingly hostile. In the next issue of *Głos* Siemieniecki labeled Krzywicki a "pseudo-radical," whose "vulgarization" of Marxism differed little from the doctrines of laissez-faire.[64] Another contributor to *Głos* implied that Krzywicki had sold out to the bourgeoisie.[65] Popławski added, a few issues later, that the so-called orthodox Marxism of Krzywicki was just "a refuge for narrow routine and intellectual backwardness."[66] Krzywicki, in turn, described the worldview of *Głos* as unstable, destined to slide toward the right. "On the pages of that paper," he wrote in his memoirs, "there appeared new names, straying ever further in their conclusions from the old populist credo and thus ever more ready to deal politely with other strata—particularly landowners and clerics."[67]

Krzywicki would have us believe that he was resisting a rising tide of conservatism among his fellow *niepokorni*, but this is not entirely accurate (at least not yet). *Głos* would, in fact, move toward the right, but it was a *new* right, one heavily implicated in the new left that Krzywicki himself was creating. *Głos* remained a radical paper, sharing many of the Marxists' basic ideals. Above all, both groups still perceived a world divided by antagonistic social strata. Only a few months after attacking Krzywicki with such hostility, Siemieniecki reaffirmed his commitment to "class struggle," criticizing the recently released papal encyclical *Rerum Novarum* for imagining that the workers could be helped by a trade union that did not recognize social conflict.[68] A revolt against the established order, against all existing hierarchies, on behalf of the "popular" class, was the glue that held the *niepokorni* together, even as they began to tear themselves apart.

This cooperative rebelliousness becomes evident if we survey the illegal activities of these young intellectuals. As was mentioned earlier, at almost the same time *Głos* was founded, an illegal organization known as the Union of Polish Youth (*Związek Młodzieży Polskiej,* or Zet for short) was created as an affiliate of Zygmunt Miłkowski's Polish League. The so-called *zetowcy*, however, were always more radical than their Geneva sponsors, more interested in direct public action, more willing to accept a worldview based on class struggle. For many years, "socialists" and "patriots" alike could find a home in Zet, and the lines between these two factions remained porous and vague.[69] Tomasz Ruskiewicz remembered the organization as an effort "to reconcile national aspirations with the slogans of social radicalism" and to create "a bridge in the form of a national socialism." The group included a combination of "those under the red and white flag, as well as those who would later fight under the exclusively red flag."[70] Another participant recalled that Zet included all "the most radical students," regardless of their specific ideological convictions.[71] Even the National Democrat Stanisław Grabski, who later emphasized his repudiation of class struggle, had to admit that socialism and *chłopomaństwo* (literally, "peasant mania") shaped all the young people in Warsaw until the early 1890s.[72] The statute of Zet suggested an affinity with *Głos*. "The leading idea of the Union," it declared, "is the desire for national independence, mainly through the planned development and organization of national strength, [and] for the transformation of socioeconomic relations in the spirit of the interests of the *lud*." Independence and social transformation were two sides of the same coin, and both were aimed at "preparing the *lud* to take an active and direct part in political life." The statute did contain one brief caveat about the dangers of "class struggle," but it went on in some detail about how workers should organize against their employers "in the spirit of defending and guaranteeing the interests of the working strata."[73] The promise of social transformation and the devotion to the popular strata suggested here were sufficient to bring many socialists into the organization, and Zet remained a common institution until 1898, when the socialists finally set up their own youth group, *Spójnia*.[74]

On May 3, 1891, Zet staged a public demonstration to commemorate the centenary of the Polish constitution of 1791. A group of students paraded down one of the central streets of Warsaw and (as expected) they were met by the police. One hundred and eighteen people were arrested, one of whom, for unknown reasons, committed suicide in jail, provoking more demonstrations at his funeral.[75] Roman Dmowski, then the president of Zet and one of those arrested for participating in the march, would later remember these events as an expression of anti-socialist nationalism, but the actual rhetoric of the day belies this recollection. In the proclamations issued for the occasion, the link between socialism (broadly defined, as it should be for the 1890s) and patriotism remained strong. It was the task of the current generation, one manifesto declared, to fully realize the national project initiated 100 years earlier by the landed aristocracy ("the capitalists of the day"): "Our path is the further development of the ideas of freedom, equality, and brotherhood, the death of absolutism, exploitation, and privilege, in whatever forms they appear; it is the continued struggle for independence, the firm, ruthless, and inexorable defense of our national rights."[76] The emphasis on the national tradition was still inextricably tied to a message of social emancipation—indeed, the nation itself was justified by evoking its presumed democratic tradition. Although this text suggested a bond of national unity between the nobility and the *lud,* a message of social division and revolution overpowered any hint of solidarity. Another document from the same demonstration equated capitalism with the national enemy: "Our people are forced by hunger to abandon in mass their fatherland; our workers, deprived of all rights, are given up to the mercy of the capitalists, who . . . build Orthodox churches for the pleasure of the government."[77] A third manifesto went even further, openly calling for a radically egalitarian national revolution. The resurrection of Poland, the text promised, would bring the collectivization (or nationalization) of all wealth, and the rich would pay for their sins:

> We are not addressing those gentlemen who sweep the Tsar's antechambers, [or] those rich men who live off of the blood and sweat of our people, [or] all of those who today live well even though the entire nation wastes away in poverty. [Instead we are addressing] you, who irrigate with your bloody sweat the beloved land that your fathers watered with their own blood. You are the root of the nation and the future belongs to you. . . . Proclaim to the worker that all the fruits of his labor belong to him; announce to the villager that the land which he

plowed and sowed is his property. From [your] great voice will arise the
fatherland, free from the blood, tears and suffering of the majority of its sons.[78]

Krzywicki, then, was either insincere or mistaken when he suggested that from 1890
his opponents at *Głos* were "ever more ready to deal politely with . . . landowners
and clerics." He hoped to characterize the polemics of the time as the inauguration
of a split between conservative nationalists and socialists, but in fact this would remain, for several years, a dispute *within* the left, between socialists of different stripes.

But if Krzywicki had mischaracterized the arguments of 1890, so had the *głosowcy*.
Aleksander Więckowski wrote at the time that "if [Krzywicki] simply cannot recognize the importance of the national side of this problem, that is one thing; if, being a
publicist with so-so theoretical training, he does not see that side, [then] he is doctrinaire, that is, a person with a narrow mental horizon."[79] Similarly, Popławski published
an essay attacking the socialists' May Day demonstration as an effort to create "a purely
international worker's solidarity."[80] This was the inverse of Krzywicki's argument: while
Marxists wanted to deny the socialist credentials of *Głos*, the *głosowcy* wanted to cast
the debate in terms of patriotism versus internationalism.

Więckowski and Popławski would have us believe that the antinationalism of
Waryński's *Równość* was carried into the 1890s, but this is not entirely correct. The
historian Tomasz Nałęcz identifies three forces pushing the socialists toward a more
patriotic stance. First, after the collapse of *Narodnaia Volia* in the early 1880s there
seemed little hope that revolution would come to Russia in the near future, and the
Polish socialists increasingly saw themselves as an independent revolutionary van-
guard, not as a mere affiliate of a broader movement based in St. Petersburg. Second, once they turned their attention toward the Kingdom, they came to realize that
this region was more industrialized than all but a few isolated oases of modernity in
Russia. However backward Poland may have seemed when viewed from Western
Europe, it was far closer to the Marxist paradigm for revolution than was Russia.
Given this fact, many socialists reasoned, continued ties to the empire might delay
Poland's own socialist transformation. Finally, and perhaps most important, once the
revolutionary intellectuals began agitating among the workers in Warsaw, they encountered strong expressions of national identity to which they had to respond.[81] Even
some of the earliest socialists in the Kingdom discovered that they could not easily
avoid "the national question." When Józef Uziembło, a Polish socialist from Kiev,
arrived in Warsaw in 1878, he quickly learned this.

> I immediately realized how much higher the Warsaw worker was than the
> Russian. . . . The average Russian worker had no understanding of political
> questions; he was deeply convinced that all that happened in the world occurred
> on the order or permission of the Tsar. . . . The Warsaw worker, on the other
> hand, raised in the traditions of centuries of political struggle, eagerly recalled
> stories about Kościuszko, Głowacki, Kiliński. . . . They were accustomed (from
> stories and in part from their own experience) to nearly perpetual conspiratorial
> work; they longed for it and attached a certain charm to it, and when they came

into contact with an agitator, they greeted him with satisfaction and said, "Well now, so something is starting again; after all, for 15 years already it has been quiet around here."[82]

Uziembło was convinced that this activism tended inexorably toward an international working class solidarity, but even he noted the importance of Kościuszko, Głowacki, and Kiliński (the last two were plebeian heroes of the Polish nationalist mythology). The workers Uziembło met were positioning the socialists, like it or not, within the tradition of 1863 ("15 years ago").

Even Stanisław Mendelson, who had been one of the most virulently antipatriotic members of Waryński's circle, came to recognize that some concept of the nation had to play a role in the rhetoric of Polish socialism. Since the first wave of social-ism had been crushed by the tsarist police, Mendelson and several of his colleagues had been struggling to sustain an organizational presence in the emigration, prima-rily by publishing a magazine called *Przedświt* (The Dawn).[83] In 1891 an editorial essay in this forum suggested a new approach to the national question. The 1863 Uprising, Mendelson argued, had demonstrated that there was a clear distinction between the "national question" and the agenda of "noble Poland, the Poland of the privileged classes." Given this, "people having the good of the country as a goal" would now have to "turn to the class that constitutes the foundation of the nation, the entire nation." Poland had to be based on a new class, one dedicated to "emancipa-tion" and not to the "oppression of other social strata." Mendelson identified this class as the "working *lud,* the *lud* that creates everything with its labor, the *lud* that nour-ishes the entire society, the *lud* that wants the emancipation of labor and of man." This argument led Mendelson to the conclusion he had once resisted: independence.

> In our society there are only two parties, two camps: on one side stand the exploiters and those living from privileges, on the other side the exploited and those from whom the fruits of labor have been stolen. . . . There are only two parties—listen to me, Mr. Politician, you who want independence above all. Understand that without a conscious popular organization, without a social revolution, you won't get a free Poland. There are only two parties! One socialist, *ludowe,* working for Equality and Freedom, the party of the future, the party of victory. The other is the nobleman's camp, bristling with government bayonets, the party of oppression and slavery, exploitation and darkness, the party of death.[84]

Without softening his rhetoric of class struggle, Mendelson appropriated the patri-otic argument by defining the nation in terms of the working people and by exiling the capitalists and landowners to the party of death. Perhaps equally important was Mendelson's use in this essay of the term "*lud*" rather than "proletariat" or "worker." Later *Przedświt* offhandedly announced that terminology was irrelevant: "We can exchange the word 'worker' with the word '*lud*' a thousand times and it will not change reality. Strength does not lie in a word, but in the real state of things."[85] As long as Marxists like Mendelson could adjust their rhetoric in this way, they could continue to share common ground with the *głosowcy*.

Unity on the left became *Przedświt*'s driving goal in the early 1890s. Mendelson insisted that there was a place for both urban and rural activists, both "socialists" and "patriots." Like Krzywicki a few years before, Mendelson (unjustly) accused the "patriots" of imagining that socialism was possible without class conflict. He derided his opponents as "bourgeois radicals" and even "little girls" (*panienki*), but he was nonetheless convinced of the need to cooperate. "After the battle we will begin our courtship," he wrote, "but meanwhile the issue is the survival of the revolutionary elements and the success of socialist slogans." Mendelson believed that "a union of all the revolutionary forces can take place," and the victory of socialism be assured, if a consensus was reached on the issue of independence. Then a coalition could be built, based on "a program of all those who suffer and all those who have been wronged." The workers would participate in such a coalition "demanding for themselves not class rule but social justice."[86] The first sign that some degree of unity had been achieved came at the Congress of the International in Brussels in late August 1891. Here a wide array of socialists, from all three partitions and the emigration, formed a single delegation and issued a proclamation that they would work together "in the interests of the development of socialism in Poland and in the interests of international socialist politics."[87] For the next year talk of unity continued, facilitated (and made more urgent) by the fact that there were very few activists with whom one could talk (arrests kept the opposition tiny throughout the early 1890s).

Against this background, perhaps the meeting of Polish socialists in Paris on November 21, 1892, was primarily of symbolic importance. Eighteen activists representing a variety of revolutionary groups met at that time to give some organizational form to *Przedświt*'s talk of unity, creating the Polish Socialist Party (*Polska Partia Socjalistyczna*, or PPS). The PPS existed mainly on paper for the time being, since none of the "delegates" in Paris really had any direct contact with the Kingdom. Only when Stanisław Wojciechowski traveled to Poland a year later to hold talks with local activists did the PPS really come into existence.[88] Bolesław Limanowski was unanimously elected chair of the conference, thus indicating what sort of socialism the delegates had in mind: the *eminence gris* of radical patriotism would now be a model, not a heretic. The first words of the party program, composed mainly by Mendelson, clearly announced that the days of socialist antipatriotism had passed: "One hundred years have passed since the moment when the Polish Republic, fallen upon by three neighboring powers, proved incapable of creating from its bosom enough strength to resist the invaders. With the loss of state existence, with the snuffing out of the active political life of the nation, the development of our social relations stagnated and the whole country suffered from the inabilities of our ruling classes."[89] *Przedświt* would return to this theme repeatedly, insisting that the restoration of Polish independence would be in the interests of the working class, because it would free Poland from its ties to "backward," Russia, with its "brutal Asiatic government."[90] A proclamation issued by the PPS on the occasion of Alexander III's death in 1894 put it this way: "We want to raise the consciousness of the entire working class, and (since we understand our own problems) we want to govern ourselves. The basic condition is for us to attain the possibility of broad organization and free propaganda. Such conditions are possible only in a country possessing wide political freedom, free from the oppression of conquerors. Well understood class interests, therefore, compel us to demand an independent Poland."[91]

Poland, then, was suffering from two "yokes" (as the PPS program put it): both "internal reaction" and the "disgraceful cohabitation with tsardom." A manifesto from 1894 declared that "along with the Russian subjects of the Tsar we bear the oppression of an autocratic government, but aside from that they abuse us as non-Russians, as non-Orthodox."[92] The PPS would struggle against each type of oppression, thus linking the tradition of the uprisings to the coming socialist revolution. "When the last warriors of the Polish cause [in 1863] contemptuously threw in the eyes of the victorious Tsar the cry, 'Poland has not yet died,' these unknowing representatives of the noble estate probably did not understand that only on the ruins of their Poland, the noble Poland, would a new socialist Poland, with a more certain future [and] invincible strength, arise."[93] Nearly every PPS manifesto would end with the words, "Long Live Independent Workers' Poland!"[94] The two adjectives here had to go together, because either taken separately was only half the message of the PPS. The party was committed to both national cohesion and social unrest, and they joined the two by locating the final realization of the nation at the end of a historical narrative that was driven by "class struggle." That is, the nation could fully come into being only after the revolution, when the people (or the workers) came to define the national interest; until then Poland would be a site for social conflict. The nation was a *goal,* to be attained both by regaining Polish independence and by establishing the hegemony of the proletariat. The whole worldview of the PPS was held together by this faith in history, this conviction that social disorder was tolerable in the present because national unity was guaranteed in the postrevolutionary future.

It followed that the Polish socialists were not interested in preserving some imagined "Polish culture"—this was just a meaningless phrase, according to Kazimierz Kelles-Krauz. "Culture! That is one of those expressions which, like progress, organic work, civilization, and even the fatherland, must at all times be unmasked by socialists, so as to distinguish the contradictory class interests hidden within. . . . If a worker and a capitalist see in Mickiewicz their own poet, then each has a different Mickiewicz before their eyes. . . . for some, Adam will be above all the poet of mushroom collecting, for others the poet of conspirators."[95] Such rhetoric would have been anathema to a older patriot. For most of the *niepokorni,* however, it was seen not as a critique of the national tradition, but as a necessary purification of a concept they desperately wanted to preserve. This passage returns us, in fact, to the prospectus of *Głos*, where Popławski described two civilizations in Poland, that of the wealthy and that of the oppressed. A world of both social and national exploitation was common to both the PPS and the "patriots" at *Głos* and Zet; to Krzywicki, Krauz, and Mendelson on the one hand and Popławski, Balicki, and Dmowski on the other. Historians would like to imagine clear genealogies distinguishing the two circles, but for much of the 1890s they are better understood as factions, not at all incompatible, within the same antitsarist, anticapitalist, socialist-patriotic (or patriotic-socialist) opposition. Indeed, many members of the PPS joined Zet and the Polish League, and Balicki himself belonged to the émigré branch of the PPS. Only Róża Luksemburg's tiny splinter group, the Social Democrats of the Kingdom of Poland (which would remain virtually invisible within Poland until the end of the decade), remained truly apart, because of its consistent antinationalism.[96]

While the socialists organized the PPS, the patriots created their own conspiratorial group: the National League. It would be misleading, however, to date the origin of the twentieth century's great ideological divide from this moment. Even as these two organizations took shape, the boundary between them remained porous. The National League was the creation of three men we have already met: Roman Dmowski, Zygmunt Balicki, and Jan Ludwik Popławski. Balicki, as we have seen, had been a member of the Polish League from its inception, and in 1887 he had organized the Union of Polish Youth (Zet). In April 1893 Balicki met with Dmowski (then the president of Zet) and Popławski (the editor of *Głos* and a fellow member of the Polish League), to discuss the weaknesses of the national movement. These three engineered what they later characterized as a coup against the émigré leadership of the League, changing the group's name to the National League, relocating its central committee to the Kingdom (that is, to themselves), and tightening their conspiratorial methods. The reformed group got off to a slow start and for many years was restricted to the Russian partition. It grew steadily there, however, and by 1904 it had more than 350 members.[97] This figure made it a relatively large underground organization by the standards of contemporary East-Central Europe, but the actual impact of the National League extended far beyond this core of committed activists. By sponsoring a number of organizations, both secret and open, the National League contacted thousands of Poles even before Dmowski decided to announce publicly the existence of the League in 1899. Among these organizations were the Publishing Society, (a cooperative founded in 1897), Zet (which gradually fell under National League influence over the course of the 1890s), and the small *Collegium Secretum* (for nationalist priests). But all these projects were overshadowed by the National League's successful work among the peasantry, which transformed the Endecja from yet another underground conspiracy into a mass movement. In 1896 Popławski began editing a monthly magazine for the peasantry called *Polak*. The simple language of this publication and the practical information it contained made it quite popular among the increasingly literate villagers, even in the Kingdom (where it was illegal). Some 3,000 to 4,000 copies of *Polak* were distributed each month, but these figures do not take into account the large audience created when subscribers read aloud to their neighbors. Even more important was the work of the Society for National Education, which was formed in 1896. The purpose of the Society was not only to spread literacy among the peasants—several organizations with this purpose already existed—but to encourage the villagers to "become aware" of their national identity. Thanks to the growing strength of all these groups, the League's organ, *Przegląd Wszechpolski* (The All-Poland Review), became one of the most influential underground papers by the turn of the century. It had a rather narrow base of readers at first, with a print run of under 500 copies per issue until 1901, but then this figure shot up to nearly 1,700 (rivaling *Prawda* and *Przegląd Tygodniowy*, which were both legal). In the Kingdom, moreover, each issue would be read by several people. Thanks to all these efforts, when a public political space was created in the Kingdom after 1905, the Endecja was immediately a potent political force.[98]

Stanisław Wojciechowski, later president of Poland and then an activist in the PPS, recalled that in the early 1890s the socialists and the National League were friendly rivals, even printing each other's literature if the need arose.[99] Such conflicts as did exist between them were always kept quiet and (until 1905) no one ever exposed an opponent to the Russian authorities.[100] Once, when a loyalist student at Warsaw University tried to take advantage of the growing hostility among his more rebellious colleagues by proposing that socialists be banned from all student organizations, an overwhelming majority, without regard to ideology, voted to ban him instead for even suggesting such a thing.[101] When the National League organized a public demonstration on May 3, 1893 (the anniversary of the old Republic's final, abortive constitution), the PPS was upset about the possible competition with their own commemoration of May Day, but they were not opposed in principle.

> Our nationalists want to establish May 3 as a permanent national holiday, as a day on which the Polish population of all estates is supposed to demonstrate against the political oppression that exists among us. Such a goal by itself, *as an attempt to strengthen in our country the forces of resistance* against a demoralizing oppression, could find only support in our ranks. . . . [However], a project to establish a general national holiday, despite all the progressiveness that one could give a demonstration on May 3 . . . will be hindered by the demonstrations of May 1. There is no way to set up two days of demonstration coming so soon after each other.[102]

This was cast as a tactical dispute—primarily a scheduling problem—between two groups allied in a common struggle against tsardom.

On April 17, 1894, the National League staged its first really successful public demonstration, the so-called *Kilińszczyzna*.[103] On that day, a hundred years earlier, a cobbler from Warsaw named Kiliński led a local rebellion in conjunction with the Kościuszko Uprising. The occasion did not belong to the great anniversaries of the nationalist tradition, but it appealed to many of the *niepokorni* because Kiliński represented both an assertion of Polish identity and a revolt of poor craftsmen in the name of radical revolutionary slogans. Early in the morning of the 17th a crowd of students gathered on the Castle Square in the center of Warsaw, then walked the short block to St. Jan's Cathedral. They had prepared in advance by arranging for a mass to be said for the recovery of a sick child, which they intended as a metaphor for the restoration of Poland. After the service a small procession, 300 to 400 people, made its way through the old town of Warsaw to the home of Kiliński. The police intervened at this point, arresting 253 participants. The sentences were modest by the standards of the day: only 140 were actually punished, most with two to four months in prison followed by two to three years of exile to remote parts of the empire. None of them served out their terms, thanks to an amnesty at the accession of Nicholas II a year later. Perhaps the most important immediate consequence of the *Kilińszczyzna* was the blow it struck to student activism. Most of the members of Zet were removed from Warsaw as a result of the demonstration, and Potocki and Popławski (the editors of *Głos*) were jailed for joining the students. This was the excuse the authorities needed to close down *Głos*.

The response of the PPS to the *Kilińszczyzna* was revealing. While the party resisted commemorating the centenary of the Kościuszko Uprising in the emigration because they felt that other émigrés were giving the anniversary an excessively conservative tone, they made an exception in the case of the Warsaw demonstrations. "The only place where the Kościuszko commemoration was to have a revolutionary meaning," *Przedświt* wrote, "regardless of the party that managed it, was the Russian partition." Certainly the PPS did not agree entirely with the plans of the patriots, who wanted to treat the Kościuszko Uprising solely as a national commemoration—in contrast, the socialists would have liked to "clarify the real meaning of the Kościuiszko Uprising, all its bad and good sides." Nonetheless, thanks to the common pressure of tsarist "despotism," the demonstrations "were greeted by us with sympathy, despite the fact that they did not in any way have the character of a conscious political action of the proletariat. The thought that alongside us one can find other warriors opposed to the government filled us with joy." The goal of the PPS was to take part in the plans for the demonstration, and in doing so "give it a totally different, much more powerful character." Unfortunately, concluded *Przedświt*, the patriots ruined everything by staging the event where they did. "What can you expect," the paper wrote, "from people who are not able to find a more appropriate place for a demonstration than a church?"[104] Even this mild criticism provoked a letter of protest to the editors. There was nothing wrong with holding a protest in a church, a correspondent insisted; after all, for nonbelievers like the socialists it was just another large hall. *Przedświt*, this author wrote, should recognize its close ties to the patriots.

> You proclaim the same antigovernment speeches, you condemn the same
> governmental acts and decrees, directed at decreasing freedom of speech,
> freedom of holding state offices and many other limitations. You also forget that
> those same patriots constitute a rather broad segment of the readers of your
> journal. . . . Patriotism is for them a feeling of resistance against despotism, a
> feeling which, under the right circumstances, could be changed into action and
> give no less service than feelings directed against economic exploitation.[105]

The editors of *Przedświt* did not agree with the correspondent, but their response was defensive. "We did not at all condemn [the Warsaw demonstration] for the fact that it was patriotic," they wrote. "On many occasions we declared that patriotic demonstrations can only make us happy, since they would be evidence of the existence outside of our ranks of groups opposed to the government. Our only concern is when and how those demonstrations are managed." As to the suggestion that many patriots were reading *Przedświt*, the editors claimed not to be surprised, "since life is convincing them at every step that the desire to merge together the entire nation is utopian. Once they break with that idea, they will proceed along the path of logical development to a recognition of the socialist program."[106] The socialists were frequently forced to confront the fact that many people in the Kingdom, particularly outside of Warsaw, did not really understand the difference between the PPS and the patriots—or rather that these activists inhabited a world in which the disputes between the two factions of the *niepokorni* were minor disagreements within a common front. It was even possible for a rural "patriot" like Maksymilian Malinowski to write that his hero was the socialist theoretician Ludwik Krzywicki.[107]

Contemporary texts from the National Democrats reflected the same sort of openness and willingness to cooperate. A series of brochures from 1892 to 1895 called *Z Dzisiejszej Doby* (From the Current Day) was uniformly friendly toward socialism. One contribution to the series even equated the PPS and the National League, tracing the roots of both groups to the socialists of the 1870s (!), described here as "champions fighting for the rights of the working *lud,* for a new Poland, a socialist Poland." This author wrote that *Przedświt* and *Z Dzisiejszej Doby*, "despite different points of departure, are more or less in agreement."[108] Another issue of this series, discussing some strikes in Łódź in 1893, called for all patriots to support the cause of the proletariat: "Today the national interest irrevocably demands that in this struggle, which the working class above all engages with the Muscovite despotism, the entire Polish democratic and patriotic intelligentsia must stand openly and honestly on its side."[109] In Dmowski's own contribution to this series, a brochure entitled "Our Patriotism," the tone of reconciliation was even more pronounced. True patriotism could not be concerned with the interests of one class alone, he cautioned, but this did not imply that all social groups should be treated equally. "In political practice," Dmowski wrote, "the honest national position leads one to defend the interests of those classes whose elevation and welfare lie in the interest of the nation." He argued that the workers and the peasants best represented the nation because the capitalists and large landowners would always support a strong government, even if that government was foreign.[110] The editors of *Przedświt*, while not uncritical of Dmowski's booklet, were conciliatory. "Patriotism," they wrote, "as formulated in the brochure under review, is no longer an opponent of the class struggle of the proletariat. Quite the contrary, it even looks on us with sincere sympathy."[111] In 1895, when the Endecja inaugurated its monthly magazine, *Przegląd Wszechpolski* (The All-Poland Review), Dmowski felt compelled to write to Limanowski, assuring him that the new journal would not necessarily be antisocialist.

> I look upon the work of our socialists from a certain idiosyncratic position. You might not praise that position, but as an honorable man you will admit that it flows from good will and from a conscientious digestion of theory and fact. I am neither an unqualified glorifier of what they do nor an enemy of activities which are supported by sincere inspirations and in part by good results (with, however, a huge waste of energy on useless or even harmful things). . . . I offer [the socialists] friendly but stern criticism.[112]

The *Kilińszczyzna* of 1894, and the arrests that followed, produced a lull of several years in the *niepokorni*'s activism. Things began to revive only in 1897, when a protest was organized against some particularly polonophobic Russian professors. At about this time the cooperative attitude between the Polish opposition groups began to break down. A symbolic turning point may have been the unveiling of the Mickiewicz statue in December 1898. The National League felt that it could subvert the loyalist content of this event by joining in it, staging alongside the official ceremony a program of events to teach peasants and workers about the greatness of Mickiewicz as a national hero. The PPS rejected this tactic and planned to stage a demonstration on the day of the unveiling to protest what they saw as the unavoidable loyalist implication of the monument. The disagreement was mainly tactical, but it produced a powerful image: as the statue was unveiled, the leaders of the National League stood at the base of the monument alongside the loyalists (and the Russians) while the socialists were being arrested on the other side of a police barricade.[113]

Things went rapidly downhill after this. Zet finally split apart in 1898, and in November 1899 the PPS declared that none of its members could belong simultaneously to the National League.[114] By the first years of the twentieth century the invectives described earlier were common fare. In hindsight the socialist–nationalist divide seems obvious and the relative harmony of the 1880s appears unstable, if not inexplicable. A closer look, however, reveals a puzzle. If it is true that both the *głosowcy* and the Marxists were mischaracterizing each other back in the late 1880s— if the debate was not, at the time, between budding conservatives on one side and uncompromising cosmopolitans on the other—then what really motivated their dispute? What sparked the argument that would transform the united (or at least cooperating) antitsarist opposition into two bitterly hostile political parties?

The Abandonment of Historical Time

To understand the origins of the great divide between socialists and nationalists in Poland, we need to return to its founding moment: the polemical exchange of 1889–1890 between Ludwik Krzywicki and *Głos*. On one level, that debate was a local manifestation of a controversy that was then raging among revolutionaries all over the Russian Empire, between those who continued to believe in the possibility of an agrarian socialism based on the *obshchina* (the commune) and those who placed their faith in the coming of capitalism and the rise of an industrial proletariat. The Russian translation of Karl Marx's *Capital* came out in 1872, complete with a passage that would spark this controversy:

> Intrinsically, it is not a question of the higher or lower degree of development of the social antagonisms that spring from the natural laws of capitalist production. It is a question of these laws themselves, of these tendencies winning their way through and working themselves out with iron necessity. The country that is more developed industrially only shows, to the less developed, the image of its own future. . . . One nation can and should learn from others. Even when a society has begun to track down the natural laws of its movement—and it is the ultimate aim of this work to reveal the economic law of motion of modern society—it can neither leap over the natural phases of its development nor remove them by decree. But it can shorten and lessen the birth-pangs.[115]

Georgii Plekhanov was one of the first Russians to perceive the challenge that Marxism posed for a populist. No revolutionary could stop the march of time, he argued: "This process sometimes takes place over a very long period, but once it has reached a certain degree of intensity it can no longer be halted by any 'seizures of power' on the part of this or that secret society." That degree of intensity had already been reached in Russia, insisted Plekhanov, and further capitalist development was inevitable. Both the willful actions of the revolutionaries and the ancient traditions of the *obshchina* were "powerless and defenseless before the logic of economic evolution."[116]

Not all Russian revolutionaries were convinced by Plekhanov's reasoning, because it threatened to foreclose the possibility that the individual could do anything to alter the course of history. Vasilyi Vorontsov, for example, retained his faith in the power of revolutionary action: "If we are able to interest society in our plans, if we can evoke in the individual the feelings, wishes, and thoughts necessary for us, we ourselves can destroy the notorious law of history and create a new one in its place."[117] Nikolai Mikhailovsky was less hopeful, but even as he wavered in his opposition to the Marxist vision of history, he continued to insist that individuals had to act *as if* they could change the world.

> Let it be, in fact, a fatal mistake and useless folly, a futile attempt to stop the inexorable movement of history which, all the same, will take its own course and mercilessly crush all who oppose it. But at least admit that there was in this neither exaggerated deference toward the West nor disdain for the hopes and needs of the great majority of the people. . . . Concerning the fatal mistake and useless folly, I think that it is not at all a rare occurrence in history for people to be actually condemned by fate to a futile opposition against a clearly evident and far advanced historical process. And this is not from obstinacy, but from the same motivation that leads one deliberately to dive into the water at the risk of one's own life to save a drowning man who is past saving.[118]

As was mentioned above, the revolutionaries in the Kingdom had close ties to their Russian peers and predecessors, and they participated in many of the same disputes. As always, though, Polish intellectuals appropriated Russian (and Western) arguments according to their own distinct polemical needs. Krzywicki had declared in 1889 that the peasantry would inevitably be destroyed by the forces of progress and so it was senseless to try to help them. It was better to encourage their proletarianization, so as not to prolong their agony. Aleksander Więckowski and the others at *Głos* were disturbed by this claim, and they responded with arguments similar to those offered by Vorontsov and Mikhailovsky. But in the Kingdom this debate had ramifications that extended beyond the original issues of economic development and the efficacy of revolutionary action. The Polish situation differed from the Russian in two fundamental ways. First, the discussion about a "separate road" to socialism had limited resonance in the Kingdom. Not only did Poland lack a tradition of communal land ownership, but by the 1880s Warsaw, Łódź, and other Polish towns were industrialized enough to make it impossible to imagine that capitalism might be avoided. More important, there were (as always in Poland) *national* implications to this debate. When Krzywicki defended the iron laws of history and denied the power of free will, he brought into the open the great tension at the heart of the *niepokorni*'s reconciliation of social change and national unity. The writers at *Głos* responded to Krzywicki's Marxist determinism by reiterating their ability to change the future and by insisting that they wanted to improve the lives of the poor and oppressed *today*, without waiting for the amoral and uncaring forces of history to take their course. They were going to worry about the actually existing peasants and workers instead of remaining fixed on the ultimate triumph of a prophesied revolutionary proletariat. This decision became part of a broader turn away from historical time, toward social space. With this move, *Głos* took the first step away from the comforting conviction that national disunity in the present could be resolved by the march of progress. This seemingly innocuous conceptual shift went to the very heart of the *niepokorni*'s worldview and laid the foundation for the "new right" of the twentieth century. The "patriots" thought that they could remain on the left without a telos. They were wrong.

The focal point of this debate was the definition of the *lud*. Więckowski explored this term at length in a major essay series entitled "The *Lud* in Democratic Programs," published in 1890 in response to the controversy with Krzywicki. Więckowski accused Krzywicki of using the term *lud* as "a name without meaning, a verbal sign without content." In contrast, Więckowski wrote, *Głos* defined the *lud* as a concrete social formation consisting of "various social groups—such as factory workers, rural workers, craftsmen, small landowners, and so forth." All these people were linked by their status as "the direct producers of material value." Więckowski was *not* setting the peasants against the proletariat, and the disputes that followed were not between rural populists and urban socialists. In fact, in this particular article Więckowski devoted most of his attention to the urban poor.[119] Więckowski contrasted his devotion to the "real" interests of the *lud* with the prophetic idealism of Krzywicki. Marxism, wrote Więckowski, lost sight of the eternal struggle between the powerful and disempowered, because it posited a fanciful story of progress within which only some of the oppressed gained historical agency. *Głos*, in contrast, offered a timeless vision of the *lud* which:

> with one thread, ties together all the phases of the political development of
> societies. . . . It is a fact that the division of political societies into *ludowa* and
> non-*ludowa* parts encompasses the whole field of their economic and social
> antagonisms. This is the background on which, over the course of centuries, the
> changing picture of the struggle for the bread and rights of some, and for the
> privileges of others, has appeared. Against this background, in our day, threatening political problems rooted in the economic relations of capital and labor are
> taking shape, [and these] constitute only a new form of the same eternal
> essence.[120]

Więckowski accused Krzywicki of a narrow, doctrinaire attitude that allowed him to see only a limited class struggle, instead of "perceiving the more general opposition arising from the division of society into *ludowa* and non-*ludowa* masses." The *głosowcy* imagined a bifurcated world, where the specifics of any social conflict were mere variations on a universal theme. The *lud* was the rhetorical key that made this argument possible. As Więckowski put it, "We have a group of people engaged in physical labor, materially disinherited, intellectually debased, economically exploited, socially handicapped, giving the most to society [but] taking from it the least—a group of all those who, in contrast to the group of those truly privileged in every respect, we call the *lud*."[121]

This concept of the *lud* would provide the contributors to *Głos* with the tools needed to argue that they were listening to the voices of the poor and oppressed rather than imposing their own agendas. If one did not believe in a specific historical narrative, one had to serve the "real" needs of the people as they appeared at any given moment. Indeed, *Głos* would be programatically (so to speak) opposed to all programs. Więckowski described two types of democratic action:

> [The first] has as a goal the direct improvement of the existence of that class, or the elevation of its social role. [The second comes] from that personal idealization of the relations of life that disposes an individual to sacrifice his personal interests for general [interests]—and then it has in mind the realization by the *lud* or in the *lud* of certain ideals of progress, justice, humanity. In the first instance the *lud* appears as the subject of the act, in the second, as its object. In the first instance the act is, so to speak, the work *of the lud* for itself; in the second, it is the work *of someone* for the *lud*."

Więckowski argued that the dreams of the intelligentsia were irrelevant to a real democrat. "Whatever we might think of their interests, they will give them full priority. Whether the ideals of progress, humanity, [or] justice fit with their class aspirations or not, they will struggle for existence." Deploying a phrase that had become loaded with implications of passivity, Więckowski described Marxism as "social science," and contrasted this with the "practical knowledge" that underpinned *Głos*' program. The latter, he wrote, "deals with the subjective side of development; that is politics." The *lud*, it followed, was a "political term."[122] In other words, Więckowski saw Krzywicki's historical vision, like that of the positivists, as a disempowering narrative that made the people mere objects of a grand project to be realized at some point in the future. As such, it made it impossible to act—to apply will to shape the future. The program of *Głos*, Więckowski believed, was "subjective," and thus "political," because it was burdened by no such historical teleology.

Krzywicki and the members of the PPS, in contrast, would continue to perceive their actions within the boundaries of historical destiny. They would try to apply pressure at the edges of a preordained narrative, shaping it as best they could, trying perhaps to hurry it along, but always confident that the future was with them. The members of the PPS were still part of the generation of the *niepokorni*, so even as they replaced the old positivist conception of progress with their own, Marxist alternative, they continued to look for ways to "act." This would remain a creative tension (one might even say contradiction) within the worldview of Polish socialism. As we will see in the next chapter, the easiest way out of this impasse was to agitate among the workers in the hopes of unleashing forces of disorder and rebellion that were (supposedly) already latent, ready to explode.

While Więckowski was removing the *lud* from Krzywicki's controversial historical narrative, he was placing it into an ethnographic formation that would prove to be equally rigid. After discussing the *lud* in a series of articles published from June 7 to September 23, 1890, Więckowski ended with a definition: "The *lud* is the national mass of the working classes with the international proletariat at its head."[123] He was still close enough to socialism to posit the existence of an "international proletariat," but he subdivided this amorphous entity into national communities. He wanted to classify people "according to the real characteristics of the individual: . . . ethnographically, according to nationality, and economically, according to class."[124] In a revealing slip *Głos* once subtly reformulated its slogan about "subordinating" all interests to those of the *lud,* describing its program instead as "recognizing the *lud* as the main element of *national* life."[125] At first glance this idea was nothing new—we have already seen that the *niepokorni* were driven by a desire to restore Poland's independence, and socialism offered a means of reconciling revolutionary agendas and patriotic goals. But *Głos* put this puzzle together in a new way. Since they had freed themselves to concentrate on the "real" problems of the *lud*, they could focus on its *sociological* rather than *historical* existence. "Realism" did not simply require that people be removed from abstract teleologies; it necessitated that they be reconceptualized within new categories marked by immediate material needs and, more significantly, ethnolinguistic attributes.

Więckowski contrasted his "realistic" definition of the *lud* (as an actually existing ethnographic formation) with the "abstractions" of Krzywicki. But this was still supposed to be a socialist argument, as some young authors tried to make clear in 1892 when they founded a short-lived but ideologically significant journal called *Przegląd Socjalistyczny* (The Socialist Review) in Paris. This was a collaborative project of Bolesław Limanowski and some more recent émigré members of Zet (including Zygmunt Balicki and Roman Dmowski). The magazine's programatic statement began with a bit of wishful thinking that was essential to its argument: "[Now that] the working class, emancipated to a large degree from the influence of the socialist intelligentsia, has itself taken control of the movement, the socialist program has come down to a real foundation, aspiring gradually toward the removal of everything that stands outside the sphere of the struggle between labor and capital." *Przegląd Socjalistyczny* wanted to be a voice for the "real" class struggle, in contrast to the "dogmatic" Marxism of those devoted exclusively to the proletariat and its historical role. In fact, the paper wanted to remove the class struggle entirely from history. "The workers' party of a given country ought to consider itself to be a part of the international organization of the proletariat," the editors wrote, "and thus in its ultimate goals aspire to the transformation of the current system; but in its practical, ongoing tasks it [ought not to] go beyond that which directly or indirectly constitutes the needs of the proletariat as a class."[126] At issue were the "needs" of the workers; the revolution was subordinated and transformed from a historical inevitability to the vague outcome of some future struggle.

But *Przegląd Socjalistyczny* had its own "abstractions," its own imagined communities. After self-righteously proclaiming their desire to serve the "real" needs of the peasants and workers, the editors proceeded to educate the *lud* about the vices of excessive materialism. "The Polish worker," they wrote, "despite all the duties that are placed upon him by the current class struggle, cannot and should not forget that economic interests are not his only interests and that, defending these in the class struggle, he ought at the same time to stand in defense of national rights wherever they are trampled." This was a distinctly national socialism, one that could accommodate both solidarity and class struggle. "The forces in the struggle for independence are not limited to the working class, to that part of society conscious of socialist goals. It rests on the entire mass of the *ludowe* strata and on that part of our intelligentsia which has nothing in common with the Western 'bourgeoisie.'"[127] Despite all the emphasis on the proletariat, *Przegląd Socjalistyczny* returned to the *lud*, defined with amazing breadth so as to include even the intelligentsia. Without the ability to posit the union of all Poles at some point in the postrevolutionary future, it was necessary to insist that the unique situation in Poland (allegedly so unlike "the West") had created a *ludowa* solidarity in the present. A pseudonymous author (probably Balicki) tried to convince other socialists that this posed no threat to the primacy of class struggle. "Those who fear that the slogan of an autonomous Poland might surrender the socialist movement into the hands of the patriots," he wrote, "can be assured that any political movement, whatever its tasks, as long as it is based on a separate workers' party, could never be exploited by anyone except the socialists, because no party except the socialists' is based on the class struggle."[128] The degree to which Balicki and Dmowski would be able to retain their own acceptance of class struggle, however, was now in question. They had taken the first step toward constructing (or imagining) national solidarity in the present, and this would have profound consequences. These men, the founders of National Democracy, already recognized that the people might not be devoted to the national cause—thus their injunctions against excessive materialism. This realization would push them toward a discourse of order and discipline, designed to enforce national unity and cohesion. As we will see in the next chapter, socialists and patriots alike would attempt to impose new forms of order on the disorderly masses during the last decade of the nineteenth century, but the importance and meaning of authority would differ greatly between these two factions of the *niepokorni*. Limanowski, Krzywicki, and the others in the PPS could wait for the national organism to coalesce in the future, so broad social unity was unnecessary, or even harmful (insofar as it might delay the revolution). They would talk about proletarian unity against the class enemy, but their focus on social disruption would attenuate any authoritarian impulses. The patriots, in contrast, could no longer share the socialists' optimism about the future or their faith in a revolutionary moment; they were no longer convinced that the united nation would come into being on its own accord, or that the path toward its creation would pass through a chiliastic moment of social unrest. If Dmowski, Balicki, and their colleagues wanted unity, they would have to enforce it, actively, and willfully, in the present.

6

Organization

In the 1880s, while the young intellectuals of the Kingdom—the *niepokorni*—were trying to define the *lud* on the pages of their legal and illegal periodicals, the actual peasants and workers were raising their heads and voices. Their activities were particularly evident in the cities. Throughout the entire decade of the 1870s there were only eighteen strikes in the Kingdom, but during the 1880s there were more than forty, involving 27,000 workers (mainly in the textile center of Łódź, the mines of the Dąbrowa basin, and Warsaw).[1] These had little to do with the agitation of the intelligentsia: after Waryński's group was broken up by the police in 1886, the number of strikes only increased (to seven in 1887 and eleven in 1888, including one in Łódź that mobilized 8,000 workers). One study has estimated that during the 1880s, before the development of an "organized" labor movement, nearly one out of five factory workers in the Kingdom struck at least once.[2] In 1883 there were violent confrontations between rioting workers and police in the town of Żyrardów, and two years later a huge crowd gathered for a demonstration in the center of Warsaw—all without the intelligentsia's leadership or even involvement. During the 1890s labor unrest continued sporadically, rising rapidly after the turn of the century toward the crescendo of the 1905 Revolution.

While the workers were mobilizing, the countryside remained comparatively quiet. The Russian authorities believed that the land reform decree of 1864 had left the peasants eternally grateful to the Tsar, while Polish nationalists were convinced that patriotism would inevitably—and very soon—spread to the villages. Neither view, however, was unambiguously verified by the actions of the peasants themselves, who remained shrouded in myth for both opposition intellectuals and state officials alike. In 1905 this veil was lifted in a dramatic way when agricultural strikes broke out in 41 of the Kingdom's 84 counties, encompassing half of the largest estates. Activists from the intelligentsia (mainly the National Democrats) tried to co-opt and

direct the peasant unrest, but they were unable to do so. The peasants were demanding higher pay for farm labor, more land, and restoration of traditional access rights
to forests, rivers, and pastures. Even when they directed their ire at the government's
denationalization policies, they hesitated to accept the leadership of the "patriots" in
Warsaw, not to mention those in the local manor house. The peasants demonstrated
their hostility toward both the Russians and their "fellow Poles."

The decades leading up to 1905 were marked by the rise of mass politics, not
just in Poland but all over Europe. As Stephen Kern has put it, there was a "general
cultural reorientation" around the turn of the century "that was essentially pluralistic
and democratic."[3] Literacy had become pervasive enough to support a popular press,
and mass-circulation dailies were appearing even in peripheral cities like Warsaw.
"The people" were becoming involved in political life all over the continent, whether
or not electoral institutions existed within which they could legally express themselves. In this environment neither parliamentary politics in Western Europe nor
opposition politics in the Russian Empire could remain the exclusive domain of educated elites. Robert Blobaum has argued that the truly revolutionary quality of 1905
was not so much the way it changed the governing institutions of the tsarist state but
the way it exemplified and helped bring about a profound transformation, even "democratization," of political culture.[4]

But nearly all revolutions are followed by counterrevolutions, and in this case
new forms of discipline were arising from within the very forces that were "democ-
ratizing" the public sphere. If modernity, in the political sense, is characterized by
the increased participation of the masses in the determination of public policy and in
the conduct of partisan conflict, then the modern world carries within itself its own
negation. This chapter offers an example of how authority, modernity, and democratic rhetoric were inextricably intertwined in turn-of-the-century politics. The
modernization of political culture may have created a more pluralistic and democratic world, but it also facilitated the construction of new styles of social control.
As Foucault so famously put it, the "democratization of sovereignty was fundamentally determined by and grounded in mechanisms of disciplinary coercion."[5] The
nation of the people, in this modern era, would become the site for the reconfiguration
of authority. In Poland the democratization of politics was accompanied by the contested ordering of the masses within a limited repertoire of discursive frameworks
and ultimately by the disciplining of the people within a hierarchical nation. Of course
the actual "people" would not always accept these new categories, and when they
did use terms like "nation," "worker," or "peasant," they often appropriated them in
their own creative ways. But this reaction only exacerbated the situation, because
the intelligentsia's disciplinary desires had been inspired by precisely this gap between their conceptual universe and the various images of community circulating in
popular culture.

If we are to understand the rise of mass politics in Poland, we must grasp a fundamental paradox: just as the narrow conspiracies of the nineteenth century were
developing into the broadly based political movements of the twentieth, the rhetoric
of Polish nationalism was growing ever more authoritarian. As both Partha Chatterjee
and Florencia Mallon have argued (in different contexts), modern national move-

ments generally begin with evocations of popular action, only to be subsumed later within what Chatterjee calls "a discourse of order."[6] Diversity and plurality are silenced as new narratives are constructed to make sense of and give shape to the national modernity. When historians work within these narratives, they are often blinded both to the ways in which peasants, workers, women, ethnic minorities, and others resist, constitute, amplify, and modify the intelligentsia's national imaginings, and to the techniques deployed by elites to restrain and domesticate such variety. The recovery of the voices lost within the totalizing narratives of modernization and nationalization is one of the most challenging tasks facing historians today, but before we can even begin to identify and listen to those voices, we must first understand the mechanisms by which they have been (and continue to be) silenced. This chapter, then, will explore the ways in which power and discipline penetrated the rhetoric of Polish nationalism in the late nineteenth century, eroding what had once been a revolutionary discourse and transforming it into a vehicle for order and authority.

René Rémond has argued that the "new type of right" which emerged around the turn of the century arose from "the ground of the old right wing." According to this interpretation, there are genetic links between the early nineteenth-century right of the counterrevolutionary aristocracy and the early twentieth-century nationalist right.[7] The authoritarianism that emerged as such a powerful force beginning in the 1890s is thus cast as a revolt against earlier democratization and liberalization, as a desire to go back to a (mythical) time of secure hierarchies and social discipline. In Shulamit Volkov's words, the fin de siècle right was marked by "popular antimodernism."[8] More recent scholarship, however, has demonstrated convincingly that the "new right" was indeed new, with roots in the late nineteenth-century left and (more generally) in the cultural and social context of modernity.[9] The authoritarianism of the National Democratic movement was not a conservative reaction to the modernization of Polish political culture; rather it was a *product* of that modernization. As the labor movement grew in the 1880s and 1890s and as the peasants made their voices heard in 1905, it was clear that they could not be easily squeezed into any of the intelligentsia's revolutionary or insurrectionary dreams. The newly mobilized masses did not seem to fit into *any* of the conceptual frameworks that had been debated on the pages of *Głos*, *Przedświt*, or *Przegląd Tygodniowy*: socialists complained that the workers did not demonstrate an understanding of their "real" class interests, and patriots bemoaned the lack of enthusiasm for the national cause. In 1874 the Russian revolutionaries had "gone to the people" only to be ignored and rejected; in the late 1880s and 1890s the Polish "people" similarly demonstrated that they did not speak the same language as the Warsaw intelligentsia. The *niepokorni* were forced to confront the gap between the way they perceived the world and the way workers and peasants did, and the resulting dilemmas went to the very heart of the democratic, populist framework cultivated on the pages of *Głos*. What could a revolutionary do if the people did not behave according to any of the imagined narratives of revolution? The answer to this question was predictable: before long, terms like "organization," "order," and "discipline" began to penetrate the rhetoric of the "democratic" opposition.

But not all of modernity's political vocabularies were equally vulnerable to Chatterjee's "discourse of order"; not all impositions of authority were equally authoritarian. Up to the mid-1890s the rhetoric of the *niepokorni* seemed surprisingly open to the possibility that the subaltern might indeed speak. In a typical comment that would be echoed across the political spectrum, one student activist recalled that he and his colleagues longed for an ideology that could "flow from [the peasants'] feelings and instincts."[10] The Polish Socialist Party (the PPS) and the National Democratic movement (the Endecja) would both try to realize this ideal, but each would confront the challenge in a different way. For the socialists to sustain their vision of a utopian future, they had to ensure that the proletariat behaved according to an established revolutionary script. The flesh-and-blood workers (not to mention the peasants) did not always cooperate, and as a result some socialists began discussing the need for "discipline." This would always be a dangerous undercurrent within the rhetoric of the PPS, but most socialists managed to subdue the more authoritarian implications of concepts such as "the dictatorship of the proletariat." In 1905 the party demonstrated that it remained comparatively open to what it misleadingly described as spontaneous popular action. The socialists were by no means impervious to the discourse of order, but (with a few notable exceptions) they were able to tolerate a great deal of disorder, finding ways to ride the waves of popular unrest without stepping outside their ideological parameters. The same cannot be said for the nationalists: by the turn of the century the National Democrats had grown preoccupied with disunity and disobedience, and had started to extol the virtues of strict social and political hierarchies. It might seem obvious that socialists would retain more margin for diversity, disorder, and popular initiative than would nationalists, but this fact appears self-evident only in hindsight. As we saw in the last chapter, the "patriots" at *Głos* were sincerely convinced that they were the only true democrats, having liberated the people from the "abstractions" of the Marxist historical narrative. The *głosowcy* believed that by rejecting the idealist historiosophy of Ludwik Krzywicki (and, by extension, Karl Marx), they made it possible to listen to the "real" needs of the people. However, even as they were turning away from a socialist conception of progressive time, they were formulating their own, equally confining vision of ethnographic space (the nation). It was this combination of a synchronic and sociological frame of reference that ultimately generated the Endecja's authoritarianism.

Agitation and Organization

The publications of the *niepokorni* often observed ruefully that the radical intelligentsia looked upon "the people" much as Polish landlords had long viewed their serfs. *Przegląd Społeczny*, for example, complained that "the peasant is treated—in accordance with the traditions of the nobility—at best as a dead lump of earth, from which only the noble hands of the aristocracy can manage to create something. . . . But counting on the *lud* failed, because he could not be used as a tool. He was not so deprived of reason and memory as to trust those under whom he suffered for so many centuries."[11] Popławski once argued (in a passage that would later seem self-accusatory) that educated activists should respect the individual talents and the wisdom of the peasants.

We are still held back by the old bad habit of looking down on people who do not belong to the privileged professions. . . . Often even people of good will would like to lock those strata into some sort of caste exclusivity. They imagine the peasants as honest but ignorant. . . . They use in writing [and] in speech the expression "my brothers," but they speak to them not as brother to brothers, equal to equals, but as guardians, as teachers, with indulgence but from on high.[12]

In this passage Popławski even switched from the totalizing term *lud* to the more internally differentiated expression, *ludzie* ("people" instead of "*the* people"). He had discovered that there were real people within the people, and he hoped to work *with* them for a common future, not *on* them to realize the intelligentsia's goals.

Like Popławski, Zygmunt Balicki (later one of the Endecja's most authoritarian figures) was originally committed to a radically participatory version of democracy. In 1886 the young Balicki wrote a three-part essay in *Przegląd Społeczny* entitled "Democracy and Liberalism." Here he critiqued parliamentary government as a disguised means of imposing force upon the people, even while promising freedom. The root of this hypocrisy was the tendency of liberals "to see society as a totality, contained within a state form. . . . In relation to society, liberalism considers the legislative body to be an expression of the majority, and the majority to be the expression of the totality." The young Balicki, like the young Popławski, was opposed to any ideology that erased individuality and transformed the subalterns into an undifferentiated mass. It was senseless to talk about the needs of the whole, he wrote, because "the whole of a social organism does not have spiritual direction and thus, as such, it cannot have needs and corresponding aspirations, aside from the needs and aspirations of individuals." It followed that real democracy "takes as its point of departure the interests of the citizen just as he perceives them himself." Balicki concluded unequivocally that "there is no place [in a democracy] for hierarchy, for bureaucracy."[13] A few years later he was even more direct: "We will only achieve more perfect forms of the social system when the leading intellectual strata democratize their instincts to rule, [when they] come off the pedestal of 'older brothers' and merge with the *lud*."[14]

Despite such properly democratic sentiments, the *niepokorni* found it difficult to really subordinate themselves to the needs and (worse) the desires of the *lud*. Kazimierz Bystrzycki captured this dilemma when he ridiculed any educated activist who would

abandon all those characteristics that make him privileged, throw away higher culture and accept the culture and ideals of the *lud*. . . . Looking critically at our *lud*, it is difficult not to see that its ideals are not always of a positive nature. Centuries of hard and demoralizing conditions of existence must have cultivated in [the *lud*] some negative aspirations, directly contrary to the healthiest ideals of the intelligentsia. The uncompromising subordination of the intelligentsia to those aspirations would be, therefore, a hard and unrewarding sacrifice; in many cases it would only be a retreat backwards in progress, which is neither desirable nor possible.

But having said all this, Bystrzycki insisted that he had no intention of "forcing upon the *lud* those ideals that the intelligentsia considers best." This apparent contradiction was the dilemma of the age: how could one work on behalf of a group that did not share one's vision of progress; how could one retain "higher" ideals while simultaneously embracing "democracy"? Bystrzycki's solution was awkward. He suggested that intellectuals should "momentarily discard" some of their ambitions until "the conditions of life . . . create in the *lud* corresponding aspirations." Until that day arrived they should search for anything "that can serve as a bridge for joining the *lud* and the intelligentsia."[15] The dream expressed by Popławski that the intellectuals would turn to the people "as brothers to brothers, equals to equals," seemed beyond the reach of most of the *niepokorni*. The best that could be hoped for was that the educated activists would seek bridges between their "enlightened" goals and the "backwardness" of the masses. For some, this would be a lifelong dilemma and an unrealized goal. For others it would soon become a discarded ideal not worth pursuing.

Both the orthodox Marxists and the heterodox *głosowcy* wanted the people (or the proletariat) to become active forces in history, but both would retreat before the sight of a "mob" that did not share their objectives or ideals. The socialists had to confront these tensions often in the 1880s, when rising unemployment and falling living standards sparked several "spontaneous" strikes in the Kingdom. The most memorable of these came in 1883, with a strike at an Austrian-owned linen works in the town of Żyrardów, just outside of Warsaw. In response to layoffs and pay cuts, about 180 women walked off the job on April 23; by the next day that number had doubled, and soon the strike encompassed hundreds of women and men. When the police moved in, the resulting confrontation left three strikers dead (including a fifteen-year-old boy) and many more wounded. So far the script was familiar, but the workers responded to the police violence in a manner incomprehensible to observers from the intelligentsia: they launched a pogrom against Żyrardów's Jews. Some of the slogans shouted at the time suggest how distant these events were from the world of the *niepokorni*. Referring to the Warsaw pogrom of 1881, workers were reported to have complained (in what must have seemed to the intellectuals to be a series of non sequiturs), "in Warsaw, during the Jewish pogroms, no one shot down the people [i.e., the non-Jewish rioters], but in Żyrardów, when we don't want to work for Germans [i.e., the Austrian factory owners], they kill our brothers and children."[16] The Żyrardów strike, with its fascinating intersection of gender, class, nation, and race, deserves a monograph of its own, but for now I want to note only the vast gap between these autonomous acts of protest and *any* of the rhetorical alternatives available to the *niepokorni*. When intellectuals tried to assign agency to the *lud*, they invariably confronted this gap.

The "mob" reared its head again two years later, this time in the center of Warsaw itself. The continuing recession of those years generated widespread unrest among the recently urbanized and rapidly growing population of the city, and throughout February 1885, there were almost daily confrontations between jobless workers and the police. These culminated in a huge demonstration on Castle Square on March 2. A petition for the Russian Governor-General was prepared, but when the crowd tried to deliver it the police intervened, arresting 146 people. Significantly, this event is missing from nearly all of the opposition narratives of the late nineteenth century. Socialist historians would later refer to the May Day demonstrations of 1890 as the first major sign of public action since the January Insurrection, while nationalist scholars point to the May 3 protests of 1891; neither group claims the events of March 1885 within their tradition. Significantly, the only intellectual directly engaged with the crowd on Castle Square that day was a Serbian adventurer named Andra Banković, who just happened to be in Warsaw at the time.[17]

Against the backdrop of events like this, socialist intellectuals began emphasizing that infamous phrase, "the dictatorship of the proletariat." This was not, as an author in *Walka Klas* recognized in 1884, "a democratic expression," but it was nonetheless a crucial part of socialist teaching. The idea of dictatorship, he wrote, had a dual meaning: on the one hand, it referred to the need for the working class to "enclose entirely the arena for the formation of social relations" so that reactionary forces could not turn back the revolutionary tide; on the other hand, this was a dictatorship of the radical intelligentsia over the "unconscious" masses. Such authority was needed, this author continued, because the working class had to be "organized and conscious of its interests" if it was to be strong.[18] *Walka Klas* had no doubts about who would do this organizing: "The initiative of introducing to our social life the aspiration to social revolution belongs to our revolutionary intelligentsia. . . . Gifted with stronger initiative, possessing a broader social morality, it will, together with that kernel of a worker's organization, be able to be a sort of moral leader for the entire movement."[19]

An anonymous socialist later recalled that the situation in the Kingdom in the early 1890s was ripe for revolution. "It would have been possible to create a more serious organization," he wrote, "were it not for the lack of intellectuals-agitators."[20] This last phrase—agitators—brings us to the fundamental distinction between the socialist effort to give order to the people *in time* and the nationalist dream of establishing order *in social space*. Like all the activists of his generation, this author wanted to give order to the new politics of the 1890s, but the sort of organization he imagined was disrupted by the concept of agitation. The socialists dreamed of a chiliastic moment of salvation, a revolution that would overturn the entire world and bring a new dawn, and they positioned their imagined social unity within this utopia. Their vision of revolution implied a moment of disorder, chaos, and systemic destruction—to be followed, of course, by the construction of the new socialist order. This eschatological dream determined how the PPS approached the concept of organization and how they acted to shape the emerging forms of mass politics. Like all underground opposition groups, the socialists were concerned with the institutional structure of their movement, but they had no need to discuss in advance (that is, before the revolution) the organization of society (thus the infamous vagueness of nineteenth-century Marxist thought regarding the postrevolutionary world). The socialist Adam Próchnik explained the distinction between propaganda and (as he put it) "politics":

> As long as the capitalist system was criticized and socialism was derived from its
> foundations, we remained on scientific, reasoned, rationalistic ground. However,
> whenever we reached toward the past [or] whenever we penetrated into the
> sphere of social revolution, we found ourselves at once on metaphysical ground.

> We imagined social revolution as a transcendent phenomenon, as a great
> elemental change, the foundations of which we did not know and did not know
> how to find. . . . Since, therefore, all those social changes would be the mere
> result of that great transformation—social revolution—there was no need to
> conduct a political struggle. . . . It was only necessary to prepare as many
> talented people as possible to accept socialism. The greatest necessity, therefore,
> seemed to be not political struggle but propaganda [and] preparatory work.[21]

Once Próchnik accepted the inevitability of the great moment of salvation, he was driven to "agitate" and spread "propaganda," to foment unrest so as to hasten the day of transformation. The entire raison d'être of a socialist party in a capitalist world was disruption, division, and discord, which would allow the PPS to attract an enormous following during the chaotic months of insurrection in 1905. Indeed, the PPS helped spark the events of that year by provoking a violent incident between demonstrators and the police. Even if they did not bring about *the* revolution, they accomplished an important goal: as Robert Blobaum has put it, they "contributed to the creation of an atmosphere charged with confrontation."[22] This was precisely what they wanted: to heighten the "class contradictions" of Polish society, to sow unrest, to hasten the apocalypse. Within their narrative of rupture and utopia, the liberation of the *lud* and the *naród* alike could come only after passing through the storm of social conflict. As the socialists participated in the ordering of mass politics, they were thus compelled to retain wide spaces for disorder.

Even within this framework, however, the lure of social discipline could overwhelm the commitment to revolution. When this occurred, the socialists tended simultaneously to lose their faith in progressive historical time. In 1906 recriminations for the failures of the revolution exacerbated existing disputes within the PPS, and the party split into two groups: the PPS-Left and the PPS-Revolutionary Fraction. Historians of this division point to tactical disputes over the use of paramilitary violence or over competing priorities of national restoration and social revolution, but in fact the division rested on a deeper foundation. The PPS-Left (by far the larger faction in 1905–1906) believed in the virtues of social disorder, while their opponents in the PPS-RF stressed the need to *organize* the proletariat. Significantly, the leading figure among the latter group was Józef Piłsudski, who many years later would become interwar Poland's authoritarian leader. Piłsudski had long been involved in the socialist movement, but by the early twentieth century he was already moving away from the PPS's vision of revolutionary disruption and utopia. He revealed his thinking in a private letter in January 1905, in which he wrote that the party must be ready for organized action. "We must be prepared for the moment, so as to weigh in on the course of events not as an impotent and irresolute mass, but as a consolidated and well-led force. That is why it is necessary to create an organization with a military character, which can give direction to the future uprising."[23] The PPS-RF's organ, *Robotnik* (The Worker), emphasized the dangers of an undisciplined proletariat: "Only anarchists imagine that a victorious revolution will be sufficient, even if the masses are not yet entirely conscious. We, however, know that it is not enough to attain power; one must be able to hold onto it and know how to benefit from it, and only a conscious proletariat can accomplish this."[24] The socialists around Piłsudski had given up their faith in time, their belief that history itself would propel the future forward after the moment of revolutionary disruption. Instead, they became increasingly worried about creating that future, and to do so they needed to *organize* the proletariat, not just agitate among the workers.

The majority of PPS activists, however, distanced themselves from this vision of a militarized social-patriotism. In the first years of the twentieth century most Polish socialists continued to imagine mass politics in a way that retained wide room for *disorder*, and most considered Piłsudski and his supporters to be heretics. Even among those who accepted the need for some sort of paramilitary organization, the goal of social revolution remained paramount. Socialism undoubtedly gave conceptual order to "the people" and "the proletariat," but it did so within a diachronic perspective that allowed for disruption in the present so as to lay the foundation for an equation between *lud* and *naród* in the future. For most socialists, the revolutionary moment was imagined as a time of creative destruction, as the old order was overthrown so that something new could arise. For most, historical time served as the antidote to order, discipline, and authority.

From Democracy to Discipline

The socialists were not the only ones struggling to make sense of modernity's mass politics, of course. The other branch of the *niepokorni*, the so-called patriots at *Głos*, were equally concerned with these matters, and like the socialists they succumbed to the temptation to assume the role of "the elder brother" (as Balicki had put it). The *lud* provided all Polish intellectuals with a way to embody their social imaginings, to "clothe the national spirit in the body of fact" and "turn the word into flesh" (as Zygmunt Wasilewski put it).[25] If we thus understand their fin de siècle fascination with "the people," we can hardly be surprised that it was difficult for them to listen to the unmediated voice of the people. The "national spirit" could not get *too* mired in its "body of fact," lest the *lud* challenge the intelligentsia's ideals. But the form of elite leadership would differ significantly between those who imagined themselves within a historical teleology and those who could perceive only synchronic social space. The PPS talked about the dictatorship of (and, implicitly, over) the proletariat, but their eschatological worldview allowed them to retain a message of subversion and disorder. In contrast, the National League, with its roots in *Głos*' repudiation of "abstract" visions of the future, found it difficult to tolerate any diversity or division within a community that existed in the present. The nation, as imagined by the members of the National League, eventually became a site for talking about authority, discipline, and power, and the *lud* had to be reconceptualized so as to support, rather than subvert, organization. The result was a discursive framework that allowed Polish nationalists to claim a popular foundation while at the same time facilitating control over the peasants and workers as these "masses" were being drawn into the political process. All discussions of class struggle were eventually banished from the pages of National Democratic publications, leaving space only for the "duty" of the workers and peasants to subordinate their own needs to a higher cause and to obey their betters. Insofar as any "particularism" was allowed to exist within the nation, it was carefully contained and disarmed.

At the heart of National Democracy—indeed, embodied within the very name of the movement—was a fundamental tension: on the one hand, the Endeks claimed to be popular and democratic, committed to bringing the *lud* into political life; on the other hand, they could not allow the demands of the workers or the peasants to undermine "national unity." The first issue of *Pochodnia*, the party's underground organ in the Kingdom, opened with a call for populist action: "So on your feet, anyone who is alive! Get to work with the *lud* and among the *lud*."[26] The National Democratic peasant magazine, *Polak* (The Pole), reminded its readers that "the true Pole does not only think of the independence of the Fatherland, but also wants freedom and civil equality for all of its children, as well as the sort of social order which would abolish the unjust differences between people."[27] The 1903 program of the Democratic National Party declared that "the interests of the *lud* . . . are today, in all respects, equivalent with the interests of the nation." Later in the program, however, the party cautioned against "sowing hatred and sharpening class tensions," lest doing so "hinder the development of feelings of social solidarity and national unity." By 1903 the Endecja was demanding that all "class, denominational, corporate, regional, and local" interests be subordinated to the (singular) national interest.[28]

There was a long path between the young revolutionaries of the 1880s and the disciplinarians of 1903. As we saw in the last chapter, the "patriots" of *Głos* and the Polish League had initially accepted social division and class struggle. When Zygmunt Miłkowski founded *Wolne Polskie Słowo* (The Free Polish Word, the Polish League's émigré magazine) in 1886, he announced that socialists were welcome to contribute, and they did so for a while.[29] He published articles describing "the idea of repairing the contemporary manifestation of the world" as a volcano that would soon explode in the form of "a great and universal Social Revolution."[30] A speaker at a meeting of Polish émigrés in France was quoted with approval when he declared, "among us, patriotic impulses must go together with social transformation."[31] An unsigned review of the poetry of Jan Kasprowicz identified the sort of socialism *Wolne Polskie Słowo* could endorse.

> His socialism, as we see, does not preclude the love of the fatherland—instead he considers love of the fatherland to be the source of universal brotherhood. We agree with this sort of socialism—with a socialism identifying as the goal of its aspirations the improvement of the lot of those whom the social order currently oppresses. We are also socialists of this sort! This Democracy has a goal—a goal pointed out by Christ and carried on by those who strive to bring to life a beautiful, exalted science of justice, penetrated by the enormous love of the Son of God.[32]

Patriotism, democracy, socialism, justice, and the Kingdom of God: all were focused on the future, on the eradication of all that was wrong with the world. Such a synthesis between patriotism and social revolution, however, would prove to be unsustainable on the pages of *Wolne Polskie Słowo*. The *głosowcy* in Poland and Miłkowski's émigré circle in Geneva were living in a postpositivist world, a world in which the rhetoric of science determined how one spoke about social life. As we saw in the last chapter, the "patriots" believed that science required them to cast their gaze on society as it was in the present, instead of dreaming about the nation of justice and harmony that was yet to come. This was no longer the world of Mickiewicz and Hegel; it was not even the world of Spencer and Marx. The structures of sociology had vanquished both the romantic narratives of history and their liberal and socialist successors. All that remained was an indeterminate future—one that could be created through an act of volition, if only an appropriately willful subject could be identified.

The nation would be that subject, but once *Wolne Polskie Słowo* entered the world of synchronic sociology, it had to discover scientific definitions of both *naród* and the accompanying expression, *lud*. A dangerous question was then raised: who, exactly, was·a member of "the people," and how did the people fit within the nation? Back when the *lud* had been a metaphor for social justice and the *naród* had stood for national freedom, such questions were beside the point. Now, in a world filled with sociological communities, these terms could be used only if they were filled with demographic content. Once this problem was raised, it had to be resolved in a manner ensuring that the patriotic commitment to the people would not threaten national unity. An anonymous author from 1892 distinguished "democratic" from "socialist" definitions of "the people": "Democrats, in terms of civil rights and duties, consider all strata, classes, and estates to be equal, [and all of them] combined constitute the *lud*." Socialists, he complained, excluded the bourgeoisie, the aristocracy, the intelligentsia, and the peasants from the *lud*, leaving only the proletariat.[33] Two years later another contributor proclaimed simply, "The *lud*—that's all of us."[34] If the émigré patriots wanted to serve both the nation and the people, then neither could be allowed to challenge the other. The easiest way to prevent this was to make the terms synonymous: if national unity could not be prophesied, as it had in Limanowski's work, then disunity had to be defined away. Henceforth, for these authors, there could only be one object of oppression: "all of us." And "we" certainly couldn't exploit "ourselves."

But if the *lud* was "all of us," then how could the growing social unrest in Poland be explained? There could be only one answer: "agitators" were disturbing the peace. Even as early as 1887 Miłkowski complained about those who tried to "disturb the social harmony."[35] This would prove to be an insidious phrase, undermining Miłkowski's progressive understanding of the nation and driving a wall between patriots and socialists. In a telling moment, Miłkowski proposed to his colleagues that Bolesław Limanowski be placed on the Polish League's central committee, but the idea was met with strong resistance and had to be withdrawn. At about the same time, in 1887, an anonymous author tried to defend the socialist label: "Our sin, the mortal sin of which they accuse us, is our professed socialism. It is true, we are socialists—but what of it?" He then proceeded to offer a long list of Polish national heroes who had embraced the socialist label in the 1830s and 1840s.[36] Aleksander Guttry, who had been a democratic activist in the Prussian partition since the 1830s, was quick to respond. In a letter published in the next issue he called socialism a "foreign idea" based on a narrow class egoism. He proposed instead an agenda that emphasized "freedom, not for one estate or caste, but for the entire nation."[37] Another correspondent wrote that the patriots of the 1840s "did stand on a social foundation, that is true, but they derived their political and economic principles from the living needs of the nation, not from foreign theories."[38]

If "class egoism" undermined the nation and if socialism was "foreign," then it was only a short step to the demand that all good patriots work to suppress social discontent. This step was taken in an unsigned series of essays published in 1889, entitled "The Threats to Our Nationality." The author began with a familiar (but untranslatable) usage of the term *lud*: "Our urgent need, above all of our other needs, is to merge the social classes into a *ludowa* totality for the struggle with the enemy of the nation."[39] Again, the *lud* was equivalent to the nation itself. As the author put it in the next installment, "Our strength, in hibernation, lies in the Polish *lud*, but in the entire [*lud*]— not in the peasants alone, not in the workers alone, not exclusively in the nobility, not in the bourgeoisie or the Jews, but in the entire Polish *lud*."[40] This was as inclusive a concept as one could imagine, embracing even the Jews within an amorphous, all-encompassing Poland. Alongside this *lud*, however, the author juxtaposed some surprising Spencerian rhetoric, complete with a reference to *Principles of Sociology*. "The contradiction of interests," he wrote, "the natural phenomenon of the struggle for existence, is a fact that cannot be denied, a fact . . . existing not only between classes, but among individuals." If left unchecked, this "fact" would lead to the destruction of the human race in a war of all against all. How could this fate be avoided?

> A certain *lex suprema* has been found that will mediate and soften the struggle
> for existence, making it dependent upon the conditions in which laws, duties,
> and morality are built. This is shaped over the centuries "by gradual differentia-
> tion" (Herb. Spencer). Above that increasingly magnified clash of interests there
> stands a general task, interesting the members of a given society both together
> and individually. Along this path are formed national, political, [and] patriotic
> interests, against which individual, group, class, [and] estate interests diminish,
> lose value, and withdraw into the shadows.[41]

The purpose of national unity was no longer to bring justice to Poland and to the world. Instead, unity was posited as a solution to the struggle for existence, a means of mediating between the competing interests within society, so that the nation could turn toward its enemies with one voice. We find here a *prioritizing* of interests against a Spencerian backdrop instead of a collective submersion within a universalist agenda. And with this, the definition of the *lud* had to change yet again: "We stand before the enemy, who divides us and oppresses us through differentiation. Are we to help him? 'Through the *lud* and for the *lud*' certainly does not mean [that we are to] implant dissatisfaction into the midst of the *lud* and hand Poland over to our enemies."[42] The people, once the object of so much hope, had become a threatening force for disruption and disunity. The "patriots" had now come full circle: from the *lud* as a disenfranchised underclass requiring protection, through the *lud* as "all of us," and finally to the *lud* as a dangerous sectional interest. The imperative had once been to help the people; now it was to ensure that the mob did not break loose.

Miłkowski took the final step toward a discourse of discipline in April 1890, in the longest article ever published in *Wolne Polskie Słowo*. Here he printed a defense of socialism by an anonymous correspondent from the Kingdom, followed by an editorial response. The youth of today, Miłkowski wrote "neither perceive nor understand that such theories lead to discord between the social strata, [and] that social quarrels damage any sort of organization of national defense." Instead of socialism, Miłkowski now called for the "enlightenment" of the people in the name of "national defense." "When Polish independence is attained," he concluded, "then we will find—perhaps—that socialist formula which to this day has not yet been found anywhere, and which is supposed to be a guarantee of social justice."[43] This was the voice of a disillusioned radical, who still wanted to believe in both social solidarity and social justice. By then, however, Miłkowski felt that he was being compelled to make a choice between the two, and he opted for the former, putting off the latter—"perhaps"—to some future date, after Poland regained its independence. As an anonymous correspondent put it later, it was a question of priorities: "For us the point of gravity ought to be, above all, to regain Poland."[44] As the 1890s progressed, the antisocialist rhetoric at *Wolne Polskie Słowo* became increasingly harsh. One author could ask, "What lies at the bottom of a socialist's soul? Envy, jealousy toward those who possess, hatred toward those who give them work."[45] When some socialists tried to join in a commemoration of the January Uprising in Paris in 1893, a correspondent protested, "Go demonstrate somewhere else, but do not show yourselves at émigré gatherings."[46] By the mid-1890s essays equating socialism with loyalism, or even with "the Muscovites" themselves, were common.[47] By then *Wolne Polskie Słowo*'s authors could speak of social change only in the most qualified way, subordinating all discussions of social injustice to the needs of the nation.

The younger patriots in the Kingdom were slower to adopt such harsh rhetoric—the radical traditions of *Głos* were too strong—but eventually they also began to move from democracy to discipline. To be more precise, they gradually reconceptualized "democracy" so that it would serve the cause of social discipline. Popławski, a founding editor of *Głos*, had once been strongly committed to the idea that the *lud* was an oppressed underclass which had to be defended against exploitation. As late as 1897 he could write, "By 'the people' we understand all those strata of society which to this time, as a result of cultural neglect, have been cut off from conscious participation in national life and deprived of influence in the improvement of their material and spiritual existence, deprived of the ability to independently defend their interests."[48] This definition, however, suggested the possibility of divisive social conflict, and by the late 1890s Popławski, like Miłkowski before him, had stopped believing that such disunity could be resolved by a utopian teleology. Without the solace of prophecy, he had to work for social unity in the present. "In national politics," he wrote later the same year, " . . . one must push to the forefront that which unites all strata, not that which divides them."[49] To accomplish this, Popławski relocated the "great majority" of society within the *lud*. He explained that by "the people" he meant workers, craftsmen, and even the "intellectual professions"—anyone who "exclusively or primarily" earned a living from personal labor and contributed to the national welfare.[50] Zygmunt Balicki offered an even more expansive definition of the *lud*: "that social whole which remains on a certain territory occupied by one state."[51] Here was an all-embracing *lud* that included virtually everyone, rich and poor, noble and peasant, exploiter and exploited.

In a fascinating transitional text from 1898, Balicki took his initial steps away from the socialist eschatology toward a dehistoricized commitment to social harmony in the present. He still claimed to believe in "the elimination of all forms of the class system" and the "erection of new arrangements based on solidarity," but he no longer cast this familiar utopia as the product of a proletarian or populist victory. It was, instead, something that the proletariat had to create today. The workers had to become "quintessentially national," building the classless society not by fighting for their own hegemony, but by voluntarily subordinating their own needs to the common good. Class consciousness, for Balicki, was a destructive force when it "measured everything by its own standards" and "recognized the common needs of the totality of society in its entirety only insofar as it suited its special needs." Balicki would oppose any attempt to place "class interests above the welfare and interests of the nation."[52] As he put it elsewhere, "One should not spread propaganda (especially negative propaganda), but above all organize; when influencing the masses, one should not play off of their egoism, but off of their communal, social, and national feeling."[53] Gone was the call to work for the good of the people in order to serve the nation; now the material needs of the workers were marginalized as expressions of "egoism" which must not be provoked lest they weaken the force of "communal, social, and national feeling."

The Endecja would continue to claim the mantel of democracy, but they did so by turning their populism into a tactical maneuver aimed at strengthening the nation. Back in the late 1880s Popławski had written on the pages of *Głos* about "subordinating the needs of all strata to those of the *lud*." By 1897, when he composed the program of the Democratic-National Party, his wording was significantly different: "*In today's system* of social and political relations the general interests of the people are equal to the interests of the nation. We therefore place first in our social aspirations the spiritual and material interests of the popular strata, subordinating *where necessary* the interests of other strata."[54] Popławski's straightforward declaration of a decade earlier was so heavily revised as to be almost unrecognizable. The people and the nation were still one, but only provisionally and only because the nation required it to be so. As a National League declaration of 1900 explained, "If we step forth as a party, it is not because we represent the interests of one stratum, but because . . . in organizing the popular masses for political life we see the most important task of national politics."[55]

Popławski imagined, in an optimistic moment in 1898, that the people would easily recognize the importance of the national struggle. "The people have not been won over by anyone," he wrote, "either by the government or by the Polish intelligentsia! Simply advancing in the development of education and political understanding, [the *lud*] understood that it is itself Poland, that national oppression is its slavery, that the independence of Poland is its freedom!"[56] More typical for the Endecja, however, was the doubt expressed by a four-page pamphlet in 1899 in which the author proclaimed that "the struggle with the Russian government and its allies in our society has become ever more clearly a struggle for the Polish *lud*, for influence on it, for its soul." The only way to win this struggle was to demonstrate greater organization than the enemy: "The nation . . . must keep its public life under the restraint of an organization, open or secret, capable of directing the totality of its aspirations and efforts and aiming persistently toward the attainment of the goal. The strength of the nation, just like the strength of a state, rests in its organization."[57] The people were thus transformed from "all of us" into a trophy of war, a prize over which the Russian government and the Polish intelligentsia were fighting. And to win this fight the Poles needed organization.

The Endecja's 1903 party program made it clear that the oppression of the people was no longer a problem in its own right; it was merely an obstacle to national unity. This document still highlighted the need to strengthen the *lud* "economically and culturally" and transform the peasants into a "politically active social element." The justification for this agenda, however, was now "so that the nation as a whole can follow others in progress and effectively defend its interests."[58] *Polak*, the Endecja's peasant magazine, similarly explained that greater social equality was a means to ensure that "we will have order among ourselves and strength for the struggle with [our] enemies."[59] The National Democrats appropriated the language of populism (or rather, they reconfigured it, since they had been among its creators in the 1880s) so as to redirect *and contain* demands for social change. They recognized that the social context for political action was changing and that the *lud* was starting to raise its own voice. "Whether with regret or enthusiasm," Dmowski wrote, "one must agree that in our times only the masses can achieve great things."[60] But the National Democrats did not allow this situation to lead them toward radical democracy or popular empowerment: instead, they concluded that democracy was the most effective means to organize politics in the modern era, the most efficient way to discipline the desires of the masses.

In order to imagine a democracy that would not be threatened by the pursuit of "egoistic" desires, the Endecja had to envision a form of political participation, engagement, and mobilization that would be tightly organized and disciplined. In the 1897 party program Popławski wrote that the Endecja's task was to "transform society into an organization of autonomous citizens, deciding consciously about their own fate." This did not, however, imply any support for such "external" freedoms as voting rights, free speech, or free assembly. Rather, Popławski wanted to establish "internal" freedom by instilling in the masses a sense of citizenship, a belief that they were participating in the national community. It did not matter what was done, or even if anything specific was accomplished: the point was to mobilize the masses, to involve them in "public life."[61] Władysław Jabłonowski, a rural activist for the Endecja, wrote in his memoirs that the movement's goal was not to focus on the material interests of the peasants, but to convince them that they were citizens, and as such were "just as responsible for the fate of the nation as its enlightened strata."[62] This was a concept of democracy that contained ample room for leadership. Although the people were to be integrated into the political process, the intelligentsia had to "express" or "represent" their needs—otherwise the "immaturity" or "backwardness" of the masses might lead them to advance socially divisive demands or become preoccupied with irrelevant concerns about material welfare. Dmowski's formulation was carefully worded: "Politics becomes national in the modern sense only when it steps forth as the representation of the aspirations of the national masses." Although he believed that a politician should not try "to impose upon the mass desires foreign to it," he still assigned to the intelligentsia the role of formulating a program articulating the "living desires of the masses."[63]

No matter how authoritarian the Endecja became, its publications continued to claim that the "popular strata" generated the movement's goals and policies. The voice of the people, however, had to be carefully mediated by more "mature" elements of society. In 1897 Dmowski defined a word that he assumed the peasant readers of *Polak* did not know: "democracy." Significantly, he located this vocabulary lesson within a conversation between Jan and Mateusz, two fictional peasants who had an ongoing discussion on the pages of *Polak*. Jan asked his friend the crucial question, "Just what is democracy?" Mateusz responded that it is something that exists in other European countries, where a parliament elected by "the nation" controls the government. Within such a system, the *lud*—if it was "enlightened" and if it "understood its own affairs"—would elect delegates who would defend its interests. Those who represented the people in parliament were, in turn, called "democrats." Jan then asked what a democrat could do in the Muscovite system. "He gives the *lud* books and newspapers," Mateusz responded, "enlightens [the *lud*] about its situation, attempts to get closer to the peasants in order to give them advice and help."[64] In a later installment Mateusz clarified that this enlightenment would be attained when the peasants came to understand their national identity and realize that the Tsar was not their rightful ruler. The peasants needed to "destroy ignorance [*ciemnota*, darkness] and establish education, a true Polish education," which would teach people that "things go better for those nations that have their own national government."[65] In other words, the enlightened peasant would recognize authority *within* his national community rather than outside of it. The call to democracy thus became a means of locating "the people" under a "national government," subject to new hierarchies.

Perhaps no one articulated the theme of organization more insistently than Balicki. As was cited above, in 1886 he had attacked liberalism for ignoring the "real" desires and needs of concrete individuals and for substituting representation for "real" democracy. At the turn of the century Balicki was as hostile toward liberalism as ever, but by then his critique was based on the inability of liberalism to ensure sufficient communal coherence. In a two-volume work from 1900 entitled *Parliamentarianism*, Balicki cautioned against the dangers of the unorganized mob. This term—"the mob"—was used by Balicki to describe the dark side of the people: "The spiritual characteristic of a mob consists of the peculiar feature, that as an accidental collectivity it does not have any permanent collective feeling (selfhood), any preformed personality." For a group to move out of this state, it had to construct a "tradition" that would allow it to act in an organized manner in the pursuit of specific goals that the community would set for itself in a "conscious" manner. A democracy could function, Balicki argued, only if the voters had been organized—if they were no longer a mob.[66] In a move typical of the National Democrats, Balicki shifted the focus of politics from "rights" (long a basic term in the vocabulary of Polish patriots) to "duties." In 1905 he wrote that democracy existed only when "the organization of society" was structured so as to involve "the widest social strata" in the "fulfillment of national obligations." The involvement of the masses in the public sphere was predicated upon their acceptance of a set of civic duties; only after one's "national obligations" were carried out could one enjoy the "rights" of a citizen. Balicki's democracy did not even claim to be egalitarian: instead, it was based on a "general hierarchy of social functions" which gave everyone a place in society and put an end to the "atomization" of individuals. He admitted that he was describing an "antiliberal democracy"—one that would prevent "rule by the mob" as well as "rule over the mob."[67]

The denouement of this line of reasoning came several years later when Dmowski, speaking at Popławski's funeral, completely inverted his old friend's slogan about subordinating everything to the needs of the *lud*. Popławski, said Dmowski, "bravely advanced the formula that the good of the *lud* is the good of the fatherland, that to raise up the *lud* was in the national interest. And he presented the principle that the *lud* should be just as concerned with the future of the fatherland as the other strata of the nation. . . . He loved the *lud* with all his heart, because he loved Poland in them."[68] This turned the message of *Głos* upside down. Having transformed the peasants back into a singular noun, the National Democrats argued that the most pressing need was to unite them/it behind the national cause. Dmowski had long ago abandoned the idea that the *lud* deserved protection for its own sake, and he had passed through the inclusive "all of us" phase. By the twentieth century Dmowski's *lud* was once again a subordinate stratum, but one that deserved praise and support only insofar as it embodied the nation.

With this sort of argumentation the National Democrats began to sound more and more conservative—a label that would have been anathema to any of the *niepokorni* in the 1880s or 1890s, but one the Endecja embraced in the early twentieth century. In 1903 *Przegląd Wszechpolski* called for the creation of a conservative party that could balance the "excesses" of democracy. "National society is like a living organism, in which the past, the present, and the future are tightly bound together," this anonymous author wrote. "It is necessary, therefore, to have a conservative party that will take great care so that the thread binding tradition with the demands of the current moment are not violently severed."[69] The movement's conservatism was not merely about preserving tradition: it was also a means to fortify Poland's existing elites. Balicki admitted that the Endecja's goal was to persuade the peasants to stop troubling the "rural citizenry" (*obywatelstwo*—an archaic and in this case highly ironic synonym for the nobility) in the name of "economic antagonisms," and turn instead "against the Russian invaders in the name of Poland."[70] Similarly, the National Democrats tried to prevent the industrial workers from upsetting the new urban hierarchies. The proletariat, warned the 1903 party program, lacked a "tradition" and an "ethical foundation." It was isolated from the rest of the nation by "divisive foreign influences," and had no "civic impulses." Therefore "improving the existence of the working stratum cannot be aimed at increasing its earnings or decreasing its working hours—more urgent today, still, is work on the toiling masses to ensure that increasing wages and hours of rest . . . will be used to elevate [the workers] to a higher level of human existence." Not surprisingly, this higher level entailed a "development of national feeling" and a "sense of union with all of society," so that the workers would no longer be vulnerable to "the slogans of class struggle and the international unity of the proletariat."[71] An 1899 essay in *Pochodnia* argued that strikes were appropriate only when they were directed against a foreign government. The same sort of industrial action would not be right if aimed at *Polish* factory owners, because then it would undermine national unity.[72]

By the early twentieth century the National Democratic attack on the socialists had broadened as the movement's preoccupation with social discord deepened. The result was an unprecedented emphasis on obedience and hierarchy. The workers, complained *Przegląd Wszechpolski*, were "recruited from among the darkest land-less population" and required firm leadership, but this was impossible as long as the socialists were inspiring distrust and hatred toward "the more enlightened elements of society." Thanks to the socialists, the workers were provoking the otherwise vir-tuous factory owners and starting unnecessary conflicts. "Today, when the worker looks on every superior as a person who drinks his blood with delight, that superior begins, despite himself, to repay the worker with the same." This author did not oppose the labor movement as such, but he insisted that it be separated from the "universal ambitions" of socialism and used as a tool to bring order to the working class.[73] The Endecja tried to accomplish this by forming the *Narodowy Związek Robotniczy* (Na-tional Worker's Union). One NZR manifesto proclaimed that the group would wel-come all those who wanted to work "for the good of all Poland and the concerns of the workers" (most emphatically in that order). All members of the Union, the text declared (in a revealing play on the old slogan of *Głos*) had to "subordinate their own interests to the needs of the nation."[74] As a National Democratic economist explained, the purpose of a trade union was not to "defend labor against the exploi-tation of capital," but to create institutional structures to better organize production and conflict resolution.[75]

The National Democrats made some attempts to develop their own theory of national political economy to accompany and justify their growing hostility toward labor unrest. On the simplest level, *Polak* tried to convince the peasants that eco-nomic injustice and inequality were caused by national oppression. An anonymous author declared that "the main cause of the lack of land, the backwardness, and in general the poverty of the Polish people is the rule of foreign governments in our country."[76] Another approach was represented by Stanisław Grabski, who attacked liberalism for "positing as the goal of the nation its material welfare, its economic development."[77] While such things were certainly important, Grabski admitted, they could never be taken in isolation, nor elevated as an ultimate objective. The highest goals were the independence and strength of the nation, and these required social co-hesion. It followed that the pursuit of development must never be allowed to weaken existing social hierarchies. "The goal of political economy," Grabski wrote, "is the most profitable formation of economic functions and the fullest development of the produc-tive forces of the nation *on the basis of the governing social system*."[78] Bolesław Nidzicki, another National Democratic economist, insisted that "the art of skillfully directing the economic functioning of society (that is, political economy) cannot, of course, see its task only in giving one class that which it takes from another. It must look above all at the entire economic life of the nation and its productive forces, which it ought to nurture." Nidzicki even opposed the eight-hour workday, because (he believed) it would cause capital to flee abroad. In fact, he wrote, any "experiments" would almost certainly backfire, so calls for fundamental changes were just "demagogy."[79]

This dramatic move to the right did not imply an acceptance of all aspects of the governing social system: the National Democrats were never comfortable with the principles of laissez-faire. The "blind play of competitive forces," Grabski wrote, would only lead to "social atomization," and this in turn would undermine national unity. Instead, the nation must "grant itself not only the right but the duty to consciously shape the mutual relations of the classes, as well as their relation to the national wealth. . . . In order to avoid the danger of the extreme atomization caused by economic forces that threaten the normal development of the national organism, [the nation] must aspire to gradually replace competition with coordination (in all the spheres of economic life where this is possible and necessary); the blind struggle of diverse interests [must be replaced by] planned cooperation."[80] In 1903 Piotr Panek argued that in any well-functioning economy there had to be clear lines of authority so as to facilitate central planning. "There must be someone who directs the work," he wrote; "there must be someone who distributes work to everyone and supervises its execution."[81]

That someone would be the National Democrats themselves, who would assume this role whether or not Poland quickly regained independence. In 1900 the National League announced that it was "strong enough to claim openly the national leadership."[82] Angered by assertions like this, the conservative writer Erazm Piltz complained that the Endecja was arrogantly and illegitimately assuming the role of an underground national government.[83] Balicki admitted that some National Democrats thought of themselves as the "moral government" of Poland, but he felt that this role was better described as an aspiration, not a reality. For the time being, he wrote, the Endecja was limited to "moral influence" rather than "moral compulsion," since it did not yet enjoy a "political monopoly." Nonetheless, Balicki continued, the National League was more than just an opposition party: it was, instead, a "governing party, working on behalf of the still nonexistent, but future Polish government."[84] Helena Ceysingerówna, an activist in the Society for National Education, believed that her superiors wanted to create "a sort of superstructure that . . . could replace to a certain degree the most important aspects of [the nation's] own statehood."[85] On one level none of this was new: in the 1840s (as we saw in chapter 1) August Cieszkowski attempted to create a "moral government," and in 1863 the leaders of the uprising formed a "national government." However, when placed within the worldview of National Democracy, the term "government" became darkly authoritarian. This was no longer a mere organizational form, a *means* of attaining a collective goal. The concept of order had been transformed into a fundamental prerequisite of national existence.

Balicki wrote in 1903 that society could be compared to one "great, independently living brain." Whereas he had earlier defended individuality against the tyranny of the majority, now he accepted "the existence of social soul distinct from the consciousness of individuals." This "soul" had its own structures, motives, needs, and goals: "The social spirituality possesses its own unconsciousness, its own selfhood [*jaźń*], its own individuality, its own method of thinking and a whole range of manifestations of feelings, thoughts, and will."[86] It followed from this integral vision of the nation that the first priority of any national movement had to be (as an anonymous author put it in 1900) the formation of a "national brain." A collective central nervous system would ensure "*unity, indivisibility*—these are the slogans of the Polish *raison d'état*. In these [slogans] lies the concept of the nation as a system with *one undivided life*."[87] Here was the voice of Żeromski's "romantic in a positivist hat," the idealist who longed to discover the national soul and the scientific realist who favored biological metaphors. More important, here was the voice of the authoritarian. Discipline—and the social cohesion it enforced—was much more than just a means to attain some national objective. Now the very existence of the nation's "one undivided life" depended on the presence of a national brain.

The Endecja would be that brain. A schoolteacher remembered how his life changed when he became a member of the National League in 1897: "Adjusting to organizational directions, my work became more coordinated and subordinated to the general program of the organization."[88] Documents from the time stress the need to "guard with the utmost care the unity of the movement," and the National League's statute affirmed "the principle of strict centralization, based on the unconditional obedience of lower organs to higher ones."[89] Superficially, none of this was unusual. Any illegal political group in the Russian Empire had to employ conspiratorial methods, and strict internal discipline was a matter of survival. But the National Democrats went far beyond this tactical consideration, elevating authority to the level of a general principle and extending it outside the bounds of the movement. The 1903 program of the Democrat National Party expressed the desire to "spread the organization across all the regions and all social spheres," thus ensuring "the strongest possible influence on society" and "making the willful action of individuals impossible."[90] According to an internal party document from 1894, the Union of Polish Youth (Zet) had been established in order to "train members for work in political organizations, to cultivate discipline in [those organizations] . . . [and thus] to direct the entire youth movement."[91] One National League member recalled that he had been instructed to "attain influence on society" by "organizing society into legal, cultural, and economic institutions" which he would then lead.[92] An anonymous author in *Pochodnia* lamented the existence of institutions outside the League's control. Otherwise intelligent and honest individuals, he complained, were working for the Red Cross or (worse) for state-run educational programs. Such activities were a result of "naïveté" and testified to the "collapse of political thinking." Could people not see, he wrote, that these groups were part of a plot by the Russian government "to deprive us of the unity of opinions, to bring out different viewpoints, to deprive us of unanimity." But there was a solution to this crisis: "It is necessary [to create] an organ, a machine working quietly and effectively, the commands of which must be obligatory for all. Today such an organ, such a moral government, is the National League, and its point of view, its tactics, its position must be unconditionally obligatory for all. . . . Today there is no social work here that can be conducted without us or alongside us."[93]

In 1904 Dmowski wrote that the National League deserved credit for "crystallizing opinion" in Poland. Because the movement was "an expression of the opinion of [society's] healthiest part," it was able to "guarantee the obedience" of Poland's "undisciplined elements."[94] A report he sent to Miłkowski echoed this theme. People in the Kingdom, the document affirmed, "have begun to look on the League as the only element of leadership, as the only internal authority able to hold the youth in check, capable not only of calling forth a movement but also of directing it and, if necessary, stopping it."[95] Often this approach was cast in military metaphors. As Dmowski put it, "The only salvation for us is to stop being an incoherent, loose mob, and change into a strongly organized, disciplined army."[96] The programatic statement for *Teka* promised "to create from [the youth] a strong and (insofar as possible) an organized whole—a disciplined army that they cannot dissolve. . . . Arming the soldier, it is still necessary to teach him to maneuver in accordance with his unit—it is necessary to create an army. We have written a lot about organization. It alone can teach order, discipline, and precision."[97] Elsewhere *Teka* dismissed "false ideas about individual freedom. Our real misfortune is that untimely criticism which commands us to reason when it is necessary *to act*."[98] Taken to its logical extreme, this reasoning could generate totalitarian desires. In 1901 one National Democratic author described his ambition to "bind more strongly than ever, than anywhere on earth, all thoughts, desires, and feelings of all strata of the nation into one feeling."[99]

This sort of proto-fascist rhetoric was just below the surface at the turn of the century, kept there by the memory of *Głos*. Even as the split with the socialists deepened beyond repair, most patriotic activists continued to cling to the tattered remnants of their youthful radicalism. This restraint ended in 1905. This year of revolution brought the specter of social unrest before the eyes of the National Democrats as never before, thus confirming their worst fears of disorder. Afterwards the rhetoric of discipline and authority became sharper than ever, and whatever democratic pretensions the movement still had were finally jettisoned. Universal franchise had once been sacred to the *niepokorni*; now *Przegląd Wszechpolski* expressed *fear* that the revolution might bring democracy to the Russian Empire.

> The right to vote is not a natural right, with which every inhabitant enters the world, . . . but is really an obligation placed on citizens. . . . Denying this to those elements which constitute the strength of the nation, in which the nation expresses its vitality, would be a great loss, and thus [our] party hopes to expand [the vote] to the politically mature or maturing popular elements. However, being guided by a doctrine which commands that this be granted to everyone conceals within itself the danger of warping the political life of the country.[100]

One manifesto issued by the National League in 1905 declared that "the recent events in our country have clearly demonstrated the danger that threatens us because of a lack of a broader organization." Strikes were one manifestation of disorder, but the National Democrats promised to put an end to such foolishness. The movement would gather together "all thinking elements" of society into a national party dedicated to "the creation in the country of a strongly organized national opinion, ensuring it internal order, the moral direction of all collective action, and through this the assurance that society would not be forced into acts contrary to its will."[101] As one Endek later recalled, in 1905 the campaign against russification was a secondary concern, because the National League was primarily mobilized against the forces of disorder and social division within Poland.[102] Dmowski wrote to Miłkowski at the time that the socialists had "turned for vengeance on their own society, destroying it with strikes, robbing, murdering bourgeois industrialists and nationalists (the latter sometimes paid them back in kind). . . . Such are the characteristics of our situation. A struggle with two anarchies, both governmental and socialist."[103] According to a leaflet from 1905, the workers' movement had "turned above all against its own society," serving the interests of the Russians. "Strength does not depend on letting mobs loose," the brochure argued, "but on the ability to rule over them and direct them to a goal, predetermined from above."[104] In an often-reprinted 1905 article, "The Foundations of Polish Politics," Dmowski declared that "excessive tolerance for divisive views and aspirations would be national suicide." He considered it imperative "to organize a strong public opinion, guarding the leading principles of national behavior. . . . We must create unity in those areas in which there is only one path for the nation. . . . The nation becomes the master of its fate not only when it has many good sons, but also when it possesses enough strength to restrain its bad ones."[105]

The unrealized goal of the Endecja was to build enough strength to restrain Poland's bad sons, to create the "state within a state" that would allow Poland to "act" once again. Independence and statehood were obviously important objectives for the Endecja, but only insofar as they served to further the authority and discipline needed to organize "the mob." After 1905, tactical considerations led Dmowski to enter the Russian Duma and thus to set aside (temporarily) his demands for independence. This highly controversial move (which led to a split in the ranks of the Endecja) makes sense if we realize that the movement's goal was not just statehood. As should be evident by now, to define nationalism as the quest for independent political existence is simplistic, and ignores the fundamental question of how the nation is positioned within historical time. For those who placed national unity (and thus the "realization" of the nation) in the future, after a chiliastic moment of revolution, statehood became an almost incidental marker of international justice. It became difficult to speak of social discipline in the present, since the future utopia could come only after a period of disorder and class conflict. A nation thus located in time could not easily become a site for authority, at least not until a moment of revolution arrived and a socialist leadership began to construct a new world. In contrast, powerful disciplinary desires were unleashed when the nation was removed from this sort of teleological narrative, when it had to construct its own internal cohesion in the present so as to survive in an eternally struggle-ridden world. For the Polish nationalists who abandoned prophetic historical time, the state became not a goal but a means: the optimal way to organize the nation along hierarchical lines so that it could face its enemies. It remained only to determine who those enemies were.

7

The National Struggle

Perhaps André Malraux was exaggerating when he said, "a man who is both active and pessimistic is a fascist or will be one," but this dictum does highlight an important link between the exaltation of "the deed," the repudiation of progressive historical time, and the emergence of the radical right.[1] Although a belief in historical evolution still dominated European intellectual life in the 1880s, several pessimistic counternarratives of stasis or degradation were already in circulation. By the early 1890s an important segment of the Polish intelligentsia came to believe that progress was an illusion, that struggle in its most violent forms defined all social relations, and that morality was based on power. This dark vision of the world did not lead to resigned passivity, because for many young people the overpowering urge for action remained. As Malraux would have predicted, when the force of will was combined with hopelessness, the result (in Poland) was a disturbing new ideological formation: National Democracy.

In 1895 Roman Dmowski wrote a series of essays called "National Unity," in which he coined a National Democratic mantra: "National thought, if it is to be vibrant, cannot be cut off from reality, cannot be derived from some sort of doctrine. Instead, it must be tied tightly to the essential conditions of life today, it must take that life into account and base its own development on it. . . . National thought, if it is to be healthy, cannot feed on fantasies but must take its nourishment from everyday experience."[2] The socialists and the liberals (and all "humanitarians") were not merely wrong, they were *unrealistic*—as judged against the Endecja's version of reality. In 1902 Dmowski described his worldview as "a philosophy of national struggle and oppression. Perhaps. But what of it, if that struggle and that oppression are realities and universal peace and universal freedom are fictions? One must have the courage to look the truth in the eye."[3] Reality, for the Endecja, was a world in which justice, rights, humanity, progress, peace, and brotherhood were naïve fantasies, and in which oppression, expansion, and conflict defined international relations. The National Democrats stripped the "struggle for survival" from its liberal moorings and embraced an unmitigated, unending war of all against all. In the process they constructed high walls of exclusion around the Polish nation, with solidarity and authority inside and hatred and violence outside.

In chapter 8 we will explore this bleak landscape in more detail, but first we need to understand how it became possible to imagine such a world—or more specifically, how this vision came to penetrate the conceptual framework of Polish nationalism, which had previously been so utopian and idealistic. On the most general level we could explain this belief in the *bellum omnium contra omnes* by referring to broad European trends—the late nineteenth century, after all, was the age of Heinrich von Treitschke and Friedrich Nietzsche, and the era in which modern anti-Semitism became a powerful force all over Europe. But even if we could identify unambiguous lines of influence (which we cannot), this allusion to a wider context in European political thought only begs the question: what made it possible for the radical intelligentsia (both in Poland and elsewhere), once so committed to building an earthly paradise, once such fervent believers in the power of revolution, to abandon all this in exchange for an unending future of "struggle and oppression"? This chapter will answer this question by examining the most prominent manifestation of such collective animosity: anti-Semitism.

Certainly the Jews had long constituted an important "other" for the Polish imagination, but difference alone is hardly adequate as an explanation for the hatreds of the twentieth century. The mere presence of diversity was not in itself enough to produce rigid social boundaries: cultural plurality had to be positioned within a doctrine of national unity and international struggle before it could generate a rhetoric of conflict and exclusion. As we have seen, the relationship between Jews and Poles could be configured in a number of ways, not all of them predicated on antagonism (let alone violent hatred). The historian Ryszard Bender repeats a common fallacy when he writes, "The Jewish population [in Poland] possessed a particularly strong position in trade. . . . This fact provoked, in some years, a boycott of Jewish stores. . . . The fact that in interwar Poland one quarter of the secondary school and university students were Jewish caused nationalist campaigns for introducing a *numerus clausus* in higher education."[4] But the "fact" that Jews were concentrated in trade and had higher rates of school attendance became meaningful—became a *cause* of violence— only when "the Jew" was defined as "the enemy." Before it became possible to hate the Jews, it was necessary to perceive them as irrevocably alien, both invulnerable to assimilation and implacably hostile. The Polish–Jewish conflict did not simply emerge from objective social conditions; it was necessary to give meaning to difference before difference could become meaningful. Diversity is always present in the world, but the idea of an antagonistic and eternally unfamiliar "other," the *concept* of "them," has a specific intellectual history. And that history, though obviously linked in some general sense to a particular socioeconomic environment, developed according to its own internal dynamics, which we will explore in this chapter. Too often scholars have taken popular anti-Semitism to be a cultural constant which cynical intellectuals and politicians exploit in order to gain support.[5]

Without denying the existence of popular stereotypes and even animosities, I argue that these gain political meaning (and virulence) only when they become part of a public discursive framework—and such frameworks are always more than just emanations of popular attitudes.

For most of the nineteenth century judeophobia existed alongside but distinctly *outside* the patriotic tradition. Until the 1880s Polish patriots were constrained by the concept of "for our freedom and yours," or by the less lofty but no less universalistic vocabulary of liberalism, and to find anti-Semitism one had to look to the Church or to the peasantry. "Good patriots" considered it vulgar (or at least counterproductive) to reinforce anti-Jewish stereotypes or to encourage Polish–Jewish conflict. Populist, antimodernist anti-Semitism first appeared in the press in the 1880s, parallel to similar developments in France, Germany, Hungary, Austria, and Russia, but even then most urban intellectuals and political activists—even most conservatives—remained aloof. A "respectable" Polish patriot was not supposed to be openly anti-Semitic, and a fundamental reconfiguration of nationalism was necessary in order to bring explicit hatreds to the public realm. When this happened, the Jews were not the only ones affected. The Jews were the first community to be defined by some Polish intellectuals as an irredeemable other, but the rhetoric used to discuss the "Jewish question" soon spread. By the mid-1890s it was possible for the authors at *Głos* to perceive a world filled with conflict and conquest, not only between Poles and Jews but between Poles and Germans, Russians, Ukrainians, Lithuanians, and (in theory) just about anyone. The doctrine of struggle would serve as a virus that would weaken and transfigure the intellectual landscape in Poland, setting the stage for the emergence of the twentieth-century radical right.

And this returns us to the central question: how did it become possible for "good patriots" to imagine such a hate-filled world? For this to occur, a number of tendencies within the Polish intelligentsia had to intersect: (1) the national ideal had to become a "real" human community; (2) the optimism that had been sustained even in the 1870s had to be abandoned; and (3) the vocabulary of sociology had to merge with an agenda of action. As long as Poland was a transcendent object of desire, an ideal that motivated and guided human action, it was unnecessary to discuss issues of diversity or homogeneity, conflict or cooperation. The nation of the romantics was not (or at least not only) a sociological entity, so its ethnic composition, its geographical borders, and its social and political form were all of secondary concern (and sometimes entirely epiphenomenal). To speak of the nation in the 1830s was to talk about history and meaning, not about the boundedness of social space. The lasting contribution of positivism was to bring disrepute to this style of national imagining. Świętochowski, Prus, and the other liberals at papers like *Prawda* and *Przegląd Tygodniowy* relocated the nation within a "realistic" and "scientific" discourse and cast their gaze on the linguistic and cultural features of Poland. From the time these papers attained their dominant position in Polish intellectual life (from the early 1870s), it was deemed important to consider what language people spoke, how they worshiped, and where they lived. Society became an object of empirical study, and ethnography was transformed from a foundation for historiosophical hermeneutics into a sociological database.

But the positivists' scientistic worldview was only a necessary antecedent—not a sufficient cause—for the emergence of the fin de siècle rhetoric of hate. Because the positivists continued to believe in historical time (in the progressive force of the liberal narrative), they were able to sustain tolerance for diversity even as they concentrated on the social foundations of unity. The positivists were fundamentally optimistic, believing that *with time* the Jews, Ukrainians, Belorussians, and Lithuanians would be assimilated to the "higher" and more "progressive" culture of the Poles. Świętochowski and his colleagues introduced a new attention to sociocultural cohesion, but they did not need to be obsessed with heterogeneity because they thought it was destined to fade away. This position may not seem like enlightened multiculturalism by our standards, but neither was it equivalent to the violent doctrine of struggle and exclusion that would develop later. This was the progressive intolerance of liberalism, not the chauvinistic intolerance of the extreme right. Although the two might be related, the one does not inevitably lead to the other.

When intellectuals began to question these hopeful prophecies in the 1890s, it became harder to sustain the idea that Poland could be open and pluralist, even temporarily. As we saw in chapter 4, the young radicals known to historians as the *niepokorni* ("the defiant ones") longed for a return to action, because they could no longer believe that history, on its own, would bring about the new world of freedom and justice. Embedded within even the wildest dreams of the students of the 1880s was a fundamental pessimism, a fear that if they did not *do* something, neither revolution nor independence would ever come. This preoccupation with action led to a concern for identifying collective actors, and we saw in the last chapter how the various factions of the *niepokorni* tried to cast the Polish *lud* (the people) in this role. This brings us to the final piece of the puzzle: in the postpositivist age it was necessary to specify with greater precision than ever before who constituted the Polish *lud*. The positivists had already provided an answer to this question by defining Poland as an ethnocultural space, but for the young National Democrats that space no longer existed within a historical narrative, and it was no longer possible to predict optimistically that cultural unity (a necessary predicate for mass political action, they believed) would come at some future date, thanks to a process of gradual assimilation and acculturation. The National Democrats had to *create* such unity, just as they thought it necessary to intervene actively in history in order to create the future. In the positivists' world of historical progress, the obstacle to unity was "backwardness"; in the Endecja's world of willful subjects, the disunity within Poland and the country's lack of independence could be explained only by uncovering the intrigues of a national enemy. Within this Manichean framework, Spencerism took on a frightening new meaning.

Unleashing the Struggle for Survival

Before 1863 there had been little room for hatred in Polish discussions of the nation. The slogan "for our freedom and yours" was not just a statement of universalist idealism, but a reflection of the deeply felt need to support the Polish cause with a theory of justice. Whatever the romantic patriots really felt about the Russians, they found it difficult to talk about collective animosity. Even anti-Semitism was momentarily silenced (albeit not actually banished) during the 1863 Uprising. The collapse of the insurrection and the rise of positivism initiated a move away from such an open worldview, but the change was gradual, tempered by the liberalism of the *młoda prasa.* The positivists made the community concrete (and thus bounded), and they introduced the dangerous new motto of "the struggle for survival," but they also reconfigured their Spencerism within a Bucklean framework of "intellectual progress." This evolutionary perspective made the positivists as universalistic as the romantics, and they could not easily articulate hatred toward any foreign community. The very concept of "foreign" played only a minor role in their vocabulary; their real enemy was backwardness (much as the enemy in 1863 had been tyranny). They wanted to "develop" the nation, so fighting (or hating) was pointless.

The positivist approach to communal boundaries can be seen most clearly in their approach to the "Jewish question." When we look back on the *młoda prasa* through the prism of twentieth-century anti-Semitism, they appear benign in comparison. They considered themselves well disposed toward the Jews, and both contemporaries (usually opponents) and some historians have described them as philo-Semitic.[6] An author in *Przegląd Tygodniowy*, for example, called anti-Semitism "an echo of medieval instincts . . . like rust disfiguring the physiognomy of our century."[7] During the era of positivist dominance in Warsaw (from the early 1870s to the early 1880s) Jewish conversion dropped off precipitously even as the Jewish population of the city was rising, suggesting that Jews felt more able to assert their identity *as Jews.* The Kingdom's only Polish language, assimilationist Jewish newspaper, *Izraelita*, was barely able to attract 450 subscribers (at a time when the Jewish population surpassed one million).[8] Despite these tentative manifestations of security within the Jewish community, the positivists' redefinition of the nation closed the door on a form of multicultural nationalism that had, for a brief moment in 1863, seemed possible in Poland. The romantics had been able to embrace the Jews as Jews, because the nation of the early nineteenth century depended on the "act" rather than on any external characteristics. The positivists, on the other hand, literally *embodied* the nation—that is, they defined it as a corporeal community, marked by observable sociological features such as language, folk practices, and place of residence. Describing the nation in this way invariably entailed the construction of boundaries and the establishment of membership criteria. The positivists embraced those Jews willing to become Poles, but only if they looked, sounded, and behaved like Poles. It was no longer enough to join the national cause; now Jews were going to have to *be* Polish.

In the 1860s it momentarily appeared that Polish intellectuals might soften their uncompromising insistence that assimilation was the price for tolerance. Even the positivists, whose commitment to ethnography made it hard to imagine a multicultural nation, maintained a tactful silence regarding "the Jewish question" well into the 1870s. Only later did this issue become unavoidable. On the one hand, an increasingly vocal anti-Semitism was emerging in Russia, Germany, Austria, and Hungary, and by the early 1880s such voices could be heard in the Kingdom as well. On the other hand, Jews themselves were exploring new forms of identity within the Zionist movement and eventually within the socialist *Bund*, thus challenging the idea that Jews and Poles ought to be seen as two elements within the same nation. Pressured from both sides, the Warsaw liberals began discussing Jewish identity, assimilation, and anti-Semitism. When pogroms broke out in Russia over Easter weekend in 1881, Aleksander Świętochowski warned Warsaw's Jews that they needed to accelerate the pace of assimilation for their own safety. He still retained a host of anti-Jewish stereotypes (he spoke often of their "Asiatic" ways), but in good liberal form he imagined a better future in which Jews would become Poles (or rather, Europeans) and the threat of anti-Jewish violence would simply fade away.[9] A few weeks later he spoke with pride about the calm in Warsaw during the Russian pogroms. The Poles, he boasted, "knew how to control their impulses," and the Polish press had effectively appealed for calm. With this in mind, he repeated, the Jews ought to repay the "hospitality" and "honest protection" they enjoyed in Poland by assimilating. He drew a sharp distinction between "real *Jews*, that dark Asian mass which uses a foreign language, lives by different customs, and grafts onto the national trunk only insofar as it is necessary to suck out its living juices," and "those who in civil documents figure as believers in the Old Testament, but in spirit and life, aspirations and goals are Poles." The latter had nothing to do with the "Jewish question," Świętochowski claimed, because they had "fulfilled their obligations." The former, however, had to be forced "with the most strict ruthlessness" to assimilate. The government should not permit "even one Jew to escape general education, even one Old Testament organization or even one school to exist."[10]

These arguments were intensified after Christmas of 1881, when a violent pogrom in Warsaw destroyed the peace Świętochowski had described with such pride. For three days riots continued in Warsaw, until the Russian authorities finally decided to intervene, arresting 2,600 people. The Warsaw pogrom left two people dead, twenty-four injured, and almost a thousand families financially devastated. In the months that followed about one thousand Jews from Warsaw emigrated to the United States.[11] Świętochowski was forced to admit, in an article entitled "Without Illusions," that "among the European nations we do not constitute an ideal exception." He was unsparing in his criticism of the intelligentsia for not doing enough to combat the hostilities of the *lud* and for not welcoming assimilated Jews as Poles. At the same time, however, he repeated his attacks on "Jewish fanaticism," which he considered just as bad as "Christian fanaticism." He made a revealing parallel between the Jews and American Indians: both groups, he believed, were destined to be absorbed by a "higher" European culture.[12] Eliza Orzeszkowa responded to the 1881 pogroms with a small book entitled, *On the Jews and the Jewish Question*. As she put it, her reaction to the "Warsaw tempest" could be summarized in three words: disgrace, pity, and regret. "Disgrace over the antisocial and anticivilized acts; extreme pity for the suffering; burning regret that the fruits of so many years of effort by noble and enlightened minds had once again fallen into the flames of hatred." Like Świętochowski, she condemned her compatriots for their "prejudices and superstitions, derived directly from the treasury of medieval legends." Orzeszkowa's only complaint about the Jews of Poland was that they remained separate and resistant to "enlightenment."

In this regard, she continued, they were similar to the Polish peasants, who were also excluded from the nation by their ignorance and their lower level of "civilization."[13]

By the mid-1880s the positivists were drawing a sharp line around the Jewish community. They welcomed assimilated intellectuals and businessmen with open arms, but only if they stopped calling themselves Jews. When Józef Nusbaum, a famous biologist, wrote in 1886 that he wanted to be both a Jew and a Pole at the same time, Prus reacted angrily: "Mr. Nusbaum is not a Jew, because instead of going around in a dirty gabardine and eternally unbuttoned pants, he dresses in a European manner. Instead of speaking jargon [Yiddish], he speaks perfectly correct Polish. Instead of reading the Talmud, he studies natural law. Instead of becoming a dubious mediator, a usurer, a fence, or the manager of a public house . . . he took up medicine and literature. Jewishness does not so much refer to descent and religion, but rather to darkness, pride, separatism, laziness, and exploitation."[14] But despite all this obvious, often ugly prejudice, the positivists were never able to close the doors to the Polish community—their nation was both bounded and open, carefully delineated yet permeable. Because their appropriation of the struggle for survival was linked to intellectual progress rather than violence and conquest, they found it dangerous to talk about any sort of conflict between Jews and Poles. Instead, they cast both communities within an evolutionary narrative that would ultimately lead everyone toward "civilization." This utopia resembled their own world much more closely than it did Jewish society, but the assertion of universality was significant, even if its substance was grounded in European, Christian norms.

Insofar as the struggle for survival played a role in the *młoda prasa*'s rhetoric—and we have seen how they contained and domesticated this dangerous idea—the Jews and the Poles were rarely cast as opposing communities. They were, instead, striving toward the same goal: a "civilized," secular, all-encompassing nation. Świętochowski did evoke the struggle for survival when talking about the Jews, but he used this phrase to call for tolerance and assimilation, not conflict. "The exclusion of masses of nominal or actual believers in the Old Testament from the bosom of the nation," he wrote, "deprives us of a very significant sum of strength in the struggle for survival."[15] Here the Jews were either one of "us" or an untapped resource; they were not cast as "them," the enemy. Eliza Orzeszkowa described a struggle for survival between the Polish peasantry and the rural Jews, but she quickly backed away from the consequences of this phrase. Comparing these two groups, she wrote that "one is active and sober, the other helpless and penetrated through and through with the bad habit of alcoholism. Naturally, in the struggle for survival the first must necessarily win more often than the second. . . . Is it appropriate to complain to the Jews about their nearly total sobriety and to cure them of this in order to make their strength equal to the strength of our drunken peasant villagers?"[16] Orzeszkowa was using Spencerian language, but she was not trying to set Poles against Jews in a struggle for survival. Quite the contrary: she was appropriating this slogan only as a means to advance what she saw as a broader agenda (sobriety). In the end she argued that Jews should abandon their "superstition" and Poles should discard their alcohol; both should move (together) toward "civilization."

Even as Orzeszkowa wrote this text, however, an alternative discourse had already penetrated the Polish press. As late as the 1870s the Jewish press of the Kingdom could dismiss anti-Semitism as a German problem, with confidence that if such attitudes appeared in Poland they would be rejected as contrary to the patriotic tradition or dismissed as medieval outbursts. By the 1880s, however, assimilationist papers like the Warsaw weekly *Izraelita* were forced to devote up to half of their articles to defensive polemics.[17] Orzeszkowa complained in 1881 that Poles read only foreign books about the Jews, with one unpleasant exception: "We, who have lived with ten times more Jews for 800 years . . . have [only] Mr. Jan Jeleński."[18] This was a reference to one of the most infamous writers of late nineteenth-century Warsaw, the editor of a vitriolic anti-Semitic magazine called *Rola* (The Field). Jeleński was hated by nearly everyone in the Polish intelligentsia: he was devoutly Catholic at a time when anticlericalism was in vogue, he was pro-Russian, and he was deeply conservative. But he was nonetheless important, because he was both the first Polish writer to call himself an anti-Semite and the first to appropriate the Spencerian vocabulary of struggle to describe a world of irreconcilable hostility.

Jeleński was born in 1845 in a village in central Poland.[19] His parents were from an impoverished noble line, and although they managed to put him through the Kielce gimnazjum, they lacked the money needed to send him to Warsaw University. He worked a series of jobs as a telegraph operator, a court clerk, a train conductor, and even a bricklayer, but his great aspiration was to be a member of the Warsaw intelligentsia—an ambition blocked by his family's poverty. Nonetheless, he read voraciously and even managed to publish a few articles in *Przegląd Tygodniowy* in 1872.[20] In 1875 Jeleński turned his insatiable appetite for books into a business opportunity by opening a private lending library in Warsaw. This venture proved to be amazingly successful and within a few years Jeleński was a wealthy man—a rise that led one of his opponents to admit that he was a "model of self-help" (while others insisted that he must have received financial backing from the Russians).[21] Despite a biography that reads like a Samuel Smiles tract, and despite his contributions to *Przegląd Tygodniowy,* Jeleński was no liberal. By 1874 he had already published an antiliberal and anti-Semitic brochure entitled "Our World of Finance," and two years later he released the text that his followers would later cite as their Bible, *The Jews, the Germans, and Us.* In the wake of the Warsaw pogrom of 1881, Jeleński added salt to the city's wounds by purchasing a struggling agricultural magazine and converting it into Poland's first explicitly anti-Semitic periodical: *Rola.*

It is difficult to measure the depth of Jeleński's popularity. *Rola* had about 2,000 subscribers and was able to sell two pages of ads (more than *Przegląd Tygodniowy, Prawda,* or *Głos,* but fewer than the mass-circulation *Kurier Warszawski*).[22] On the other hand, we can hardly find any members of the intelligentsia who admitted to reading the paper. Kozicki wrote in his memoirs that "everyone" in Warsaw disapproved of Jeleński's anti-Semitism, so *Rola* had to find a readership in the countryside (particularly among parish priests).[23] The positivist papers, when they did not simply ignore *Rola,* labeled it a "nest of libel," called Jeleński an "idiot," and described his "shouting" as an attempt to "fish for subscribers in the turbid waters of tribal and religious hatred."[24] *Kurier Warszawski* initially carried paid advertisements for *Rola*, but after a few months the editors began complaining about Jeleński's "noisy but usually empty clichés," and soon afterwards the paper refused to print any more of his ads.[25] Even the Catholic papers, which shared many of Jeleński's views, attacked him for "provoking the estates" and "elevating passions" (i.e., for encouraging pogroms). They called upon him to adopt a more "positive" tone, based on "Christian love."[26] Not even the National Democrats wanted to claim Jeleński. In 1898 *Przegląd Wszechpolski* described him as an "uncouth consumer of the most absurd ideas laying around the sacristy" and as little more than a "street speaker."[27] We do not study Jeleński, then, as an example of the sort of writer who could speak to the Warsaw intelligentsia, be they positivists or *niepokorni*, or even conservatives. He had violated their codes and stepped beyond the bounds of what they considered acceptable public rhetoric. He had, metaphorically, been exiled to the countryside.[28] His work can thus help us delineate the limits of the intelligentsia's world and understand what the National Democrats had to overcome before they could make anti-Semitism respectable for the writers, artists, journalists, and politicians of urban Poland.

In *The Jews, the Germans, and Us*, Jeleński introduced a new way of talking about international relations. "It is not enough to know if the Jews and Germans, as strata made up of individuals, are such or so, are bad or good, are guilty or innocent," he wrote. "It is, rather, necessary above all *to consider what sort of position we have to take right now vis-à-vis those two elements.*"[29] Jeleński dismissed the positivist discussions of the virtues of Jewish "sobriety" (as Orzeszkowa put it), their harmful "Asiatic ways" (Świętochowski's phrase), or their "ruthlessness" (Prus' favorite term). The "nature" of the Jews should be set aside as irrelevant; it was no longer a question of how the Jews could be made more like the Poles, but how "we" should deal with "them." Turning to the Germans, Jeleński asked rhetorically:

> When have we ever been in a state of agreement and friendship with the
> Germans? History will answer us: *never*. For centuries germanism has set upon
> the peaceful inhabitants along the Elbe, Oder, and Vistula, who have nothing
> rapacious in their nature, and for centuries struggle has been unavoidable. . . .
> From those prehistoric epochs to the present moment the intention of the
> Germans has not changed at all, and therefore today the struggle seems to be as
> necessary and unavoidable as it is necessary for one who is attacked to preserve
> his own individuality, his own existence.[30]

Jeleński described a "struggle between tribes," in which it was pointless to try to reform the other side. Instead, it was necessary to resolve "our" weaknesses so as to better compete with "them." A close colleague of Jeleński, Konstanty Wzdulski, wrote several years later that the Poles themselves were responsible for "the Jewish question" as long as they refused to recognize the Jews as foreigners. "We let the wolf into the sheep pen and the wolf did what wolves do," he wrote, "but the shepherd did not fulfill his obligation—he did not defend the flock entrusted to him—and the responsibility falls on him, not on anyone else." Just as wolves had an unchanging nature, so would the Jews always be dangerous aliens. To imagine that one could reform or assimilate the Jewish community was as absurd as trying to domesticate wild beasts.[31] Thus we see the two fundamental innovations mentioned above: the Jews were reconceptualized as an eternal other and (even more important) as an irreconcilable foe.

This acceptance of the Spencerian struggle for survival distinguished Jeleński from the traditional right, and *Rola*'s contributors regularly used the phrase "modern conservatism."[32] Even an unapologetic reactionary like Teodor Jeske-Choiński could write, perhaps ironically, "We are all positivists today."[33] At the same time (paradoxically), *Rola* tried to exemplify an older conservatism based on tradition, stability, authority, and faith, and Jeleński regularly praised the Church, the nobility, and even the Tsar.[34] It was not easy to reconcile the conservative ideals of the aristocracy and the clerical hierarchy while at the same time constructing a "modern" conservatism based on "science" and an amoral vision of eternal struggle. When Wzdulski proposed the immediate expulsion of all Jews, he apologetically admitted that "such seemingly inhuman ostracism" would return Polish law to the Middle Ages. He was angered by the "need" to adopt a brutalized Spencerism in his war with the Jews.

[The Jews] are the most dangerous and most threatening representatives of the struggle for survival, against which gentleness, sweetness, patience, and above all justice and Christian morality are only infantile illusions. The Jews are a nation of positivists—and they will never betray the principle of "whoever is stronger is better." For several thousand years before the appearance of today's positive-materialist science, they were total positivists in practice—and aside from matter, that is, earthly wealth, they saw nothing more lofty.

This reasoning drove Wzdulski to a point of frustration often demonstrated on the pages of *Rola:* he wanted to embrace an unqualified vision of struggle, but he could not do so. He believed that "the idea of brotherhood is a false idea . . . it has brought those societies which believe in it not gains, but losses." Nonetheless, Wzdulski described this as a "Christian" idea, for which countries like Poland had to pay a heavy price. The same "moral" principles that he offered as the mark of Christian superiority were also, in his view, the cause of Poland's downfall.[35] Similarly, Jeske-Choiński recognized the conflict between an ideology of struggle and any ethical system, be it Christian or "modern":

The struggle for survival is not a song of forgiveness and mutual love, because [it involves] a defense of the exploited against the exploiters. And wherever people defend themselves, the meaning of "humanitarian considerations," even the most just, vanishes. . . . Unqualified tolerance, particularly regarding religion, is a valuable achievement of our century. It is only unfortunate that the struggle for survival has formed us differently, that it forces us necessarily to exclusivity. There are too many Jews among us and we have too little time to attempt to incorporate them into our organism. Anyway, would such an experiment be successful? . . . Let us learn solidarity and exclusivity from the Jews.[36]

This tone of regret was common. It was as if Jeske-Choiński were accepting a doctrine of unending struggle and exclusivity against his will.

With this cluster of arguments Jeleński cut himself off from nearly all his contemporaries. Catholics and conservatives could not accept his Spencerian vocabulary or his critique of Christian ethics, the positivists could hardly approve of someone who directed most of his ire against liberalism, and the *niepokorni* were deeply opposed to his loyalism.[37] *Rola*'s anti-Semitism might seem to constitute the first step from positivism to National Democracy, but we cannot get from Jeleński to Dmowski without identifying a respectable way for a progressive urban intellectual to talk about eternal communal conflict and hate. Such a formula would be hard to find: if it was difficult for a Catholic like Jeleński to cope with the ramifications of unmitigated struggle, it would be even more troubling for democrats or socialists to do so.

The first to try to find a point of contact between irredeemable struggle and liberalism would be a paradoxical figure named Ludwik Gumplowicz (1838–1909). Gumplowicz was a self-defined liberal who deprived liberalism of its ethical foundation, a Jew who developed a brutal theory of "racial struggle," and a professor at the University of Graz who published most of his work in German while claiming that his ideas "grew from Polish soil."[38] Although he was a Krakovian by birth, his liberalism ensured that he would find a wider audience in the Kingdom than in Galicia, and he contributed regularly to the Warsaw press. Gumplowicz first attracted international attention with his sensationally titled 1883 book, *Der Rassenkampf*, and his reputation was firmly established two years later with the more systematic *Outline of Sociology* (the Polish version of which was translated and revised by Gumplowicz himself in 1887).[39] "Not an idyllic state of peace," he wrote in the latter text, ". . . but eternal war has been the normal state of humanity for all time. Indeed, the history of humanity, just as the living present, offers us a picture of unending struggles of tribes against tribes, peoples and nations against peoples and nations, states against states. This is the main content of history. The goal of these struggles is always the same, namely (to use the most general expression), to exploit others."[40] Gone was the Spencerian faith that such violence was part of an evolutionary process, that this struggle might lead anywhere or accomplish anything. Gone even was the suggestion that violence might someday be replaced by a less destructive "industrial war" (as Spencer himself had proposed). For Gumplowicz, the rapaciousness of humanity ensured that savagery would never end. As he put it, "Only when strength fails does strife cease."[41]

This image of conflict was not limited to international relations. Gumplowicz defined the state as "the organized control of the minority over the majority" and traced its origin to the efforts of a "superior class" to "make the most productive use of the subject classes." Regardless of the form such "oppression" took, all social relations were based on exploitation.[42] Writing in *Prawda* in 1884, Gumplowicz scoffed at the idea that nations were based on feelings of solidarity: "The nation did not grow from the family, and its moral principle is not familiarity. It grew from the soil of the state, the principle of which is not family love, not mutual dedication but— even if it sounds ugly—mutual exploitation, forced dependence on one another, a government based on the dominance of some over others."[43] This argument did not lead to a socialist conclusion, because Gumplowicz refused to accept any moment of revolutionary transcendence, or even any theoretical alternative to exploitation. He denied justice any role in his world and he accepted the Hobbesean conclusion that only the state could establish peace. "As strivings increase," he wrote, "the state, which was called into being to satisfy them, is driven to further conquests of territory and power. But the same tendency that animates the state as a whole also animates each social division within it. The only difference is that its manifestation is limited by established political relations to a struggle for control by peaceful means, while outside the state it breaks out in bloody and destructive wars."[44]

Paradoxically, Gumplowicz considered himself to be a liberal, with a preference for peaceful social norms and "civilized" culture. He wanted to believe in a better world, but his sociology would not allow him to do so. Even the most glorious products of art and literature, he wrote, were possible only because a privileged elite had gained the time and resources necessary for creative activity by exploiting the masses. As he put it in *Prawda*, "In the end one must acknowledge that without conquest, domination, and exploitation, there would be no civilization."[45] But regardless of the state's foundation in violence, regardless of the fact that "property everywhere and always arose as a result of *conquest* and constitutes a *means of domination*," there was no alternative. "Maybe it is unfortunate," he wrote, "but there is no other choice. Either anarchy and barbarism, or personal property as a means of domination."[46]

Gumplowicz thus constructed a vision of society characterized by eternal conflict. A conservative might contend that the state was a source of stability and justice in a vicious world, a nationalist might argue that the integral community could overcome the tensions of class conflict, a socialist might claim that the proletarian revolution would end all wars, and a liberal might believe that, with time, progress and the free market would replace violence. But Gumplowicz affirmed *both* class *and* national struggle, so he could not employ one as a solution to the other. Because he took humanity outside of dynamic historical time and repositioned it in an unending war for survival, there could be no respite. He demystified both class and nation and made it impossible to sustain a faith in the emancipatory potential of either. Gumplowicz could explain human interactions, but he could not imagine "progress." He believed that his principles applied to "all international relations, all political history, without regard to differences in time or [differences between] the societies of Europe, Asia, America, or Africa and Australia." The only distinction he granted was the tendency for "civilized nations" to conceal their brutality behind "flowery excuses" and "noisy slogans."[47]

It followed that ethics and rights were just illusions.

> The conditions established by force and accepted in weakness become rightful if
> peaceably continued. . . . Individuals can consider ethical requirements, they
> have consciences, but societies have none. They overwhelm their victims like
> avalanches with irresistible destructive power. All societies, large and small,
> retain the character of wild hordes in considering every means which succeeds to
> be good. Who would look for fidelity, veracity, and conscience in the intercourse

of the "most civilized" states of the world? Lying and deceit, breach of confidence and betrayal is on every page of their history.[48]

Gumplowicz accepted, therefore, that "greater might is the better policy—as things stand now."[49] These final words are revealing, because they mark the great point of tension in Gumplowicz's work. Although he repudiated the idea of progress, he implied here that force might someday cease to be the standard of justice and that things might not always be "as they stand now." He based this qualified, cautious optimism on a thin foundation. Liberals had given evolution a telos in order to escape the darker consequences of their own reasoning, but Gumplowicz could not accept their solutions. He foresaw no utopia, but only an endless process of aimless change. Even a "civilized" society would eventually be torn apart by either conquest or the rebellion of a proletarian "horde." Instead of a straight line toward a glorious future, history appeared in Gumplowicz's work as a set of overlapping cycles without any destination.[50] On this, Gumplowicz rested his liberal hopes. Progress, albeit temporary progress, was still conceivable within any given society, and this possibility should inspire people to perform "moral acts," to make "sacrifices for the whole," and to "work for one's neighbors." The fact that in the end "it all must die" should not stop one from acting.[51]

Similarly, the inevitability that large nations would always and everywhere devour small nations should not cause the latter to despair. Gumplowicz's vision of cyclical collapse allowed him to imagine a moment when a seemingly powerful state (such as the Russian Empire) might expand beyond its limits and disintegrate. The mighty would conquer the weak, he reiterated, but in some cases this eventuality would be complicated by the "strongly developed nationality" of a defeated community. In this case, if the vanquished had been "cultivated by centuries of development," they would retain their cohesion even in defeat, and the conqueror's attempts to incorporate them would be "highly dangerous."

> A nation, which is the product of a long period of development, is such an
> exclusive unit that the attempt to incorporate it must tax the strength of the
> conquering state and render it for a long time incapable of future external
> activity. That is to say, it is neither simple nor does it promote humanism and
> healthy morality to subject a foreign people by violence. Though simple
> conquest and annexation cannot be treated as "crimes" without characterizing the
> whole history of mankind as one long crime, yet every violent attempt to destroy
> a nation, which is a product of history, is after all immoral and inhuman.[52]

All the tensions of a liberal discussion of struggle emerge here. Gumplowicz was convinced that "in reality the desires of states know no boundaries," but at the same time he warned of the dangers of conquest.[53] He could not call international violence a crime, yet he considered it immoral and inhuman (without being able to explain this distinction).

Not surprisingly, Gumplowicz was widely criticized by his contemporaries in Poland. The positivist press was polite (Gumplowicz was, after all, one of their own), but they could write favorable reviews only by glossing over or cautiously criticizing his most basic ideas. Adolf J. Cohn acclaimed Gumplowicz's work in *Prawda*, but noted almost as an aside that "what he says against the fact of intellectual progress does not stand up to criticism and can easily be knocked down by universally known facts."[54] The *niepokorni* had no reason to be so kind. Nationalists attacked Gumplowicz for failing to understand that a strong society could cultivate voluntary cooperation, thus bringing class struggle to an end.[55] Socialists expressed amazement that Gumplowicz could be so perceptive when describing the roots of the bourgeois state in class struggle and exploitation, without seeing the emancipatory potential of revolution. Edward Przewóski wrote that Gumplowicz had ignored recent research about the history of class struggle and that he had overlooked the vital role that human will can play in history. Przewóski wrote with biting sarcasm, "What a pity that we have become familiar with the theories revealed by Mr. Gumplowicz so late; if they had been known in the eighteenth century [i.e., in 1789] no one would have lifted a finger." Gumplowicz's system, this review concluded, "has no value," except insofar as it shed some light on class conflict.[56] Later that year Ludwik Krzywicki offered a more sustained response to Gumplowicz, writing simultaneously in both *Głos* and *Prawda*.[57] In the latter journal (to which Gumplowicz himself contributed) Krzywicki's tone was respectful. He credited the *System socyologii* for pointing out the importance of "struggle" and the illusory nature of all the liberal slogans used to conceal the workings of power within the state, but he expressed surprise that Gumplowicz would deploy his analysis of politics as a defense, rather than a critique, of state power.[58] Krzywicki's tone in *Głos* was less restrained. Here he referred to the "philistine hypocrisy" of liberals, who were nothing more than "defenders of a social order based on private property, the separation of the masses of society from state power, etc., etc." At least Gumplowicz was honest, Krzywicki wrote, about the centrality of exploitation to the liberal state.[59]

As with Jeleński, then, we do not study Gumplowicz because his work appealed to his contemporaries—clearly it did not. Like Jeleński, Gumplowicz had repositioned "the struggle for survival" outside the boundaries of a liberal telos. He had demonstrated that science need not be a doctrine of hope and progress, and he had staked out new frontiers for Polish Spencerism. Thanks to the contradictions within his work that allowed him to sustain his liberal creed, Gumplowicz was never as marginalized or as ridiculed as Jeleński, but in many paradoxical ways the liberal Habsburg Jew had a lot in common with the conservative Warsaw anti-Semite. Both are remembered more for the opposition their ideas aroused than for any obvious (or admitted) influence they exerted on other authors. Nonetheless, the very act of standing *against* these doctrines of struggle expanded the boundaries of political discourse. Gumplowicz in particular could not be ignored: his prominent position in *Prawda* and the wide circulation of his *System socyologii* made him a force to be reckoned with. Similarly, although the intelligentsia may have preferred to turn their eyes away from Jeleński, as the circulation of *Rola* grew they had to pay attention (if only to ridicule him as a demagogue). These two authors, then, opened up the uglier ramifications of the Spencerian world that the positivists had worked so hard to contain. It was only a matter of time before the *niepokorni* began to explore this newly expanded discursive frontier.

Resisting the Struggle for Survival

None of the *niepokorni* wanted to believe in the world of Gumplowicz, and in their early writings they used the concept of "struggle" with great care. The young authors at *Głos* were just as fascinated by Spencer as the liberal press had been, and they tried to increase their circulation by offering a free copy of *First Principles* and (later) *The Principles of Sociology* (translated by Józef Potocki, the co-editor of *Głos*) with each paid subscription. Potocki accepted the idea that "to be capable of life means to [be capable of] struggle," and he praised Spencer for bringing science to the study of society. Nonetheless, he argued that the tendency to apply a Darwinian worldview to the understanding of social relations was yet another marker of "decay" in European culture. "All social disasters and misfortunes," Potocki wrote, "have come from those cases in which competition persisted where cooperation ought to have spread. . . . [T]he unrestrained competition of individuals, being the basic feature of wild life, cannot be the foundation of social life."[60] Such ambivalence was typical. In late 1886 an anonymous author described the intensity of Franco–German hatred but dismissed any notion that things could be otherwise.

> A living creation is condemned to struggle: it must struggle *always, everywhere*, and with *everyone* over *everything*. . . . Contemporary man will never repudiate struggle, and one must doubt that [struggle] will ever be neglected. Needs grow and diversify infinitely, and satisfying those needs, even the most idealistic, demands that one take up the struggle, because struggle is an unavoidable necessity and a law of nature, an inexorable law. And there is probably nothing more noble in humanity than a struggle for a lofty interest.[61]

This may have seemed like a Gumplowiczean vision of struggle, but there was an important difference. The *głosowcy* had to struggle *for* something, preferably for a great and worthy cause, for an ideal. They could talk about the struggle for survival only by conceiving of existence as an unending quest for growth and diversification. This author began by recognizing a conflict between two communities, but transformed it into a "struggle for a lofty interest."

True to their roots in the radical intelligentsia, *Głos* rejected Jeleński's hate-mongering. Józef Hłasko, a member of the paper's editorial board, later recalled an evening when he and his colleagues had broken into *Rola*'s offices to "take part in an adventure" and embarrass the "hated" Jeleński.[62] In early 1888 Popławski criticized the "principle of tribal exclusivity" and the "arrogant, blind chauvinism" which had brought "wild racial cannibalism" to Europe. "The evil, base, obscene instincts of human nature," he wrote, were suffocating "all the more noble impulses."[63] Potocki tried to counter *Rola*'s influence by advocating friendship with the Jews, which he defended in terms of "simple considerations of civic honor."[64] The Jewish publicist Henryk Nusbaum was even invited to contribute a few lines to *Głos'* prospectus, and he took the opportunity to call for mutual tolerance between Christians and Jews within a common Polish home. "I am a Jew," he proclaimed, "and nothing could make me consider changing religion, because I consider religion to be a purely personal matter, touching the most internal essence of the soul."[65] For Nusbaum, relations between Christians and Jews should be governed by mutual understanding and respect, not conflict or rivalry.

The members of the Polish Socialist Party (the PPS) were particularly opposed to the idea that violence was eternal or that solidarity was powerless against animosity. Class struggle was acceptable because it was embedded in a narrative that promised a revolutionary transcendence, after which mankind would live in peace. The war-of-all-against-all, on the other hand, was unimaginable. The coming revolution, the party declared in an 1894 leaflet, would transcend all national differences: "Comrades! In this struggle we will have allies. The proletariat of all countries, joined with us by bonds of international solidarity, has already declared that it is behind us. The Russian comrades will stand with us. Finally, we will call to battle those millions from various peoples who, like us, are held in the chains of tsarist slavery. Faced with such a force, the power of the Tsar will not stand. And then, from the free breasts of free people will rise the shout: *Long live our worker's cause! Long live the free, Polish lud!*"[66] There could never be room for an unending struggle for survival in the world of the PPS. Stanisław Heybowicz-Herburt refused even to use the phrase in his major study of nationality, *Zarys pojęć o narodzie* (An Outline of the Concept of the Nation), retreating instead to an idealist vocabulary that fit better with the party line. He defined a nation as "an idea, a spiritual impetus to work for self-improvement," which was embodied in the form of an ethnolinguistic "nationality." This sort of nation was safely embedded in a rhetoric of "rights" and "law," protected from the threat of a Gumplowiczean struggle (which Heybowicz explicitly condemned).[67] When faced with the threat of conflict—worse yet, *popular* conflict—between two communities, the socialists called upon Poles to uphold a commitment to universal salvation. After a wave of pogroms hit Russia in 1903, the PPS issued this manifesto:

> Comrades! We are the champions of truth and justice, we are the warriors of the idea of human brotherhood . . . everywhere, therefore, where tears of injustice burn the tightly closed eyelids of people, where the groans of strangled victims ring out—we must be in all such places, to support the wronged and ensure the triumph of our ideas. Therefore we call upon you, comrades, to energetically step forward against the government-run anti-Jewish propaganda. . . . If, despite this, the government succeeds anywhere in exploiting the darkness of still unenlightened people and in bringing about riots against the Jews, we call upon you to actively defend the Jews.[68]

The PPS wanted to portray itself as the defender of the powerless and an advocate for international justice, and this agenda virtually compelled the party to "defend the Jews."

These "universal ideals"—this desire to work for the freedom of all mankind rather than just for national independence—would be put to the test when the *niepokorni* discussed the social and spatial boundaries of the national community. Among the many rights that Polish radicals of the 1880s wanted to establish, probably the most important was right to national self-determination. In the days before ethnicity became important, one could deploy this slogan with ease. In the early nineteenth century there were no Ukrainian or Lithuanian national movements, and Ruś (Ruthenia) and Litwa were just regions within an idealized "Poland," alongside Małopolska, Wielkopolska, and Mazowsze.[69] Moreover, as we saw in chapter 1, the idealist conception of the nation allowed one to speak of national freedom without worrying much about where any given nation would fit on the map or whom it would include. By the 1880s such conceptual laxity was untenable: once the nation was brought down to earth (literally and symbolically) by the positivists, attention had to be paid to the details of marking cartographic and sociological boundaries. Specifically, Ukrainian and Lithuanian nationalists had begun challenging old assumptions about Poland's eastern borders. Even calls for a multicultural, pluralistic national identity were suspect, since such claims could be interpreted as a polite way to talk about Polish irredentism. A Lithuanian nationalist could, understandably, perceive Polish calls for inclusivity as a way to ensure that Vilnius would be governed from Warsaw, subordinate to an all-encompassing (even if "tolerant") Polish nation. In this environment, it began to seem that the "right to national self-determination" would reduce Poland to a relatively small space, delineated by ethnography or by some future plebiscite.

Nonetheless, until the late 1880s nearly all the young Polish radicals continued to insist on an unqualified and universally applicable right to self-determination. *Przegląd Społeczny* presented the "right of every nationality to preserve and develop its cultural and ethnographic distinctiveness" as a general principle, applying equally to so-called historic nations (like Poland) and the "new" nationalities (like the Ukrainians).[70] A Polish socialist from Vilnius wrote to the party's central committee that the Lithuanians deserved their own separate organization because of their linguistic distinctiveness. Using the same criterion, this correspondent suggested that the *tutejsi* ("the locals"—a term for the then uncategorized Slavs of the old Grand Duchy of Lithuania, a group we now call the Belorussians) did not merit such a distinction, because they did not yet constitute a clearly defined ethnic community. "Saying this," the author cautioned, "we do not prejudge state boundaries for the future."[71]

Głos initially took a similar position. The young Popławski felt that he could not complain about violations of Poland's national rights unless he were willing to grant the same rights to other groups, and he attacked "that shameful solidarity which forgives every sin, every dishonor, just because it is 'ours.'"[72] The accusation that Poles were violating the rights of other nationalities was so damning, Popławski argued, that it should be avoided at all costs: "One should rather give more than necessary, so that no one will feel wronged by us." He lamented that this had not been the case vis-à-vis the Ruthenians, whose accusations against the Poles "if not entirely justified, are [nonetheless] inspired by our actions."[73] Popławski conceded in 1888 that "national policy can be based only on the principle of ethnicity."[74] Józef Potocki agreed: the goal of recreating Poland in its historical boundaries, he wrote in 1887, was an illegitimate ambition. "As a principle of *state* policies such a program is a negation of *nationality*. Poland . . . would have to deprive other peoples of national distinctiveness, it would have to divide and dismember tribes with populations in the millions, and it would thus have to create for itself internal and external enemies precisely where, in the natural order of things, it ought to find allies. Evoking here our traditions, our political tolerance, would make no sense."[75] A few issues later Potocki added that a "consistently conceived and realized program of 'historical Poland' would have to be an unpatriotic, antinational program, in the deepest sense of that expression." He based this dramatic assertion on the conviction that the only way to sustain such a state would be to oppress the non-Poles who ended up within its boundaries. This, in turn, would corrupt the Poles, draining the strength of the nation and leading to its collapse.[76]

If someone wanted to form "some sort of federation of equal and mutually independent nations," Potocki believed, such a creation would have to be a totally new political entity, not a resurrection of the old Polish Republic.[77] This comment was a response to Bolesław Limanowski, who advocated a more expansive vision of Poland and resisted the move toward ethnically defined polities. Even Limanowski, though, justified his ambitions with the vocabulary of freedom and rights.

> In my opinion, *ethnography* alone does not suffice to explain the question of *nationality*. Even more important, it gives [the concept of nationality] a certain exclusive character which could grow into a monstrous mania of oppression, as is now the case in Prussia. Ethnography allows one to recognize national material, but we learn from *history* how that material is developed and how it shapes the moral essence of the nation. . . . The nationality question, which appears currently most sharply in Eastern Europe, is really a question of *equal rights* for nationalities. Wherever political freedom provides a foundation for those equal rights, the relations between nationalities loses its sharpness and continues its further evolution peacefully.[78]

For the members of Limanowski's short-lived National-Socialist Commune (which he set up in 1889), the nation had to be grounded in freedom, or it was not worth reconstructing at all. An essay by H. Polanowski in the Commune's organ, *Pobudka,* declared that the old borders of the Republic should be thrown out "along with the whole archive of national barbarity" and replaced with treaties based on the "will of the oppressed *lud.*" The Poles had to stress that they had no "aggressive intentions vis-à-vis Lithuania or Ruthenia," but at the same time insist that a truncated "ethnographic Poland" was based on a fundamental misunderstanding of what the nation was all about. There was only one reliable metric for national membership, according to Polanowski: "The hero dying on the scaffold for the national cause does not need a degree in the Polish language or a patent of Polishness from our ethnographers, but a burning feeling of his nationality and solidarity with the concerns of his nation. The same can be said regarding the masses. We have no right, on the basis of language, to deny or to force upon the people any nationality." Both sides of this last sentence were crucial: no one could force people to be part of the Polish nation if they did not wish to be, nor could such membership be denied to anyone who wanted to belong. It followed that a nation had to be the product of a plebiscite, though Polanowski quickly drew back from this risky conclusion by assigning to the intelligentsia the task of building popular support for the most appropriate boundaries (which, coincidentally, approximated the Poland of 1772).

> Instead of prematurely slashing out a map of Europe, it would be better to energetically take up revolutionary propaganda among the *lud*. This is the mission of the Polish intelligentsia. . . . We therefore consider controversies about the borders of a state that does not yet exist to be at least premature today, in the conviction that the borders of the future Republic will not depend either on political-philological or political-historical doctrines, but on the borders that will be drawn by the victorious revolution. We should strive above all for this victory.[79]

Like Limanowski's *Pobudka*, Miłkowski's *Wolne Polskie Słowo* was committed to a broad, multicultural vision of Poland. The paper's program of 1887 contained a "profession of faith" that predicted "a free and independent Polish Republic, organized on the basis of a union of the free with the free and the equal with the equal, both in a social and a political sense." This implied, the editors clarified, a union of all those in Eastern Europe who longed for freedom, even if they were not historically tied to the Polish state. In a grandiose conclusion, the program imagined a confederation not only between Poles, Lithuanians, and Ruthenians, but also Czechs, Hungarians, Romanians, South Slavs, and "even Germans and Russians" as long as the latter two broke with their aggressive and chauvinistic traditions.[80] Another contributor to the paper argued that ethnic boundaries were meaningless, because Poland should be assembled "from the voluntary union of nations, affirmed by centuries of common martyrdoms, pilgrimages, exiles, scaffolds, and bloodshed."[81] In perhaps the grandest version of this scheme, Feliks Górski wrote that Poland had to have a federal structure, because it was destined to "gather together the Slavic peoples with a second Union of Lublin and become the nucleus of a great federation of European nations."[82] These ambitions were more important than "superficial" characteristics like language. One correspondent for *Wolne Polskie Słowo* noted in 1889 that one "could be a Polish patriot even if circumstances did not allow one to learn the language of the fatherland."[83] In response to a letter to the editor that equated Polishness and Catholicism, Miłkowski insisted that anyone could be a Pole. "There are many Orthodox, Calvinist, and even Muslim Poles," he wrote. "Jews are not Catholic and they do not speak Polish, yet they are Poles."[84]

Despite their many differences, *Przegląd Społeczny*, *Przedświt*, *Głos*, *Pobudka*, and *Wolne Polskie Słowo* all imagined boundaries based on universal principles of national rights and voluntary affiliation. Many, following Limanowski, wanted to envision a nation that was open to the Ukrainians, the Lithuanians, and the Jews: all could be part of Poland if they wished, and the intelligentsia assigned itself the task of convincing them that they should. At the same time, no one could foresee a future

Poland based on forced assimilation or the denial of national rights to any group. Most Polish intellectuals in the 1880s seemed to understand that the rhetoric of national inclusivity and multiculturalism, when spoken in Warsaw, could be heard in Vilnius or L'viv as an aggressive desire for Polish expansion. Those Poles who challenged the idea of a multicultural nation based their doubts on the suspicion that any pluralistic Poland would breed conflict and oppression. An aversion to the world of Gumplowicz and Jeleński, an unwillingness to see communities as mutually exclusive and inevitably antagonistic, ran through the entire debate. Few intellectuals in 1886 challenged the claim that national rights were inviolable and universal. Unfortunately, this resistance to violence, conflict, brutality, and oppression was about to weaken, as the *głosowcy*'s denial of historical progress created an opening for "the struggle for survival." The repudiation of determinism described in chapters 4 and 5 would undermine faith in the right to self-determination, just as it had corroded the *niepokorni*'s commitment to democracy. The first manifestation of a new vision of irredeemable conflict would come when *Głos* addressed "the Jewish question."

Nationalism Begins to Hate

A letter to the editor of *Przegląd Wszechpolski* in 1895 spoke with great satisfaction about a change in the intellectual climate in Poland. "One cannot deny," this anonymous author wrote, "that one of the most important phenomena of our life recently is the incredible increase in anti-Semitism in all spheres, in all positions and in all possible forms." This author credited Jeleński with giving impetus to the new anti-Semitism but regretted that *Rola*'s audience was limited to "half-intellectuals" and that the paper was inspired by "Russian agitation." Much more important than *Rola*, for this correspondent, was *Głos*, where he believed anti-Semitism became respectable, sophisticated, and modern.[85] Dmowski remembered the rise of anti-Semitism in a similar way: "It was striking, back then, that in the 'progressive' and democratic magazines, anti-Semitic tendencies began to emerge. Anti-Semitism was then represented, in a very sharp form, by Jan Jeleński, the founder of the weekly *Rola*, which was strongly Catholic and was based mainly on the support of the rural clergy. Anti-Semitism had been treated as an expression of reaction, so *Głos* made all that much more of an impression."[86] The *głosowcy* were well aware that they were repositioning Polish anti-Semitism and giving it legitimacy for the radical intelligentsia. The magazine argued in 1890 that anti-Semitism "does not stand in the way of the progressive movement of humanity" and should be understood as a "positive phenomenon, testifying to the strengthening of consciousness and social solidarity."[87]

This brings us to the fundamental transformation mentioned in the title of this book: the moment when it became possible to speak of hatred within the discourse of nationalism. Demagogues like Jeleński had been propagating anti-Semitism in Poland since the early 1880s, and (on a deeper level) tensions had existed between Christians and Jews as long as the two groups had lived side by side. But Polish nationalism had not heretofore been directed against the Jews. It was certainly not inevitable that anti-Semitism would ever transcend the narrow confines of aristocratic and clerical conservatism, and Jeleński, with his aggressive hostility toward the entire intelligentsia, had done little to increase the appeal of his doctrines. But the tolerance and openness of the intelligentsia had, to this point, been rooted in a firm belief in the power of historical time. Mickiewicz and his contemporaries had located the nation in the realm of the ideal, where one's actions on behalf of the national cause mattered more than one's language or folkways. The positivists had focused attention on the "real" characteristics of the national community, but they too had positioned the nation within a narrative that promised the transcendence of diversity by a universal "civilization." The *głosowcy*, in contrast, denied the "abstractions" of historical progress and demanded that one serve the needs of the people here and now. They could no longer imagine any future resolution of cultural difference; they could only perceive social conflict as it existed in the present. With their rhetoric of sociological realism, they cast the Jew as a cultural "other," and with their synchronic mind-set they saw such otherness as eternally fixed. If time alone (progress) would not make ethnic, religious, and linguistic diversity go away, and if this diversity mattered (as it did in the postpositivist world), then one had to strive actively to eliminate it. This was no longer a question of furthering "development" and "civilization" (and thereby softening the tensions resulting from difference); this was a program aimed at the abolition of difference as such (or, worse, at the destruction of those who were different). The "Jewish question" was taken out of historical time, and this shift opened the doors to the world of Gumplowicz. A nationalism without recourse to progress quickly dissolved into a rhetoric of hate.

As was noted above, *Głos* was initially opposed to anti-Semitism. However, even in 1886 (the year the magazine was founded) there were signs that its tolerance rested on an unsteady foundation. A two-part editorial entitled "Anti-Semitism and the Jewish Question" appeared in the fourth issue, revealing some of the tensions to come. The arguments seem familiar at first reading, well in line with a long-established liberal approach to the Jews: the goal of any society must be the assimilation of the Jews, but force should never be used because it was "morally repulsive." A closer reading, however, reveals some Jeleńskian undertones. "The main reason for antipathy toward the Jews," the editors wrote, "is not that they are worse or better, but mainly that they are different." For the positivists, the goal had been "improvement," as both Poles and Jews progressed toward "civilization." For *Głos*, historical progress was not guaranteed and difference in the present had become a more serious problem. The editors suggested that Poland was suffering from a "pathological" anti-Semitic movement (Jeleński) because a "foreign body" (the Jews) had infected the social organism.[88] The threat of disease had pushed aside the assurances of historical time.

The dangers inherent in this new approach were frighteningly exposed in this same 1886 essay when the editors wrote, "Every society, in relation to the Jews, must work to destroy them—whether we will call this extermination, expulsion, or assimilation does not change the essence of things. Both judeophiles and anti-Semites want to destroy the Jews as Jews, that is, as representatives of a separate society." Having equated assimilation and genocide, the editors of *Głos* emphasized that the latter option was neither possible nor morally acceptable. Since they believed that forced assimilation was impractical on a mass scale, the only remaining alternative was "civic assimilation," which would "make Jews members of our society, Poles of Semitic descent and of the faith of Moses."[89] The authors thus concluded with a call for emancipation and the inclusion of the Jews within a common Polish home, but how they got to this point is more important than where they ended up.

The tension between *Głos'* stated position of tolerance and the rhetoric cited above proved to be unsustainable. The use of that good liberal slogan, "Poles of the faith of Moses," could not entirely compensate for the discussion of extermination. By 1888 the *głosowcy* had entirely abandoned the liberal approach to the "Jewish question," and the editors had grown defensive about their earlier position: "It is false to state that Mosaism [sic] finds full tolerance in *Głos*. *Głos* has discussed the Jewish question several times and probably even Mr. Jeleński will not accuse us of excessive sympathy for Jewry. However, we only speak about the Jews when their activities in some way or another touch the native interests of our society; we cannot get involved in the internal life of that segment of our country's population, even if for no other reason than that we do not understand it."[90] Here the Jews were segregated off as "the other," part of the "country's" population but certainly not one of "us." This segregation had been so firmly established in the minds of the *głosowcy* that they could admit unapologetically to ignorance about Jewish "internal life," as if one could not be expected to know much about those inscrutable foreigners. From this foundation it was but a short step to the repudiation of assimilation—a step first taken in late 1888, by Józef Hłasko. In France, he argued, Jews had all the rights and liberties they could want, yet they "remained Jews, only speaking French, just like the Irish remained Irish, even though they have accepted the English language." For Hłasko, the existence of the *Alliance Israélite Universelle* was the best evidence of this separatism, because it proved that assimilation did not run very deep.[91] Starting from the assumption that national identity was unitary and exclusive, Hłasko could not imagine that a seemingly assimilated Jew could really be a Frenchman if he also belonged to an international Jewish organization. The only meaningful assimilation was *total* assimilation, the complete abnegation of one's former identity, allegiances, and cultural practices. There could be no "Jewish Poles" or "Polish Jews," there could be no "Poles of the faith of Moses"; there could only be "Jews" and "Poles." To belong to the *Alliance Israélite Universelle* was to betray the nation.

An 1888 essay by A. P. Ordyński demonstrated how corrosive anti-Semitism could be for the ethical foundations of the *niepokorni*. For Ordyński the Jews were a "force of disintegration and destruction" in the countryside, and the peasants had to be "emancipated" from this alien body. The Polish–Jewish conflict, complained Ordyński, had fatally undermined traditional notions of morality. "The ethical views serving in a given village as a standard for relations between peasants do not restrain them at all in relations with the Jew," he wrote. "It is hard to imagine that theft, robbery, and fraud would be tolerated in the village in general, but regarding the Jews these are practically considered an honorable duty."[92] Ordyński did not quite approve of such behavior, but he claimed that such harsh methods were employed only out of necessity. This author still clung to a concept of morality, but he had already recognized that the needs of the struggle for survival could obviate existing ethical codes.

From this point *Głos* rapidly slid toward unqualified anti-Semitism. Articles about the Jews began to appear with much greater frequency, and their rhetoric became more violent. *Głos'* last call for tolerance came in the summer of 1889 but was followed shortly by a strong repudiation of assimilation.[93] By late 1889 Popławski noted that "the times have long since passed when a magazine would have to make an act of contrition" for writing against the Jews.[94] In fact, soon *Głos* would even cite *Rola* as a source of statistical information about Jewish society.[95] Even Potocki, once such an advocate of tolerance, was insisting by 1890 that the Jews were a separate culture, a homogenous entity with distinct ethics and "racial" characteristics. "This entire mass seems like one huge ant hill of exploiters . . . in a word, millionaire exploiters on one extreme and impoverished exploiters on the other. . . . Between the millionaire Jew and the impoverished Jews is only a difference of degree, but there is no conflict of interest."[96] In 1890 Świętochowski rebuked Popławski for some misrepresentations about the Jews printed in *Głos*, and the younger man replied with frustration, "Enough of all this about what the Jews are like; it is sufficient that they are different from us."[97] Perhaps Potocki put it most dramatically when he declared that "if Catholic usurers exploited us three times worse than Jewish ones, even then we would prefer [the Catholics] ten times more."[98] Exploitation was no longer the issue: the Jews *as such* were.

The Jews, according to *Głos*, were not just alien, but *eternally* alien. This was the crucial innovation offered by these young intellectuals: they had taken the Jews out of progressive historical time and located them in the realm of nature, which never changed. Any changes that did occur were epiphenomenal; it no longer mattered what the Jews were like, it only mattered that they were Jews and that *as such* they would be forever different and forever hostile. This new approach was exemplified by Witold Ziemiński's ten-part series from the summer and fall of 1890, "What Is Israel?"[99] The Jews, in this presentation, were not only deprived of all internal heterogeneity, but cast as inscrutably alien: "The relations of Israel to other peoples can perhaps serve as clear evidence of how mistaken the principle of the intellectual homogeneity of the human race is. For 2000 years we see the descendants of Jacob living among other peoples in total separation, not understanding them and not understood by them."[100] Zieminski imagined the Jews to be a coherent "them," marked by "Semitic" traits derived from "the East." Their racial bonds were so tight that even assimilated, "enlightened individuals" were still marked by their essential natures, differing from their "orthodox brethren" only in form, not substance.[101] Ultimately Ziemiński's argument came down to a basic question: "Can two distinct social types inhabit the same territory?" His answer was an unequivocal no.[102] This "no" stemmed from Ziemiński's conviction that the Jews' difference lay in the realm of eternal, unchanging nature, not the realm of mutable, progressive historical time. Once again, the repudiation of history marked the final step into the new world of the twentieth-century radical right—a world of hatred and conflict without end.

At this point an even darker message emerged, one rooted in a Gumplowiczean despair that the "better" combatant in the struggle between Pole and Jew might not win. Just as Ordyński had lamented that moral standards were irrelevant when one was dealing with the Jews, Ziemiński believed that the "higher" values of "European" society might have to be abandoned if Poles were to emerge victorious. "Science" had convinced him that "higher individuals" did not necessarily survive; instead, a "more perfect organization" often weakened the resistance of an advanced organism, thus "increas[ing] its susceptibility to negative influences." Because of this phenomenon, the struggle for survival could lead to retrogression, as "lower types" defeated "more noble" entities. Just as a parasite could infect and kill a human, he concluded, so could the Jews destroy civilized Europe.[103] In Ziemiński's scheme of evolution (or rather, devolution), there was a "dominance of the elements of hatred, the destructive elements, over the creative elements of organization."[104] Ziemiński wanted to believe in an ideal of European civilization, standing against "Jewish" cosmopolitanism and materialism, but he was unable to show how the "Western" body could overcome the "Asian" parasite—except to suggest that the Jews be "eliminated" by being sent to Palestine.[105] Any other solution, any more direct engagement with the Jews in the struggle for survival, would require the Poles to embrace the ruthless standards of competition in which Jews, allegedly, excelled. Writing in *Przegląd Społeczny*, Alfred Nossig (himself, amazingly, an assimilated Jew) put the dilemma most clearly: "The Jewish type is, on average, stronger in the struggle for survival, but morally it stands lower than the non-Jewish [type]; it possesses more shrewdness and perseverance, but also more ambition, laziness, and dishonesty." As a result, the mere coexistence of Jews and Christians on the same territory inevitably forced the latter to "resort to the policies of their ancestors," that is, to abandon the fruits of modern civilization in the name of the struggle for survival. The only alternative for Nossig was to hope for a "victory of the human spirit over the forces of nature."[106]

But "nature" had broken into the world of the *niepokorni*, and Nossig's hopes would be hard to sustain. The doctrine of the struggle for survival, having entered the paper on the back of the "Jewish question," began to penetrate other aspects of their worldview. In 1890 Popławski wrote a positive review of some new legal texts portraying law as a reflection of the will of the strongest.[107] This did not sit well with some of the other *głosowcy*. A few months later an author using the initials A. P. contributed an essay called "The Struggle for Survival and Morality," in which he argued that these two ideas were mutually contradictory. Progress entailed the development of social sentiments, he claimed, and these were the antidote to our animal nature, to "the atavistic struggle for survival."[108] But A. P. was swimming against the tide. During the last few years before *Głos* was shut down by the police in 1894, the theme of "struggle" would push its way to the surface. No author typified this better than a university student who began contributing book reviews to *Głos* in 1891: Roman Dmowski.[109]

In February 1892 the young Dmowski published his first major article, a two-part essay entitled "From the Economy of Spiritual Interests." In this short space, fewer than five pages, he opened up a frightening new world for the *niepokorni*, a world in which conquest and colonization were justified and in which cultural assimilation flowed toward the strongest. The argumentation would not have seemed novel for an English or French audience, accustomed by 1892 to apologies for colonialism, but for "progressive" Poles this was something new. This was the Spencerism that Spencer himself had tried so hard to avoid, the struggle for survival with the gloves off. Dmowski's opening assumption was artfully expressed in both the language of "science" and "spirit," the combination the *niepokorni* wanted to see. "There are social phenomena," he wrote, "in which the main and even the only factors are the spiritual interests of a certain social group. Acting on behalf of those interests creates competition between specific groups." The first such interest was expansion, the "incorporation of as many individuals as possible into the sphere of its spiritual interests." To a certain extent, Dmowski wrote, such incorporation could be accomplished by "raising up" the poor and uneducated within one's own society, but ultimately colonization would be necessary. Since every other "social unit" would be trying to do the same, competition would inevitably result. Dmowski cast his discussion of cultural assimilation within this framework: one group would attempt to draw members of another group into its "sphere," while the latter would strive to "increase its spiritual assets" so that it could survive. But such conflicts could not be limited to culture wars.

> The colonization of wild countries by European nations takes place generally in
> a manner that is not very humanitarian, because it is accompanied by the mass
> extermination of the local wild population. Thus, on the one hand, [colonization]
> makes the customs of the often peaceful local tribes militaristic and wild; on the
> other hand, it lowers the level of human sentiments in the colonists themselves.
> Nonetheless, one must agree that the process of colonization, quickly increasing
> the size of the civilized races and thus filling up heretofore wild territory, creates
> new centers of civilization and becomes the salvation not only for the races
> occupying a given territory but for humanity as a whole.

In the metaphor-ridden, aesopian world of the Polish press no one had ever dared discuss colonization in such a manner. This was a justification not only for conquest but for extermination. Dmowski, of course, was not about to allow this reasoning to return to him in the form of a justification for Russian expansion. He clarified that the process he was describing was "progressive" only when dealing with "uncivilized" tribes; in the case of groups possessing the "spiritual assets corresponding entirely to the level of contemporary civilization," such aggression could not succeed. Nonetheless, Dmowski wrote, "in the majority of cases" conquest, colonization, extermination, and assimilation were "useful not only for the group in question, but for universal progress."[110]

Throughout this essay Dmowski employed the vocabulary of progress, but this was not at all the sort of progress envisioned by either liberals or socialists. For Dmowski, civilization would advance, but violence and hostility would never end, because these were the basic motive forces for human action. Dmowski was caught in a transitional moment: like the rest of the *niepokorni*, he had grown to doubt the promises of any historical destiny, but he was still so rooted in the postpositivist world that he could use a word like "progress," even as he eviscerated it of most of its progressive content. Since the dawn of time, Dmowski wrote, the main creative force in social development had been the "organic repulsion toward everything that is psychologically alien to a given ethnic unity." While "mutual familiarity" was leading to a decline in "unjustified contempt" and the methods of competition were becoming more humanitarian, Dmowski claimed that antagonism had actually intensified. "One must seek the cause of this in the fact that the place of contempt has been occupied by a recognition of one's own interests," he wrote. The "enlightened strata" that understood the needs of their society, therefore, were working to better equip themselves for the struggle for survival: "In the next phase of the processes currently taking place we must expect above all that ethnic groups without a literature corresponding to the demands of civilization will create one, or else they will lose their ethnic distinctiveness and enter into culturally superior groups, drawn by their rich spiritual assets."[111] The familiarity of much of Dmowski's argument made its novelty all the more striking. This was not yet a world entirely without progress, not yet (quite) the dark vision of amoral struggle he would later develop, but it was nonetheless a world in which conflict and violence would *never* be transcended. It was, more important, a world without a moral standard. Even extermination was justified in the course of colonization and assimilation. The fate of the "often peaceful tribes" that would be wiped out by "civilized" nations was, for Dmowski, irrelevant. The only restraint on Dmowski's vision—and this was by now a very thin reed—was his belief in progress. He was still willing to hope that with time the *methods* of conflict would become more "humanitarian" and "gentle," and he was able to argue that cultural development could save a nation from destruction. But he had clearly turned the corner and entered the world of Gumplowicz.

Anti-Semitism, then, was the point of entry for the doctrine of "struggle," the first space within which the *głosowcy* could talk about eternal hostility, within which they could subordinate (although not yet eliminate) ethical norms and moral considerations to the imagined needs of international conflict. It was, as a consequence, the first space within which they could define the Jews (and eventually the Ukrainians, the Russians, the Germans, and just about anyone) as irrevocably "them." The boundedness of this worldview was disturbing, but even more troubling was its timelessness. For the romantics and positivists alike, all communities had existed in history and even the most apparently intractable social divisions were destined to fade with the passage of progressive time. The *głosowcy* perceived no destiny; they saw only synchronic social space in which each nation had to act for its own self-defense. Instead of "liberals" or "progressives" doing something about "backwardness," *the Poles* had to do something about *the Jews*. Thus we see the final consequence of the abandonment of history: a world in which the mere presence of diversity became the foundation for an unending struggle for survival. The nation emerging from the pages of *Głos* was compelled to insulate itself behind high walls of exclusion and hostility, and the open, universalistic, idealist nation of Mickiewicz was lost.

Polish Imperialism

Dmowski's colonialist rhetoric was almost unprecedented in 1892. No "progressive" intellectual in Poland had ever declared so openly that the "process of colonization" might bring "salvation . . . for humanity as a whole." For most of the nineteenth century, Poles had preferred the language of the victim, of the small nation consumed by rapacious neighbors. Slogans like "for our freedom and yours" made it hard to justify colonial expansion and the extermination of lesser "tribes." Even the positivists had condemned the aggressive tendencies of the European powers—they could not allow the struggle for survival to become a justification for conquest, lest the same reasoning be turned on Poland. Świętochowski believed that "the poor, the weak, the uneducated also want to live," and he complained about those who saw in small communities "nothing other than vanishing species."[112] Dmowski, in contrast, had not only justified but glorified imperial expansion, all in the name of progress (by then an almost empty term for him). His essay could not have been shocking to the *głosowcy*, however, because the foundation had been well laid for such an argument. In discussing the "Jewish question," they opened the doors to a Gumplowiczean vision of unending struggle, and Dmowski was merely exploring the possibilities of this new discursive framework.

But there were still limits to how much could be said in defense of colonization and conquest—very concrete limits imposed by the Russian censors. One could speak about the expansion of European civilization against an undefined other, but one could not talk about the role of Poland in this process. Throughout the late nineteenth century the tsarist authorities were engaged in a campaign to russify their state, and even if they could not denationalize the Kingdom, they could at least (they thought) prevent the Poles from ever reclaiming their hegemony over the vast eastern territories of the old Republic, the so-called *kresy* (the borderlands) encompassing what we today call Lithuania, Belarus, and Ukraine. It followed that Poles could not legally express any colonial ambitions over the lands and peoples of this region, at least not in the Warsaw press. In Geneva, however, Miłkowski's *Wolne Polskie Słowo* faced no such restrictions (indeed, this is why the paper was called "The Free Polish Word"), and he provided both exiles and correspondents from the Russian Empire with a forum to explore the possibilities of a colonial discourse. Like the *niepokorni* in the Kingdom, Miłkowski was drawn to the rhetoric of science, and by the 1890s *Wolne Polskie Słowo* had embraced a Spencerian vocabulary. However, unlike the younger intellectuals in Warsaw, the émigrés were less inclined to abandon all faith in history, less likely to embrace a vision of an unmitigated war of all against all. As we saw in the last chapter, Miłkowski found it difficult to resist the authoritarian implications of "modern" political rhetoric, but even as *Wolne Polskie Słowo* slid closer and closer to the National Democrats, it was never as committed to discipline and order as was Dmowski's own *Przegląd Wszechpolski*. Similarly, when the Geneva émigrés followed the path set by *Głos* and began to discuss Poland's role within an eternal struggle for survival, they stopped short of the dehistoricized, conflict-ridden world that would soon be articulated by the National Democrats. Miłkowski's worldview, described as it was with the rhetoric of liberal imperialism, would be familiar to the West Europeans among whom he lived. This approach would generate some regrettable intolerance and would certainly undermine the old slogan of "for our freedom and yours." It would, furthermore, fulfill the fears of those Lithuanians and Ukrainians who predicted that the idea of a multicultural Polish nation would serve to justify Polish dominance over the Eastern "borderlands." However, Miłkowski's approach would always be linked to a historiosophy that promised an end to struggle, and this would prevent him from stepping entirely into the dark world of Gumplowicz.

As was noted above, Miłkowski never severed all ties with the rhetoric of romantic nationalism, which he had been fed as a young man and which he had spoken during the 1863 Uprising. In the 1890s, however, we can trace the gradual erosion of this framework as younger voices from *Głos* began to dominate Miłkowski's Polish League. The old colonel himself soon found it impossible to avoid "the struggle for survival." As early as 1888 he used this idea to defend the principle of violent insurrection. "Our uprisings take on various physiognomies and do not resemble each other," he wrote, "but all are manifestations of one and the same natural law, recognized by science: the struggle for survival. . . . The fact of the uprisings does not depend on our will and it is irrational to protest against them. . . . It is thus not necessary to prepare an explosion, but to prepare *for an explosion* that is necessary, natural."[113] Miłkowski frequently described insurgents as mere "executors of natural law," insisting that Poles *must* rise up, whether they wanted to or not.[114] In a moment of particular despair in 1890 he even suggested that Poles had to defend themselves alone because there would be no justice on earth unless they fought for it.[115] Such rhetoric was safe as long it was linked to this idea of justice, as long as the imperative for insurrection was still embedded in an idealist vision. The force that compelled Poland to rise up was now described as a natural law, but it was still positioned within a narrative of progress that promised the victory of freedom—as a universal principle, not as an isolated Polish accomplishment. Poles had to fight for justice, but at least Miłkowski could still imagine such a goal.

The historical narrative articulated on the pages of *Wolne Polskie Słowo* was therefore still rooted in the "politics of Mickiewicz," even as it was described with the language of the fin de siècle. Mickiewicz and his peers had used the metaphorical potential of a poetic style to describe their enemy as "tyranny" or "injustice," but if the struggle for progress was going to be inserted into the language of social science, a more concrete collective opponent had to be found, and the obvious candidate was Russia. At the same time, this specific foe could fit within Miłkowski's increasingly awkward hybrid discourse only if it continued to represent something else, some historical force that had to be overcome on the path to the utopia—and this provided the point of entry for a corrosive orientalism that would ultimately undermine *Wolne Polskie Słowo*'s idealism. The Poles were not just fighting the Russians, Miłkowski believed; they represented Europe in an epochal conflict with the "Asiatic horde" of Muscovy. An anonymous author began an essay in 1888 with a familiar description of Poland as the embodiment of freedom, battling a Russian Empire that was "organized on the foundation of absolutism." In this presentation, however, tyranny and freedom were not just general principles; they were embodied in a symbolic dichotomy between Russia and Poland "in which one represented Asia, the other Europe." "Who can deny," the author asked, "that Moscow is the heir of the idea of the state and the political aspirations of the Golden Horde? . . . From this it follows that Moscow is the enemy of Poland—an enemy in the full meaning of this word and with all its implications—an enemy with whom rapprochement and understanding is impossible."[116]

Instead of a mutual struggle for a universal revolution against a single oppressor (the Tsar), *Wolne Polskie Słowo* offered a more complicated image of the Polish nation fighting a Russian nation that was oppressed but too uncivilized to realize it. In a four-part series in 1893 with the revealing title "The Liberation of the Russian Nation," an anonymous author granted that Russia and Poland were imprisoned by "one chain," but he insisted that each community had responded to its bondage in a different way. "The Russian nation, itself remaining in slavery, is, in the hands of the Tsar, the tool that holds the Polish nation in slavery." This paradoxical positioning of the Russian people made it almost impossible to imagine revolution there, this author argued, and insofar as there was a Russian opposition movement, it was only thanks to the support provided by the Poles. "You complain about oppression, about the draft, about taxes, about injustice, about the bureaucrats . . . but do you know why [you are oppressed]? The grievances of Poland are on your conscience. You want things to be better for you—then right those wrongs!"[117] Despite this appeal, the contributors to *Wolne Polskie Słowo* were not satisfied with a mere request for justice; they were going to fight for it, simultaneously *against* and *for* the Russians.

With Poland representing Europe in a battle for "civilization" against the "Asiatic horde" to the east, new possibilities were created for talking about the people caught in the zone between the Poles and the Russians. *Wolne Polskie Słowo* affirmed that "Poland, faced with the threat to civilization posed by Moscow, will answer to history and humanity not only for itself, but also for Lithuania, for Ruthenia, for Slavdom, and for Europe."[118] These responsibilities were not all structured in the same way: Poland *represented* Europe, while *protecting* the Lithuanians and Ruthenians. In the very first issue of *Wolne Polskie Słowo*, right after the paper's "Program," there appeared an essay called "Ruthenia and Poland." The author explained that this subject had been given pride of place in the new paper because "we openly recognize that there is no more important question than this." The emphasis here was on unity: "Poland without Ruthenia, Ruthenia without Poland—each of these alone is weaker by half against Moscow." Not really by half, though, because the two sides of this imagined alliance were hardly equal. "The Ruthenian nationality," the author wrote, "exists in reality, as has been demonstrated by the appearance of popular literature, but over the course of centuries it has not achieved those properties of civilization demonstrating a political idea of nationality."[119] Thus it fell to the Poles to play the role of the older brother, educating and defending their younger siblings to the east. This did not imply that the Poles wanted to denationalize the Ukrainians, Miłkowski insisted repeatedly. As one correspondent put it in 1890, "the Poles, hoping to obtain freedom, can never hope to deprive the brother Ruthenian nation of this. We want to be free and we want to free others."[120] *Wolne Polskie Słowo* even claimed that the very term "Poland" was used only as a convenience; what they were talking about was a federation that included Lithuania and Ruthenia as well. Within such a union, "We would not even think of polonization."[121]

This freedom, however, was based on the presumption that the Ruthenians would freely chose to federate with Poland. Another author, even while evoking the model of Switzerland, insisted that Poland had to be recreated in "its old borders, extending as far as possible."[122] The generosity of *Wolne Polskie Słowo*'s contributors wavered with the first signs that the Ruthenians might decide to be "Ukrainians." By 1890 the "Ruthenian question" had become a frequent topic for front-page editorials (presumably by Miłkowski, but usually unsigned). In September of that year the paper complained about the "chronic illness in Ruthenian diplomacy" that was provoking anti-Polish sentiments in East Galicia. The Ruthenians needed to demonstrate "reason, reason, and once again reason" and try to understand that the Poles had no intention of standing in their way.[123] Miłkowski knew that new political forces were transforming the *kresy*, but he refused to grant these legitimacy.

> Calling for its independent existence, Poland simultaneously calls for the existence of Lithuania and Ruthenia, for returning them the freedom of national, autonomous development. Our demand—for Poland in its prepartition boundaries, "whole, free, and independent"—is based on this. "But circumstances and conditions have changed," explain the politicians for whom such demands seem exaggerated and who babble on about ethnography. Certainly, circumstances and conditions have changed, but the basic Polish essence has not changed, and it corresponds exactly to just the circumstances and conditions which arise from the principle of nationality.[124]

This "principle of nationality" was configured so as to recognize the rights of the Ukrainians and Lithuanians while still insisting that they all remain within Poland. Polish statehood would protect the nationality rights of ethnic minorities, as long as political divisiveness was precluded. As *Wolne Polskie Słowo* put it a few years later, "The autonomous existence and the development of the Ruthenian nationality depends entirely and unconditionally on a federal union with an independent Poland."[125]

An 1890 letter to the editor of *Wolne Polskie Słowo* insisted that there had been no national oppression in the old Polish Republic, but in doing so the author exposed the fatal flaw of *Wolne Polskie Słowo*'s inclusivity: "Doubtlessly 'the free with the free' and 'equals with equals' were joined together back then. Doubtlessly (with very few exceptions among political thinkers) there was no conscious desire that one half would rule over the other and oppress them. However, there was no force that could resist the higher culture, the higher intelligence, the greater wealth, and the dynamic civilization, and so what happened had to happen—that is, Ruthenia succumbed to the higher Polish culture."[126] Just as an orientalist discourse had allowed *Wolne Polskie Słowo* to escape the full consequences of the "struggle for survival" in talking about the Russians, a colonial discourse made it possible to sustain Poland's domination over Ruthenia without suggesting that the Polish nation was engaged in conquest. The prospect of "natural" assimilation, however, was preserved. As was explained in an 1891 front-page editorial, there was a huge difference between forced denationalization and natural assimilation. Poland would never engage in state-sponsored polonization, but it was quite normal for some "tribes" to merge with "superior" nations "all by themselves."[127]

As a letter signed only "from the Dnieper basin" put it, the Ruthenians were developing a sense of national distinctiveness, but they lacked the "social stratum that could give that feeling expression." This author believed that "from the Dnieper far to the north, far to the west, to the sea in the south, to the Black Sea, in all that vast space there is no other enlightened social stratum capable of expressing Ruthenian national aspirations, no other element conscious of the common grievances, except the Poles. . . . Let the Ruthenians be Ruthenians in spirit and in truth and they will come to us all by themselves and extend to us the hand of brotherhood."[128] The rhetoric of brotherhood and an image of a common struggle were firmly in place, but so was the unshaken conviction that Poles alone could constitute the enlightened stratum that would lead and give expression to the aspirations of the Ruthenians. If some Ruthenians did not recognize this fact, another author wrote, this was simply evidence that they did not know what was good for them. "The Ruthenians, being culturally inferior to the Poles, would like it a lot if, thanks to Austria, the *Lachy* [a derogatory term for the Poles] would be knocked in the head. . . . In the stated goals and aspirations of the Galician Ruthenians there is no rhyme or reason. They do not necessarily know what they themselves want." The Poles, according to this author, had to give the Ruthenians what they needed and not pay attention to what they asked for.[129]

By the turn of the century Zygmunt Miłkowski had long since faded from view. He had retired from *Wolne Polskie Słowo* and was disbursing funds from his National Treasury to the Endecja with few questions asked. However, in 1902 he raised his voice once again with a book called *The Ruthenian Question in Relation to the Polish Question*, released by the National League's publishing cooperative in Lwów. Here he declared his love for the "Ruthenian *lud*" and applied to himself the old moniker *gente Ruthenus, natione Polonus* (he was born in what is today Ukraine). Anyone who was a "real Pole," Miłkowski wrote, could never be an enemy of the Ruthenians, but it was necessary to recognize that they were "a nation of a 'lower species'" and should be treated like "younger brothers." This relationship implied that the Poles should take care of the Ruthenians, but also that the latter should show appropriate deference to their older siblings. If the Ruthenians would just stop acting as if the Poles were their enemies, Miłkowski insisted, then they would be provided with all the schools, theaters, and academic societies they needed. If the Ruthenians succeeded in developing their own separate network of schools, Miłkowski continued, "Polish cultural superiority" would ensure that the Ruthenian schools would always remain inferior. Only common schooling—indeed, common institutions throughout the region—could help elevate the younger brothers of the East. Miłkowski concluded by describing his ideal future nation: "Poland for the Poles, Lithuania for the Lithuanians, Ruthenia for the Ruthenians. Poland, Lithuania, and Ruthenia joined together with the bonds of *united states*. This is the ideal of our common statehood, the ideal toward which everyone individually and all together—Poles, Lithuanians, and Ruthenians— ought to aspire, an ideal more rational today and for the future more beautiful, more honorable, and more useful than mutual struggle, wrangling, and slander."[130] Miłkowski's reference to the United States was not coincidental, because he imagined a future "United States of Poland" that would include all the peoples of the region. But this was indeed the inclusivity of the United States—and the Ukrainians were to play the role of the American Indians.

The language of *Wolne Polskie Słowo* will no doubt be recognized by anyone familiar with the rhetoric of West European imperialism or American discussions of manifest destiny. This was the tolerance of those who felt they could afford to be tolerant because time and history were on their side. This was also, of course, the *intolerance* of those who could only conceive of cultural diversity within strict limits, of those who drew sharp lines of inclusion and exclusion around national entities. Miłkowski, it seems, genuinely wanted to remain within the tradition of "for our freedom and yours," but he was finding it increasingly hard to do so. In a world of ethnonational diversity he could retain his expansive vision of Poland only by resorting to the historiosophy of imperialism, which located cultural plurality along a spectrum of progress and accepted diversity only insofar as "they" could be defined as "our younger brothers." This was not, in fact, a Swiss model (as *Wolne Polskie Słowo* occasionally claimed), but an American model—not a vision of equal partners within a common national home, but one of an eviscerated diversity that accepted local dialects and folk customs as long as everyone eventually assimilated to a "higher" common culture. It was a model that worked only as long as the younger brothers were willing to accept their designated role.

For a surprisingly long time this approach did in fact serve West European and American intellectuals (to the detriment of colonial subjects and domestic minorities), but it could never work very well in Poland. On the one hand, the Lithuanians, Ukrainians, and Jews refused to see themselves as inferior to Polish "civilization." On the other hand, the Poles themselves clung only precariously to the status of "European" and "modern." Not only did Poland stand on the edge of Europe, both conceptually and cartographically, but the Poles were incongruously occupied by other powers even as they applied a colonialist rhetoric to the eastern borderlands. Poles were perhaps unique in that they saw themselves as a European society engaged in a civilizing mission vis-à-vis a set of Eastern peoples, while simultaneously being subjected to imperial domination by one such "Oriental" land (Russia). The bewildering contradictions arising from this dual status as colonizer and colonized, as both underdeveloped and "civilized," made it hard to consistently apply the worldview cultivated by *Wolne Polskie Słowo*. It might serve an audience of Polish émigrés, but back in the Kingdom the National Democrats were coming up with a much more persuasive alternative, one that did not depend on any dubious predictions about the future—indeed, one that rejected historical time altogether. For all his limitations, Miłkowski remained within the world of the nineteenth-century liberal-democratic left. Dmowski and his colleagues were about to enter the world of the twentieth-century right.

8

National Egoism

We are often told that by the late nineteenth century (if not earlier) the new sciences of ethnography and linguistics provided the conceptual tools needed to formulate a "modern" definition of the national community. The restrictive noble nation of the eighteenth century was long dead, made obsolete by the emergence of mass politics and the inclusive, democratized sociologies of the nineteenth century. Similarly, the "abstraction" of romantic nationalism, with its transcendent spirit and its mystical vocabulary, had been decisively repudiated. The prestige of the social sciences made it difficult to perceive the nation as an embodiment of the patriotic deed, and the politics of the Polish intelligentsia precluded any open endorsement of an elite hegemony over the national idea. By the turn of the century, it seems, Poles had come to accept that the nation encompassed an entire ethnolinguistic community, open to all those who spoke the same language (regardless of class), but closed to those who did not exhibit certain demonstrable markings of Polish ethnicity.

Although this narrative is compelling, the development of a "modern" and "democratic"—but also potentially chauvinistic—conception of the nation was hotly contested, and its victory was by no means assured. Instead of interpreting fin de siècle nationalism as the culmination of the "modern" idea of Poland, we need to focus instead on the *crisis* of national identity that generated so much intellectual ferment in the 1890s. The intelligentsia of the day was more fractured and less committed to empiricism and democracy than we might expect. This was a time when none of the available frameworks for imagining the nation could win unqualified acceptance. Positivism provided a conceptual foundation for a definition of the nation based on language and cultural practice, but many political activists were uncomfortable with the rigid boundaries and narrow scope of an ethnic community. This sort of national vision established walls of exclusion that would prevent Ukrainians, Lithuanians, and Jews from identifying with the Polish cause, thus limiting the territorial ambitions of the future nation-state to narrow ethnolinguistic frontiers. Moreover, it was already obvious at the turn of the century that it would be nearly impossible to draw such boundaries on the complex ethnographic map of Eastern Europe. What would one do with Lwów, Wilno, and other eastern cities inhabited mainly by Poles and Jews but surrounded by Lithuanian or Ukrainian peasants? What would one do with the fervently patriotic Polish nobility scattered over lands as far east as the Dnieper River—individuals who had ruled over their estates for centuries but who were cut off from any sizable population of Polish-speaking peasants? Equally troublesome was the idea that the nation was an expression of popular sovereignty (a "daily plebiscite," as Ernest Renan put it in 1882).[1] In 1898 one patriotic activist did in fact suggest that the territorial limits of the future Poland be established by referendum, but this proposal found little support.[2] Aside from all the practical difficulties of organizing such a vote, many intellectuals were frightened by the prospect of placing their cherished national dreams before a tribunal of millions of peasants who seemed to possess little or no national consciousness. It was one thing to say that the nation was rooted in "the people," but quite another to imagine that the actual peasants and workers would determine who was a Pole and where Poland was to be located. As we saw in chapter 6, the intelligentsia could talk about "the people" only if they could place "the mob" within an organized, disciplinary framework (be it the historical trajectory of the socialists or the synchronic national space of the patriots). Until the intellectuals gained the power to enforce order and impose their own versions of national identity (i.e., until they won political independence), they had to figure out how to be Polish in a world where many of their supposed compatriots did not recognize all the social labels discussed in Warsaw and where national indoctrination was difficult or impossible.

In this book I have added some complexity to the familiar narrative of national modernization, moving beyond the unidirectional story outlined by Benedict Anderson and beyond the neat, mechanistic phases of "nation building" itemized by Miroslav Hroch.[3] National identity is not something invented by the intelligentsia and then spread to the masses, but neither is it a sociological phenomenon, emerging from an *ethnie* and given ideological articulation by a national elite.[4] Instead, the term "nation" has been used to describe a wide variety of identities, an array of possible human communities which can be located in social space and historical time in many different ways. Under different circumstances the term might be used on a regular basis by millions of people, or it might be restricted to the conversations of a narrow patriotic elite, but in either case the word is distinguished by its flexibility, its semantic indeterminacy, its ability to fit within multiple ideological frameworks. Perhaps at no time was this variability more evident than during the last years of the nineteenth century, during what Jacques Le Rider has described as "modernity's crisis of identity."[5]

To understand this crisis—and the forms of nationalism that emerged from it— it is useful to follow Robert B. Pippin's distinction between *modernity* and *modernism*. According to Pippin, the *ancien régime* was not merely replaced by an alternative world, because by the 1890s the teleologies and historiosophies that had sustained the nineteenth century's critical (often revolutionary) "modern" projects were themselves under siege. In other words, we should understand modernity as a socioeconomic process (urbanization and industrialization) as well as a critical and deconstructive cultural process (secularization and rationalization). These socio-cultural transformations produced, around the turn of the century, an intellectual crisis known as "modernism," a sense that the old world had been thoroughly torn apart but that nothing had replaced what had been lost. Modernism, Pippin concludes, should be seen as the climax (and not merely the product) of modernity—a last attempt to seek some stable ground against the onslaught of critical reason, before reason itself would disintegrate into postmodernism.[6] Fin de siècle intellectuals had to reconfigure their identities within a world that had been stripped of all certain narratives, a world in which old hierarchies and social norms were long gone but in which liberalism's "progress" had been called into question, leaving "the struggle for survival" as the only law. Some intellectuals—mainly socialists and liberals—would cling to the comforting secular and rational prophecies of the nineteenth century and continue to look forward to a future of progress. Others, less sanguine, would pursue doubt and skepticism to the bitter end, discarding as utopian and unrealistic the hopeful historiosophies of a previous age in exchange for a darker—but, they argued, more honest—worldview. In France, Georges Sorel grew disillusioned with Marxism and began his long quest for a new "myth" that would generate a revolution even if history could not promise one.[7] In Italy, Filippo Marinetti abandoned the idea that the future would grow out of the past, demanding instead a radical, willful break with historical time.[8] In Germany, Friedrich Nietzsche's writings—even when poorly understood—inspired a wide variety of thinkers to discard the verities of the nineteenth century as they searched for an "overman" who would impose his own meanings on a meaningless world. And in Poland, the National Democrats would resolve their own crisis of identity by embracing what they called "national egoism."

On the simplest level, national egoism was an ethical principle that commanded one to place the needs of the nation above all other considerations. As Zygmunt Balicki put it succinctly, "When one goes against the interests of one's own nation, one becomes immoral."[9] More profoundly, though, national egoism was a means of reconceptualizing both the nation and the ego, a way of reformulating the relationship between the self and the other—and the nature of both—so as to cope with the crisis of modernity. In this sense, it was a quintessential manifestation of political modernism. Le Rider observes, following Paul Ricoeur, that identity is constituted in the space between the "I" and the "not-I"; it is necessarily a relational concept rather than an introspective assertion of the self.[10] In the 1890s this linkage had been shattered by the uncertain status of both the individual and the community. The National Democrats (the Endecja) offered a new nation that could act in a world plagued by the unending war-of-all-against-all and thus serve as solid ground for the atomized individuals who had lost their place in time, their position within a progressive narrative. In this way the National Democrats resolved the crisis of identity by relocating the self within a redefined community. By the first years of the twentieth century they had constructed a radically new style of nationalism, one based on hatred, violence, oppression, and exclusion. They cast aside old slogans like "for our freedom and yours" and offered instead a chauvinistic vision that continues to haunt Polish intellectuals. They put aside the crisis of modernity and recovered their identity, but the price they paid was high.

Modern Poland, as conceived by the National Democrats, was not merely the ethnolinguistic community of the positivists, although the Endecja did make use of the empiricist rhetoric of social science. Dmowski and his colleagues found meaning in the anthropological distinctiveness of the Poles, and under the right circumstances they were willing to envision a nation thus bounded by language and culture. But the Endecja emerged from the cauldron of fin de siècle modernism, not the comforting teleologies of nineteenth-century modernity. Their worldview was not the culmination of a clear and unidirectional historical development toward democracy and sociological realism; instead they were trying to make sense of a world in which history no longer seemed to go in any obvious direction and in which the old liberal stories of progress were no longer persuasive (at least not to the National Democrats). As a result, they could accept the importance of ethnography (a product of liberalism's modernity, with its scientific approach to the study of society), but they also demanded something more, something that could survive all the challenges that were then eroding the confidence of liberalism's telos. Believing that nothing was certain, that history made no promises, the National Democrats could not confidently predict that the masses would someday "realize" their ethnicity and act in the way self-defined patriots thought they should. They needed a definition of the nation that took ethnolinguistic markers into account but also allowed the individual patriotic activist to transcend the confines of empiricism. They were searching for a way to talk about the nation as a sociological category while still retaining wide spaces for the application of individual will. They had to go beyond ethnicity, beyond the social sciences of modernity, in order to resolve their crisis of identity.

They did so by turning to the rhetoric of *power* and *struggle*. The nation envisioned by the National Democrats was supposed to have the power to enforce homogeneity, to *make* the cohesive ethnolinguistic community that history had not generated (and would not generate) of its own accord. The nation, thus conceived, was entitled to impose authority (mediated by its patriots), precisely *because* it had to contend with an unending, nonteleological struggle. Once it was decided that history was not going anywhere and that there could be no absolute standards of ethics or morality (above the needs of the national struggle), then the nationalists were free to impose authority, discipline, and homogeneity in the name of the nation, without concerning themselves with "justice," "equality," or "liberty" (all terms that had once stood at the center of the Polish intelligentsia's vocabulary). This grim worldview once again brings us back to the primary theme of this book: the relationship between the definition of the nation and the configuration of historical time. Because the National Democrats helped create a style of thought which denied all the historiosophies that had sustained the Polish intelligentsia throughout the nineteenth century, they were defenseless against the consequences of that expression (so firmly rooted in public rhetoric since the 1870s): the struggle for survival. As was discussed in the last chapter, the repudiation of historical time made it possible to articulate a new style of anti-Semitism on the pages of *Głos* and to see Poland as a participant in an endless battle for national existence. "Struggle" was no longer the engine of history; it was now a part of a timeless "nature." It was no longer the means by which humanity moved toward a liberal (or socialist) utopia; instead, it was a permanent feature of the human condition. The National Democrats stood before the abyss of this dark vision, looking out over the bleak landscape of the nineteenth century's failed ideologies, searching for a way to stabilize their identity as Polish in a world that offered no solace for the victims of injustice. Their solution was novel (for Poles): they insisted that they were *not* victims, that they had no need to appeal to any higher cause or ethical standard to justify their existence or their identity. They felt Polish, they declared, because they were part of a national community that was just like any other collectivity in nature. Their Poland had to assert its existence (no longer expressed in terms of "national rights"), and they had to serve that nation simply because it (and they) existed, not because it (or they) participated in some higher scheme. Anyone who stood in their way—be it in the name of "humanitarian justice" or in the name of some other national community— was the enemy and had to be defeated, perhaps destroyed. This was more than just an ideological program; it was a resolution to the modernist crisis of identity. This was a way to solidify a sense of belonging in a post-teleological and postpositivist world, a way to use the vocabulary of ethnography and linguistics to talk about the nation, without being confined to the static limitations of sociological formations. This was a way to restore will to science, a way to avoid the paralysis of critical reason without falling back into liberalism's or socialism's faith in historical time. National egoism offered a way to act on behalf of the nation even if one could no longer believe that the nation stood for anything—other than itself.

Grounding the Modern Self

The sense of fin de siècle crisis shared by so many intellectuals in the 1890s was expressed eloquently by Roman Dmowski in 1894 in a lamentation about modern urban life published in *Głos*. He described the major cities of Europe as "maelstroms for the human soul. . . . The human essence, enveloped by that sphere, is pushed by necessity, drawn toward a whirlpool in which souls are smashed together like ships in a maritime chaos. The strongest individuals disintegrate, tearing themselves into pieces. They cannot withstand the extreme moral pressure. That pressure is created directly or indirectly by the free competition that reigns in the large cities in full bloom." This defense of the individual against the forces of competition was familiar, but it was leading in a new direction. Dmowski concentrated on the "trivial struggles" that bombarded urban residents at every step. Contending with these challenges, he wrote, forced individuals to "make themselves into small change, to constantly tear themselves to pieces." It became impossible to strive for greatness, because more immediate needs raised so many distractions. Worse yet, the unquestioned rule of the market forced even geniuses to compete for physical survival by accommodating their abilities to the desires, institutions, and norms of the masses. The result was a fatal "leveling."

Dmowski's most fundamental concern was that a fractured and contentious modernity had destroyed the integrity of the individual, reducing the cohesive personality to "small change." The autonomous "I" could not be sustained within the boorish and brutal urban spaces of contemporary Europe; there was no time to cultivate the self when one had to spend all day worrying about petty problems of survival. The promise of the modern world had been that the rational individual could become free, both politically and ontologically, but Dmowski recognized that the nineteenth century had not realized these goals. Liberty (even in the strangled form it took in the Russian Empire) led to the vulgarization of political and cultural life, and positivism naturalized the human personality so thoroughly that one could no longer even conceptualize a self existing outside sociological or biological laws. Dmowski confronted these frustrations while critiquing the work of Friedrich Nietzsche in 1894 (the only time he directly engaged his more famous contemporary). Dmowski agreed with Nietzsche's attack on bourgeois Europe but would not follow him along the path toward unchecked individualism. If one really wanted to cultivate a space for the genius, Dmowski wrote, one had to liberate him from daily cares, and only a strong society could do this. Nietzsche, Dmowski wrote, "declared his full hatred for society, in which he saw the enemy of individuality, which he elevated to a moral level second to none. The philosopher, however, aimed his blow badly: society and cooperation (the foundation of existence) has created the only foundation from which individualism can grow. The enemy of individualism in society is the antisocial element."[11] This formulation was not paradoxical: Dmowski was attempting to transcend modernity by bracketing its struggle and vulgarity within another sphere, placing firewalls around the war-of-all-against-all so that he could create a space within which the genius could escape the "trivial problems" of life.

That space would be the nation. As Dmowski put it in 1905, "Only a strong national organization, based on a deep respect for tradition, is capable of guaranteeing human society moral health over the centuries. . . . Thus national ethics is the foundation of interpersonal ethics. . . . Wherever [these ethics] perish, all of social life will gradually dissolve, society will atomize, all moral bonds will be broken, mutual obligation with disappear, and we will reach the state of *homo homini lupus*."[12] But Dmowski did not really fear such chaos, thanks to his faith in Spencerism. "*Homo homini lupus* does not rule without restraint," he wrote elsewhere. "Thanks above all to the struggle of groups with groups, cooperation has developed within groups."[13] Dmowski displaced struggle without even trying to resolve it: battles between nations became the answer to conflicts between individuals. Struggle, in this presentation, was not a problem but a necessary safeguard against social decay.

This view was not merely a reclamation of Hobbes, because Dmowski's goal was not (or was not only) to establish order: he wanted to find a space for the exertion of *will*. Whereas Hobbes had imagined the Leviathan as a repository for individual autonomy (in the name of security), Dmowski's powerful social collective was a means of facilitating individual expression and volition. The fatal weakness of the modern world, he thought, was the inability to *act*, to *create*. "Our youth is very moral," he wrote, "if one judges them from the perspective of everyday morality, as the average person understands it: a passive morality, consisting above all of not doing anything wrong. But alongside that morality there exists another one, consisting of doing many good things, of generally doing a lot, so as to live life as intensely as possible." In contrast with the morality of action, he complained, the average Pole considered "the summit of morality to be vegetation."[14] According to Dmowski, passivity—the morality of vegetation—had caused the great cultural crisis of his era. He summarized his argument in one rambling sentence:

> Today, when brutal egoism, elevated to the level of a principle, rules in social life; when bourgeois Europe, emancipated from all moral standards, presents in the most influential spheres an image of final collapse; when interests, understood in the most superficial way, whether stated honestly or hypocritically concealed under a cover of cheap clichés, determine the spirit of all political programs; when the subject matter of fine art, purged of ideals, has become the lowest form of exploiting life; when true religion has survived only among the dark masses, losing in the minds of educated people its first foundation—honest faith; when some make of [religion] a display of fashion, while others abuse it with the foolish grimaces of literature and art that go under the great name of neo-Christianity; [faced with all this] the mind needs something morally positive, and not being able to stand under its own strength, the only clear perspective is opened by that social gospel [socialism]; simple, accessible to the reason of even the least educated, simplifying in an often naïve manner things that are very complex, but having a strong moral foundation—the good of humanity, a goal of sincere aspirations, understood in a fresh, not a used-up manner.[15]

The quest for order, beauty, and faith within a just society culminated in socialism—or (as Dmowski put it) in "socialist decadence." This false (in his view) resolution to the crisis of modernity was the product of humanitarianism, which he linked, in a sharply gendered maneuver, to an imagined feminization of Polish culture. Because of the lack of a proper educational system, he wrote, Polish boys were raised by their mothers, "whose humanitarianism differs in its passive character from the human feelings of men." Such training, Dmowski believed, led to polite children who would do nothing wrong, but who were capable only of "crying and complaining whenever they encounter injustice."[16] Dmowski was convinced that Polish culture and political thought had become effeminate, superficial, decadent, egotistical, and *thus* socialist. National Democracy, in contrast, was going to provide "masculine" virtues that were firm, realistic, and above all ruthless.

The nation would serve, in this vision, as the incubator for masculine individuality, a place where men could be(come) men. This is the context within which, in 1896, Dmowski first used the expression "national egoism."[17] He praised England as the model nation precisely because others criticized it "for embodying egoism, for negating in its actions humanitarian principles, for working only for itself." All this was true, Dmowski wrote, but in displaying such egoism England had performed "the greatest service for that humanity. It has served it by not living according to imitation." One could not say the same about Poland, Dmowski lamented. Here one was taught to be a cosmopolitan, to think of Poland as a birthplace, but nothing more. Only someone who "possessed a extraordinary individuality" could overcome this indoctrination and avoid becoming "the owner of nothing, a pauper living on scraps seized here and there." This sort of person "does not know how to create anything, and only imitates everything." Such "imitators" could offer nothing to mankind, because "humanity, in order to progress, needs workers who will show it new and better forms of life than heretofore known, who will open new perspectives of thought."[18] Here, as elsewhere, Dmowski employed the term "progress," but this was no longer the teleological advancement of liberalism or socialism. This was a progress that men *made*, through the force of their will, and it had no relation to any transhistorical ideal, any vision of where such progress might be heading. The agent of this progress was the autonomous individual, and to be truly autonomous he could not be tied to any ethical restraints. But such an individual *did* have to be tied to a national community. Just as the nation freed the individual by resolving the "trivial struggles" of daily life through social organization, so would the unique core of national character allow the individual to create, to transcend the uniformity and vapidity of cosmopolitan culture. By ensuring that this core was sufficiently "realistic," without excessive emotions or morals, such a restoration of community would also transform "our 'feminine' nation" into a solid foundation for masculine identity.[19]

With this argument, Dmowski was able to exploit the vocabulary of biology, with its well-established organic metaphors, without undermining individuality. In *The Thoughts of a Modern Pole*, which became the canonical text of the National Democratic movement almost immediately after it was serialized in *Przegląd Wszechpolski* in 1902, Dmowski wrote, "Just as organic development depends on the ever tightening mutual dependency of tissues, organs, and [the organism's] constituent cells, so does the development of society lead to the ever tightening mutual dependency of certain strata and [society's] constituent individuals. The more a society is advanced in development, the more it is a society, the less an individual in relation to other members of the society can be that which he wants to be and the more [he will be] that which he must be." What he "must be" was whatever the community needed him to be. Dmowski recognized the authoritarian implications of this argument, but he insisted that he was not weakening the autonomy of the self. When national solidarity is strong, he wrote, "it only simplifies the development of individual distinctiveness on a higher level." This argument forces us to read more deeply into the Endecja's apparent negation of free will and personal liberty. When Dmowski wrote that the true Pole should "treat all of [society's] affairs and interests as his own, regardless of whether they are personally close to him," he was repudiating egoism so as to restore the self, to repair the fragmentation and chaos of modern life so that men (if not women) could once again cultivate their own personalities.[20]

Whereas Dmowski stressed the problem of modernity (the inability of genius to rise above social chaos), Zygmunt Balicki concentrated on the solution (the nation as a locus of order and discipline). In 1895, writing for a French audience in the *Revue Internationale de Sociologie*, Balicki seemed to be unconcerned about the fate of the individual. "What is the individual from the point of view of society?" he asked. "He is only the point of intersection of various collective currents, of various organizations, a synthesis of his own instincts and the tendencies of society. . . . The social integration of modern times operates on the basis of the common needs of ad hoc groups and not on the individuals who constitute [those groups]." Like Dmowski, Balicki argued that this integral bond with society was the only thing that prevented the struggle for existence from "dominating without restraint." But while Dmowski had appealed to the resulting cohesion as a means of freeing the individual for personal development, Balicki seemed to be interested in the community for its own sake. "Each group has its own interests and needs—the community is not merely the sum of all the individuals that make it up—and in a developed society the individuals serve these common needs. Individuals change, grow, are replaced by others, but the common needs of the collective interest remains constant."[21]

Ultimately, though, Balicki followed Dmowski in the quest for a stable center, a secure identity. "Happiness," he wrote in 1900, "is the state of our self-awareness that we feel as a lasting unity." To be satisfied with life we must possess a sense of "harmony," and there must be a "methodical" quality to our inner selves. Unhappiness, in contrast, was a feeling of "constant bifurcation" and "dissonance," accompanied by an erosion of spiritual energy. According to Balicki, "Pain and physical suffering constitute only a trivial, meaningless fragment of the suffering that we endure." Much more distressing was the sense of not knowing who we were, the feeling that our essential nature was being torn apart and that the day-to-day petty struggle for survival made it impossible to establish a secure foothold in the fin de siècle urban environment. This concern drove Balicki to search for a new Archimedean point, and he found it in "society." If the problem was bifurcation, then the resolution (he believed) was to be found in "the influence of opinions, feelings, prejudices, and customs." Individuality could be fully realized only if one reflected the "dominant tendencies in society."[22] Identity was not a question of self-image, nor was it a reflection of some sort of essential inner nature; it existed not within the soul but at the point of contact between the self and the social world. Balicki argued that the turmoil of modernity had severed this link, leaving humanity adrift in a world where the only choices were egoism or oblivion.

Paradoxically, Balicki's apparent negation of individuality was rooted in a quest for personal happiness and harmony. He deprived the individual of autonomy because he believed that the regrounding of the self within the community had to be based on a "real" bond, not a free choice.

> In order that the internal bond of personal contentment and the impersonal happiness of the whole may really create a firm spiritual harmony, it must flow spontaneously from a deep social instinct, it must be free from all internal force and reflection. Then even sacrifice, if it becomes necessary, ceases to be a sacrifice: the person himself is not capable of differentiating between bearing [the sacrifice] for others and for himself; egoism and altruism do not contradict, but merge into one feeling flowing from the deepest stratum of human nature.[23]

In contrast, if one's bond with society was a product of "reflection" rather than a "deep social instinct," then the distinction between altruism and egoism reemerged and one was faced with painful choices between personal interests and the needs of society. To opt for egoism in such cases would transform the individual into an isolated particle, adrift and without identity, lost because it could no longer recognize anything with which to identify. Similarly, if one consciously abnegated personal interests for the common good, then the self would be submerged and obliterated. Either way the harmonious interaction between "I" and "we" was lost.

Balicki offered a means to attain harmony by imagining the collective as a social subject in its own right.

> There exists a whole category of positive and negative feelings that are above all collective, social feelings. They are transferred onto the individual only insofar as he feels solidarity with the whole, insofar as he appears as one of its constituent parts. It is not the individual entity which feels pain or satisfaction in such cases, but the social entity; the latter is the primordial source of those feelings. . . . This brings us to the conclusion that social hedonism, as a whole, is a primordial phenomenon, not only taking precedence over individual hedonism, but containing within itself all its basic features. . . . The interests and welfare of the individual are decisive only insofar as they are in accordance with the interests and welfare of society, and influence [society] directly or indirectly.

There followed from this a simple ethical principle: "Everything which, according to the dominant ideas of society, brings a feeling of satisfaction to the community is called good; that which is a source of suffering in collective life is called bad." There is no such thing as an individual conscience or a private morality, Balicki argued, because "all morality is public."[24]

Balicki developed this principle into a fully elaborated ethical system in his 1902 book, *Egoizm narodowy wobec etyki* (National Egoism and Ethics). He based his argument on a critique of what he called "detached" moral principles—those that claimed to transcend time and place. No act could be immoral or moral in isolation; different social conditions necessitated a variety of ethical rules, so social context "constitutes the most important, the only decisive ethical measure." The idea that ethics should be contextualized and flexible was common currency among European philosophers in the 1890s (to the outrage of conservatives), but Balicki turned this premise in an unexpected direction. The quest for a universal moral code, he argued, was both an impossibility and a profound danger.

> The ethic of ideals, absolute in its essence, unable to create a feeling of universal duty, shatters society in terms of morality, introduces into it chaos and spiritual anarchy. Creating a situation without an exit, it strikes a wedge between the heart and the brain, sows unrest and irresolution, discord and hysteria; it makes the community nervous and creates from it a type without character. In the pursuit of perfection people stop being good members of society, in the pursuit of honor they stop performing adequately their personal and civic duties. These are not at all the foundations upon which one could base the moral rebirth of the nation![25]

Such a fate could be countered, Balicki believed, only by the "social instinct," which compelled people to identify with the "common interest" and to express "solidarity with the egoism of the collective whole." The ultimate goal of the moral individual was to recover his link with the community and in this way to resolve his bifurcated identity. "The rule for [the individual]," Balicki wrote, "will be to create from himself a unified, harmonious, and strong type, corresponding to his own individuality (self-conscious egoism); to join his individuality to the appropriate circle, sphere, group, and entire society (self-conscious altruism); finally, to merge spiritually with his society and accept its welfare, desires, and goals as his own (collective egoism)."[26] Balicki believed that even the most "self-conscious" individuality would be incomplete and even the greatest selflessness would be insufficient if the two did not find a point of contact in the community. It was from this intersection that identity would be discovered, or salvaged.

These arguments could have served a socialist as well as a nationalist, and at least one reviewer of *Egoizm narodowy wobec etyki* understood the volume to be a generic appeal for social commitment.[27] Midway through his book, however, Balicki subtly switched his terminology: "The preservation, the independence, the development, and the strength of the highest social individuality, as is the nation, has as a foundation self-conscious national egoism, before which any other egoism, whether individual or collective, although in itself the most justified, must give way."[28] The collective egoism he spoke of earlier became here the national egoism of the book's title. Any other social group could claim some loyalty from its members, but only as a subset of the national whole, and those who placed the interests of a "lesser" group over those of the nation were immoral, regardless of their good intentions. The nation, Balicki wrote, was the "highest social collective" and "the only natural society." All ethical injunctions, he concluded, "are and must always be national. Social ethics demand that everyone feel himself to be a member of his nation and not only show solidarity with its interests, but merge his entire social essence with its essence and live its life. If one is not devoted to the nation, one is a cosmopolitan individualist. Socialists and Jews, claiming to express their social attachments through a love of humanity, are just insincere."[29]

This is what it meant to be "moral" for the National Democrats. As a contributor to *Przegląd Wszechpolski* wrote:

> The propagation of our political principles and the elevation of the level of political thought in society will go a lot quicker if preceded by effective moral propaganda. . . . Love of the fatherland, placing the national good above everything, the duty to sacrifice oneself, to make personal sacrifices for its defense and expansion—these main foundations of our public morality must be made evident, presented in an accessible way in everything that we do. In the name [of this morality] we must fight the power of egoism, be it personal or caste, be it declared with brutal honesty or veiled with the impoverished clichés of false humanitarianism.

Moreover, for a political movement to be moral it had to be willing to *enforce* these principles upon a reluctant society. As this author wrote, "The propagation of ethics among society is closely tied to the moral control of its public life." The patriot must strive to "remove from [the nation] elements that employ excessively low ethics."

Ominously, this author considered it "an obvious fact that the ethics of nearly all our opponents are incredibly low in comparison to ours."[30]

Dmowski and Balicki had resolved modernity's crisis of identity by regrounding the atomized individual within a national community, thus locating (or constructing) a point of stability and a source of social solidarity. Imbedded within this vision, however, was an evocation of discipline and authority, of the "moral control" that had to be imposed upon unruly "elements." This introduces the central irony of the Endecja's nation, and the "modern" nation in general. On the one hand, their Poland was a focus for order and authority in a chaotic world, a place where people would be compelled to be "that which they must be." On the other hand, the nation was a "natural society" held together by innate bonds of association, not voluntary or willfully imposed affiliation. The National Democrats were mixing the language of "ought" (or "must") with the language of "is." They wanted to talk about Poland with the vocabulary of science but at the same time they had configured the nation within a moral discourse. This tension would shape the Endecja's idiosyncratic and complex definition of the nation.

Beyond Ethnicity: Defining the Modern Nation

The nation, as imagined by the Endecja, had to be a point of unity for a fragmented population, an anchor in a chaotic world. It had to be modern and democratic, in the sense that it encompassed and incorporated the masses, yet it also had to be organized and stable, invulnerable to the transitory whims of its less enlightened members. It had to be a positive force for moral control, so as to encourage and enforce unity and discipline—a natural phenomenon, existing independently of the willfulness of its members. It had to be real, subject to scientific laws, yet it had to inspire people with great ideals. To accomplish all this, the Endecja's Poland had to be, on one level, an ethnolinguistic collective—something that could be talked about with the vocabulary of social science. It had to be based on innate, natural similarities and affinities, not voluntary, contractual affiliation. But it had to be more than this: for the National Democrats, Poland would be *both* a sociologically defined community *and* an autonomous subject, a transcendent spirit that could confine and command the actions of individual Poles. This spirit, moreover, would itself be constrained by a set of natural laws that would determine how it interacted with other nations and with its own population. The nation could thus be both ideal and real, both an independent source of volition and morality and a dependent component of an amoral natural world. This was the complex concatenation of ideas and images that constituted the National Democrats' vision of Poland, allowing the nation to become in their minds an agent for struggle and (eventually) conquest. In the Endecja's definition of the term *naród* (nation), all the elements discussed in this book came together: the use of patriotic rhetoric to enforce social discipline, the construction of high walls of inclusion and exclusion around the national community, and the insistence that international relations were based on conflict. The doctrine of hate sustained a paradoxical vision, simultaneously freeing the nation from the confines of ethnicity while facilitating the imposition of both cultural and political unity. That is, it allowed the Endecja to imagine a nation that was based on, yet could rise above, the narrow bounds of the ethnolinguistic community without leading to the conclusion that Poland might be a pluralistic, diverse space.

As was discussed in chapter 4, the intellectual atmosphere in the Kingdom in the 1880s and 1890s was both antipositivist and postpositivist. The young radicals known as the *niepokorni* (be they "socialists" or "patriots") rejected the "sterile" and "small" worldview of the liberal press, without escaping the appeal of scientistic rhetoric. The National Democrats participated in this ambivalent legacy when they talked about and defined the nation. Some scholars, citing Popławski's early writings and noting Dmowski's willingness to accept (temporarily, for tactical reasons) a smaller, more ethnically homogenous Poland after World War I, have argued that the Endeks thought of the nation as an ethnolinguistic community. Most historians agree, however, that the National Democratic conception of Poland was more complex and less socio-logical.[31] Dmowski did indeed describe the borders of 1772 as "geographical non-sense" demarcating "a monstrosity," but he was equally scornful of those who be-lieved that Poland "could exist only in the concepts of philologists, not politicians."[32] He was skeptical of the view (propagated by Limanowski, Piłsudski, and others) that Poland should be a multicultural federation, but this skepticism did not lead him to accept a narrow vision of an ethnolinguistic nation. Dmowski, Balicki, Popławski, and their colleagues tried to be "modern" and "scientific," yet they could never fully accept the limitations of sociology, linguistics, or ethnography. To resolve this di-lemma, they looked back, selectively and creatively, to the rhetoric of romanticism.

In 1892 the literary critic and National Democratic author Zygmunt Wasilewski had already begun to question the positivists' emphasis on ethnicity and language, and on the empirical world in general. His return to romanticism was more explicit than most, as he combined his metaphorical search for "great ideas" with a literal sojourn to a pocket of Polish romanticism: an émigré museum of Polish artifacts and documents in Rapperswil, Switzerland.[33] Visiting the museum, he wrote, was like entering "a strange world of the moon," where one could not help but succumb to the appeal of romanticism. Wasilewski's stay there changed his life.

> I fell into history. My shore, from which I had looked upon the Polish present
> from the perspective of its existence and aspirations for the future, while turned
> away from a past that I did not know at all, drifted away from me. . . . If, while
> in Poland, one operated according to concrete details in the expectation of action,
> then here one could not be surprised at any allegories or patriotic symbols, a
> feeling of martyrdom, a messianic vision. Poland itself became a symbol, and it
> would be the task of the literary critic to understand its drama from the remains
> that a previous epoch had left behind, were it not for the fact that the same critic
> is drawn into the drama, condemned by the émigré tumult.

While working in the museum library, Wasilewski formulated his definition of the nation: "I understood then that one cannot consider the nation in solely political, territorial, geographical, and economic categories. Instead it is necessary to see it as an individual civilization, capable of producing and using individuals of genius, elevating that individuality to the highest level of European civilization. National civilization, as the creation of one soul, must therefore present a cohesive organic whole."[34] Wasilewski's nation was not a social collective but a *singular* spiritual entity ("the creation of *one* soul"). It had been taken from the sociologists and returned to the realm of literary metaphors.

Not all National Democratic writing was as explicitly neoromantic as this, but Wasilewski's unwillingness to rely on positivism's sociological and ethnographic definition of the nation was typical. Already in the third issue of *Przegląd Wszechpolski* (in 1895) an anonymous author argued that Belarus was an integral part of Poland, regardless of the ethnolinguistic characteristics of the region. He realized that the *Białolachy* (as he wanted to call them) neither spoke Polish nor shared Polish cultural norms—he simply believed that such things were irrelevant in the face of deeper historical bonds.[35] Similarly, Popławski rejected both race (as an abstract and meaningless concept) and language (as a mere descriptive category without political significance). He initially hoped to retain "culture" as an emanation of the "national spirit," but soon he abandoned even this metric of national membership in exchange for more flexible metaphors.[36] Dmowski believed that a Pole was measured not by his language or place of birth but by a commitment to the nation's struggle for survival. His very definition of the nation thus implied a call to action. He returned Poland to the world of the deed:

> We are a nation, a single, indivisible nation, because we possess a feeling of our
> unity, we possess a common, collective consciousness, a common national spirit.
> That national spirit is . . . created though centuries of common state existence, [it
> is] a feeling of unity in the struggle for common existence, in success and
> collective failure, in the aspiration to collective goals, a feeling of its distinctive-
> ness from the alien traditions of [our] neighbors. That national spirit, created
> through a long process of history, in history finds the justification for its
> existence and its aspirations. Clearly, *historical rights* is not an empty phrase,
> not an empty formula without meaning. Yes, we are one nation, because we are
> joined by a common feeling, a common national thought, finally a common will
> directed toward one national goal that every Pole, even if only a little educated,
> is aware of.[37]

This dense passage contains the essential ingredients of the National Democratic conception of the nation. Most important was the "national spirit," which removed Poland from the confines of language and ethnicity and elevated it to a higher realm. Whenever the National Democrats confronted evidence that a certain population was not really Polish, according to some historical, sociological, ethnographic, or cultural measure, they could always respond by evoking the national spirit that transcended all such mundane considerations. This spirit, in turn, was defined as a "feeling," an awareness of a collective goal. Dmowski claimed that Poland was a nation because it possessed a "feeling of unity," a sense of common purpose and a united devotion to the national struggle. Similarly, Popławski believed that "neither common descent, nor a similarity of languages, nor a doubtful cultural bond suffices. Political solidarity must be based only on a solidarity of aspirations and interests," which in turn arose from the "historical idea" of the nation.[38] "National individuality," Popławski wrote in 1898, "depends not only on the external properties of tribal distinctiveness, but above all and primarily on a psychic distinctiveness (which is, in a sense, a crystalization of the historical tradition of the nation, in the broad sense of that expression) and on the natural conditions of its existence in the past and present. Language is only an external manifestation of national individuality, without which [the nation] can still exist (for example, the Irish nationality) and which, without the support of other factors, does not protect [the nation] at all."[39]

Popławski opposed those who wanted to draw state boundaries solely according to ethnographic standards, as well as those who pursued policies of forced assimilation in order to create ethnic unity. He presented this argument most clearly in 1900, in a lengthy passage that must be cited in full to capture its polemical force. Here Popławski criticized

> the simplistic, mechanistic understanding of nationality affairs, [which is]
> pervasive among us, particularly in radical circles. This mechanistic view,
> pointing to the need to shift borders and create ethnic territories, does not take
> into account the facts of reality, and under the pretense of humanitarianism and
> freedom is a justification for the brutal violation of national individuality. The
> fact of being born or living on a certain territory and [having a certain] tribal
> descent cannot decide the nationality of thousands and millions of people, or
> even a single person. Centuries of common political life, a community of
> spiritual and material culture, a community of interests, etc., mean one hundred
> times more than a community of descent or even language. That supposedly
> humanitarian view is only the opposite side of another, centralist [view],
> demanding in the name of state interests or cultural interests—which always
> comes down to the interests of the majority—the elimination of national
> differences and distinctiveness. . . . These are precisely Bismarckian views, this
> is precisely the cult of brutal strength—it is all the same if one calls this the
> omnipotence of the state or the omnipotence of the national majority.[40]

This was a double-edged critique, attacking on the one hand the idea that ethnic groups deserve independence, while at the same time evoking a well-established (but soon to be abandoned) commitment to diversity. Such an argument allowed Popławski to defend Poland's national distinctiveness against the Germans and the Russians while maintaining territorial ambitions in the multiethnic *kresy* (the "borderlands" of Ukraine, Belarus, and Lithuania). It allowed him to repeat an old Polish complaint about forced denationalization (perhaps the last time any National Democrat would speak positively about "difference") while repositioning the discussion of ethnography so as to strip it of all meaning. Because language and culture were of secondary importance, Popławski believed, the construction of both national and state boundaries could never be based entirely on ethnicity. Cultural practices change all the time, he argued elsewhere, and it would be foolish to try to intervene in this process in any way, or to use such shifting sands to demarcate national frontiers.[41] "In general," he wrote in 1903, "for the normalization of mutual relations between two nationalities, ethnolinguistic criteria are insufficient and even improper."[42] Only the historical community, the bond of common aspirations, and the collective participation in the struggle for survival could define a "real" nation.

All these references to history and difference can be misleading, because neither Dmowski nor Popławski believed that Poland should be shaped according to some specific historical geography, nor (paradoxically) did they think that Poland could exist if divided by diversity. One will find few references in National Democratic writing to the maps of 1772, 1648, or any other significant date in Poland's past. Their idea of history was not limited by any cartographic images: it was a reference to a timeless engagement with the national cause, a patriotic devotion that extended across generations into the past and the future. *Timelessness* (a more precise term than "history" in this case) and *social discipline* were the keys to National Democracy, because these concepts resolved an apparent contradiction. Dmowski based his nation on a "common will" and a shared goal, but even he recognized that many people whom he considered Polish were not, in fact, "aware" of the identities imagined by the Warsaw intellectuals. The gap between the community of common aspirations and the actually existing, "unenlightened" peasantry was easy to bridge for the National Democrats, thanks to a concept that would become one of their hallmarks: the potential Pole. True patriotism, Dmowski wrote, "is a love for all of Poland, a feeling of duty toward it and the ability to sacrifice for it. That feeling, which has developed to varying degrees in varying people, even when not evident, [nonetheless] exists in the average Pole in a dormant state, in (so to speak) a potential state."[43] The power of this concept cannot be overstated, because without it the National Democrats could not have made their nation concrete and "realistic." Dmowski's potential Pole allowed the nation to exist even before national consciousness was widely propagated. From this foundation the Endecja could spread the message of patriotism among the peasants with an evangelical zeal and with confidence that they were, in any case, already Polish. The National Democrats could imagine a popular nation without opening themselves to the vagaries of the popular will, and they could speak about the national future without resorting to a deterministic historiosophy. The peasants were already Polish, but only through the willful actions of the National Democrats would this potential identity be made manifest.

In a frequently cited passage from *The Thoughts of a Modern Pole*, Dmowski expressed his contempt for those who were not yet "conscious" of their nationality, without surrendering the conviction that such people were nonetheless bound to the nation. Once again, the key to his argument was the timelessness of the nation.

> I do not want to share my thoughts with those for whom the nation is a dead
> statistic, a collection of individuals speaking a certain language and living in a
> certain area. I will only be understood by those who see in [the nation] an
> indivisible social whole, organically cohesive, binding the human individual
> with innumerable knots, some of which have their beginning in the distant
> past—the creators of our race—others in the history that is known to us—the

creators of our tradition—and others, finally, enriching the content of that race, tradition [and] national character, being created today so that in the future [the national bond] will be tightened even more strongly. I write not for those who must still obtain their Polishness, but for those who deeply feel their bond with the nation, with its life, needs [and] aspirations, who recognize the duty to participate in its work and struggles.[44]

Here the nation existed beyond those who did not (yet) "feel their bond," beyond the "dead statistics" of ethnography, beyond even the devoted patriot. Dmowski's Poland was an organic whole that linked people across generations. He may not have wished to speak to the unpatriotic, but he had already included them within the nation (the Polishness they did not feel was nonetheless "theirs").

There was no room in this conception of the nation for Renan's "daily plebiscite," despite the Endecja's emphasis on a "feeling of unity" among all Poles. For Balicki, the nation was a community "which the individual does not choose but into which he is born."[45] Wasilewski described the nation as an "organic" union standing above all "individual rights, desires, and centrifugal tendencies."[46] Dmowski put it even more forcefully:

Patriotism is not a philosophical system which people of equal intellectual and moral development accept or reject: it is a moral relationship of the individual to society; recognizing it is a necessity at a certain degree of moral development, and rejecting [it] testifies to moral immaturity or collapse. . . . We are gradually becoming ever more a society in the higher, modern meaning of that word; the internal bonds are increasingly tight, uniting us in a cohesive whole—bonds which in their essence are not voluntary but result from a system of social relations, from the dependence of the individual on the whole; [these bonds are] therefore more certain, more durable, less dependent upon momentary intellectual atmospheres.[47]

Dmowski took this argument to its furthest extreme in an article entitled "The Foundations of Polish Politics," published in the tenth-anniversary issue of *Przegląd Wszechpolski* and later reprinted as an annex to *The Thoughts of a Modern Pole*. "The moral union of the individual with the nation," he wrote, was "independent of the individual will." One who is joined with the nation "does not have free will but must be obedient to the collective will of the nation." The "instincts" of national obedience could command not only that an individual risk his life in times of war, but that an entire generation sacrifice itself for the timeless continuity of the nation.

The highest moral satisfaction for me is to love and honor that which my father and my grandfathers loved and honored, to recognize the same duties as they did. . . . In this union with the old, with the most ancient generations of the nation, I see the highest sanction for moral behavior in national affairs, a sanction that allows one to sacrifice the entire contemporary generation if it is not faithful to the national duty. That ethic permits one to decrease or even destroy the welfare, peace, and happiness of the contemporary generation, if this sacrifice is necessary for retaining the continuity of national existence, for rescuing that which the past has left us, for the development of that existence in the future. . . . That ethic indicates as a source and goal the nation, not only today's [nation], living for the moment on its territory, but the entire nation in time, with all generations that preceded us [and] all those that will follow us.[48]

"One might say," Tadeusz Grużewski wrote later, "that the value of the nation consists of the personal qualities of its sons, but this would only be half the truth. The nation does not only accept individuals just as the race presents them, but educates them over the course of generations."[49] Needless to say, the Endecja saw itself as the source of this "education."

The National Democrats began with a moral injunction to sacrifice for the national whole but ended with a conception of the nation that deprived the individual of the autonomy needed to make a moral choice. Once again we see the creative tension at the heart of National Democracy: the conflict between "ought" and "is," between the nation-as-ethical-standard and the nation-as-integral-organism. Insofar as the former presumed that the individual was an independent moral actor, the latter turned the nation into the locus for authority and discipline. As Dmowski wrote in 1905, the collective spirit of the nation should ultimately

seize more and more from the spirit of the individual on behalf of the whole, on behalf of the great, collective spirit of the nation; [the nation] could create the strongest known collective moral bond in the history of humanity, the breaking of which, if it lasts long enough, will stop depending directly on the will of the individual. Someone is a Pole, an Englishman, or even more so a Japanese—for Japan presents the most classic example of the nation, the highest of the known levels of national collectivity—not only because he likes it, but because it could not be otherwise. With the greatest effort of will he would not be able to tear out from his spirit the feeling that holds him within the nation [and] ties him with its past [and] with its goals, and which constitutes his national conscience.[50]

Ten years earlier Dmowski had set out to find a place for the "genius" within the "maelstrom" of modernity. He and Balicki had offered the "organic" community as a source of stability, a refuge from the "trivial struggles" of everyday life and an incubator for masculinity. Pursuing this imagery over the course of a decade, they came to believe that such a community had to be "reflexive" and "instinctual." This conviction pointed toward a nation defined according to objective markers like language, cultural practices, religious affiliation, or place of residence, and the National Democrats were indeed interested in these things. They may have moved toward neoromanticism, but they always remained postpositivist. Nonetheless, against the backdrop of the political and social unrest leading up to 1905, the need for the nation to enforce discipline and loyalty grew in the minds of the Endecja's leadership, making it impossible to rely entirely on ethnography. To utilize a purely sociological definition of the nation would entail accepting political diversity within the national com-

munity (acknowledging that "true Poles" could be socialists) while recognizing that
wide swaths of territory previously thought of as Polish would have to be surrendered to the new nations of Lithuania, Ukraine, and perhaps even Belarus. From the
National Democratic perspective, a more flexible vocabulary was needed, one that
still sounded scientific and modern, but one that could be configured so as to exclude the Endecja's political opponents from the national whole while simultaneously
marking the ethnically diverse eastern lands as Polish. As Andrzej Walicki has suggested, they needed a normative definition of the nation that could take them beyond
their descriptive (ethnolinguistic) approach.[51] They would resolve the tension between
their political ambitions and their postpositivist heritage with a creative appropriation of the old slogan, "the struggle for survival." For the National Democrats, the
legacy of Polish Spencerism would provide a "realistic" way to push their conception of the nation beyond mere empiricism.

The Ethics of the Struggle for Survival

Stanisław Kozicki, in his unpublished memoirs, described a terrible dilemma facing
someone who was both a patriot and a Christian. In the contentious world of the international struggle for survival one had to be willing to take whatever actions were necessary to preserve and strengthen the nation, yet on a personal level one was constrained
by the commandments of the Church. "How can this be reconciled?" Kozicki won-
dered.[52] Zygmunt Balicki resolved this dilemma in his 1902 work, *National Egoism
and Ethics*, where he offered a new system of morality to correspond to his new definition of the nation. Between individuals the precepts of Christianity retained their force,
Balicki argued, but in judging the actions of nations (and of individuals in service to
their nation) there could be only one standard: success in the struggle for survival. A
year before Balicki's book was published, Dmowski wrote to Miłkowski that he and
his colleagues had decided to "discourage references to any sort of humanitarian feelings."[53] In this spirit, Tadeusz Grużewski complained about "an aversion to making
sacrifices for the common cause [that] easily assumes the mask of peaceful humanism.
. . . We see a weakening of the national group's collective egoism on behalf of the egoism
of the selfish individual."[54] Elsewhere Grużewski praised the turn toward "national
instincts," away from "pseudo-humanitarian slogans, the source of which was supposed
to the summit of universal ideals, but which in reality oozed from those moral swamps
created by the psychology of slavery."[55] The National Democrats conflated humanism
with selfish egoism and servility, and when it came to the nation they repudiated all
universal standards of behavior. Whatever worked was, by definition, right.

These values would have been inconceivable (or at least unspeakable) even a
few years earlier. Miłkowski's Polish League had cultivated the old dream of a revolutionary alliance of oppressed peoples, sure that "the victory of the principles of
justice throughout Europe will hasten the moment of obtaining our independence."[56]
At the League's annual meeting in 1887 the delegates passed resolutions calling for
greater cooperation with socialists and Ukrainian nationalists, on the assumption that
all those working for justice should stand together.[57] A brochure from 1893 even

promised collaboration with any Russians "who aspire to the destruction of the contemporary Russian monarchy," because such revolutionaries "will necessarily become defenders of our cause."[58] When Dmowski, Balicki, and Popławski transformed the Polish League into the National League, they initially retained this internationalism. In 1894 they prepared a series of manifestos to announce their new organization, addressed in turn to the Poles, the Slavs, the Ukrainians, the Lithuanians, "all the oppressed peoples of Russia," and "Russian Society" (общество). The declaration to the Lithuanians was typical: "Lithuanians! On the hundredth anniversary of the struggle for our freedom and yours, we call upon you: unite with us against our common enemy, unite with us in the name of political and national freedom and universal equality—in the name of eliminating all oppression. Down with slavery! Down with tsardom! Long live the brotherhood of both nations!"[59] The same slogans could be found in the manifesto to the oppressed minorities of the Russian Empire. Here the League called (in French) upon all the subjects of the Tsar to rise up in "la défense de la liberté. . . . Sur les étendards de nos insurrections vous trouverez la devise: 'pour notre liberté et la votre.' A nom de tous les peuples opprimés par la Russie, marchons à la lutte, en rangs serrés, la main dans la main!"[60] Even the first issues of *Przegląd Wszechpolski* carried the imprint of these older traditions of national thought. In Dmowski's introductory article he professed his faith in "the possibility of the harmonious cohabitation of various nations alongside each other" and promised that his new magazine would work for "international justice and the brotherhood of peoples."[61] Dmowski later spoke with embarrassment about these early texts and claimed that he wrote them only to attract readers. In those days, he recalled, overt expressions of national animosity were outside the bounds of polite discussion, and young people "felt it necessary to justify their patriotism, to 'ennoble' it by tying it to socialist ideology."[62] Whether Dmowski was sincere or not in 1895, it is certainly true that most of the *niepokorni* still wanted to believe in universal justice, and they dreamed of a revolution for Poland *and* for all humanity.

The first signs of change, however, can be found in these same brochures and manifestos from 1893 and 1894. The proclamation to the Slavs revealed the two voices of early National Democracy. It began with an unprecedented assertion that the Poles were not seeking any international aid in their struggle: "We ask for help from no one. We are fighting above all for our existence, for our rights, [and] we will depend upon our strength." At the same time, however, the author proclaimed that the National League's slogan would be "the free with the free, equals with equals."[63] The manifesto to "Russian society" presented an even more awkward combination. The tone of the document was assertive, even aggressive.

> One hundred years of oppression . . . have not weakened our strength, have not made us doubt our faith in the manifestation of the ideals of truth, justice, freedom, equality, the brotherhood of nations. With you or without you, in accordance with your intentions or against those intentions, we will continue to conduct our struggle for our freedom and yours. The moment will arrive when the enslaved nations will arise in agreement, an uprising of all the oppressed and plundered . . . and there will be no more strong or weak, slaves or masters,

nationalities without rights or states artificially held together. . . . The struggle for an independent Poland is a struggle for a free Russia.[64]

The universal principles referred to here were from an earlier era, but now all of Russia was described as a collective enemy. Polish nationalists had long distinguished between the evil Tsar and the innocent Russian people, but this text indicted Russian "society" as a whole (although the term общество is ambiguous, suggesting "high society" but perhaps not "the people"). Struggling to combine this verbal attack on the Russians with the slogans of brotherhood, the Endecja promised to save the Russians from themselves: For your freedom and ours, whether you like it or not.

This ambiguity faded after 1895. A manifesto from March of that year complained that most Poles were "ready to naïvely judge that the national and political oppression to which we are subjected depends above all on the good will of this or that tsar. It is hard for us to understand that *Russia* is oppressing us." The text "reminded" the Poles that the greatest weapon they had at their disposal was "hatred."[65] Another document from the same period points even more clearly away from the rhetoric of the Polish League toward the conflict-filled universe of National Democracy. "We will answer strength with strength, violence with violence, cunning with cunning," this leaflet promised. "They must give way to us, give us the rights that belong to us, if only we can fight for [these rights] with courage."[66] The National Democrats were still talking about "rights," but they had also entered a world in which violence and cunning were necessary. Struggle was moving to the forefront of the National League's message, and the vocabulary of conflict began to replace the vocabulary of justice. As a brochure from 1894 put it, "A careful observation of what is happening in the political world ought to teach us that it does not pay in political affairs to demand anything in the name of justice, the Christian love of one's neighbor, etc. If justice played any role here, we would not have been driven to the state in which we find ourselves today. Whoever wants to obtain anything must appeal in the name of strength."[67] Dmowski wrote at the time, "No government will ever make concessions to which it was not forced by internal struggle or external disaster!"[68]

This was what the Endecja considered a "realistic" approach to international politics, one based on "experience" and "real life" instead of "abstract thought."[69] In contrast, argued Dmowski later, the "doctrine of justice" was hopelessly unrealistic. "Contrary to all historical scholarship, this [doctrine] tells us to believe that justice in international affairs will triumph, and with the goal of hastening this triumph we are told to act justly toward all."[70] The National Democrats called on their countrymen to reject such advice, to recover a more militant spirit. An unsigned article in *Przegląd Wszechpolski* derided those who believed that Poland could obtain its independence "from the will of God or as a result of the triumph of the principle of justice." Poles should realize, the author wrote in a Bismarckian spirit, that "nations have always obtained freedom with blood and iron and political reason, and we are not a chosen people for whom a higher will can change the laws of history."[71] References to Bismarck were common on the pages of the National Democratic press. Balicki credited the (then) Prussian Chancellor's victory over France in 1870 with opening his eyes to a dark "reality":

The Franco-Prussian war came, and the voices of the victors resounded [with the a cry of] "strength before rights." That was a real clap of thunder, which struck dormant but not entirely despondent minds and simply pulled out from under our feet the traditional ground of our national faith. Not because we had counted on defeated France as an ally and savior—we were disillusioned of that hope during the [1863] uprising itself—but because France, fairly or unfairly, was in our eyes the representative of right and justice in international relations, just as Prussia evoked for us brute force. So all of our spiritual strength was based on a sense of rights, on the necessary triumph of justice in the life of nations.[72]

Since Balicki was only twelve at the time of the Franco-Prussian war, with several years as a socialist still ahead of him, we should not take this "memory" as a reflection of his personal experiences. But the reference to 1870 was nonetheless important, because by rooting his might-makes-right ideology in a specific historical episode, Balicki was able to fortify his claim to "realism." He would have us accept that "experience"—not "doctrine"—drove him to national egoism.

On one level the Endecja's call to arms was familiar. Ever since the partitions, Poles had retained an enthusiasm for armed rebellion, and since the mid-1880s the *niepokorni* had been dreaming of a return to action. But the National Democrats went a step further. Dmowski was not only attacking those who longed for some imagined "Kingdom of Justice" that would right all wrongs: he was demanding that Poles stop worrying about "acting justly" toward others and concentrate instead on the application of strength, the use of "blood and iron." Balicki not only was calling on Poles to recover what had been taken from them: he wanted his countrymen to become more militant in general, to embrace a Gumplowiczean world of unending struggle. He even argued that the nation should be willing to go to war with a neighbor over a few square kilometers of worthless territory. "For self-conscious patriotism it is not a question of interests but a question of character, a question of the inviolable and strong individuality of the nation, prepared to bear the greatest suffering so as to preserve untouched its type and its essence. On precisely this depends the ethical superiority of self-conscious national egoism."[73] Dmowski went further yet, arguing that national struggle ought to penetrate private life so that "every Pole will be an enemy of every German he meets."[74] But even for Dmowski there were limits to this hatred—very revealing limits. Although he thought that everything bad for Germany was good for Poland, he could not applaud the massacre of a group of German colonists in Africa, "people of the white race, by black African barbarians." In such a case, he said, "it is all the same to me if they are Germans, or English, or Portuguese." He was not a true chauvinist, he claimed, because he valued (Caucasian) "human life" even more than he hated his enemies.[75]

Previously those who had supported armed revolt had imagined a specific end to their struggle. The most committed idealists believed that Poland's victory would initiate a new age of justice and brotherhood, while more modest patriots hoped that the defeat of Russia would at least bring Poland back into the community of nation-states. For the National Democrats, however, there was no end to the battle. A small political victory would help organize the nation, which in turn would assist in the eventual armed struggle for independence, which would provide the necessary mechanism—a state—for further struggle and expansion. Struggle was part of the world order, not a means of obtaining a specific goal. There was no National Democratic utopia, because unlike every previous version of Polish nationalism, theirs was explicitly nonteleological. The struggle would continue forever, even after Poland itself had passed away, and the best the Poles could do was join in the battle for survival and obtain as much as they could. Dmowski resigned himself to this deeply pessimistic view. "Our task as members of the nation is not to guarantee its eternal existence, but only to derive from it as much strength, acquire for it through struggle as wide, as rich, in every sense as full a life as possible."[76] Ultimately, he believed, the nation would die, but in the meantime it could fight.

When Leo Tolstoy began preaching that violence should be met with nonviolence, the Endecja reacted with scorn. An article in *Wolne Polskie Słowo* depicted Tolstoyan ethics as "an attack on Polish patriotism," and argued that only a "nation of brutes, such as explorers have found in Africa, Australia, and some of the islands of Oceania" could show love toward an enemy. A civilized nation, in contrast, would always defend itself, and no Christian preaching could stop this.[77] Balicki argued that those who followed Tolstoy's teachings of nonresistance were in fact accomplices in evil and were thus "fundamentally immoral."[78] Tolstoy's commandment to love one's enemy, Balicki wrote in a book called *Hedonism as a Starting Point for Ethics*, was a "principle taken from idealistic, imaginary human relations." Such injunctions could be honored only in "exceptional conditions," because they contradicted "real social feelings."[79] A National Democratic priest (using the pseudonym Father Pole) tried to convince his fellow clerics to join the Endecja despite this apparently anti-Christian ethical system. "The religion of Christ is sublime; it does not command us to be stupid," he wrote. "And it would be stupid to listen blindly [sic] to the first good tyrant who imposes his power on us by force."[80]

By abandoning "rights" and "justice," the National Democrats were left with only one ethical metric (as stated in their 1897 party platform): "Everything that brings us closer to the goal, to political independence, is good, and everything that pulls us away from [that goal] is bad."[81] An anonymous contributor to *Przegląd Wszechpolski* wrote (also in 1897) that the only appropriate principle for a patriot should be "the famous Roman maxim *Salus reipublicae suprema lex*, a maxim that an old Englishman put more precisely and more exactly: '*Right or wrong—my country.*'"[82] An author signing his name as "Civis" suggested an even more succinct slogan: "We are Poles." He believed that this "would suffice to throw out all those formulas, all those doctrines, with the help of which we demonstrated to others and to ourselves that our concerns were the concerns of freedom and progress, the concerns of the European balance of power, of European civilization, of social justice, and God knows what else." It would not matter to Civis if the Polish cause entailed a negation of "the freedom of people, progress, civilization, and social justice, all those beautiful things"—even then he would still love his nation.[83] This was not an isolated sentiment. Popławski himself felt that "even if our struggle for independence [and] our national aspirations had nothing in common with democratic principles, humanitarian ideas, [or] social progress, our cause would be just as good today, our rights just as sacred. . . . Legitimating that patriotism, contriving some ideological affinity for it, reduces its honor."[84] For the National Democrats the national movement was not *about* anything other than the nation itself.

Despite such an unquestioning devotion to their nation, the National Democrats insisted that they were not chauvinists, if one means by this term an inordinate and unquestioning national pride, a conviction that one's own nation is superior to all others. National Democracy was not about national pride, but about international *struggle*. In a world of incessant conflict there was no right and wrong, only us and them. As Dmowski wrote, "I am a Pole—that means that I belong to the Polish nation on all of its territory and through all the time of its existence, both today and in the centuries past and future. . . . Everything that is Polish is mine: I can deny nothing. I can be proud of that which is great in Poland, but I must accept also the humiliation that falls on the nation for that which is pitiful."[85] Dmowski felt that Poles were "dirtier and lazier" than other nations, but this opinion did not weaken his patriotism.[86] Elsewhere he boasted that "no contemporary movement in Poland criticizes as strongly the national deficiencies, none searches for a way to remove them, none works so hard in the field of education as the Democratic National Movement."[87] This was the "realistic" side of National Democracy, the side that could (under the right circumstances) describe Poland as an ethnolinguistic community. But contained within these same passages was the other side of the Endecja, the normative conception of the nation which Dmowski and his colleagues used to organize and give ideological content to the national whole. This was an "objective" community, independent of the will of its members, but it was also a site for the imposition of "education." For the National Democrats, this pedagogical agenda was not just about eliminating "dirt and laziness"; Dmowski stressed that alongside hygiene and the work ethic, it was necessary to teach people about the evils of "false humanitarianism."[88] Moreover, as we saw in chapter 6, for the Endecja, education was closely linked with hierarchy, discipline, and authority.

Not only did the National Democrats debunk national pride, they even questioned the importance of a sense of national belonging. As Władysław Studnicki wrote in 1902:

> Patriotism based on love for one's own nation, supported exclusively by images of the solidarity of interests within the bosom of that nation as well as solidarity with other peoples, is a patriotism good for that unrealized golden age when all social and national antagonisms will disappear. But such patriotism is ever more foreign to our civilized world, which contains in its bosom so many antagonisms. The society that lives on [this idea] will be unfit for the struggle for its existence, for the conditions of its development. . . . Today's patriotism is associated with national antagonism.[89]

In the end the National Democrats did not love Poland as much as they hated Poland's enemies. Their patriotism was not merely burdened by a message of international antagonism: it was virtually defined by hate.

It followed that anyone who questioned the Endecja's hatreds was not a good patriot. In a 1903 letter to Miłkowski, Dmowski complained about the "cosmopolitan dreaming" of all those who placed "utopian" and "doctrinaire" ambitions above the needs of the nation. In a subtle criticism of his patron (who had long fought "for our freedom and yours"), Dmowski implied that those who believed in universal human rights were not true patriots. They might be "valiant people" and "in their own way good Poles," but they were guilty of the gravest sin: cosmopolitanism.[90] Balicki even argued that to show compassion for the fate of foreigners was immoral. "Cosmopolitan philanthropy," he wrote, ". . . is always a hidden egoism, because when one gives to others one passes over one's own people." It would be a grave wrong, for example, for a Czech to give to a German charity or a Pole to help the starving in Russia: those who did such things were immoral because they shifted attention from their "real" community toward an abstraction (humanity).[91]

> Whoever gives more, whoever sacrifices the interests of his own nation without receiving anything in return, commits a crime against [the nation and] violates its healthy instinct of self-preservation. Historical justice will never leave such a violation without punishment. . . . Only a nation with a strong individuality, able to fight for and win its [independence], able to oppose force with force, avenge the wrongs it has endured and ensure for itself the superiority of justice, has the right to independent existence. . . . All altruistic sacrifices made in the name of and at the cost of the nation are evidence of its inability to [sustain] independent existence, a property which everyone will willingly take advantage of, but which will not elevate in anyone's eyes its authority or charm. . . . Wanting to organize international solidarity, [cosmopolitans] begin by disorganizing their own nation. Altruism toward others arises almost always at the cost of one's own interests and needs.[92]

During a famine in Russia in 1899 some Poles tried to organize emergency aid for the starving, and in response *Pochodnia* complained about those who gave money to this "foreign" cause. The editors recognized that some Poles had succumbed to sympathy for the hungry, but they warned that "if some sort of political charlatan tries to pretend that in this way a love for the Volga horde has been inculcated into the hearts of the Polish people, he will doubtlessly fail."[93]

Not only had Dmowski, Balicki, and their colleagues abandoned the old slogan of the Polish patriot, "for our freedom and yours," but they had abolished the distinction between the good and bad foreigner. They were no longer engaged in a struggle between justice and injustice—theirs was a world in which "we" were fighting against "them." The new identity they had constructed for themselves—the new nation they had imagined—not only had opened up unprecedented spaces for the exertion of authority and discipline, but had established a wall between Poles and non-Poles such as had never before existed. They made it possible for a Polish patriot to talk about "them" as an undifferentiated, hostile unity, against which "we" had no choice but to fight with all available means. Before the 1890s, Polish patriots were always careful to leave a door open for cooperation with Russian revolutionaries, because it was assumed that the tsarist regime constituted a common enemy. Since the 1870s, as we have seen, there existed close ties between revolutionaries in Warsaw and their counterparts in St. Petersburg, Moscow, and Kiev. Many Poles would continue to seek such alliances (and many Russians would reciprocate), but the National Democrats made it possible to articulate a very different approach.

In discussing Russian policy toward Poland, Dmowski argued that oppression and denationalization was not just "a policy of the moment, dependent upon some or another activist, on some or another leader."[94] Instead, russification was part of an "entirely natural process of exploiting the strength of the state by the nation for the spreading of its faith, language, culture . . . an expression of certain political tendencies created by the whole history of the state." Dmowski went so far as to argue that the government was not to blame, because it was just responding to irresistible natural impulses emanating from the nation itself.[95] In 1893 a delegate from Moscow University visited the Kingdom to ask his Polish peers to join in an all-empire student demonstration (thus demonstrating once again that slogans like "for our freedom and yours" were more than just words). Dmowski vehemently opposed this proposal, arguing (as he put it many years later), that "Warsaw University does not have anything in common with the Russian universities, since it is in Poland and has Polish youth, [and thus] the Warsaw youth may not join with the Russian youth in any kind of action."[96] Though seriously ill at the time, Dmowski fought hard against his "internationalist" opponents and managed to prevent any coordinated action between Russian and Polish youth. Two years later a student wrote to *Przegląd Wszechpolski* that relations between the two national groups at Warsaw University had indeed been poisoned. "There can be no talk of any sort of union, even on a foundation of general and purely student interests. . . . A reconciliation will *never* occur. . . . Science is neutral and knowledge is cosmopolitan, but today—even under the wing [of science]— the struggle must continue and one cannot think of an alliance."[97] This was an exaggeration, because Polish socialists were continuing to cooperate with their Russian counterparts, but even to imagine such a fissure as a positive development was a disturbing novelty.

Polish patriots (along with many Russian liberals) had long treated the bureaucrats and russifiers in the Kingdom as a distinct breed, not representative of all Russians. In 1895 *Przegląd Wszechpolski* urged its readers to abandon this belief in the "good Russian," even if they thought they had met such people. Those who seemed so friendly in Moscow or St. Petersburg, the paper warned, would be just as bad as any Warsaw official if they had the chance. All Russians were alike, constituting an "entirely different ethical type," and it was the Russian nation that was oppressing the Poles, not specific bad individuals.[98] Studnicki ridiculed the idea that Poles could fight the German or Russian governments "without struggling with the German or Russian societies—societies on which those governments depend and which support them in their struggle with us."[99] In 1899, on the occasion of another set of Russian student strikes, the underground student government of Warsaw University (then controlled by the Endecja) issued the following declaration:

> The national youth protest strongly against establishing a sense of brotherhood with Russian youth. We do not count on their support, because they have always let us down. We count on our own strength, on sacrificial civic work, in the

conviction that in serving above all the tasks and goals of our nation we also serve the national interest. Giving the protests an all-student character was nothing other than an uncritical transference of international slogans of class solidarity to student affairs. It was a repudiation of all distinctions, a triumph of the principle of supporting the movement for its own sake, the demonstrations for their own sake, without considering their goal or meaning. . . . All Poles, particularly the young intelligentsia of our nation, ought to exert all their strength and direct it toward the defense of national existence and toward the deepening of our cultural distinctiveness, which is ever more threatened by attacks from, on the one hand, tsardom (as a form of political oppression that has introduced into our social organism forms of government alien to us) and on the other hand, Russia, as a culture, the influence of which is spreading, aspiring to an annihilation of the individuality of our national soul even worse than [could be achieved by] the oppression of a despotic government.[100]

Even an expression of appreciation for Russian art or literature was unacceptable for the National Democrats. On the occasion of an empire-wide festival in honor of Pushkin, *Pochodnia* proclaimed that "Mickiewicz and Pushkin today are two extremes, two mutually hostile figures. A real Pole, during the jubilee days of Pushkin, will allow himself only one demonstration, namely, to lay flowers at the feet of the monument to our Adam." In life, Adam Mickiewicz and Alexander Pushkin had great respect for each other, but the Endecja needed to transform them, as emblems of hostile cultures, into enemies.[101] In an essay provocatively entitled "Our Chauvinism," a National Democrat signing his name as B. O. urged his countrymen to reject the literature of Tolstoy and Pushkin. One would not accept the friendship of a brutal criminal just because he was occasionally polite, B. O. argued, and for the same reason one should remain hostile to all things Russian, no matter how appealing some works of art may seem when considered in isolation. "The struggle is engaged not only with the government," B. O. wrote, "but with the entire society. . . . Russian society from top to bottom is oddly unified, consistent, and clear in its relations with us." Personal experiences to the contrary should not be allowed to soften this stereotype; indeed, a *real* understanding of Russia was inversely related to one's actual familiarity with live Russians. As this author put it, "One might dare say that those who remain in relations of social intimacy with Russians know the least about the Russian character." The boycott of Russian society and culture could permit no exceptions, because one should always remember that if a Russian was invited into the home and introduced to one's daughter, "such an acquaintance might end in a marriage."[102]

These same arguments were directed toward the Germans. According to Popławski, Poland was struggling not against specific nationalist parties in Germany, but with "the entire German society" in an "inexorable struggle for life or death."[103] He believed that "every policy—whether Prussian or Polish—is rapacious in its relations with other nationalities; it must always strive to obtain new territories or regain lost ones."[104] An unsigned article in *Przegląd Wszechpolski* from 1896 warned that a particular politician in Berlin might decide that denationalization was ineffective, but the nation as a whole would never change. "Germanization from the German point of view is a political necessity, not only a task for the state, but for the nation."[105] In 1898 Dmowski argued that the partitions themselves were a political necessity for both Russia and Prussia. "The historical process that forced Prussia to rapacious aspirations toward Poland," he wrote, "had its beginnings in very distant times. . . . The partition of Poland was necessary for the further development of Prussia and Russia, and those states were, so to speak, forced to carry it out." Dmowski concluded that the Germans either had to denationalize the Poles or the Poles would denationalize them; coexistence was inconceivable and the "desire to exterminate" was universal.[106]

What made this argument particularly novel was the way it exonerated the partitioning powers of malicious intent. The National Democrats did not argue that the Germans or the Russians were unusually expansionist or oppressive: to the Endeks, all nations were by definition aggressive. Many Poles, of all political persuasions, viewed the Russians with contempt or animosity, but only the Endecja inserted these prejudices into a broader worldview of unremitting and universal antagonism. Józef Piłsudski, for example, represented a strong faction within the PPS that was reluctant to cooperate with (let alone depend upon) the Russian revolutionaries, and he shared familiar stereotypes about the "*Moskale*." Like the National Democrats, the Piłsudskiite socialists tended to blur the distinction between the tsarist government and the Russian people. But the Endecja took this attitude an important step further by casting the Russo–Polish struggle as an example of a general principle of international relations. Many Poles disliked the Russians because they were (allegedly) backward and brutish; the National Democrats disliked the Russians simply because they were not Polish.

The National Democrats refused to think of themselves as victims. As early as 1895 a contributor to *Przegląd Wszechpolski* by the name of Stanisław Komornicki proposed that the Poles should stop complaining about their enemies and start engaging them on their own terms. Aggression was natural and should be welcomed as a means to clarify the national struggle.[107] In *The Thoughts of a Modern Pole*, Dmowski argued that one should deal with one's enemies without emotion, soberly confronting them in the struggle for survival. He saw the Germans and the Russians as opponents, but he did not believe that they were behaving inappropriately. "In my opinion no German or *Moskal* is discredited by the fact that they use in an honest way their strength for expanding their national culture, for winning for their nation new territories, for assimilating foreign elements; on the contrary, this elevates them as valiant citizens. . . . And precisely this feeling that I am not a victim, that I have no right to complain about my fate to anyone, means that I must fight."[108] In these arguments there was a strong undercurrent of confidence. Studnicki felt that the "new" Poles would no longer "complain about the 'cynical world of strength,' because they know that we are not without strength ourselves, that our strength can be increased."[109] The National Democrats, in rejecting the role of victim, argued that Poland was becoming a force in the region, overcoming decades of oppression not only to defend itself against Russian and German aggression, but even to attack back. As an anonymous author put it in 1897, the Polish people "are beginning to understand that when the struggle begins, the best defensive tactic is to attack the enemy—*die beste Deckung ist der Hieb*."[110] Just as the Russians and Germans were not to be condemned because they engaged in "natural" acts of aggression and expansion, so the Poles were not to be praised because they had been victimized by such violence. Dmowski insisted that "the moral strength of the nation is not its defenselessness [or] its innocence, as we hear often among us today, but the passion for a wider life, the desire to multiply the national wealth and influence, as well as the readiness to sacrifice for the realization of national goals." The problem with the Poles was not they were insufficiently virtuous, Dmowski argued, but that they were insufficiently active. He realized that it would be hard for "old patriots and democrats" to "accept the thought that the national question might demand of them the use of force against [foreign] peoples, that for [the nation's] good it will be necessary to impose something on others against their will." Nonetheless, Dmowski argued, the Poles would have to use force and compulsion; these were the weapons of the national struggle, and Poland could not abandon them lest it cease to grow, and therefore to exist.[111]

The "old patriots and democrats," however, were not the only ones to resist the uncomfortable implication that Poland was morally equivalent to the partitioning powers: the National Democrats themselves tried to escape the uglier consequences of their own reasoning. Balicki, for example, imagined a world filled with "citizen-soldiers" who would devote all their energies to the survival of the nation and would fight all opponents with unquestioning loyalty and obedience. But even as he wrote this, he recognized that he had offered no way to restrain this citizen-soldier in his pursuit of national glory. To avoid the conclusion that *any* act would be moral and justified if performed in the name of the nation, Balicki awkwardly introduced a concept of honor (as distinct from ethics) to guard against unchecked brutality. "A nation that is spiritually strong," he wrote, "a great force of self-conscious national egoism, does not lower itself to abuse and violence, because it values highly its dignity, it has respect for its own culture and honor for its flag." Balicki insisted that the citizen-soldier would never resort to "cruelty, violence, or the murder of the defenseless, because not the superiority of force, but the superiority of justice will be in every case the stimulus for his actions." The true soldier would be guided by the "knightly spirit" rather than the "spirit of militarism." Suddenly, incongruously, justice was once again a transcendent value, something that stood above naked force. Balicki even insisted that the National Democratic doctrine of national expansion was not really a doctrine of violence or force at all.

> A nation, as a living organism, has a moral right to expand not only at the cost of passive, unthinking and socially amorphous elements, but even at the cost of other nations, as long as that expansion is natural and is not based on brutal strength, force, or exceptional laws. This is cultural politics and historical expansion, not conquest. . . . A leading idea and not thoughtless appetite; noble ambition and not arrogance; the desire for influence and not the lust for domination; a high feeling of one's own honor and not the desire for forced homage— this constitutes the moral shape of self-conscious egoism in the nation.

In other words, if one's intentions were good, conquest was acceptable, but if one was driven only by appetites, arrogance, and lust, the same sort of domination was bad. This ethical system allowed Balicki to criticize Germans for polonizing Poznania while praising virtually identical Polish ambitions in Ukraine.[112] This desire to move away from violence, to stop short of the final conclusion toward which the concept of national egoism was heading, was also apparent in Dmowski's *Thoughts of a Modern Pole*: "One can, after all, recognize the fact that in relations between nations there is no right or wrong, that there is only strength and weakness. . . . and at the same time, calling one's society to strong and decisive politics of the national interest, not recommend either brutal violence or dishonesty (or deceit), which in the truly civilized and morally developed man must arouse deep disgust."[113]

One could selectively quote from National Democratic texts to show that they supported unqualified aggression, or to demonstrate that they were benign advocates of patriotism and national solidarity. Neither image would be inaccurate, but both would be incomplete. Clearly the publicists and activists at the turn of the century *preferred* to use "honorable" means in the pursuit of the national cause, but they had deprived themselves of the rationale for excluding more brutal methods if a perceived need arose. Grużewski argued in 1903 that "spiritual forces" and military might were equally important and that the national future depended on "not only physical strength but also intellectual [strength], moral [strength], and above all [strength] of will and character."[114] These more peaceful forms of struggle were important to the National Democrats; in fact, they consistently opposed plans for another uprising and they criticized the use of terrorism as futile and counterproductive. Nonetheless, they no longer had the rhetorical means to condemn violence or brutality as *wrong*, as anything worse than dishonorable or (more commonly) impractical.

For our purposes, the most important implication of the Endecja's doctrine of struggle was not that it led to violence (though it certainly could, and later did), but that it helped constitute a vision of the nation based on hatred of all those outside the community and on authority and discipline toward all those within. This was the glue that held National Democracy together, the justification for everything else they believed in. Even Balicki did not defend "organization" for its own sake; the nation required social hierarchies and obedience in order both to ensure success in the struggle for survival and to control the wild forces unleashed in the heat of battle. Balicki argued that a nation able to govern itself was sure to gain and sustain its independence.

> Among the nations accustomed to social self-government, every public task undertaken by the citizens themselves is conceived in an organized form. A dispersed mode of activity, based on the individual efforts of people of good will, is our special property and our weakness at the same time, a legacy of our old political-social system, consumed by our divisive individualistic instincts. If it were necessary to summarize in one word our national defect . . . one could answer that we must cure ourselves of individualism and attain a talent for collective public work and organization.[115]

Balicki was thus able to return to his favorite theme—discipline and organization—in order to avoid the conclusion that Poles should resort to violent struggle. In 1898 an anonymous correspondent in *Przegląd Wszechpolski* reached a similar conclusion, arguing that violence would be effective only if it were carefully planned and directed by a central authority. The use of force, if employed carelessly, would be nothing more than a "riot."[116] In *Polak* the National Democrats cautioned that although struggle was inevitable, another uprising was not appropriate at the time. "Nations rarely take up arms, but they struggle from day to day for their existence, for their success, for their rights. He who teaches his brothers about social obligations, who spreads useful books among them, who resists the abuses of the government . . . every one of these is struggling with the government."[117] More useful than violence, then, was the distribution of "useful" reading and the preaching about "obligations." These acts could further national unity and discipline, while a "riot" would spread discord and disorder.

   We thus come full circle. The National Democratic commitment to the struggle for survival was linked to their demand for social order and discipline. These were the two sides of the Endecja's coin: because Poland had to fight for its existence, it had to be well organized and unified; if Poles were obedient to the authority of "honorable" men, such fighting would not lead to brutality. The Endecja's dark vision of international relations helped sustain a cohesive imagined community that was rooted in "nature," yet was not subject to the transitory measurements of ethnography, linguistics, or historical cartography. This style of nationalism was "scientific" because it spoke the language of Social Darwinism, yet it could escape from the "small ideas" of liberal individualism by denying the teleologies of Spencer, Mill, Świętochowski, or Prus. Like the positivists of the 1870s, Balicki and Dmowski did not want to unleash unrestricted violence on the world, but unlike their liberal predecessors, the National Democrats could not envision such barbarism fading away with the advance of historical time. Instead of casting the struggle for survival as the engine of progress, they used it to justify authority, thus defining the nation in terms of both conflict and discipline. Spencer could be the prophet of struggle while still insisting he was a pacifist, because he believed that progress was taking mankind beyond the stage in which overt violence was needed, toward the ultimate liberal utopia in which cooperation and harmony would finally be possible. The Endecja predicted no such transcendence, so their only escape from an unmitigated war-of-all-against-all was the disciplinary force of national hierarchies. This was a nation for the "modern" world, a nation that encompassed all "the people" and could be described with the language of "science." But it was also a nation based on unending antagonism and strict order. This was the nation of the twentieth-century radical right.

National Expansion

Przegląd Wszechpolski summarized the Endecja's primary goal in 1897: "Every nation that is increasing its spiritual and material wealth, that is capable of creating and developing its own culture, that is aware of its individuality and the distinctiveness of its interests, must strive to obtain political independence."[118] Popławski believed that if his compatriots ever abandoned the quest for statehood, "the Polish question would cease to exist, because we would cease to be Poles."[119] This was more than just a polemical overstatement: the National Democrats placed the collective will to fight for "existence" at the center of their definition of the nation. Once again "the deed" acquired fundamental significance, but this notion was not a mere reprise of the romantic conception of nationhood. For the patriots of 1863, one expressed identity with the nation by acting on behalf of the national cause; for the Endecja, the nation itself (as a collective entity) was real only if it could act. "The vitality of the nation is measured by its aspiration to preserve and defend the marks of its collective individuality," Popławski wrote. "A nation that is capable of autonomous sociopolitical and cultural creativity will not waste away in the worst conditions, and will rise again in a favorable environment," but a nation that had to live within an "alien form" for any length of time would "lose its distinctiveness, . . . waste away and die, just like a biological organism placed in conditions unsuitable to its nature." Although the nation was not determined by its state, it could survive only if it pursued this goal.[120] Even when the National Democrats decided to play down their hopes for independence in 1905 (in order to participate in elections to the new imperial Duma), they justified this move by arguing that if a Polish state were to arise at that moment, it would be too small to survive.[121]

The National Democrats wanted to claim the mantle of realism, but they were not satisfied with race, language, ethnicity, or even culture as the measure of national membership. Their way out of this dilemma was to emphasize the role of the state, which became for them the point of contact between the timeless national whole and the "real" world of politics. The state, moreover, was the best means to ensure the national cohesion and social discipline that was so fundamental to National Democracy. Popławski described the state as a material expression of the national spirit, an embodiment of "its traditions and national character, its political, social, and economic relations, its mentality and the natural circumstances of its existence."[122] Dmowski used similar terminology: "The nation is the essential moral content of the state, and the state is the essential political form of the nation. The nation can lose its statehood and not cease to be a nation, if it does not sever the ties of moral union with the state tradition, if it does not lose the nation-state idea. . . . Otherwise the nation will descend to the level of a tribe." Twice in this article he repeated the phrase, "the nation is a creation of state existence," but he simultaneously argued that the state was only the physical form of the national spirit. This was not a contradiction, but rather a reflection of the intimate relationship between these two concepts. As Dmowski put it, "The state and the nation are indeed indivisible concepts. The state is national, and through its very existence it creates the nation."[123] The national spirit was expressed through a collective commitment to the idea of statehood, and the state in turn allowed the national "raw material" (Grużewski's phrase) or its "tribal existence" (Dmowski) to thrive. The nation was the great combatant in the struggle for survival, while the state was the best means to ensure discipline in that struggle. Without organization (the highest form of which was the state), the nation could not exist, and without a national foundation, no state had a reason to exist.

Within this framework, the idea of the state (i.e., social discipline) was inextricably paired with the idea of the nation, but the specific form that national organization might take at any particular moment depended on circumstances. National unity and expansion were basic imperatives, but political independence was only one (albeit the best) way to achieve these goals. Popławski described the needs of any "vivacious organism" in 1899:

> Poland, regardless of the circumstances in which it arises, must be obtained with blood and iron, for neither historical experience nor sober and logical consideration, taking into account the demands of reality, show any other paths or methods for regaining lost independence. Moreover, in whatever form, in whatever boundaries that Poland arises—even if it is a mini-state or an autonomous part of a great whole—if it is to be a vivacious organism it must aspire to dominate the space that constitutes its natural inheritance, bounded by natural borders that correspond to its national and economic interests.[124]

This space within which national authority and domination were to be applied, included (in addition to the Kingdom) the lands we now call Ukraine, Lithuania, and Belarus, along with the "Polish" territories of the other two partitions (Galicia, Silesia, Poznania, Pomerania, and even East Prussia). As Dmowski put it, "State independence is not at all treated here as a final goal, but as a means, as the most important condition for broad national development."[125] This ambiguous expression—national development—was used in two ways. It could refer to the "internal" growth of the nation, the expansion of national awareness to the peasantry and the deepening of Polish patriotism. But to single out this less objectionable side of National Democracy is to ignore an equally common meaning of the phrase "national development": territorial expansion.[126]

The great innovation of National Democracy was to remove aggression, violence, and expansion from the realm of the immoral, and transpose it to the realm of the natural. If they had simply called on their fellow Poles to return to action—even armed action—against the partitioning powers, they would have fit well within the existing boundaries of a Polish patriotic discourse. But when they identified conflict *as such* as both an irredeemable part of the natural world and a marker of national virtue, they pushed the edges of those boundaries, creating something frightening and new. This stance allowed them to cast their imagination far beyond the struggle with Russia and Germany and to dream about their own expansion in the future. Once the National Democrats accepted Russian and German aggression as inevitable and moral, they could endorse with a clear conscience a similar program of conquest for themselves. If Grużewski could *praise* the Hungarians for resisting the demands of the Croats, Slovaks, Serbs, and Romanians in 1848 and for showing a "decisive" disregard for the slogans of the "freedom and the brotherhood of peoples," and if Dmowski could support British actions in South Africa even as he admitted that they were committing injustices, then it became possible for Popławski to claim for Poland what would have heretofore been unthinkable: a policy of national expansion.[127]

As was noted above, the earliest National League brochures and even the first issues of *Przegląd Wszechpolski* repeated the Polish League's slogans about respecting "national rights." If this message was ever sincere, it was unambiguously jettisoned by the end of 1895. In December of that year *Przegląd Wszechpolski* complained about the so-called exceptional laws that restricted Polish language and culture in what the Russians called the "western gubernii" and the Poles called the "eastern borderlands" (*kresy*). Poles had often criticized these severe regulations, but this article took a novel approach, attacking the exceptional laws because they "created for us an artificial boundary, justified by an ethnographic, bureaucratic doctrinarism [and] violating the rights of the civilizing development [*cywilizacyjny rozwój*] of nations." These territories, historically part of the Polish state, had served as a "natural outlet for our excess strength," and by closing them off to Polish influence the Russians had "locked us into an artificial territory."[128]

The "outlet" was a favorite National Democratic metaphor and was embedded within a Polish version of the *Lebensraum* argument. The nation was growing, the Endecja maintained, because of both its expanding population and its increasing "national energy." If no means of expression could be found for this energy, the national life would be stifled and eventually extinguished. As Dmowski put it in *The Thoughts of a Modern Pole*, "A nation that is quickly civilizing, increasing its spiritual strength, wanting to retain its health in the realm of the spirit, must to a corresponding degree expand the sphere of its action, its interests, its expansion of all sorts, so that the aggregation of ever more complicated tasks will consume a corresponding increase in the energy of the national spirit." The territory of a nation was never permanent, he continued, but was always "expanding, reducing, or shifting." Whether Poland grew or declined depended upon its ability to expand, and if it lacked the potential for territorial conquest then it would eventually "shrink and even die."[129] For Dmowski, organic work among the peasants and the propagation of national consciousness could never be enough to satisfy an "energetic" patriot. "A nation on the same level of civilization and spiritual development as ours," he wrote, "creates in every generation an enormous legion of people whose thoughts and energy cannot find satisfaction in this work, who need a wider field and who can only be engaged by a much more complicated task." These people had to be satiated and their energy had to be exploited if the nation was to survive. "Expanding the sphere of national activity" was, for Dmowski, "a question not only of spiritual health, but of life itself." He itemized three ways in which Poles could utilize this energy: (1) by spreading national awareness in all three partitions; (2) by "increasing our influence" in the borderlands; and (3) by establishing colonies abroad.[130]

This argument for expansion was often explicit, without any comforting metaphors or soothing aesopian language—without even the rationalizations of Miłkowski's liberal imperialism. Piotr Panek, in his 1903 book, *The Principles of National Economy*, argued that the only way one could expand a national economy was "to acquire new tracts of land," so it followed that territorial expansion was the foundation of any "wise national policy."[131] An anonymous contributor to *Przegląd Wszechpolski* wrote in 1900, "Until a given nation feels in itself the desire to expand, it will be a passive force, it will succumb to the stronger [nations] that exploit the general trends of history for their benefit."[132] The Democratic-National Party's 1903 program was unambiguous:

The national interest demands not only the defense of that which the nation possesses, but the acquisition of that which is necessary for life and for occupying an honorable position in the ranks of other nations; not only holding steady in the boundaries of today's possessions and influence, but expanding these as far as possible. Directing national activities to a defense against denationalization, against being expelled from those places from which we have not yet been excluded, is to condemn the nation to a slow destruction, because a nation, if it wants to preserve its existence, must pursue others in progress, in the development of physical and spiritual strength. A nation that does not want to acquire anything, does not want to create anything new in the future, that has no demands, but is satisfied with what it has, must shrivel and ultimately die. . . . An essentially national position demands that one increase as much as possible a society's civilizing qualities, give its individuality the greatest possible content, and open up for the national strength as wide a field of activity as possible.[133]

A puzzling term here was the adjective *cywilizacyjny* (civilizing). This was usually a dynamic expression, referring to the ability of powerful nations to spread "civilization" to weaker and more backward "nationalities." Miłkowski had softened his imperialism with a liberal teleology, and doing this allowed him to claim (and perhaps even believe) that the spread of Polish culture to the east was part of a progressive agenda. The National Democrats searched for no such historiosophical justifications. They were not interested in Ukraine or Belarus because they wanted to bring these lands into the modern world; they intended to fight for these lands in order to prevent Russia from winning them. Rather than a space for colonial development, the *kresy* became a battleground. The Endeks had no sense of a "white man's burden." For them, civilizing implied not education, but conquest.

Dmowski perceived no nations between Russia and Poland, and he believed that this vast region was open for the cultural expansion of whichever of the two proved to be the stronger.

The Polish lands of the Russian partition present today all possible degrees of Polishness, and if we depart from the basis of historical laws we must agree that a rather considerable portion of it no longer belongs to us. Precise boundaries between the Polish West and the Russian East have been lost—between us and Russia there has been created a wide belt of land not belonging culturally to anyone, land on which two mutually hostile influences do battle, which is destined for whomever will be able to conquer it culturally. Between us and Russia there is, moreover, no clear geographical boundaries, which means that the rivalry between the two nations and the two civilizations must continue without pause into the very distant future.[134]

The eternal battle between Russia and Poland was not that of an evil oppressor and a subjugated victim, but a conflict between two aggressive nations vying for control of the "empty" space in Eastern Europe. The Kingdom might have been temporarily subjugated by the "Oriental" Russian Empire, but in reality Poland remained a European nation with an irrepressible drive to spread outward and colonize "unoccupied" and "uncivilized" lands. Popławski made the same point, arguing that Poland had vital interests in both the east and the west. In Poznania and Pomerania the Poles had to fight for access to the sea and defend the "cradle of our nation" against German aggression, while in the east they struggled for "the further growth of our nation." "Our ethnic territory," he wrote, ". . . occupies a space of not even 5,000 square miles. In such a space, in such natural conditions, one cannot develop a great nation that believes in its future. Only in the east do we have the space appropriate for the development of our strength, our national creativity."[135] Of course the National Democrats realized that this land was already populated, but they considered it to be effectively deserted because of the cultural "backwardness" of the local inhabitants. One of the Endecja's manifestos, released in Vilnius on the occasion of the unveiling of a new statue to Catherine the Great, spoke as if the only significant contestants for the region were the Poles and the Russians: the Lithuanians themselves faded from view: "Lithuania, although destroyed and led to ruin, has remained ours, because they have not managed to make it Muscovite."[136]

Popławski believed that Poland should stretch from the Oder to the Dnieper and from the Baltic "not only to the Carpathians but perhaps even to the Black Sea."[137] An anonymous contributor to *Przegląd Wszechpolski* wrote in 1896 that the essential issue between Poland and Russia was "that great contested territory from the Bug and the Niemen and, as some assert, also from the San, all the way past the Dnieper and the Dvina." This author recognized that not all the people in this vast space were ethnically Polish, but he considered this irrelevant. Once Poland controlled this region, "regulating nationality relations" would simply be a matter of "internal politics."

> Practically speaking, it would be simply impossible to renounce our rights or
> claims to Lithuania and Ruthenia. . . . That country [*kraj*] has been our property
> for five centuries, and we defend this not on the basis of historical rights, which
> have no real meaning, but because we occupied it with our blood and our labor
> and strengthened in those possessions our intellectual and political culture.
> Nearly everything that has any lasting value at all, [nearly all marks of] civiliza-
> tion are ours, because everything is the result of Polish thought and Polish will,
> Polish institutions and traditions.

This author recognized a duty to support the "tribal consciousness" of the Lithuanians and the Ruthenians, and he promised that the future Polish state would protect "the equal rights of nationalities," but he was adamant that the borderlands would remain Polish.[138] The Democratic-National Party offered to establish good relations with the Lithuanians and the Ukrainians, assuming that these groups would recognize Poland's dominant cultural and economic position. If not, "the party will work to weaken hostile tendencies on all sides by ruthlessly resisting unjustified pretensions, by simultaneously and all the more energetically strengthening the Polish elements and their civilizing efforts on a given territory."[139]

This argument introduced a troublesome tension in the National Democratic worldview. They constructed a hierarchical relationship between themselves and the Ukrainians, Belorussians, and Lithuanians, and they described this in terms of their own greater "spiritual development" and "level of civilization." The idea of development, however, implied some concept of progress, and the Endecja maintained that progress did not exist. In a dexterous rhetorical maneuver Dmowski solved this tension by creating a vision of progress based only on his concept of struggle. Without suggesting any teleology, he made advancement dependent solely on strength. There was, he wrote, no international law protecting the rights of ethnic or national minorities, because if such a principle had been accepted in the past "we would have come to possess in the middle of Europe half-barbarian peoples, suspended in development, constituting a restraint on civilization." Having suggested the possibility of development, however, he then denied that there was any historical impetus to progress. There was no telos in Dmowski's world

> because permanent improvement and progress is not an inborn property of man—the majority of those today populating the earth stand in place, not moving forward at all. And the most important impetus to progress is competition, the need for the permanent perfecting of the weapons serving to protect one's existence. . . . For since there are no exams for peoples in cultural progress and there are no tribunals able to judge their value for civilization, the only . . . criteria for the fitness of a people to work for universal progress . . . is this: does the nation know how to obtain and sustain, in struggle with others, independent political and cultural existence?[140]

This is the only reference in *Thoughts of a Modern Pole* to universal progress, and Dmowski defined this concept very narrowly. Within his framework there could be no general standard for progress, no clear objective to the march of civilization. There was, ultimately, only struggle, and whoever emerged on top was, for the moment, the most advanced.

This framework created new opportunities for talking about the Ruthenians as objects of Polish expansion. When the National League was organized in 1894, it issued a proclamation to "the Ukrainian nation" calling for cooperation in the fight against Russian tyranny, but only a few years later Dmowski would tell his younger colleague, Zdzisław Dębicki, that there was no such a thing as a Ruthenian—there was only a "pitiful type of Pole." In order to protect these people against Russian expansionism, Dmowski said, the Endecja had to turn them into "good Poles." Those who argued for the creation of a Ukrainian state were imagining "a Ukraine that never did exist, does not exist, and will not exist." Such people were "ruled by sentiment . . . and in politics there are no sentiments, there is no poetry, there are only interests."[141] Dmowski was somewhat more polite in his public statements. In 1897 he admitted that the Ruthenians possessed a rich and distinctive popular culture, but he still insisted that this did not make them a nation. "[Ruthenian] culture could only become the foundation for a movement with an exclusively cultural character," he wrote. ". . . In order for cultural separatism to be accompanied by political separatism, it would be necessary for the given tribe to have some sort of political tradition that was clear and as fresh as possible." Since the Ruthenians had no such tradition and as a result could neither hope for statehood nor resist the aggressive intentions of the Russian Empire, they had but one choice: to join the Polish nation.[142]

Since the turn of the century scholars have grouped Polish nationalism together with apparently similar movements in such diverse locations as Ukraine, Lithuania, Slovakia, the Balkans, and even the Caucuses.[143] The National Democrats, however, resented the implication that Poland could be categorized alongside these communities. Dmowski believed that such collectivities were destined to succumb to the superior force of organized, well-disciplined nations (such as Poland). "The Ruthenian who longs for a free Ukraine in the same way that I [long for] an independent Poland is a voluntary or involuntary actor who is only copying me," Dmowski wrote. "I do not want to say by this that someone cannot foster such dreams; I only think that one should not take them too seriously."[144] In 1905 Dmowski claimed that the very concept of nationality was contrary to Poland's national goals. "The Polish question is not the question of the rebirth of a politically assimilated tribe lacking a higher spiritual culture—it is the question of a nation. . . . The nationality movements . . . were and are enemies of the Polish national idea, as a nation-state idea, and not its allies. . . . The Polish question was not born of the nationality idea of the nineteenth century and it will certainly not share its fate."[145] A contributor to *Teka* derided linguistic and cultural "awakening" as "a slogan for the weak." Poland, in contrast, should have "great aspirations" to restore its position as a "great nation"; otherwise it would fall to the level of "some sort of Montenegro or Bulgaria."[146]

Popławski was somewhat more gentle than Dmowski, but ultimately he was just as intolerant of the Ukrainian national movement. As late as 1900 he assured his readers that the National Democrats had "never stepped forward against the national aspirations of the Ruthenians or the Lithuanians." He cautioned, however, that the Poles would defend their own national interests against any competing claims.[147] This statement was actually quite generous, because it implied that the Ukrainians and Lithuanians were legitimate competitors in the struggle for survival—that is, they were "nations," not mere "nationalities." By 1903, however, Popławski had backed away from this suggestion. In that year he argued that Poles and Ruthenians could normalize their relations and work together for economic prosperity, but only if the latter recognized the superiority and leadership of the former. For Popławski, normal relations would entail an increase in the number of Polish Roman Catholic parishes (staffed by priests who were "called to national work"), the establishment of a network of Polish schools and libraries, and above all, an expansion of Polish landownership. "The development of Polish colonization [in the east]," he wrote, "will convince the Ruthenian politicians more effectively than any arguments that the norm of relations between our two nationalities cannot be struggle, but must be peaceful cohabitation and cooperation."[148] This was not a repudiation of the Endecja's doctrine of struggle; quite the contrary, it was an affirmation of this principle. There was no need for Ruthenians and Poles to fight, Popławski believed, because they were part of the same nation. It followed that they had to remain united against "external" dangers. The Ruthenians might constitute a separate ethnicity—Popławski considered it "an immature fantasy" to dream of polonizing so many people—but they certainly did not merit national autonomy.

The National Democrats abandoned the idea that national membership could be based on ethnicity alone, and this allowed some of them to accept what Popławski called "tribal distinctiveness" within Poland.[149] In their party program the Endeks stated that they would support the Lithuanian national movement as long as the "Lithuanian tribe" (*szczep*) accepted "political union" with Poland, recognized the right of Poles to carry out "cultural work" wherever they wished, and agreed to "draw upon Polish civilization" whenever their own language "did not suffice."[150] Many National Democrats, however, were reluctant to tolerate diversity within the nation, even under these conditions. Dmowski insisted that "The state, if only it is healthy and based on a strong foundation, will always assimilate foreign tribes politically and culturally, whether through violence or not. . . . The state will always and everywhere, more or less consciously, aspire to create cultural unity."[151] The differences between Popławski and Dmowski on this point were significant, but they should not be overemphasized. Both agreed that the Polish nation had to expand as far eastward as possible and neither would have accepted the Ruthenians or the Lithuanians as *national* communities. Popławski simply believed that it would be impossible to assimilate them in the short term, while Dmowski was somewhat more optimistic. Both wanted to facilitate Polish growth and both wanted to impose discipline and organization on the national community. If some "tribal distinctiveness" could fit (at least temporarily) within these goals, then it could be tolerated. Popławski thought it could; Dmowski argued that it could not.

National Democracy and the Jews

In the world of "struggle and oppression" described here, the Jews occupied a peculiar position. The National Democratic movement is justly known as the principle manifestation of anti-Semitism in Poland; there were anti-Semites who were not National Democrats, but there were no National Democrats who were not anti-Semitic. One can speculate whether anti-Semitism would have become as pervasive as it did in Poland were it not for the Endecja, but the fact remains that National Democracy was the principle vehicle for its dissemination. Anti-Semitism was, moreover, the point where all the various strands of the Endecja's worldview came together. The National Democrats used their image of the Jews to direct the doctrine of struggle toward domestic as well as foreign enemies. By defining the Jews broadly, Dmowski and his colleagues could place any ideological or political enemy within this imagined circle of subversive, antinational "elements." Anti-Semitism thus joined the two themes of this book: the construction of exclusionary walls of identity and the exertion of authority and discipline.

For the National Democrats, the Jews were not a nation. "One might be able to call Zionism Jewish nationalism," wrote Popławski in 1902, "if Jewish society had created the necessary national organism. But it is not and never really was such an organism." The term "organism" was a loaded expression in this context. Popławski was not suggesting that the Jews lacked the cohesion or hierarchy that marked an "organic" community; rather, he was arguing that Judaism had never expressed itself as an aggressive historical actor, that it had never participated in the struggle for survival on the same terms, or with the same goals, as proper nations. The Jews, Popławski believed, were marked by their indeterminate identity. "The religious and socioeconomic exclusivity of the Jews . . . has created a surrogate for national-tribal distinctiveness. A sectarian-economic organization has become a peculiar nation— without its own language, without a fatherland, without a state tradition, and in general without historical [traditions]."[152] Stanisław Głąbiński, a leader of the National Democratic movement in Galicia, considered the Jews to be chameleons. He wrote in his memoirs that at one time "the Jews were Germans," but after 1880 they seemed to become Polish; shortly afterwards they changed yet again, embracing socialism as their new identity.[153] It was this indeterminacy that made the Jews such a danger, according to Dmowski. Instead of occupying a clear position in the taxonomy of nationalities and nations, "the Jewish population is undeniably a parasite on the social body of whichever country it inhabits."[154]

This image of the Jewish parasite shaped the Endecja's anti-Semitism. It facilitated the construction of the Jews as irrevocably alien, without granting them the status of nationhood and without inscribing them with any specific cultural, linguistic, or religious features. To occupy their place in the National Democratic universe, the Jews had to remain amorphous and ephemeral, often unseen yet always present. The impossibility of assimilation had to become axiomatic. In fact, in a sharp break with all previous Polish judeophobes, the National Democrats directed as much hostility toward the small number of polonized Jews as they did toward the Yiddish-speaking majority. Dmowski considered assimilation an "intrusion of Jewishness" (żydowszczyzna) into the midst of the nation. "We said loudly," he wrote, "that not everyone using the Polish language is equally a Pole, that membership in the Polish fatherland demanded something more."[155] Popławski believed that even those who "accepted the external appearance of culture" in fact retained all the "specific properties of their race," and were therefore "alien to Polish society."[156] The National Democrats realized that many Jews learned the Polish language, dressed in Polish clothing, and even become practicing Catholics: nonetheless, the Endecja maintained that all this was irrelevant, because Polishness "demanded something more." The Jews were marked by a "spirit" that persisted even when all external features changed. The Jews, according to Popławski, "were and are foreign to the society in which they live," because they could not "understand or feel its aspirations and interests."[157]

This reference to the aspirations and interests of the Polish nation linked Popławski's anti-Semitism with his vision of an eternal struggle for survival. The most distinguishing mark of a Jew, he believed, was the inability to appreciate a host nation's need to fight for existence and expand. Instead, Jews were preoccupied with universalist and humanitarian ideals, which flowed naturally from their own status as a transnational community but which were necessarily contrary to the interests of any particular nation. It was for this reason that the "Jewish parasite" was such a danger to the Polish body: it was a psychological and spiritual infection that weakened the will to fight and introduced false moral inhibitions to Polish expansion. This argument allowed Popław-ski to claim that socialism was "to a considerable extent [a Jewish] creation."[158] He recognized that there were sincere Poles in the PPS, but he insisted that most members of the movement were either "morally and intellectually unstable," or Jewish. He professed to understand why this was so. "Oppressed, derided, scorned over the course of so many centuries, it is no surprise that they have in their blood the desire for revenge, that they hate everything that reminds them of the degradation, the slavery, the wrongs done to them, that they would want to destroy everything."[159] This was what Popławski thought both socialism and Judaism were all about: destruction. He contrasted these harmful tendencies with the "creative" struggle for survival that characterized all genuine nations, even Poland's enemies.

In a 1905 report prepared for Miłkowski (the National League's largest donor), the Jews and the "socialist cosmopolitans" were grouped together under the rubric of "antinational elements." Their common sin, according to this text, was to "exploit the Polish *lud* for foreign goals, for a struggle for a Russian constitution, and through this for Jewish rights in Russia." These "unknown agitators, mainly Jews" were urging workers to go on strike, and in doing so they were "severing [the nation's] social bonds . . . as if they were mainly concerned with disorganizing and weakening Polish society."[160] The charge of spreading disorganization was a persistent theme in the Endecja's anti-Semitic writing. This was summarized succinctly in a 1903 essay in *Przegląd Wszechpolski*, which tried to explain why the Jews were drawn to socialism. "Above all," the author explained, "they were drawn to socialism by a hatred of an organized, Aryan, Christian society, of a modern nation as such, and [they were drawn by] the desire to disorganize [the nation] with the help of the slogans of the international solidarity of the proletariat."[161] The Jews, in other words, were an alien force, a parasite that was spreading disorder, disobedience, and weakness, thus undermining Poland's struggle for survival.

In Dmowski's mind the Jewish threat was even greater than this: by 1902 (if not earlier) he became convinced that a massive Jewish conspiracy was working for the conquest of Poland. "There is no doubt for me," he wrote, "that this movement among our Jews [Zionism] is developing according to a plan, that conscious thought is directing it, and that it possesses a very well-developed internal organization." Dmowski could not believe that this plan was aimed at the creation of a state in Palestine, because he did not consider this a realistic goal.

> The truly realistic, sober people among the Zionists must turn their attention in a different direction, namely in the direction of the territory that today constitutes the main seat of the Jews. That country is of course Poland. Not waiting on the future promised land, it is necessary here, above all, to organize the Jews into a nation, to build here the main corps of that great world army. Undoubtedly people with more courageous minds, based on the rapid growth of the Jewish population, even believe that in the future the Jewish element will obtain dominance in our country and that today's Polish territory will become a settlement for the Jewish nation. The more sober do not really go so far into such a fantastic realm, which does not hinder them from understanding that the most

suitable terrain for organizing the Jewish nation is precisely the country that possesses their greatest percentage.

Dmowski argued that it was time to abandon the concept of "Poles of the faith of Moses," because for him it was obvious that "the Jews want to be Jews." The Poles, he concluded, had to realize what a dangerous enemy the Jews were and confront them as such.[162] While a "healthy" nation would never permit the continued existence of an alien element within its ranks, the devotion of Polish patriots to "cosmopolitan" ideals of justice prevented them from eliminating this "disease" from their social organism. "The healthy, strong body," he wrote, "for which all functions occur normally according to the order determined by the laws of nature, is the least suitable foundation for the development of parasites."[163]

In a seminal article from 1902 Dmowski combined all of these themes: the doctrine of struggle, the metaphor of the parasite, and the imagined Judeo-socialist. There was a deep divide in Polish society, he wrote, one that was far more profound than a mere difference of opinion. This arose from "a deep psychological difference that cannot be destroyed in the course of one human life, a difference in the moral structure of man. Here there can be no talk of persuading each other—that would lead to nothing; here one must accept the existence of a certain type and not only strive to limit its growth [but] try, in the interest of the national future, to eliminate it as soon as possible." This "type" was difficult to identify, because they did not look different, they did not act differently, they did not even speak an alien language. But they *were* different, because they "did not accept the duties that fall upon every one of those who profit from Polish life, did not bind with the aspirations of the national whole for self-preservation, for the attainment in the future of autonomous existence in conditions of complete development." In addition to this alien element there were others who had "lost their ties to the aspirations of the nation, who, considering themselves Poles, recognize Polish interests only insofar as they do not contradict the interests of other peoples." Together these people have become an "internal enemy, trying to weaken national bonds."

> For us Poland is above all the Polish nation, with its culture and tradition, with a separate soul and separate civilizing needs; it is a living, organic union of people having common needs and interests in a certain area, a union placing upon [its members] specific duties (including personal sacrifice) [and] demanding work for collective needs and struggle in the defense of common interests. For them [the nation] is a loose collection of individuals, groups, or strata, having nothing more in common than that they live on one land [and] that they speak one language (but not always); they are not bound by deeper moral ties, they do not have common needs, nor common duties above the needs of justice. . . . While they consider it possible to occupy an impartial position "in accordance with justice" in all conflicts between our nation and foreigners, we recognize an extensive sphere of matters in international relations in which there is neither right nor wrong, only competition between irreconcilable interests, in which one stands on one or the other side not from a feeling of justice, but from a feeling of

solidarity with one of the combating sides. They want always and everywhere to
be only people, standing on guard for nonexistent or ridiculed laws, [but] we
demand of everyone that in relations between their nation and foreign [nations]
they feel above all that they are Poles.

Dmowski believed that if Poland could not defeat this subversive element, if it could
not develop a "realistic" vision of the international struggle and purge itself of all
those who would inhibit the quest for survival and expansion, then the nation was in
grave danger. "This is not a question of how Poland will be," Dmowski concluded,
"but whether it will be." In the final words of the article, set aside as a separate, one-
sentence paragraph, Dmowski offered a blunt solution to this problem: "The race of
'half-Poles' must disappear" (*Rasa 'półpolaków' musi zginąć*).[164] Dmowski took the
old idea of the "alien element," stripped it of its cultural, linguistic, and religious
content, gave it political meaning by including his ideological enemies alongside the
Jews, then placed all this within a doctrine of struggle in order to justify the elimination of the "race of half-Poles." This deliberately ill-defined category encompassed
both assimilated Jews and non-Jewish opponents of the Endecja, thus equating Judaism with a specific political stance and transforming the "humanitarian" left into a
racialized "other."

The National Democrats were ambivalent about pogroms, because their hatred of
the Jews conflicted with their commitment to "organized" political activity. When an
anonymous contributor to *Przegląd Wszechpolski* suggested in 1897 that Polish candi-
dates to public office in Galicia should openly state their anti-Semitic views, Popławski
expressed confidence that this tactic could be adopted without fear. "The Polish people
in Galicia have sufficiently matured politically so as not to be tempted into disturbances
against the Jews, even if there was agitation in this direction," he wrote. However,
Popławski continued, as the peasants took a more active role in political life, their natural
hatred of the Jews would be strongly represented. "One cannot imagine popular politics in the Galician conditions which would not be more or less anti-Jewish."[165] When
pogroms did break out in Galicia the next year, Popławski described these events as
threatening, but he cautioned that one always had to take reports of such events with a
grain of salt, because, he believed, the Jews often tried to gain sympathy by bringing
such disturbances to public attention. In any case, he concluded, anti-Jewish violence
was a reasonable response to the increased power of the Jews.[166] In 1903 *Przegląd
Wszechpolski* printed a declaration calling on the residents of Warsaw to resist the urge
to violently attack the Jews, because the Russians were supposedly trying to instigate
such disturbances to spread disorder in Polish society and blacken Poland's reputation. The manifesto emphasized that "we should never close our eyes on Jewish exploitation" but cautioned that "beatings and the shedding of blood will not remove this
exploitation."[167]

The Jews, then, symbolized for the National Democrats all that was threatening
in their world. Portrayed by Dmowski, Popławski, and their colleagues as parasites
and ethnic chameleons, the Jews were seen to be weakening the internal cohesive-
ness and organization of the nation. In the Endecja's vision, the Jews were the embodiment of disruption and disorder, so it was virtually inevitable that socialism

would become, in the National Democratic imagination, a quintessentially Jewish phenomenon. But the Jews were not cast just as enemies from within: by supposedly sponsoring international conspiracies and by making deals with Poland's opponents, the Jews played a role in the struggle for survival, even though they were not autonomous national players in that great conflict. Roman Dmowski's sober demeanor seemed to break down when he wrote about the Jews, and even before 1905 he made outlandish claims about vast Jewish conspiracies. But this was not merely a neurotic obsession that marred the personality of an otherwise rational man; nor was it a supplemental element of National Democratic ideology. The Jews were the focal point of the Endecja's vision, the place where organization and struggle converged and were negated. *Głos* had already defined the Jews as irredeemably alien, and by the turn of the century many Jews themselves were affirming this idea (through Zionism or the *Bund*). Given these developments, there was no way to locate the Jews within a cohesive, disciplined, unified Polish space. On the other hand, the Jews (with the possible exception of the Zionists) did not appear to be engaged in the struggle for survival in a way the National Democrats could understand. If the Jews could not be Polish and could not be a national "other," they could only be a monstrosity.

Conclusion

> But even though it was a delusion our fathers served, it
> was a wonderful and noble delusion, more humane and
> more fruitful than our watchwords of today.
>
> Stefan Zweig, 1943[1]

In the 1880s many of the young intellectuals of Warsaw rejected liberalism because
it seemed so "small," because it offered no great ideals, because it led to acquies-
cence in the face of an unjust world, because it stifled action. But the ensuing return
to "the deed" turned out to be difficult, because the rhetoric of science was by then
too entrenched. Any renewed political activism would have to measure itself against
the standards of "realism" (however these might be set), eschewing the "fantasies"
that had driven an earlier generation to the disastrous uprising of 1863. The desire
for action and the need to sound scientific intersected in the fundamental transformation that characterized the political imagination of the 1890s: the abandonment of
dynamic historical time. As we saw in chapter 4, the *niepokorni* rejected the positivist idea that all Poland's problems would be resolved by the march of history. The
positivists, using a teleology they had creatively appropriated from West European
liberalism, had promised that the invisible hand of progress would bring about the
restoration of Poland if only the Poles would adopt a better work ethic, if only they
would "modernize" their culture and society. But the *niepokorni* could not be so
patient; their frustrations while growing up in an increasingly russified Kingdom and
their sense that economic development was leading to misery led them to repudiate
such confident predictions. They were convinced that they needed to *act* to change
the world; they had to do more than merely work hard until the sum of their individual efforts generated a liberal utopia. History was not going anywhere on its own,
they argued: only willful intervention in the world could bring about change.

This book has described the enormous consequences of this change in temporal
perception. In short, nationalism shifted to the radical right when it became an ideology without a historiosophy. The young "patriots" who would later constitute the
core of the National Democratic movement did not begin their public lives dedicated
to authoritarianism and anti-Semitism, and their commitment to "the nation," taken

alone, certainly did not necessitate such a stance. Polish nationalists had long wedded their patriotism to a revolutionary agenda of social emancipation and international harmony, and it was not particularly hard to sustain this. Only in the 1880s, when trust in the promises of dynamic historical time began to wane, was this linkage between the nation and the left strained, leading to a deep split in the once unified "generation of the *niepokorni*." On the one side stood the National Democrats, who had consistently (one might say ruthlessly) pursued the consequences of their synchronic worldview; on the other side stood the socialists, who had retreated back into diachronicity rather than face a world that had no moral laws other than survival, no social cohesion without authoritarianism. Those who would create the Polish Socialist Party still wanted to appear modern, but they did so with the help of Marxism, which returned them to a teleological framework and introduced an unresolved (perhaps irresolvable) tension between their desire to act and their need to believe in an optimistic, prophetic determinism. In a sense, the socialists lost their nerve: they rejected liberalism because it was too fatalistic and would not allow them to dream of social justice, but they soon realized that they had to believe in progress— in history—in order to remain on the left. As we saw in chapter 6, when "the people" did not act according to the revolutionary script, the intelligentsia had to either place their faith in the future evolution of popular consciousness, or resort to authority and discipline. Once the socialists recovered their belief in the power of time, they could deal more easily with the "national question." There was no need to be concerned about cultural diversity, there was no need to worry about national conflict: all this would fade away with time. Even if the revolution did not solve everything, then certainly the forces of development and progress would finish the job. By preserving a prophetic vision of history, some socialists in Poland were able to retain space for disruption, and thus for difference and disorder, without giving up their commitment to the nation. Georgii Plekhanov once wrote that "history is the ally of the socialists," but this phrase turned out to be true in a way he could not have imagined.[2]

The National Democrats, who resisted the return to teleology in the name of "realism," could find no such comfort. For them, national conflict became a force of nature, ever present and irredeemable. In their world, cultural unity had to be *made*, since it would never develop on its own. In their world, cultural enemies had to be destroyed, because conflict would never be transcended by time or by the spread of humanitarian ideals. Many scholars have argued that the socialist belief in a predetermined future was at the root of the Soviet Union's brutality. According to this interpretation, the Bolsheviks were able to excuse suffering in the present in the name of the coming utopia. Adam Michnik, for example, contends that "pseudo-knowledge about the secrets of the *Weltgeist* can have the most criminal consequences. For it is this purported knowledge of the imaginary laws of history that convinces some people that they must 'lead onto the road of reason and progress' thousands of others who are not in the least aware of the need or the inevitability of the New Order. Moreover, the *implementation* of such plans for the New Order and the Kingdom of Progress necessarily leads to contempt for people, to the use of force, and to moral self-destruction."[3] Perhaps this is true, but prophetic visions can be liberating as well as enslaving. In fact, the *denial* of progress turned out (at least in Poland) to be the source of the radical right's decoupling of social equity and the national interest. Without progress, all the National Democrats had was "reality."

Stanisław Kozicki, a leading National Democrat, claimed that his colleagues replaced the "mystical methods" of earlier Polish patriots with empiricism and an understanding of natural laws.[4] Dmowski asserted that "our program—in the area of national policy the only realistic program—was born of the political experiences of the most recent times as well as from modern political knowledge."[5] Dmowski even remarked in 1905 that his worldview was so uniquely a product of his generation's experiences that it could not be understood by anyone over 40 years old (significantly, Dmowski would turn 41 in August of that year).[6] Not only was the National Democratic program "realistic," it was "scientific." In an 1899 article in *Przegląd Wszechpolski* (the first one Dmowski signed with his real name), the National Democratic leader emphasized that modern science had convinced him to accept "the cult of strength." As he put it, "The hard conditions of life unite here with the influence of the spirit of modern knowledge and create a certain ruthlessness, alien to all compromises, in [the pursuit] of national aspirations."[7] Finally, the National Democrats believed that their teachings were in accordance with the needs of modern politics. As Popławski put it in 1899, "The popular masses are already starting to take an active role in political life, or [at least] indirectly influencing it, which . . . is expressed, for example, in the growth of so-called chauvinism, which fundamentally is a strongly condensed feeling of national distinctiveness, loudly proclaiming the principle: right or wrong, my country."[8]

Thus did the National Democrats imagine reality. They argued that xenophobia and aggression met the demands of the real world, corresponded to the teachings of (Spencerian) science, and satisfied the genuine interests of the people. But the National Democrats realized quite early in their political careers that not everyone perceived reality as they did. They were opposed not only by their former colleagues, the socialists, but also by thousands of workers and peasants who placed "selfish" class needs above those of the national struggle. These "politically immature" masses even believed in the power of history: they believed that a future world might not be as oppressive or violent as the present and that "humanitarian" ideals might govern a postrevolutionary utopia. Such beliefs led industrial workers (and even some peasants) to engage in acts of protest against their "fellow Poles," and in order to counter such behavior the National Democrats insisted that discipline had to be restored. Perhaps even more disturbing for the Endeks, the ethnographic map of Eastern Europe did not correspond to their expansive vision of Poland; again, reality did not match the National Democratic "reality." Since history offered no resolution for this disjuncture (since the prophecy that Poles, Jews, and Ukrainians might progress toward mutual coexistence or even toward voluntary assimilation was "unrealistic"), the only answer was to *make* the new Poland, even if doing so required the same techniques of denationalization (polonization, in this case) against which the Poles themselves had protested for so long. So, once the National Democrats gave up the solace of historical time—all in the name of realism and modernity—they lacked the means to cope with any gaps between their dreams (which they still had, of course) and their experiences, without resorting to social discipline, coercion, and even (later) violence.

"Struggle" and "authority" were thus the two constituent parts of the National Democratic worldview, and both rested on the fateful move described in chapter 4: the abandonment of dynamic historical time. This volume has traced the emergence of the ideological formation known as right radicalism, showing how the National Democrats (and undoubtedly similar movements throughout Europe) were imbedded in the intellectual traditions of the left and in the rhetoric of "modernity." But this study of the origins of National Democracy brings up a broader question: *why* did Polish nationalism evolve in such a direction? How did it become possible for Polish patriotism, once based on the slogan "for our freedom and yours," to develop into such an exclusionary and authoritarian ideology? This question is misleading, because the patriotism of 1830 and 1863, of Mickiewicz and the Polish Democratic Society, did not simply "develop" into the nationalism of Roman Dmowski. There was nothing intrinsic to the dynamics of romanticism that made it impossible to sustain: as long as Polish intellectuals believed in progress, it was easy for them to imagine that the realization of the national agenda would also bring about a new world of social justice and harmony. Similarly, liberal sociology was not to blame. The positivists brought the nation down to earth, giving new attention to the ethnolinguistic community—they made Poland "realistic," if I dare still use this term—but it was a long way from their world to that of the National Democrats. Finally and most important, it is *not* the case that nationalism became more violent when it grew into a mass movement: as we have seen, the rhetoric of hatred was entirely in place years before the Endecja gained widespread popular support, and these ideas were in no way an emanation of popular attitudes and sentiments. Quite the contrary, National Democracy was in many ways formulated *against* the "mob," as a means of instilling national discipline. We cannot explain the rise of radical right nationalism in Poland—or anywhere else, for that matter—by merely evoking the forces of modern politics, as if the sociopolitical transformations of the fin de siècle were articulated or scripted by sensitive members of the intelligentsia. To make such an argument would reproduce the Endecja's own self-image as a "democratic" movement, as an expression of the vox populi. Obviously, late nineteenth-century nationalists did not invent or construct the nation from scratch, but the intelligentsia did give *meaning* to national*ism*—just as they gave meaning to modernity itself—in ways that can be explained only if one studies the discursive formations that structured the intelligentsia's world.

Our ways of thinking and talking—our conceptions of historical time and social space, our forms of identity and community—do not necessarily dictate any specific political stance or ideological proposition, but they do set limits on the sorts of things we can envision and describe. These limits, however, are always changing, as individuals explore the fissures, contradictions, and possibilities of each discourse and as the "real world" (which our language purports to describe) changes. Neither the exclusionary, authoritarian nationalism of National Democracy nor the open, revolutionary nationalism of the Polish Socialist Party was an inevitable consequence of Poland's modernization or the internal dynamics of patriotic thought. Rather, the ideological framework of nationalism contained points of tension that could be pushed in a number of directions as different people responded to social change (industrialization and urbanization) in different ways. Both National Democracy and socialism were *possible* developments upon the foundation articulated before 1863, but both entailed a basic reconfiguration of the conceptual universe within which Polish intellectuals had previously spoken about the nation. Moreover, each style of national imagining was a response to the socioeconomic transformations of late nineteenth century Poland and to the cultural pressures of russification. No clear causal explanation for radical right nationalism can be offered, because both the Endecja and the PPS emerged from the same intellectual tradition and the same socioeconomic environment. Nothing about either the intellectual or social history of nineteenth-century Poland *compelled* the National Democrats to think as they did. At the root of their worldview was a basic choice between a synchronic and a diachronic mode of thought, between social space and historical time. It was this choice, this "act of will" (as they would have described it) that determined how key terms like "nation," "people," "class," and "state" were defined and configured.

Dmowski and his colleagues argued in the 1890s that the fundamental gap in Polish politics was between those committed to "class" and those devoted to "the nation." The members of the PPS resisted this dichotomy, but with time the Endecja so discredited the term *naród* (nation) that many on the left preferred terms like *państwo* (state) or *społeczeństwo* (society). Indeed, the term "nationalism" has assumed in Polish an exclusively derogatory connotation, as if only the Endecja and its successors merit the term. We have seen, however, that there was a tradition of nationalism predating National Democracy. As Andrzej Bryk has argued, "Polish culture has the luxury of choosing from a wide variety of different streams. One of those most powerful and appealing, albeit a little forgotten, is the tradition of tolerance and pluralism. The rebuilding of that tradition, whose lack is the greatest loss of the modern Polish educational system, will be an enormous enrichment of the present dominant interpretation of the Polish national past."[9] Such models did exist in the past, and they were not always mere veils concealing Polish aspirations to Lithuania, Belarus, and Ukraine (although this rhetoric has occasionally been exploited for irredentist ends). That it became impossible by the 1890s for Lithuanians, Ukrainians, or Jews to take seriously the idea of a truly inclusive Poland—that the culturally homogeneous nation-state seemed to be the only option—was to a large degree the bitter harvest of the process described in this book. It is not so much that the ideal of a culturally inclusive Poland in its 1772 borders was theoretically impossible, or necessarily a violation of the cultural self-determination of the diverse communities of Eastern Europe. Rather, Poland *as defined by most Poles in the late nineteenth century*—as a sociological community marked by empirical features such as language and religion—was incompatible with Lithuanian, Belorussian, Jewish, and Ukrainian ambitions. But alternative definitions of the nation had once been available. The ideal of multiculturalism is not an American invention of the late twentieth century, but a quintessentially East European dream of the early nineteenth.

Like Andrzej Bryk, I believe that it is time to reconsider the merits of these abandoned options, not in the name of reviving dreams of a greater Poland (such ambitions have long since lost their viability), but in the name of imagining a Poland—indeed, a Europe—for the twenty-first century, within which the nation-state will no longer be equated with cultural homogeneity. The secret to recovering this older style of national imagining, this idea of a multicultural Poland, is to look for the point at which the old dreams began to disintegrate, when it became hard for a patriot to envision a world of harmony among nations and diversity within nations. As this book has demonstrated, that moment came when a large segment of the Polish intelligentsia abandoned the teleological historiosophies of their predecessors and peers. Perhaps we should follow the example of Stefan Zweig, admitting that our fathers served "delusions" while recognizing that they were wonderful and noble delusions, full of potential for formulating a national politics for the modern world.

Notes

Notes on the Sources

The works of many of the authors examined in this volume are available in edited anthologies, and whenever possible I have included references to both the original sources and the more easily accessible collected editions. Except in a few cases, which I have noted, my interpretations are based on a reading of the original texts.

Dates are a problem for the historian of nineteenth-century Poland—even more so than for the historian of prerevolutionary Russia, because the Poles used both Western and Russian calendars after 1863 for all official documents and legal publications. Even the way one dated one's newspaper or magazine made a political statement: should the Russian date be listed before or after the European date? With the significance of this choice in mind, in my notes I have presented dates as they appeared in the periodicals cited. If only one date appears (as, for example, in *Przegląd Wszechpolski*), it may be assumed to be according to the Western calendar.

Introduction

1. Żarnowska, "Rewolucja 1905–1907 a kultura polityczna społeczeństwa Królestwa Polskiego," in Wolsza and Żarnowska, *Społeczeństwo*, 1.
2. Walicki, *Poland between East and West*, 60.
3. Julie Skurski, "The Ambiguities of Authenticity in Latin America: *Doña Bárbara and the Construction of National Identity*," in Eley and Suny, 375. On the tendency of the concept of "the nation" to define boundaries of exclusion and enforce homogeneity see Bhabha, 312; Cole, 35–56; Duara, 16; Parker, 3; Stephens, 7; and Woodward, 223.
4. For a survey of how the narrative of modernization has shaped our view of nationalism, see Kramer, 525–45.
5. Pulzer, 287. See also Klier, 415; Mosse, *German Ideology*, 3; Stern, 267–98; Talmon, *Myth of the Nation*, 10. For an early challenge to the teleological implications of this approach,

see Weber and Rogger, 12. On the ways in which some authors have sustained a progressive narrative of modernization in the face of what they consider "atavistic" nationalist violence, see Ben-Ghiat, 627–65.

6. Kieval, 67–74.

7. Mendelsohn, 41. A more static (and glaringly inaccurate) portrayal of Polish nationalism is reflected in Strauss, "Poland—Culture of Antisemitism," in *Hostages of Modernization*, 965, 969.

8. Llobera, 1–92.

9. See, for example, Deutsch, 29–71; Gellner, 48; and Hroch, 3.

10. Blobaum, *Rewolucja*, 189.

11. On the need to study nationalism as a dialogical process, see Eley, *Reshaping the German Right*, 11; and Mallon, *Peasant and Nation*, 315–23.

12. Chatterjee, *Fragments*, 159–60.

13. Zeldin, 3. From a slightly different perspective, see the discussion of "elite discourse" in Verdery, "The Production and Defense of 'the Romanian Nation,'" in Fox, 81, and Verdery, *National Ideology*, 6–7. For a general discussion of how "subalterns" are silenced and how one might go about recovering their voices, see Prakash; Mallon, "Promise and Dilemma"; and Cooper.

14. Platz, 60–70.

15. Nowak, 32.

16. Anderson, 22–36, 187–206. See also Chatterjee's distinction between "European historiography" and "Puranic history" in Chatterjee, *Fragments,* 76–115.

17. Duara, 16.

18. Singer, 320–24. On the construction of temporality, see Soja, 147.

19. The acronym comes from the initials N.D. (*Narodowa Demokracja,* or National Democracy) and is pronounced "En-dets´-ya." A member of the Endecja is called an Endek.

20. [Dmowski], "Walka o prawo i organizacja narodowa," *Przegląd Wszechpolski*, 9 (June 1903), in Dmowski, *Dziesięć lat walki*, 342–43.

21. Dmowski, "Podstawy polityki polskiej," *Przegląd Wszechpolski*, 11 (July 1905): 347–48.

22. Dmowski, *Myśli,* 14.

23. R. Skrzycki [Dmowski], "Wymowne cyfry," *Przegląd Wszechpolski*, 1 (15 May 1895): 147.

24. Bromke is the leading proponent of this dichotomy, but for a more sophisticated presentation, see Kieniewicz, "Uprisings and Organic Work," 395–401.

25. Toruńczyk, 15–19. See also Michnik, *Szanse polskiej demokracji*, 138–39; Walicki, *Three Traditions*, 23–24; Wapiński, "Idea narodu w myśli społecznej i politycznej Endecji przed rokiem 1918," in Gockowski and Walicki, 224; and Zimand, "Uwagi o teorii narodu," 4. For a modest challenge to this approach, see Pąkciński, 151–52. In contrast to these authors, the official writings of the communist era virtually demonized the movement. See Kalabiński for an example. Some of the interwar writing on this topic, such as Pobóg-Malinowski's *Narodowa Demokracja*, must be read with some skepticism for similar reasons.

26. See, for example, Wieczorkiewicz, "Próby modelowania nowych postaw politycznych wobec Rosji w dobie Rewolucji 1905–1907 (Narodowa Demokracja i Stronnictwo Polityki Realnej)," in Wolsza and Żarnowska, 57–74.

27. I thank both Adam Michnik and Andrzej Walicki for explaining to me the context behind their statements regarding National Democracy.

28. Sternhell, *Birth of Fascist Ideology*, 12. See also Sternhell, *Neither Right nor Left*, 25–28; and "Paul Déroulède," 46–47. More directly relevant to Poland is the comparison

between Nazism and National Democracy offered by Hagen in "Before the 'Final Solution,'" 368. In contrast, consider Payne's reluctance to apply the label "fascist" so broadly: *Fascism*, 196.

29. Kozicki, *Historia*, 472. See also Wasiutyński, 39–40; and Tomasz Wituch, "Przedmowa do obecnego wydania," in Dmowski, *Polityka polska*, 17. See also the emphasis on National Democracy's "democratic" content in Fountain, 160; and Kawalec, "Elementy liberalne w myśli politycznej Narodowej Demokracji przed rokiem 1939," in *Tradycje liberalne*, 155–68.

30. Walicki, *Poland between East and West*, 60.

31. Mistewicz, 171.

32. Blobaum, *Rewolucja*, 195; and Żarnowska, "Rewolucja," 6–7.

33. Marczewski, 93; Micewski, 60; Piątkowski, 45–65; Toporowski, iii, 386; Wapiński, "Endecka koncepcja państwa," 149–50; and Wapiński, "Z dziejów tendencji nacjonalistycznych," 828–39.

34. Mistewicz, 169–89. Wapiński seems to have shifted to this view as well. See his *Narodowa Demokracja*, 72.

35. Kern, 152.

36. For example, see Sternhell, *Birth of Fascist Ideology*, 249.

37. Giddens, 8.

38. Verdery, "Production and Defense," 96; and Verdery, *National Ideology*, 57.

39. Some Poles have also challenged the exclusively pejorative use of the term *nacjonalizm*. See Walicki, "Czy możliwy jest nacjonalizm liberalny?" 32–50.

40. Duara, 8. Ironically, an almost identical definition of nationalism can be found in the work of a political scientist whose approach (rooted in rational choice theory) differs in every other respect from Duara's (and mine): Coleman, "Rights, rationality, and nationality," in Breton, 11.

41. Gauri Viswanathan, "Religious Conversion and the Politics of Dissent," in van der Veer, 89.

Chapter One

1. Mosse, *Confronting the Nation*, 122.

2. Michel, 190.

3. On this song, see Chrzanowski, 250–74; Pachoński; and Podgórski. For a general survey of national anthems in the nineteenth century, see Mosse, *Confronting the Nation*, 13–26.

4. For some alternative interpretations of these lines, see Chrzanowski, 273; Ujejski, 189; Walicki, *Enlightenment*, 101–3.

5. For a summary of Semeneńko's essay (and the reaction to it from other émigrés), see Nowak, 206–7; Walicki, *Philosophy*, 70.

6. J. J. Rusin z Przemyski, "O śpiewach ludu polskiego," *Gazeta Polska*, 316 (1830), in Andrzej Zieliński, 67–69.

7. Joachim Lelewel, *Polska, dzieje i rzeczy jej* (Poznań, 1851–1868), as cited by Walicki, *Między filozofią, religią, i polityką*, 215. On Lelewel, see Serejski, "Joachim Lelewel i jego szkoła," in Walicki, *Polska myśl*, 30–77; and Skurnowicz.

8. On Mochnacki, see Stanisław Pieróg, "Wstęp," in Mochnacki, 5–71; Szacki, 147–203; Ujejski, 199–200; and Andrzej Zieliński, 47–48.

9. As cited by Ujejski, 199–200, and by Andrzej Zieliński, 47.

10. Mochnacki, *O literaturze polskiej w wieku dziewiętnastym* (Warsaw, 1830), in Mochnacki, 301.

11. Mochnacki, *O literaturze*, 277.

12. Mochnacki, *Powstania narodu polskiego w roku 1830 i 1831* (Paris, 1834), in Mochnacki, 361.

13. On these two senses of *duch narodowy*, the social and the transcendent, see Szacki, "Maurycy Mochnacki," in Walicki, *Polska myśl*, 21–22.

14. As cited by Ujejski, 253; and by Nowak, 38. Emphasis mine.

15. Mochnacki, *O literaturze*, 314–15.

16. This is from the manifesto of a utopian socialist group called the "Gromada Grudziąż," as cited by Adam Sikora, "Emigracyjny socjalizm utopijny," in Walicki, *Polska myśl*, 105–49.

17. Both of these citations come from Ujejski, 284–85. For more on the slogan "for our freedom and yours," see Nowak, 42–68; 94–116.

18. As cited by Ujejski, 298.

19. Nowak, 46.

20. On Cieszkowski, see Liebich; and Walicki, "August Cieszkowski," in Walicki, *Polska myśl*, 395–442.

21. Cieszkowski, *Prolegomena*, 5–7, 8, 92. On Hegel's impact on Polish thought in the 1830s and 1840s, see Walicki, *Między filozofią, religią, i polityką*, 45–99, 102–8.

22. Cieszkowski, *Prolegomena*, 13, 87. For more on the tendency of romantic authors to posit three stages of history, see Reeves and Gould.

23. Cieszkowski, *Ojcze nasz*, in Walicki, *Filozofia i myśl społeczna*, 312. Emphasis in the original.

24. As cited by Ujejski, 303.

25. Mochnacki, *O literaturze*, 318–19, 333–35, 343; Mochnacki, "Jak rozumieć powstanie polskie," *Nowa Polska*, 58 (3 March 1831), in Mochnacki, 401. See also the passages cited by Szacki, 175.

26. As cited by Chrzanowski, "Romantyzm," 285.

27. Słowacki, "List Pierwszy do Księcia Adama Czartoryskiego," in Walicki, *Filozofia i myśl*, 588, 590. This passage is also discussed in Walicki, *Philosophy*, 281.

28. On Libelt and his conception of the nation, see Chrzanowski, "Romantyzm," 287; Walicki, "Karol Libelt," in *Polska myśl*, 443–76; Walicki, "Polska myśl filozoficzna epoki międzypowstaniowej," in Walicki, *Filozofia i myśl społeczna*, 34–35; and Walicki, *Philosophy*, 173–89. The following citations are taken from Libelt, 8–50.

29. Much of what follows is taken from the informative entry on the term *lud* in Pepłowski, 124–41. See also Andrzej Zieliński, 23.

30. Jan Nepomucen Janowski, *Krótki katechizm polityczny* (1834), in Baczko, 46.

31. Tadeusz Krępowicki, "Czy jest jaka Litwa," *Nowa Polska*, 3 (3 June 1835), as cited by Nowak, 208.

32. For two alternative approaches to messianism, see Talmon, *Political Messianism*; and Walicki, *Philosophy*, 240–41.

33. As quoted by Chrzanowski, 161; and by Ujejski, 303–6. On the importance of Brodziński's ideas to his generation, see Andrzej Zieliński, 44. Actually, Brodziński was not the first Pole to use the phrase "messianism." Józef Hoene-Wroński had done so earlier, but he wrote in French and did not use the expression within the framework of a nationalist discourse. See Adam Sikora, "Antypody romantycznego mesjanizmu—'filozofia absolutna' Hoene-Wrońskiego i mystyka Towiańskiego," in Walicki, *Polska myśl*, 156–86.

34. Mickiewicz, *Księgi*, 33, 35, 45, 47, 49.

35. Mickiewicz, *Les Slaves*, 204. On the difference between *Księgi* and *Les Slaves*, see Walicki, "Adama Mickiewicza prelekcje paryskie," in *Polska myśl*, 216–72.

36. The book went through two printings in less than a month and within a year had been translated into French (with an introduction by Montalambert), English, and German. In 1833 it was first printed—illegally—in Poland (in Lwów). Lamennais read the French translation and called the book "one of the most beautiful things which has recently been written." Not surprisingly, this volume was placed on the Church's *Index*. See Maria Grabowska "Katechizm Mickiewicza," in *Księgi*, 7–8.

37. Walicki, "Millenaryzm i mesjanizm religijny a romantyczny mesjanizm polski," in *Między filozofią, religią, i polityką*, 8–44.

38. As cited by Walicki, *Philosophy*, 58.

39. On the Church's hostility toward messianism, and toward Mickiewicz in particular, see Walicki, "Polska myśl filozoficzna epoki międzypowstaniowej," in Walicki, *Filozofia i myśl społeczna*, 59–67.

40. Marx, "Communism, Revolution, and a Free Poland." For more on Marx and the Polish question, see Kieniewicz, *Historia Polski*, 165; Marx and Engels, *Marks i Engels o Polsce;* Żychowski, *Polska myśl socjalistyczna*, 42.

41. Handelsman, 210–12.

42. "Manifest T. D. P.," in Baczko, 88.

43. "Prospekt pisma politycznego i literackiego 'Postęp'" (6 May 1834), in Baczko, 56.

44. Janowski, 46. How he might have reconciled this emphasis on "the deed" with his interest in ethnicity (cited above) is unclear.

45. Kieniewicz, *Emancipation*, 111–12. Dembowski was killed in the 1846 revolt. For more examples of how the term *lud* served to limit the *naród* to the peasantry, and how this equation was contested, see Eisenbach, *Wielka Emigracja*, 264–89.

46. Djakow, 985.

47. On the difficulty of being a conservative nationalist, see Król, *Konserwatyści,* 5–6, 275–76.

48. On the relationship between secular patriots and the Catholic Church in the nineteenth century, see Boudou, 188–229; Cywiński, *Ogniem próbowane*, 45–84; Dylągowa, 85–95; Dylągowa, "Na przełomie oświecenia i romantyzmu (1795–1831)," in Kłoczowski, 373–402; Modras, 340; Wroński, 56–60; Ziółek, "Stosunki kościelno-państwowe w konstytucyjnym Królestwie Polskim," in Piotrowski, 107–16. The text of *Cum Primum* can be found in Carlen, 233–34.

49. Jedlicki, 151.

50. Mochnacki, "Być albo nie być," *Nowa Polska*, 29 (2 February 1831), and Mochnacki and Adam Gurowski, "Czemu masy nie powstają?" *Nowa Polska*, 41 (14 February 1831), in Mochnacki, 424–29, 430–34. Note the use of the plural: Mochnacki wanted to make the Polish cause the concern of all "the peoples" (*ludy*) not just the "Polish people" (*lud*).

51. Mochnacki, "Restauracja Polski," *Dziennik Krajowy* (20 August 1831), in Mochnacki, 435–39. Bolesław Chrobry (966–1025) was an early Polish king, and the Jagiellonian dynasty ruled over Poland from 1386 to 1572.

52. Mochnacki, "Restauracja i rewolucja," *Dziennik Krajowy* (22 August 1831), in Mochnacki, 440–45.

53. On Rzewuski, see Król, 51–8; Ludwikowski, *Konserwatyzm*, 47–60; *Continuity and Change*, 56–71; Walicki, *Philosophy*, 229–36.

54. Rzewuski's novels include *Listopad: romans historyczny z drugiej połowy wieku XVIII* (1845–1846), *Pamiątki imci pana Seweryna Soplicy* (1839), and *Pamiętniki Bartłomeja Michałowskiego* (1856). On this writer's small role in the history of Polish belles-lettres, see Miłosz, 255.

55. Henryk Rzewuski, *Wędrówki umysłowe,* in Rzewuski, *Pisma,* 2:106. Compare this to de Maistre, *Study on Sovereignty,* in de Maistre, *Works,* 108–9.

56. Rzewuski, 2:108.

57. On Rzewuski's circle, the so-called "Petersburg Pentarchy," see Król, 51–64, Ludwikowski, *Continuity,* 113–19, and Ludwikowski, *Konserwatyzm,* 60–66.

58. As cited by Walicki, "Polska myśl filozoficzna epoki międzypowstaniowej," in Walicki, *Filozofia i myśl społeczna,* 56. See also Alina Kowalczykowa, "Poglądy filozoficzne Zygmunta Krasińskiego," in Walicki, *Polska myśl,* 308.

59. Kowalczykowa, 337.

60. See Elżbieta Feliksiak, "Norwidowski świat myśl," in Walicki, *Polska myśl,* 546; Walicki, "Cyprian Norwid: trzy wątki myśli," in *Między filozofią, religią, i polityką,* 195–238.

61. Słowacki, "List Pierwszy do Księcia Adama Czartoryskiego" (1846), in Walicki, *Filozofia i myśl społeczna,* 591.

62. For a complete exposition of his ideas on spiritual progress and reincarnation, see Słowacki, *Genezis z ducha* (Lwów, 1872), in Walicki, *Filozofia i myśl społeczna,* 599–614.

63. Cieszkowski, *O izbie wyższej i arystokracji w naszych czasach,* trans. J. Garewicz, in Walicki, *Filozofia i myśl społeczna,* 327–33. See also *Prolegomena,* 29.

64. Cieszkowski, *O izbie wyższej i arystokracji,* 331.

65. Cieszkowski, *Prolegomena,* 98–100.

66. On Cieszkowski's ambivalent attitude toward revolution, see Liebich, 91.

67. Cieszkowski, *O kredycie i obiegu,* trans. A. Cieszkowski Jr., in Walicki, *Filozofia i myśl społeczna,* 333–36. The French original went through two more editions, in 1847 and 1884, and earned Cieszkowski some international notoriety.

68. Cieszkowski, *Ojcze nasz,* 303–4, 318–21.

69. On the acknowledged importance of Cieszkowski to Krasiński, see Kowalczykowa, "Poglądy filozoficzne Zygmunta Krasińskiego," in Walicki, *Polska myśl,* 318–26.

70. On the difficulty of expressing explicitly judeophobic views in the 1860s, see Cała, 187.

71. On the mixed legacy of the Polish Enlightenment vis-à-vis the Jews, see Jacob Goldberg, "The Changes in the Attitude of Polish Society toward the Jews in the Eighteenth Century," in Polonsky, *From Shtetl to Socialism,* 50–63; Eisenbach, "The Four Years' Sejm and the Jews," in Polonsky et al., *The Jews in Old Poland,* 73–92. For general background on eighteenth- and nineteenth-century judeophobia, see Katz.

72. Cała, 49–86, contrasts "Poles of the Faith of Moses" with the even more assimilatory expression, "Poles of Jewish descent." See also Aleksander Hertz, 35, where he calls for Jews to be recognized as "different" but not "alien." For an interesting interpretation of the Jews' status before the partitions, see Hundert, 36–45.

73. Eisenbach, *Emancipation,* 215. See also Eisenbach, *Wielka Emigracja,* 67.

74. Kieniewicz, "The Jews of Warsaw, Polish Society, and the Partitioning Powers, 1795–1861," in Polonsky, *From Shtetl to Socialism,* 83–102.

75. For more on this topic, see Sorkin.

76. On Jews during the November Uprising, see Eisenbach, *Wielka Emigracja,* 80–108; Kieniewicz, "The Jews of Warsaw, Polish Society and the Partitioning Powers, 1795–1861," in Bartoszewski and Polonsky, *Jews in Warsaw,* 160–61.

77. "Izraelici na polskiej ziemi," *Nowa Polska* (1835), as cited by Eisenbach, *Emancipation,* 315.

78. Eisenbach, "The Four Years' Sejm and the Jews," 73–92; Levine, 203.

79. On Poles, Jews, and 1863, see Eisenbach, Fajnhauz, and Wein; Opalski and Bartal; and Opalski, 68–80.

80. Bender, "Manifestacje patriotyczne i konspiracje przedpowstaniowe w Królestwie Polskim," in Kalembka, 210.

81. Eisenbach, *Emancipation*, 437.

82. As cited by Kołodziejczyk, "Przemiany społeczno-kulturowe w środowisku ludności żydowskiej w Królestwie Polskim w XIX wieku," in Meducka and Renz, 16.

83. As cited by Eisenbach, *Emancipation*, 437.

84. "Odezwa Rządu Narodowego, Warsaw, 22 VI 1863," in Eisenbach, Fajnhauz, and Wein, 77.

85. As cited in Opalski, 72.

86. See the introduction to Eisenbach, Fajnhauz, and Wein, 6–7.

87. Kramsztyk's sermon is reprinted in Eisenbach, Fajnhauz, and Wein, 13.

88. The only other such publication was a periodical called *Izraelita Polski*, which appeared during the 1830 uprising but quickly collapsed. See Fuks, 41.

89. As cited by Fuks, 51–52.

90. From a sermon by Izaak Kramsztyk, 9 October 1861, in Eisenbach, Fajnhauz, and Wein, 39.

91. As cited by Fuks, 54.

92. Meisels had been proclaiming his devotion to the Polish cause for decades. See the copy of the speech he gave in Kraków in 1848, reprinted in Żbikowski, 118–19. On Meisels, see Cała, 30–31.

93. Eisenbach, *Emancipation*, 457–58.

94. On Feliński, see Eisenbach, *Emancipation*, 457–58.

Chapter Two

1. Wiślicki's role as a creative intellectual in his own right, and not just a publisher, has been understated. See Wroczyński, 218; Przyborowski, 31.

2. "Otwarcie pisma," *Przegląd Tygodniowy*, 1 (26 December 1865/7 January 1866): 1.

3. Wiślicki, "Niezależność kobiety," *Przegląd Tygodniowy*, 1 (13/25 February 1866): 59–60; Wiślicki, "Zbytek w strojach," *Przegląd Tygodniowy*, 1 (27 February/11 March 1866): 73–74; Wiślicki, "Polscy i Niemieccy przemysłowcy," *Przegląd Tygodniowy*, 1 (12/24 June 1866): 193–94; Aleksander Kraushar, "Samuela Smilesa Self-Help," *Przegląd Tygodniowy*, 1 (18/30 September-25 September/7 October 1866): 310–11, 319–20.

4. Wiślicki, "Praca i majątek, czyli środki uczciwego wzbogacania się," *Przegląd Tygodniowy*, 2 (23 April/5 May 1867): 137–38.

5. On Wiślicki's desperate financial situation, see "Od redakcyi," *Przegląd Tygodniowy*, 2 (19 November/1 December 1867): 382. A year later he sounded more optimistic: "Na zakończenie roku. Słowo od redakcyi," *Przegląd Tygodniowy*, 3 (15/27 December 1868): 462–63.

6. On the *Szkoła Główna*, see Błaszczyk and Danielewicz, 159–84; Bogacz, 244–66; Kieniewicz, *Dzieje Uniwersytetu Warszawskiego*, 242–377; Kulczycka-Saloni, *Życie literackie*, 44. There were in fact insurgents at the *Szkoła Główna*, despite its reputation as a point of calm in the storm. See Kieniewicz, *Dzieje Uniwersytetu*, 339–47, and Kulczycka-Saloni, 46–47.

7. At the *Szkoła Główna*, Piotr Chmielowski, Józef Kotarbiński, and Aleksander Świętochowski were best friends and constant companions. Aleksander Głowacki [Prus] and Julian Ochorowicz were in the same class as Świętochowski at a secondary school in Lublin.

See Brykalska, *Biografia*, 19, 32. For some short biographical sketches of these and all the other major figures of the period, see the extensive "biographical notes" appended to Markiewicz, *Pozytywizm*, 447–513. On the eventual spread of Polish positivism outside this Warsaw circle, see Kozłowska-Sabatowska.

8. Świętochowski described Wiślicki's permissive editorial practices in *Wspomnienia*, 5.

9. Świętochowski, *Wspomnienia*, 9, 15–17; Chmielowski, *Zarys literatury polskiej z ostatnich lat szesnastu* (Wilno, 1881), in Chmielowski, *Pisma*, 265. See also Blejwas, *Realism*, 86; Jedlicki, 233–34; Rudzki, 24.

10. Świętochowski, "My i Wy," *Przegląd Tygodniowy*, 6 (17/29 October 1871), in Świętochowski, *Publicystyka*, 32.

11. After the initial round of polemics, a well-known conservative publicist named Edward Lubowski began a systematic campaign against *Przegląd Tygodniowy* in the magazine *Kłosy*. The widely distributed daily *Kurier Warszawski* followed Lubowski's lead. This opposition only gave *Przegląd Tygodniowy* more publicity, and its circulation continued to increase. See Świętochowski, *Wspomnienia*, 17, 22–23. For another perspective, see Jeske-Choiński, *Pozytywizm*, 123.

12. Poseł Prawdy [Świętochowski], "Liberum veto," *Prawda*, 1 (1 January 1881/20 December 1880). This famous essay is reprinted in at least two collections: Świętochowski, *Liberum veto*, 1:176; and Świętochowski, *Publicystyka*, 81.

13. Jeske-Choiński, *Pozytywizm*, 142. See also Przyborowski, 91.

14. Chmielowski, 277.

15. These lectures are remembered by Chmielowski, 239–40. See also Błaszczyk and Danielewicz, 173–81.

16. Świętochowski, *Wspomnienia*, 17.

17. On the minimal influence of Comte on the Warsaw positivists, see Chmielowski, 239; Markiewicz, *Pozytywizm*, 47; Ochorowicz, 52; Rudzki, 25; Świętochowski, *Wspomnienia*, 17. Bolesław Limanowski's treatise, *Socjologia Augusta Comte'a* (Lwów, 1875) was the first work in the Polish language to deal with this French philosopher in any depth. See Skarga, "Polska myśl filozoficzna w epoce pozytywizmu," in Hochfeldowa and Skarga, *Filozofia i myśl społeczna*, 12. For a rare favorable examination of Comte's ideas in the positivist press (albeit with a sarcastic editorial interjection by Świętochowski), see L. Straszewicz, "Społeczne kierunki w teoryi i w życiu," *Prawda*, 3 (6 October/24 September 1883–13/1 October 1883): 473–74, 483.

18. On the importance of Mill and Spencer to the positivists, see Brykalska, *Redaktor Prawdy*, 9; Markiewicz, *Pozytywizm*, 47; Warzenica, 33.

19. Świętochowski, "Liberum veto," *Prawda*, 1 (1 January 1881/20 December 1880), in Świętochowski, *Liberum veto*, 79. On Świętochowski's introduction to Mill, see Brykalska, *Biografia*, 18. Mill was available in Polish translation while the positivists were still young: for references to the earliest translations of Mill into Polish, see the bibliography of this volume.

20. Kozłowski, "Charakter współczesnej filozofji. Poprzednicy Spencera," *Ateneum*, 26 (September 1878), in Kozłowski, 1–38.

21. Al. G. [Prus], "Szkic programu w warunkach obecnego rozwoju społeczeństwa," *Nowiny* (11/23–18/30 March 1883), in Hochfeldowa and Skarga, *Filozofia i myśl*, 1:188–89. *Nowiny* did not carry a volume number. This piece is also reprinted in Prus, *Wybór kronik*, 40–50.

22. Kozłowski, "Charakter współczesnej filozofji," 38.

23. Świętochowski, "Herbert Spencer (Studium z dziedziny pozytywizmu)," *Przegląd Tygodniowy*, 7 (2/14 April–23 July/4 August 1872). Kozłowski's articles include: "Charakter

współczesnej filozofji. Poprzednicy Spencera," *Ateneum,* 26 (September 1878); "Pierwsze zasady," *Ateneum,* 27 (January 1879); "Podstawy socjologji i stanowisko w niej Herberta Spencera," *Ateneum,* 29 (April 1881); "Etyka Spencera 1," *Ateneum,* 31 (July 1883); and "Etyka Spencera II," *Ateneum,* 32 (January 1884). All of these are reprinted in Kozłowski, *Pisma,* 1–273. A three-part review of Spencer's ideas appeared along with the translation of *Study of Sociology*: H. G. [Henryk Goldberg?] "Co—i jak—w socyologii," *Prawda,* 4 (2 February/21 January–16/4 February 1884). For references to the earliest translations of Spencer into Polish, see the bibliography of this volume.

24. As cited in T. Długokęcka, "Miejsce darwinizmu w działalności 'Przeglądu Tygodniowego' (1866–1890)," in Petrusewicz and Straszewicz, 61.

25. Chmielowski, 270.

26. Świętochowski, "Liberum veto," *Prawda,* 2 (29/17 April 1882), in Świętochowski, *Publicystyka,* 72–73.

27. Krupiński, "Szkoła pozytywna," *Biblioteka Warszawska,* 3 (July–September 1868), in Hochfeldowa and Skarga, *Filozofia i myśl,* 1:237.

28. Ochorowicz, 64, 94.; "Ideały," *Niwa,* 3 (20 December 1873/1 January 1874): 1–4.

29. Prus, "Szkic programu," 188–89.

30. Wiślicki, "Wielka i mała polityka," *Przegląd Tygodniowy,* 4 (21 March/2 April 1871): 106.

31. [Świętochowski], "Opinia publiczna," *Przegląd Tygodniowy,* 7 (26 January 1873/7 December 1872), 3.

32. Świętochowski, "Liberum veto," *Prawda,* 1 (1 January/20 December 1881), in Świętochowski, *Liberum veto,* 1:175.

33. [Świętochowski], "Absenteizm," *Przegląd Tygodniowy,* 7 (5/17 March 1872): 81–82. Emphasis in the original.

34. "Obowiązek i poświęcenie," *Przegląd Tygodniowy,* 7 (19/31 March 1872): 97–100.

35. Prus, "Kronika tygodniowa," *Kurier Warszawski,* 67 (22 March/3 April 1887): 4, in Prus, *Wybór kronik,* 123.

36. Prus, "Kronika tygodniowa," *Kurier Warszawski,* 67 (3/15 April 1887): 2, in Prus, *Wybór kronik,* 128. Prus was responding in particular to Entuzjasta, "Polemika," *Kurjer Warszawski,* 67 (1/13 April 1887): 1–2.

37. Prus, "Najogólniejsze ideały życiowe," in Hochfeldowa and Skarga, *Filozofia i myśl,* 1:232. Emphasis mine. The editors inform us that this came from *Kurier Codzienny* but do not offer a specific citation. I was not able to locate any copies of *Kurier Codzienny* for this period and thus could not precisely date this passage.

38. On the press laws for the Russian partition of Poland at this time, see Kmiecik, "Prasa Polska w Królestwie Polskim i Imperium Rosyjskim w latach 1865–1904," in Łojek, 11–13; and Markiewicz, *Pozytywizm,* 38. On the positivists' attempts to circumvent the censorship with aesopian language, see Jedlicki, 267.

39. Świętochowski, "Herbert Spencer (Studium z dziedziny pozytywizmu): II, Psychologija," *Przegląd Tygodniowy,* 7 (18/30 June 1872): 204. Significantly, Spencer's writing is aggressive and polemical while Świętochowski's translation/summary is more self-confident. Interjections such as "naturally," "of course," and "as we know" are scattered throughout the *Przegląd Tygodniowy* version of Spencer. Compare Świętochowski's article with the original: Spencer, *Principles of Psychology,* 1:495–504.

40. Władysław Kozłowski, "Determinizm a wolna wola," *Prawda,* 6 (25/13 December 1886): 620–22.

41. "Zarys traktatu socyologii III," *Przegląd Tygodniowy,* 9 (8/20 December 1874): 442.

42. This was not a completely unanimous view, but there were very few dissenting voices. See "Wolna wola i mechaniczne jej skutki," *Prawda*, 1 (12 November/31 October–19/7 November 1881).

43. Świętochowski, "Polityka własna," *Przegląd Tygodniowy*, 11 (29 August/10 October–5/17 October 1876); reprinted in Wroczyński, 132.

44. Świętochowski, "Praca i modlitwa," *Przegląd Tygodniowy*, 7 (13/25 August 1872): 266.

45. *Pamiętnik zjazdu b. wychowawców*, 30.

46. Andrzej Walicki has also pointed out the parallel between the positivists' vision of organic work and the ideas of pre-1863 thinkers such as Trentowski, Norwid, Cieszkowski, and Libelt. See Walicki, "Polska myśl filozoficzna epoki międzypowstaniowej," in Hochfeldowa and Skarga, *Filozofia i myśl społeczna*, 97.

47. On Helcel, see Król, *Konserwatyści*, 187–89.

48. This name came from a series of articles entitled "Teka Stańczyka" (Stańczyk's Portfolio), in which these authors satirized the views of their opponents. Stańczyk was a famous jester from Polish history. Extensive excerpts from these essays are reprinted in Król, *Stańczycy*, 73–85. On the *Stańczycy*, see Bobińska and Wyrozumski; Król, *Konserwatyści*, 184–234; Serejski, 184–210; Wyka, *Teka Stańczyka*.

49. Kurkiewicz, 195.

50. Szujski, "Kilka prawd z dziejów naszych. Ku rozważeniu w chwili obecnej" (Kraków, 1867), in *Dzieła*, 1:271–88. In January 1867 an editorial in *Przegląd Polski* announced that "this brochure is influenced by the opinions and convictions of the editors . . . we must thus refer to it as we would to our program." Król, *Stańczycy*, 72.

51. Szujski, 1:274.

52. Szujski, 1:277–78.

53. Koźmian, *Rzecz o roku 1863* (Kraków, 1896), in Król, *Stańczycy*, 226, 233–34.

54. Leslie, 22–24, 245–46, describes the conservative turn to loyalism after 1846, and the aristocracy's abandonment of the national cause after 1863. On Cegielski and Cieszkowski, see Kieniewicz, *Dramat*, 78–91. On Norwid, see Feliksiak, "Norwidowski świat myśl," in Walicki, *Polska myśl filozoficzna*, 545–93; Walicki, *Między filozofią, religią, i polityką*, 195–238; Walicki, "Polska myśl filozoficzna epoki międzypowstaniowej," 58–59. On Zamoyski and his colleagues, see Jedlicki, 213–25; Kieniewicz, *Dramat*, 57–73; Ludwikowski, *Konserwatyzm*, 98–108. For more on conservatism in the Kingdom after 1863, see Jaszczuk, 63–141; Pąkciński; and Szwarc.

55. On the paradoxical similarities between positivism and conservatism, see Jaszczuk, 252–57.

56. "Praca organiczna," *Niwa*, 2 (20 December 1872/1 January 1873): 1–4.

57. Ludwikowski even describes Zamoyski as a positivist in *Continuity and Change*, 171.

58. de Maistre, 98–99; Burke, *Works*, 4: 176; *Reflections*, 85. On the use of the organic metaphor by conservatives, see Mannheim, 98–99. For a Polish example, see Rzewuski, *Pisma*, 2:85.

59. Spencer, "The Social Organism," in *Selected Writings*, 53–70.

60. Prus, "Szkic programu," 188.

61. Prus, "Kronika tygodniowa," *Kurier Warszawski*, 59 (23 May/4 June 1879): 3, in Prus, *Wybór kronik*, 20.

62. Mikulski and Świętochowski, "Praca u podstaw I. Ogólne jej pojęcie," *Przegląd Tygodniowy*, 8 (25 February/9 March 1873): 73.

63. Mikulski and Świętochowski, "Praca u podstaw I," 74.

64. Mikulski and Świętochowski, "Praca u podstaw II. Gmina," *Przegląd Tygodniowy*, 8 (4/16 March 1873): 81–82.

65. Mikulski and Świętochowski, "Praca u podstaw I," 75.
66. Mikulski and Świętochowski, "Praca u podstaw III. Szkółki wiejskie," *Przegląd Tygodniowy*, 8 (11/23 March 1873): 89.
67. Mikulski and Świętochowski, "Praca u podstaw I," 75.

Chapter Three

1. Blejwas, *Realism*, 140; Blejwas, "Warsaw Positivism," 47–54; Bobińska; Jaszczuk, "Liberalny pozytywizm w Królestwie Polskim i w Petersburgu 1870–1905 r.," in *Tradycje liberalne*, 27–37; Jedlicki, 300; Leslie, 247; Markiewicz, *Idee patriotyzmu*; Modzelewski, 27–32, 120–22; Walicki, *Poland Between East and West*, 28–29; Walicki, *Philosophy*, 340–41. For an alternative view, see Nałęcz, 17.
2. Kedourie, 9. See also Alter, 17; Breuilly, 3; Deutsch, 105; Hobsbawm, 9–10; Minogue, 154; Schieder, 24–26; Smith, *Theories of Nationalism*, 21.
3. See, for example, Kohn, *Idea of Nationalism*, 3. Even Brubaker, 16, argues that different conceptions of nationality ultimately determine how "the interest of the state" is understood.
4. Singer, 318.
5. The classic example is Hroch, 23. For some challenges to this teleological approach, see Chatterjee, *Nation and Its Fragments*, 156; Duara, 16; Eley and Suny, "Introduction: From the Moment of Social History to the Work of Cultural Representation," in Eley and Suny, 10–11; Llobera, 194–209.
6. Ibis, "List z Warszawy," *Gazeta Narodowa*, 11 (5 May 1872): 1. For more on the conservative critique of positivism, see Pąkciński, 112–13; Skarga, "Czy pozytywizm jest kierunkiem antynarodowym?" in Stefanowska, 276–304.
7. Limanowski, "W sprawie 'Przeglądu Tygodniowego,'" *Gazeta Narodowa*, 11 (18 May 1872): 1.
8. Kozłowski, "Czy pozytywizm jest kierunkiem antynarodowym?" *Prawda*, 5 (28/16 February–7 March/23 February 1885), in Kozłowski, *Pisma*, 438.
9. [Świętochowski], "Partykularyzm," *Przegląd Tygodniowy*, 11 (18/30 July 1876): 363–65. For a discussion of Świętochowski's use of the expression "particularism," see Skarga, "Antynarodowy," 285.
10. Prus, "Szkic programu," 188–89.
11. Świętochowski, *Wspomnienia*, 17–18.
12. Kozłowski, "Charakter współczesnej filozofji. Poprzednicy Spencera," *Ateneum*, 26 (September 1878), in Kozłowski, *Pisma*, 21.
13. Orzeszkowa, *Patryotyzm i kosmopolityzm*, 26, 45–46, 125–67.
14. Prus, "Kronika tygodniowa," *Kurjer Codzienny*, 189 (1897), in Prus, *Wybór kronik*, 225–27.
15. [Świętochowski], "Tradycja i historia wobec postępu," *Przegląd Tygodniowy*, 7 (30 April/12 May 1872): 147; in Świętochowski, *Publicystyka*, 48.
16. [Świętochowski], "Opinia publiczna," *Przegląd Tygodniowy*, 7 (7 January 1873/26 December 1872), 2. Świętochowski quoted this passage in Świętochowski, *Wspomnienia*, 18, as representative of his views at the time.
17. [Świętochowski], "Tradycja i historia wobec postępu," *Przegląd Tygodniowy*, 7 (30 April/12 May 1872): 147, in Świętochowski, *Publicystyka*, 37–50. For a good discussion of the use of "history" by the positivists, see Jedlicki, 272–80.
18. Kozłowski, "Etyka Spencera 1," *Ateneum*, 31 (July 1883), in Kozłowski, *Pisma*, 203.

19. "Ideały," *Niwa*, 3 (20 December/1 January 1874): 3.

20. Hłasko, 265 (1 September 1932): 5. See also "Jubileusz 'Prawdy,'" *Teka*, 3 (January 1901): 26–30.

21. On Supiński, see Barbara Skarga, "Józef Supiński i jego filozofia 'miary,'" in Walicki, *Polska myśl*, 626–64; Skarga, "Polska myśl filozoficzna w epoce pozytywizmu," in Hochfeldowa and Skarga, *Filozofia i myśl społeczna*, 12.

22. Supiński, *Szkoła polska gospodarstwa społecznego,* in Supiński, *Pisma*, 2:5. On the contrast between the animal and the human, see *Myśl ogólna fizyologii wszechświata*, in *Pisma*, 1:163. On the importance of exchange, see *Szkoła*, 3:192. On his hostility toward the state, see *Szkoła*, 3:268. Liberals elsewhere were uncomfortable with the term "political economy," for the same reasons. See Peel, 77.

23. Supiński, *Szkoła*, 3:275. Emphasis in the original. See also *Myśl*, 1:202.

24. Supiński, *Myśl*, 1:262, 334–38; *Szkoła*, 3:275. For an alternative reading of Supiński's approach to the nation, see Skarga, "Józef Supiński i jego filozofia 'miary,'" in Walicki, *Polska myśl*, 656–57.

25. Prus, "Nasze grzechy," *Opiekun Domowy* (1872), in Wroczyński, 103. I was unable to locate an original copy of this essay.

26. Al. G. [Prus], "Szkic programu w warunkach obecnego rozwoju społeczeństwa," *Nowiny* (11/23–18/30 March 1883), in Hochfeldowa and Skarga, *Filozofia i myśl społeczna*, 2:191; and Prus, *Wybór kronik,* 40–50.

27. Prus, "Szkic programu," 191–92.

28. Brykalska, *Biografia*, 279–333. In fact, the optimism of the positivists had been waning for several years. The economic downturn of 1873–1874 hit Poland along with the rest of Europe, and the positivists felt its consequences acutely. Compare the article "Wspomnienie 1874," *Przegląd Tygodniowy*, 10 (22 December 1874/3 January 1875): 1–2, with the comparable essay published one year earlier, "Wspomnienie 1873," *Przegląd Tygodniowy*, 9 (23 December 1873/4 January 1874): 1–4.

29. Świętochowski, "Wskazania polityczne," in *Ognisko*, 51. This is the only example of Świętochowski's writing available in English (although the translation used here is my own). See Olszer, 118–23. For a reprint of the Polish text, see Świętochowski, *Publicystyka*, 94–101.

30. On the reaction to "Wskazania," see Świętochowski's *Wspomnienia*, 109–12. Jeż's own response came in very guarded terms, since it was submitted to *Prawda*, and thus to the Russian censors. T. T. Jeż, "List Jeża (Odpowiedź na *Ognisko*)," *Prawda*, 3 (10 February/29 January 1883): 61. For Jeż's uncensored defense of the tradition of insurrection, see Miłkowski, *Odpowiedź;* and *Rzecz o obronie czynnej.* Significantly, when Świętochowski advertised *Ognisko* in *Prawda*, he emphasized its "sincere and serious liberalism," but when summarizing its contents, he mentioned every contribution except his own. Knowing Świętochowski, this could not have been modesty. "Jubileuszowy podarek," *Prawda*, 3 (20/8 January 1883): 25–26.

31. Świętochowski, "Myślę, więc jestem," *Prawda*, 1 (1 January/20 December 1881): 1–2. Emphasis added.

32. "'Precz z marzeniami,'" *Prawda*, 1 (18/6 June 1881): 289–90. The juxtaposition of "dreams" and "abdication" is from Świętochowski, "Bałamuctwa," *Prawda*, 3 (10 February/29 January 1883): 61–63.

33. One scholar has even felt it necessary to point out that Spencer was not the *only* source of influence on the positivists. Hochfeldowa, "Neokantyzm okresu pozytywizmu i jego wpływy w Polsce," in Hochfeldowa and Skarga, *Z historii filozofii pozytywistycznej*, 138.

34. Spencer, *Social Statics*, 416.

35. For this reason, even Spencer's friend Thomas Huxley decided to reject the "struggle for existence" in favor of an ethical evolution that transcended "nature." Huxley, *Evolution*

and Ethics, 1–86, 203. On Spencer's reaction, see Peel, 150. For more on the Spencerian conception of evolution, see Battistelli, 192–209; Burrow, 180–226; Himmelfarb, 222–26; Peel, 130–65, 192–223; Rumney, 134–37; Wiltshire, 200, 243–56; Young, 18–22. For a more general discussion of the concepts of aggression and war in nineteenth-century thought, see Pick, 75–87.

36. Spencer, *Study of Sociology*, 176.

37. Spencer, *Principles of Psychology*, 2:577.

38. Spencer, *Study of Sociology*, 180. For another example of Spencer's equation between size and progress, see *Principles of Sociology*, 1:466–69. Peel claims that this reference to "industry" as another form of militancy reflected the pessimism of Spencer's last years, but in fact this idea appeared in his earlier work as well. See Peel, 217.

39. Świętochowski, "Wskazania," 54.

40. Świętochowski, "Liberalne bankructwa," *Prawda*, 3 (28/16 April 1883): 193–94.

41. Prus, "Szkic programu," 192–93.

42. When he did discuss *First Principles*, he mentioned Spencer's arguments about small entities being absorbed into larger ones, but he placed this within the context of the formation of collectives with internal heterogeneity. Kozłowski, "Pierwsze zasady," *Ateneum*, 27 (January 1879), in Kozłowski, *Pisma*, 39–75. See also the essay by the translator of *Study of Sociology*, Henryk Goldberg, "Co—i jak—w socyologii," *Prawda*, 4 (2 February/21 January-16/4 February 1884). Goldberg gave close attention to Spencer's discussion of all the ways in which bias can distort the study of sociology, but he did not even mention the last section of the book, in which Spencer's brutality comes forth so strongly. Equally significant is the attention given to *Principles of Ethics*, published in Polish translation in 1884 by a "publishing cooperative" that included Chmielowski, Prus, Świętochowski, and several other leading positivists (but curiously, not Kozłowski), with financial assistance from Eliza Orzeszkowa. The book received an unprecedented front-page advertisement from *Prawda*.

43. Kozłowski, "Etyka Spencera II," *Ateneum*, 32 (January 1884), in Kozłowski *Pisma*, 228.

44. Kozłowski, "Etyka Spencera I," *Ateneum*, 31 (July 1883), in Kozłowski, *Pisma*, 206.

45. Kozłowski, "Etyka Spencera II," 246.

46. Orzeszkowa, *Patryotyzm*, 12, 125–32, 155–58. Feliks Bogacki made a similar argument in a review of Rudolf von Jhering's *Der Kampf ums Recht* (1872), which argued that power was the measure of all things. This was true, Bogacki insisted, only in the distant past, among "wild" tribes. Bogacki, "Źródła prawa, według Rudolfa Jheringa," *Przegląd Tygodniowy*, 12 (10/22–17/29 April 1877).

47. Spencer, *Social Statics*, 410–11.

48. George Bernard Shaw believed that Marx and Buckle would be the only two nineteenth-century writers whose legacy would survive, a judgment which, based on the secondary literature about each of them, is at best only half right. Shaw's comment is cited by Semmel, *Liberal Ideal*, 48. On Buckle, see St. Aubyn; Huth; Robertson; and Semmel, "H. T. Buckle: The Liberal Faith," 370–86.

49. On the initial reception of Buckle in Poland, see Warzenica, 27–28.

50. Świeżawski, "Buckle i Darwin," *Przegląd Tygodniowy*, 3 (8/20 September 1868). The early enthusiasm for Buckle in *Przegląd Tygodniowy* was accompanied by an embarrassing testimony to Wiślicki's poor knowledge of English (or sloppy editing). In reviewing the Polish translation of Buckle's *History*, the paper praised not only Buckle, but "Bocckle" and "Bouckle" as well, and placed him (them?) alongside such great Englishmen as "Tindhal," "Layell," "Haeskley," "Macaullay," "Drapper," and (at least he got these right) Darwin and Mill. Henryk Elzenberg, "Henryk Tomasz Bocckle" *Przegląd Tygodniowy*, 2 (26 March/31 April 1867): 110–11.

51. Przyborowski, 9; Grabski, "Warszawscy entuzjaści," 856; Świętochowski, "Liberum veto," *Prawda*, 2 (4 February/23 January 1882), in Świętochowski, *Liberum veto*, 261.

52. Buckle, *History*, 2:472. Compare this view with the pessimism expressed on 1:109.

53. Buckle, *History*, 1:96, 242.

54. Buckle, *History*, 1:358.

55. Buckle, *History*, 2:105. On Spencer's growing doubts that war had yet been supplanted by industry, even in England, see Pick, 77–79.

56. Zawadzki, "Przedmowa tłómacza"; and "Wiadomość o życiu Tomasza Henryka [sic] Buckla," in Buckle, *Historja cywilizacji*, 1:no pagination; 3:xiii.

57. "Systemat historyczny Buckla," *Przegląd Tygodniowy*, 2 (19 November/1 December 1867): 386.

58. Bolesław Limanowski, "Przegląd życia społecznego," *Przegląd Tygodniowy*, 4 (19/31 October 1869): 369. This was part of a series of essays running from 28 September/10 October to 9/21 November 1869.

59. "Ideały II," *Niwa*, 3 (15 February 1874): 74.

60. Maslowski, 165. Maslowski lived in Galicia and was not a member of the *młoda prasa* circle. However, this work was read with great enthusiasm in Warsaw. See Świętochowski, "Przegląd piśmiennictwa polskiego," *Przegląd Tygodniowy*, 7 (28 May/9 June 1872): 178–80.

61. Nusbaum, "W imię prawdy!" *Dodatek do Przeglądu Tygodniowego*, 4 (April 1885): 399. Emphasis added. For another articulation of this theme of the superiority of "moral" strength, see "Strona moralna wojny," *Przegląd Tygodniowy*, 5 (18/30 October 1870): 353. Nusbaum's essay was a response to an extensive review of an 1884 translation of Spencer's *The Study of Sociology*. The author of the review, the Marxist Ludwik Krzywicki, rejected the concept of a "struggle for survival" on the grounds that it was merely a scientific-sounding cover for laissez faire. Krzywicki, "Wstęp do socyologii Herberta Spencera," *Dodatek do Przeglądu Tygodniowego*, 1 (January 1885): 106–24. Nusbaum seemed to be avoiding the point of Krzywicki's review. Given the liberalism of the day, it is doubtful that the phrase "intelligent and moral individuals" could refer to the working poor who concerned Krzywicki. It seems that Krzywicki read Spencer for his commentary on class struggle and laissez faire economics, while Nusbaum read the same text with the nation in mind.

62. Świętochowski, "Walka o byt I (Praca)," *Prawda*, 3 (6 January 1883/25 December 1882), 1. Poles consider Copernicus a national hero. Matejko was Poland's most famous nineteenth-century painter.

63. Ignacy Radliński, "Próbka nowej historyozofii VI," *Prawda*, 2 (27/15 May 1882): 247. This series did not directly comment on Buckle, concentrating instead on the work of Gustave Le Bon. Buckle was the most popular of those offering an escape from the Spencerian version of struggle, but he was not the only source for this "new historiosophy."

64. Radliński, 248.

65. Radliński, "Próbka nowej historyozofii VII." *Prawda*, 2 (10 June/29 May 1882): 274.

Chapter Four

1. Quoted in Targalski, 43.

2. Quoted in Czarnecki, 10.

3. Cywiński, *Rodowody niepokornych*. On the dominance of those born between 1860 and 1879—the "generation" referred to here—among the political elite of the interwar years, see Wapiński, "Elita Endecka," 447.

4. Jeske-Choiński, *Na schyłku wieku*, 1. On the sense of cultural crisis in fin de siècle Poland, see Wyka, *Młoda Polska*, 1:63–64, 123–25.

5. For these and many other statistics, see Corrsin, 13–70; Drozdowski and Zahorski, 252; Dunin-Wąsowicz, "Struktura demograficzna narodu polskiego w latach 1864–1914," in *Historia Polski*, vol. 3, part 1, 98, 101; Krzysztof Groniowski, "Na przełomie stuleci," in Tazbir, 497; Naimark, *Proletariat*, 13–25; Olszewski, "Okres wzrastającego ucisku i głębokich przemian społecznych (1864–1914)," in Kłoczowski, 474. For a detailed overview of the 1897 census, see "Rozmaitości," *Wolne Polskie Słowo*, 12 (5 July 1898): 8.

6. Zimand, *Dekadentyzm warszawski*, 106.

7. On the literacy rate, see Janina Żurawicka, "Z problematyki formowania się inteligencji warszawskiej i jej świadomości w końcu XIX w.," in Kalabiński and Kołodziejczyk, 1:164–65. On the education of the Warsaw proletariat, see Żarnowska, 199–232.

8. On literacy and the growth of the periodical press, see Zimand, *Dekadentyzm*, 99; Kmiecik, "Prasa polska w Królestwie Polskim i Imperium Rosyjskim w latach 1865–1904," in Łojek, 13, 29; Kmiecik, *Prasa warszawska*, 22, 24, 35; Żurawicka, "Z problematyki formowania się inteligencji," 1:180; Żurawicka, "Zespół redakcji 'Głosu,'" 155–56.

9. On the circulation of *Gazeta Świąteczna*, see Kmiecik, "Prasa polska," 43. On rural illiteracy, see Ihnatowicz, 493; Kaczyńska, 160; Łepkowski, 487.

10. See particularly Żeromski's diary entries for the spring of 1887, in *Dzienniki*, 297–316. The lament of Popławski's wife is related by Zygmunt Wasilewski, "Jan Ludwik Popławski. Szkic wizerunku," in Popławski, *Pisma*, xx.

11. Jedlicki, "Kwestia nadprodukcji inteligencji w Królestwie Polskim po powstaniu styczniowym," in Czepulis-Rastenis, 218–19, 226–27, 259. See also Hass, 295.

12. Sadowski, 26–27.

13. Duara, 32, 91–92.

14. Wołyński, 47. On the "decentralized despotism" of the Russian administration in Poland, see Wapiński, *Pokolenia*, 20. For more on Russian attitudes toward the Poles after 1863, see Weeks, 54–59.

15. Piltz, *Nasza Młodzież*, 176. Emphasis in the original.

16. Wojciechowski, 1:6. On the linguistic russification of the secondary schools, see Konarski, 381–82; Korotyński, 29–44, 70–84; *Pamiętnik zjazdu b. wychowawców*, 30–34; Dymitr Szarzyński, *Polskie Towarzystwo Oświaty Ludowej na Rusi: szkice i przyczynki do dziejów oświaty polskiej na Rusi w latach 1870–1920* (unpublished, BNZR, akc. 8747), 7; Wołyński, 2–12. For contrasting examples of how teachers responded to these laws, see Brzeziński, 49; Kozicki, *Pamiętniki, 1875–1914* (unpublished, AHRL, sygn. P-127), 51–62; Maksymilian Malinowski, *Sześćdziesiąt lat nieprzerywalnej codziennej pracy. . . .* (unpublished: AHRL, sygn. P.52.), 29; Wołyński, 72–73, 84–85, 104.

17. Cywiński, *Rodowody*, 25; Kraushar, 26–27. On the censorship, see Kmiecik, "Prasa polska," 13; Kmiecik, *Prasa warszawska*, 18; Maksymilian Malinowski, 44–47. On the rules that governed the lives of the students, see [Dmowski], "Gimnazja rossyjskie w Polsce: szkic wychowawczy," *Wolne Polskie Słowo*, 7 (15 July 1893): 4; Kraushar, 9; Surzycki, *Kartka*, 8–10, 14–16.

18. Krzywicki, *Wspomnienia*, 1:82, 86, 124–25. For more on the use of school libraries as a tool of russification, see Wołyński, 32–34.

19. [Dmowski], "Gimnazja rossyjskie," 6.

20. Koszutski, 33–35.

21. As quoted by Kulczycka-Saloni, *Życie literackie*, 55.

22. Askenazy, 58.

23. Askenazy, 14. See also Korotyński, 100–11.

24. Kraushar, 3.

25. Kareev, 277.

26. For more on Muravev, see Weeks, 96–98. Poles faced discrimination in the Prussian partition as well. See A. Galos "Walka mas ludowych ziem zachodnich wobec dyskryminacyjnej polityki pruskiej, 1885–1900," in Kormanowa, 682–85. In English, see Hagen, *Germans, Poles, and Jews*, particularly 135–38.

27. For a reprint of the faculty's letter, along with this student response, see Nawroczyński, 222. On the so-called *murawiewszczyzna*, see Bogacz, 386–88; Dąbrowski, 19–25; Koszutski, 133–34.

28. Kmiecik, "Prasa polska," 13. For more on the importance of Warsaw, see Żurawicka, "Inteligencja Warszawska w końcu XIX w. w walce o zachowanie kultury narodowej," in Kalabiński and Kołodziejczyk, 1:120.

29. Amerykanin [Józef Uziembło], "Wspomnienia z 1878 roku," in *Z pola walki*, 52–54.

30. On the emancipation of the serfs in Russia, see W. E. Mosse; *Osvobozhdenie krestian*; and Zaionchkovskii. On the reaction of the educated Russian public to the reforms, see Kornilov.

31. Nikolai Ogarev, "The Universities are Closing," *Kolokol* (15 January 1862), as quoted by Venturi, 231.

32. As cited in Venturi, 193.

33. From a May 1869 manifesto cited by Venturi, 368.

34. For a psychohistorical analysis of this desire to merge with the people, see Wortman, 32. For a critical interpretation of the motives of the populists, see Ulam, 12.

35. From the memoirs of S. L. Chudnovsky, as quoted by Venturi, 359.

36. Venturi, 505, reports that 4,000 people were "imprisoned, questioned, or at least harassed by the police" during the summer of 1874. A more modest figure of 2,000 participants is given in Offord, 17.

37. Mendel, 89. For more on the fate of the revolutionary movement under Alexander III, see Naimark, *Terrorists and Social Democrats*.

38. Koszutski, 6–7.

39. Pigoń, 337. See also Wapiński, *Pokolenia*, 101–3.

40. Krzywicki, *Wspomnienia*, 1:211.

41. Kozicki, *Historia*, 22.

42. Radlińska, 336–37.

43. Zenon Kmiecik, "Początki ruchu młodzieżowego w Warszawie (1864–1904)," in Hillebrandt, *Postępowe organizacje*, 10–12; Targalski, 139–42. A similar group called the Warsaw Circle of Popular Education was founded a few years later. See Krzywicki, *Wspomnienia*, 1:180–81.

44. Cywiński, *Rodowody*, 56–65, gives an excellent description of the flying university in Warsaw. On secret education in secondary schools, see Wołyński, 140.

45. At the Petersburg Technical Institute, for example, 23 percent of the students were Polish. On the large presence of Poles in Russian universities, see Targalski, 22–34. On the Polish *numerus clausus*, see Venturi, 357. For overall statistics on the empire's nationalities, see M. Slavinskii, "Natsionalnaia struktura Rossii i Velikorossii," in Kastelianskii, 280.

46. "Ze wspomnień" *Przedświt*, 1–3 (January–March 1896): 1–12.

47. On Waryński and the first socialists, see Baumgarten; Blit; Józef Buszko, Ryszard Kołodziejczyk, and Stanisław Michalkiewicz, "Początki ruchu robotniczego na ziemiach polskich," in Kołodziejczyk, 215–97; Dziewanowski, 12–13; Myśliński, "Powstanie i działalność socjalno-rewolucyjnej partii proletariat," in Kołodziejczyk, 296–350; Na——Z., "Ludwik Waryński (Osobiste wspomnienie)," *Przedświt*, 1–3 (January–March 1896): 12–17; Naimark, *Proletariat;* Suleja, 11–20; Targalski; Żychowski, *Polska myśl socjalistyczna*, 91–93, 126–50.

48. On the Szymański circle, see Bogacz, 320; Jabłoński, 68–69; Toporowski, 53–54.

49. Report from the Prosecutor of the Warsaw Judicial Chamber, Trakhimovsky, 4 December 1878, in *Procesy polityczne*, 83.

50. Report from Plehve to Minister of Justice, 6 April 1879, in *Procesy polityczne*, 12–13.

51. Krzywicki, *Wspomnienia*, 1:89–90.

52. Ironically, at the time the Poles used the Russian term сходка (polonized as *schodka*) to describe their demonstration. Political activism had so faded from Polish student life that they had to employ a Russian word to talk about their small display of defiance. On the *schodka* of 1881 see Kareev, 269; Krzywicki, *Wspomnienia*, 1:166–67; 2:351; Nawroczyński, *Nasza walka*, 230; Schmidt, 16–29. For more on Krusiński, see Tadeusz Kowalik, "Stanisław Krusiński i 'Krusińszczycy,'" in Krusiński, vii–lxiii.

53. Bogacz, 304–5; Kareev, 266; Kmiecik, "Początki," 15–16; Krzesławski, 129–64; Krzywicki, *Wspomnienia*, 1:187–94, 211; Schmidt, 11. There was a great deal of confusion among Polish students about precisely what Zhukovich did, and why. Some sources claim that the Russian was angered by a dispute over a scholarship. Krzesławski, however, examined Russian documents, including Zhukovich's own letters and Apukhtin's reports, in order to clarify that this somewhat unbalanced Russian was driven by his anger over educational policy.

54. Krzywicki, *Wspomnienia*, 1:88, 212–13.

55. Radlińska, 336–37.

56. Wasilewski, "Popławski," xxviii.

57. For biographical information on Popławski, see Kulak; Wasilewski, "Popławski," 1:v–lxiv. On Potocki, see Hochfeldowa and Skarga, *Filozofia i myśl społeczna*, 625–35.

58. Janina Żurawicka, "'Głos' wobec kwestii robotniczej (1886–1900)," in Żychowski, *Studia*, 190. For more on *Głos*, see Czarnecki; Hłasko; Kmiecik, "Prasa polska," 40–43; Kmiecik, *Prasa warszawska*, 68–83; Krzywicki, *Wspomnienia*, 3:37–111; Kozicki, *Historia*, 24–32; Perl, 225–32; Toporowski, 151–94; Wasilewski, *Życiorys, 1865–1939* (unpublished: PANW, sygn. 127), 43, 47–48; Żurawicka, "Lud w ideologii 'Głosu,'" 316–40; Żurawicka, "Zespół redakcji 'Głosu,'" 155–83.

59. Perl, 231.

60. Hłasko, 5.

61. Balicki even used *Przegląd Społeczny* to present a reader's guide to the aesopian messages of *Głos*. Z. B. "Nowe pismo," *Przegląd Społeczny*, 1 (November 1886): 377–83. On *Przegląd Społeczny*, see Perl, 233–40.

62. On the *Liga Polska*, see Kozicki, *Historia*, 49–55; Toporowski, 68–89; Wapiński, *Narodowa Demokracja*, 25–26. On Miłkowski's earlier activities, see Franciszka Ramotowska, "Wizje odzyskania Polski niepodległej przed Powstaniem Styczniowym (1858–początek 1863)," in Kalembka, 154–61.

63. Bogacz, 323–25; Stanisław Bukowiecki, "Wspomnienie Stanisława Bukowieckiego o Lidze Narodowej (1931)" (Teka Stanisława Kozickiego; PANW, sygn. 30, jednostek 3), 20–30; Hillebrandt, *Polskie organizacje młodzieżowe*, 16–26; Kosmowska; Kozicki, *Historia*, 39–45, 329–37; Kozicki, *Pamiętniki*, 100–14; Pobóg-Malinowski, 59–63; Ruskiewicz, *Tajny związek*; Gabriel Sokolnicki, untitled memoir (PANK, Teka Zielińskiego, sygn. 7789); Toporowski, 126–39; Wapiński, *Narodowa Demokracja*, 26–27.

64. Wasilewski, "Popławski," xxii.

65. Ruskiewicz, *Tajny związek*, 6; Popławski, "Kronika współczesna" *Przegląd Społeczny*, 1 (February 1886), 165; and "Obniżenie ideałów," *Głos*, 2 (20 December 1886/1 January 1887), in Popławski, *Pisma*, 1:5; Perl, 35; Potocki, "Jubilaci," *Głos*, 8 (6/18 February 1893): 76.

66. Popławski, "Obniżenie," 5.

67. Czarnecki, 21.

68. On the positivists' approach to liberal political economy, and the *niepokorni*'s efforts to label the *młoda prasa* as Manchesterian liberals, see Porter, "Construction and Deconstruction"; and in Polish, Porter "Konstrukcja i dekonstrukcja." On the disinclination of Polish liberals to accept "bourgeois" economics, see Walicki, *Polska myśl filozoficzna*, 447–48. On the "new liberalism," see Richter, 267–91; Taylor; and Weiler. Some have argued that the new liberalism was not, in fact, all that new. See Volkov, 167; and Gerö, 71–91.

69. "Kronika miesięczna," *Ateneum*, 4 (November 1885): 374–76.

70. [Świętochowski], "'Praca organiczna,'" *Prawda*, 6 (16/4 January 1886): 29.

71. See, for example, E. Przewóski, "Nauka społeczna w teraźniejszości II," *Dodatek Miesięczny do czasopisma Przegląd Tygodniowy*, 2 (March 1881): 439–42. Krzywicki recalled these early forays into the liberal press in *Wspomnienia*, 2:137–39; 3:7–36. Jaszczuk goes so far as to suggest that by the mid-1880s the positivists "ceased to be liberals." See Andrzej Jaszczuk, "Liberalny pozytywizm w Królestwie Polskim i w Petersburgu, 1870–1905 r.," in *Tradycje liberalne*, 30. The occasional antisocialist article could, however, still appear: Ludwik Gumplowicz, "Socyalizm akademicki," *Prawda*, 4 (22/10 March 1884): 135–36. See also the unfriendly obituary for Marx himself in *Prawda*, 3 (24/12 March 1883): 134–35. For more on the link between positivism and socialism, see Naimark, 33–54.

72. J. L. P., "Badania ekonomiczne (Iwaniukow i S. Jevons)," *Prawda*, 2 (9 June/28 May 1883): 269–70.

73. For another discussion of this polemical exchange, see Naimark, 49–54.

74. [Ludwik Krzywicki], "Jeszcze o program . . ." *Przegląd Tygodniowy*, 18 (3/15 April 1883): 177–79. Krzywicki discusses this essay in *Wspomnienia*, 2:419.

75. "Polemika," *Przegląd Tygodniowy*, 18 (10/22 April 1883): 200–201. See also Prus' response to the initial appearance of Głos: "Kronika tygodniowa," *Kurier Warszawski*, 280 (28 September/10 October 1886): 1–3. Krzywicki responded in "Polemika," *Przegląd Tygodniowy*, 18 (17/29 April 1883): 213.

76. Ad. Zakrzewski, "Polemika," *Przegląd Tygodniowy*, 18 (15/27 May 1883): 263–64; L. K., "Polemika," *Przegląd Tygodniowy*, 18 (12/24 June 1883): 312; S. "Polemika," *Przegląd Tygodniowy*, 18 (10/22 July 1883): 360–61.

77. [Popławski], "Kronika współczesna" *Przegląd Społeczny*, 1 (February 1886), 163–69.

78. Pisarev, "Nineteenth-Century Scholasticism," in Edie, Scanlan, and Zeldin, 2:70–78.

79. As cited by Venturi, 149.

80. N. G. Chernyshevsky, "A Critique of Philosophical Prejudices against Communal Landholding," in Leatherbarrow and Offord, 207–12.

81. On this ambiguous approach to historical time by some of the populists, see Walicki, *The Controversy over Capitalism*, 115.

82. As cited by Venturi, 247–49.

83. Mikhailovsky, "The Three Stages of History," in Edie, Scanlan, and Zeldin, 193, 198. This title, which is misleading in this context, was assigned by the editors to an essay originally entitled "Teoriia Darvina i obshchestvennaia nauka," from *Otechestvennye Zapiski* (1870). For a good discussion of Mikhailovsky's sometimes ambiguous approach to determinism and free will, see Mendel, 27–30. For a similar argument from the same time, see Lavrov, "Historical Letters," in Edie, Scanlan, and Zeldin, 123–127.

84. Ceysingerówna, 708.

85. Żeromski, 455–56.

86. R. Skrzycki [Dmowski], "Młodzież polska w zaborze rosyjskim VII," *Przegląd Wszechpolski*, 2 (15 April 1896): 147–49.

87. A. Zakrzewski, "Prawo Malthusa oraz jego znaczenie w stosunkach naszych. Szkic ekonomiczny," *Dodatek do Przeglądu Tygodniowego*, 4 (January 1884): 1–41. These quotations are from pages 3 and 5. For a similar critique of "the school of Adam Smith," as this author calls it, see Kazimierz Puchewicz, "Nowe wydanie dzieł Józefa Supińskiego," *Ateneum*, 31 (December 1883): 366–88. For another example of how a Marxist could critique liberal political economy as an expression of "determinism," see Edward Przewóski, "Polityka ekonomiczna," *Głos*, 7 (28 December/9 January 1892): 14–16.

88. "Słowo wstępne," *Przegląd Społeczny*, 2 (January 1887): 1. The paper gave a lot of attention to the "negative sides" of capitalism. See Antoni Złotnicki, "Kapitalizm i moralność," *Przegląd Społeczny*, 1 (May–June 1886): 333–43, 444–53; Kazimierz Dłuski, "Objawy kapitalizmu w Polsce," *Przegląd Społeczny*, 1 (June–August 1886): 31–42; 120–29; 421–32; Robon Dion, "Zwalony Bożek. Pogadanka socjologiczna," *Przegląd Społeczny*, 2 (November 1887): 339–52.

89. *Głos*, 6 (14/26 December 1891): 626. This was from an advertisement for Potocki's translation of Lester Ward's *Dynamic Sociology*. Potocki thought Ward might offer a solution to Spencer's laissez-faire scientism.

90. Jan Stecki, "Prawa przyrody i ich wartość dla historyi," *Głos*, 9 (5/17–19/31 March 1894): 126–27, 135–37, 148–51. The copy of *Głos* owned by the National Library in Warsaw once belonged to Stecki, and he has left us some of his own marginal comments to accompany this article. He wrote alongside these passages that after the Marxists "appropriated" the positivist press, all that was left was "the struggle against religion and the cultivating of judeophilia, and finally that troublesome radicalism and doctrinaire economics."

91. J. L. "Sądy społeczne," *Głos*, 4 (17/29 June 1889): 326.

92. S. Karpowicz, "Wiedza i pesymizm," *Głos*, 5 (3/15 March 1890): 124–27.

93. "Genewa, 3 grudnia 1890," *Wolne Polskie Słowo*, 4 (15 December 1890): 5.

94. *Amerykanin*, 54.

95. Krzywicki, *Wspomnienia*, 2:9.

96. Krzywicki, "Wstęp do socyologii Herberta Spencera," *Dodatek do Przeglądu Tygodniowego*, 5 (January 1885): 106–24. A similar argument can be found in "Herbert Spencer, 'Jednostka wobec państwa,'" *Przegląd Społeczny*, 1 (March 1886): 232–35. On the "subjectivism" of Krzywicki and other early Marxists, see Dziamski, 16, 25, 30–31, 50–64.

97. E. Przewóski, "Nauka społeczna w teraźniejszości," *Dodatek Miesięczny do czasopisma Przegląd Tygodniowy*, 2 (March–April 1881): 446, 591–93.

98. "Szkice programowe," *Przegląd Społeczny*, 1 (February 1886): 97.

99. Krzywicki, *Wspomnienia*, 2:159.

100. "Genewa, 30 listopada 1892," *Wolne Polskie Słowo*, 6 (15 December 1892): 3.

101. Prus, "Kronika tygodniowa," *Kurier Warszawski*, 67 (3/15 April 1887): 1–3.

102. *Odezwa Ligi Polskiej*, 1887 (BN DŻS, IV 14560).

103. "Ustawa Ligi Polski," as reprinted in Kozicki, *Historia*, 490.

104. Miłkowski, *Rzecz o obronie czynnej*, 27–28. He explicitly described collecting money as an "act" in "W kwestji skarbu narodowego," *Wolne Polskie Słowo*, 2 (15 August 1888): 1–2. On the importance of Miłkowski's *Rzecz o obronie czynnej* among the *niepokorni*, see Piltz, *Nasza młodzież*, 20; Cywiński, *Rodowody*, 337; Dmowski, "Relacja," 418 (the original copy of this document is in the archive of the Polish Academy of Sciences in Warsaw, Teka Kozickiego,

sygn. 30); Kozicki, *Historia*, 45–58, Pobóg-Malinowski, *Narodowa Demokracja*, 36–40; Toporowski, 115–25; Kazimierz Poniatowski, "Wyciąg życiorysu i wspomnień członka Ligi Narodowej" (PANK, Teka Zielińskiego, sygn. 4485, vol. 5); Wojciechowski, 1:13.

105. Joczel, "Głos z kraju. Szkic programowy (zarys polityki biernej i odpornej)," *Wolne Polskie Słowo*, 4 (1 November 1890): 5–6.

106. *Odpowiedź na broszurę*. These authors, who openly affiliated themselves with the *Stańczycy*, went on to equate Miłkowski with *Głos* and locate both in the intellectual world of the Kingdom. This categorization was probably appropriate: Miłkowski's audience—the *niepokorni*—was in the Russian partition, not in Galicia.

107. Popławski, "Wielkie i małe idee," *Głos*, 2 (11/23 April 1887), in Popławski, *Pisma*, 1:9–14.

108. Student, "W sprawie młodzieży," *Głos*, 2 (21 February/5 March, 1887): 149–50; "Słowo o logice historycznej (artykuł nadesłany z kraju)," *Wolne Polskie Słowo*, 2 (14 March 1888): 6–7.

109. Entuzjasta, "Polemika," *Kurier Warszawski*, 67 (1/13 April 1887): 2.

110. Amerykanin, 54.

111. "Głos z kraju. Odczyt w rocznicę powstania r. 1863," *Wolne Polskie Słowo*, 5 (1 April 1891): 6.

112. No title, Warsaw, March 1891 (PANK, Teka Zielińskiego, sygn. 7783, no. 2). This same text is reprinted in Kozicki, *Historia*, 508.

113. Czarnecki, 78; Kasprowicz, "Przed pomnikiem Mickiewicza," as quoted by Weiss, 113–14; "Genewa, 25 stycznia 1891," *Wolne Polskie Słowo*, 5 (1 February 1891): 3.

114. Studnicki, 257.

115. This speech is reprinted in Limanowski, *Pamiętniki*, 2:693–94. Excerpts are in Kawyn, 26–27.

116. Socius [Daszyński], "Adam Mickiewicz jako rewolucyonista i socyalista," *Pobudka*, 1 (October/November/December 1889): 26.

117. As cited by Kawyn, 38–39.

118. As cited by Kawyn, 40.

119. On this ceremony see Kawyn, 102–31; "Obchody Mickiewiczowskie," *Wolne Polskie Słowo*, 12 (6 June 1898): 2; "Odsłonięcie pomnika A. Mickiewicza w Warszawie," *Wolne Polskie Słowo*, 13 (5 January 1899), 4–5; Pobóg-Malinowski, *Narodowa Demokracja*, 170–87; Próchnik, "Budowa i odsłonięcie pomnika Mickiewicza w Warszawie"; Wasilewski, *Pomnik*.

120. As quoted by Wasilewski, *Pomnik*, 5.

121. Wasilewski, *Pomnik*, 26–33, 79–83. See also the report on the Russian reaction to this unexpected popular response in "Przegląd polityczny," *Wolne Polskie Słowo*, 11 (1 August 1897): 3–4.

122. "Przed uroczystością," *Kurier Codzienny* (December 1898), in Kawyn, 125–26.

123. Kawyn, 124.

124. Kawyn, 118–20. This was not the original reaction of the National Democrats to the idea of a Mickiewicz statue. Popławski wrote in July 1897 that to participate in such a project would play into the hands of the loyalists. By October the editors of *Przegląd Wszechpolski* had decided to participate in the ceremonies surrounding the unveiling of the statue, since, they judged, it was not possible to stop them. See J. L. Jastrzębiec [Popławski], "Z całej Polski," *Przegląd Wszechpolski*, 3 (20 March 1897), 127–29, and "Z zaboru rosyjskiego," *Przegląd Wszechpolski*, 3 (15 May 1897), 226–27. See also the reprint of "Sprawozdanie z działalności L. N. za rok 1898–1899. Komitet Centralny Ligi narodowej do Komisji Nadzorczej Skarbu Narodowego" (1 August 1899), in "Do historji Ligi Narodowej," *Niepodległość*, 8 (1933): 269–

80; and "Warszawa, czerwiec 1897," *Wolne Polskie Słowo*, 9 (1 July 1897): 3–4. The following reports in *Wolne Polskie Słowo* seem to have been written by a National Democrat as well: "Warszawa 3 stycznia 1899," *Wolne Polskie Słowo*, 13 (20 January 1899): 3–4; "Warszawa, 3 stycznia 1899 (dokończenie)," *Wolne Polskie Słowo*, 13 (5 February 1899): 4.

125. Untitled manifesto, Polska Partya Socjalistyczna, 20 December 1898, AAN, Zbiór PPS, sygn. mf. 2552. See also, in the same file, the manifesto from 16 December.

126. Kawyn, 129–30.

127. Mickiewicz's "Songs of the Philarets" is reprinted in Kawyn, 65.

128. Hłasko, "W redakcji 'Głosu' *Gazeta Warszawska*, 277 (10 September 1932): 5.

129. "Sto lat!" Warsaw, March 1891 (BN DŻS, Teka IM). Wasilewski identified this as the central slogan of his generation, in a speech he gave to a high school reunion in 1925. Wasilewski, "Życie szkoły i szkoła życia," in Ruskiewicz, *Księga pamiątkowa*, 84.

130. "Gdzie droga?" *Teka*, 1 (15 April 1899): 107.

131. Krzywicki, *Wspomnienia*, 2:37–38.

132. Wojciechowski, 1:13.

133. Żeromski, 112.

134. Żeromski, 118.

135. Żeromski, 215. He returned to the "Hamlet" metaphor a few days later. See Żeromski, 216.

136. Żeromski, 174, 256.

137. Żeromski, 276.

138. Hłasko, "Przedmowa," in Popławski, *Szkice*, 3.

139. Radlińska, 326–27.

140. Wasilewski, "Życie szkoły," 84.

Chapter Five

1. Żeromski, 367–68.

2. Perl, 81.

3. Krzywicki, 1:164, 2:134–35.

4. Koszutski, 22–23, 44–46. See also Wapiński, "Pokolenia," 486–87.

5. Piltz, *Nasza młodzież*; and *Nasze stronnictwa skrajne*.

6. Studnicki, 1, 5.

7. Studnicki, "List otwarty do redakcyi Przeglądu Wszechpolskiego," *Przegląd Wszechpolski*, 7 (March 1901). Studnicki reprinted this letter in *Od socyalizmu do nacyonalizmu*, 86.

8. Blit, 83, estimates that there were as many as 1,500–2,000 members of the Proletariat by 1883, but he does not explain how he arrived at this figure. Myśliński offers the more realistic (and better documented) figure of 500, 400 of whom were eventually arrested for their activities. Myśliński, 342. On the difficult problem of establishing the size of these conspiratorial socialist movements, see Kaczyńska, 181–200.

9. On the antinationalism of the early Polish socialists, see Orzechowski; Walicki, *Polska, Rosja, Marksizm*, 184–251.

10. The text of the original draft of this program is reprinted in Molska, 2:688–90.

11. *Równość*, 1 (October 1879): 2–5. For a facsimile (not a mere reprint) of the program, see Koprukowniak. On the differences between the first and second drafts, see Buszko, Kołodziejczyk, and Michalkiewicz, 276; Targalski, 100–101; Walicki, "Kwestia narodowa w polskiej myśli marksistowskiej przed 1914 r.," in *Polska, Rosja, Marksizm*," 190–91; Żychowski, *Polska myśl socjalistyczna*, 93.

12. Kazimierz Dłuski, "Patriotyzm i socjalizm," *Równość*, 1 (November 1879), in Molska, 1:103–111.

13. Untitled, *Równość*, 10/11 (July/August 1880), in Molska, 1:246.

14. Untitled, *Równość*, 10/11 (July/August 1880), in Molska, 1:251.

15. Untitled, *Równość*, 1 (November 1880), in Molska, 1:265.

16. Untitled, *Równość*, 1 (November 1880), in Molska, 1:278.

17. Untitled, *Walka Klas*, 2 (June 1884), in Molska, 2:333.

18. "Sprawozdanie z międzynarodowego zebrania zwołanego w 50 rocznicę listopadowego powstania przez redakcję 'Równości' w Genewie, 1880," in Molska, 1:375–423. For more on this contentious "celebration," see Naimark, *History of the "Proletariat,"* 96–97; Żychowski, *Polska myśl socjalistyczna*, 109–11.

19. Marx's letter to the 1880 meeting, which ended with the words "Long Live Poland!" is reprinted as an annex to Molska, 2:756–58.

20. "Sprawozdanie," in Molska, 1:378, 381.

21. *Odezwa Komitetu Robotniczego Partyi soc. rew. "Proletaryjat."* Warsaw, 1882 (BN DŻS, Teka IB). A version of this text from *Przedświt*, 4 (17 October 1882) can be found in Molska, 2:9. For a similar declaration, see Tadeusz Rechniewski, "Nowe hasło," *Proletariat*, 2 (1 October 1883), in Molska, 2:104–8.

22. [Stanisław Mendelson], "Narodowość i walka klas," *Walka Klas*, 1 (May 1884), in Molska, 2:268.

23. Daszyński, 20–21. On the impact of Daszyński's book, see Władysław Jabłonowski, untitled memoir (PANK, Teka Zielińskiego, sygn. 7847), 3.

24. On Limanowski, see Cottam; Żychowski, 67–76.

25. Limanowski, *Patryjotyzm*, 4–7, 24, 25–26.

26. Limanowski, "List otwarty do Pana Władysława Wścieklicy" (20 February 1883), in *Pamiętniki*, 3:688–91.

27. His main collaborator on this project was the young Zygmunt Balicki, who also served as godfather to Limanowski's son. See Limanowski, *Pamiętniki*, 2:383.

28. "Odezwa Stowarzyszenia Socjalistycznego 'Lud Polski'" (August 1881, Geneva), in Limanowski, *Pamiętniki*, 686. All caps in the original. This same text is also reprinted as an annex to Molska, 2:758–61.

29. "Z powodu 'odezwy stowarzyszenia socjalistycznego Lud Polski,'" *Przedświt*, 3–8 (October 1881–January 1882), in Molska, 1:554. *Przedświt* also pointed out that in Limanowski's discussion of the geography of the future Polish state, the awkward *granice dobrowolnego ciążenia* (boundaries of voluntary gravitation) became clearer in translation as *les frontières de libre fédération* and граница добровольного союза.

30. Limanowski, "Świadomość narodowa," *Przegląd Socjalistyczny*, 1 (October 1893): 39–42.

31. Limanowski, "August Comte i pozytywizm, podług Milla," *Przegląd Tygodniowy*, 4 (20 March/11 April–20 April/2 May 1869): 128–29, 149–51, 159–60.

32. Limanowski, *Patryjotyzm*, 25–26.

33. Redakcya, "Nowe pismo," *Głos*, 1 (20 September/2 October 1886): 1. For more on the concept of the *lud* in *Głos*, see Kmiecik, "Oblicze społeczno-polityczne," 39–51; Żurawicka, "Lud," 316–40.

34. Władysław Kiersz, *Prospekt Głosu* (n.p., n.d.), 1. Kiersz was the publisher of *Głos* and thus had to sign the prospectus, but he did not in fact write anything for the paper. Within a year he was forced to flee Warsaw after a financial scandal, and the editorial board, led by Józef Potocki and Jan Ludwik Popławski, took over the paper.

35. J. L. P., "Otwarte karty," *Głos*, 1 (27 December/8 January, 1886/7): 17–18.

36. On Krzywicki's close personal friendship with the editors of *Głos*, see Krzywicki, *Wspomnienia*, 2:43. Other examples of Marxist writing on the pages of *Głos* include Z. Heryng, "Notatki ekonomiczne: kierunki i metody badań," *Głos*, 3 (30 January/11 February–6/8 February 1888): 63–64; 73–75; Karl Kautsky, "Przeciwieństwa klasowe w roku 1789. Z powodu setnej rocznicy Wielkiej Rewolucyi," *Głos*, 4 (29 July/10 August–16/28 September 1889); "Z ruchu klasy robotniczej w Europie," *Głos*, 3 (17/29 September 1888): 458–60; Edward Przewóski, "Nasi prawnicy i ekonomiści," *Głos*, 3 (15/27 January 1888): 41–42.

37. *Prospekt Głosu*, 1. See also Redakcya, "Pańskie i chłopskie potrzeby umysłowe, cz. II," *Głos*, 1 (1/13 November 1886): 97–98.

38. [Popławski], "Dwie cywilizacye," *Głos*, 1 (1/13 November 1886), in Popławski, *Pisma*, 1:133–40.

39. Redakcja, "Pierwsze żądło," *Głos*, 1 (27 September/9 October 1886): 18.

40. Redakcja, "Pańskie i chłopskie potrzeby umysłowe, cz. III," *Głos*, 1 (15/27 November 1886): 129.

41. J. K. Potocki, "Inteligencyja wiejska I," *Głos*, 2 (17/29 October 1887): 657.

42. Żeromski, 307.

43. Żeromski, 447.

44. Żeromski, 215.

45. Żeromski, 62.

46. W. Czetwertyński, *Na wozie i pod wozem (1837–1917). Wspomnienia z lat ubiegłych wnukom i wnuczkom opowiedziane* (Poznań, n.d.), as quoted by Wapiński, *Pokolenia*, 99.

47. J. L. Popławski, "Lud i naród," *Głos*, 3 (30 April/12 May 1888): 217–18.

48. Wasilewski, "Jan Ludwik Popławski. Szkic wizerunku," in Popławski, *Pisma*, xxxv.

49. *Przegląd Społeczny* similarly equated *lud* and *naród*. See, for example, "Szkice programowe III: program ludowy," *Przegląd Społeczny*, 1 (May 1886): 329; "Słowo wstępne," *Przegląd Społeczny*, 2 (January 1887): 1–2; Henryk Biegeleisen, "Szlachta w świetle poezji ludowej," *Przegląd Społeczny*, 2 (January 1887): 36.

50. On Balicki's ties with socialism, see Kurczewska, "Dwie postawy," 202–9; Kurczewska, *Naród w socjologii*, 207; Toporowski, 102–8; Walicki, *Zarys dziejów filozofii polskiej*, 384.

51. "Z wychodźstwa i kolonii: uroczystość w Rapperswylu," *Przegląd Wszechpolski*, 3 (15 August 1897): 374–75.

52. [Dmowski], *Nasz patriotyzm*, in Dmowski, *Dziesięć lat walki*, 266–67.

53. [Popławski], "Nasz demokratyzm," *Przegląd Wszechpolski*, 6 (March 1900), in Popławski, *Pisma*, 1:115–24.

54. Untitled manifesto, Warsaw, March 1899. Komitet Stronnictwa Narodowo-Demokratycznego (BN DŻS, Teka IB13). "Moskale" was a derogatory term for Russians. A reprint of this manifesto can be found in "L. N.," *Wolne Polskie Słowo*, 13 (5 April 1899): 1–2.

55. "*Narodowy Związek Robotniczy. Bracia Robotnicy!*" Lublin, 12 August 1906 (BN DŻS, Teka IB).

56. Kulczycki, 27.

57. Emil Haecker, "Zygmunt Balicki I," *Naprzód*, 25 (9 October 1916): 3.

58. Krzywicki, *Wspomnienia*, 2:43.

59. K. R. Żywicki, "Złudzenia demokratyczne," *Prawda*, 9 (9 February/28 January 1889): 64–66.

60. K. R. Żywicki, "Złudzenia demokratyczne," *Prawda*, 9 (16/4 February–2 March/18 February 1889): 75; 88–90. For more on this essay and the reaction to it, see Jedlicki, 335–49.

61. K. R. Żywicki, "Dekrety Wilhelma II," *Prawda*, 10 (15/3 February 1890): 73–75.

62. J. H. Siemieniecki, "Rachunek bieżący I," *Głos*, 5 (24 February/8 March 1890): 113–15.

63. K. R. Żywicki, "Tymczasowy obrachunek," *Prawda*, 10 (15/3 March 1890): 129–31.

64. J. H. Siemieniecki, "Rachunek bieżący II," *Głos*, 5 (10/22 March 1890): 142–43; "Rachunek bieżący III," *Głos*, 5 (24 March/5 April 1890): 167–68. At this point the debate became somewhat petty. "We never had a very high opinion of the scientific ability of Mr. K. R. Żywicki," Siemieniecki wrote, "and we judged skeptically his ability to write anything original." *Głos* had published his work only because they believed "that he could write a perfectly good summary of some book or article." Krzywicki, in turn, responded to the charge that he advocated laissez-faire by demanding "satisfaction." One can only assume that he was joking, since socialists were not supposed to believe in dueling. In any case, their dispute remained rhetorical. K. R. Żywicki, "Tymczasowy obrachunek," *Prawda*, 10 (29/17 March 1890): 153–55.

65. "Z prasy," *Głos*, 5 (12/24 May 1890): 254.

66. J. L. P., "Bezwiedni wstecznicy," *Głos*, 5 (14/26 April 1890): 199–200.

67. Krzywicki, *Wspomnienia*, 3:92–94. See also K. R. Żywicki, "Tymczasowy obrachunek," *Prawda*, 10 (29/17 March 1890): 153–55.

68. J. H. Siemieniecki, "Z obcego świata," *Głos*, 6 (8/20 June 1891): 295–96.

69. Dmowski, a leading member of Zet, was heard at the time singing the socialist anthem, "The Red Banner," much to his later embarrassment. See Kazimierz Czarnocki, "Przyczynki do historii PPS," in Kulakowski, 1:135. Dmowski later tried to dismiss his early socialism as an insincere tactical ploy. See Dmowski, "Relacja," 420; and Jabłonowski, 3. For different reasons, the socialists were also eager to establish that these Endeks were never "real" socialists. Emil Haecker, writing later in the socialist paper *Naprzód*, argued that Balicki's early socialism was part of a plot to infiltrate the PPS and subordinate it to the National League. Emil Haecker, "Zygmunt Balicki III," *Naprzód*, 25 (11 October 1916): 3. For another example of a socialist effort to deny the socialist content of Zet, see Kulczycki, 10.

70. Ruskiewicz, *Tajny związek*, 20–21. See also Surzycki, *Z dziejów pamiętnego 'Zetu,'* 5.

71. Stanisław Dobrowolski, "Związek Młodzieży Polskiej (Zet), 1886–1906," in Nawroczyński, 117.

72. Stanisław Grabski, "Wspomnienie o Lidze Narodowej" (Teka Stanisława Kozickiego; PANW, Sygn. 30, Jednostek 3), 43–62.

73. Dobrowolski, 112.

74. See Hillebrandt, *Polskie organizacje młodzieżowe*, 19–27.

75. Cywiński, *Rodowody niepokornych*, 343–44; Hłasko, 286 (16 September 1932): 5.

76. "Sto lat!" (Warsaw, March 1891) (BN DŻS, Teka IM).

77. "Odezwa Ligi Polskiej, 3ego Maja," in Kozicki, *Historia*, 507.

78. As cited by Pobóg-Malinowski, *Narodowa Demokrajca*, 78. The original of this document, like so much relating to the early Endecja, was destroyed during World War II.

79. A. Więckowski, "Wątpliwa pozycyja pewnego obrachunku," *Głos*, 5 (31 March/12 April 1890): 179.

80. J. L. P., "Rozwiana chmura," *Głos*, 5 (28 April/10 May 1890): 223–24.

81. Nałęcz, 6, 34.

82. Amerykanin [Józef Uziembło], "Wspomnienia z 1878 roku," in *Z pola walki*, 51. For a similar comment, see Kazimierz Kelles-Krauz, "Rachunek," *Przedświt*, 3 (October/November 1895): 11.

83. On Mendelson's significance, see Perl, 363–71.

84. "Wygadali się!" *Przedświt*, 1 (18 July 1891): 1–3. See also the very similar argument one month later in "Polityka ludowa," *Przedświt*, 1 (8 August 1891): 1–3.

85. "Potrzeba jedności," *Przedświt*, 2 (26 March 1892): 4–5.

86. "Potrzeba jedności," *Przedświt*, 2 (26 March 1892): 2–5.

87. "Rezolucyja delegacyi polskiej przedstawiona kongresowi socyjalistycznemu w Brukseli," *Przedświt*, 1 (22 August 1891): 2–3.

88. On the origins of the PPS, see Jerzy Myśliński, "Portret zbiorowy uczestników paryskiego zjazdu socjalistów polskich w 1892 r.," in Drozdowski et al., *Stulecie PPS*, 24–35; Perl, 384–99; sp., "Wspomnienia z dwóch lat (1892–1893)," in *Z pola walki*, 28–34; Suleja, 24–30; Wojciechowski, 48–52; Żarnowska, "Wokół zjazdu paryskiego polskich socjalistów w 1892 r.," in Drozdowski et al., *Stulecie PPS*, 12–23.

89. "Szkic programu Polskiej Partyi Socyalistycznej," in *Materyały do historyi PPS*, 8–9.

90. M. Kelles-Krauz, "W kwestyi 'równoległości,'" *Przedświt*, 3 (July 1895): 19–22. On the PPS's contempt for Russian socialism at the time, see F. P., "Geneza naszego programu politycznego," *Przedświt*, 3 (October 1894): 7–11. This could come dangerously close to orientalizing anti-Russianism, as in "Etapy," *Przedświt*, 3 (September–October 1894): 1–4; 1–6.

91. Untitled Manifesto, PPS, 9 November 1894 (AAN, Zbiór PPS, sygn. mf. 2552). This text was also published as "Odezwa PPS," *Przedświt*, 3 (November 1894): 23.

92. Untitled Manifesto, PPS, 8 September 1894 (AAN PPS, sygn. mf. 2552).

93. "Szkic programu PPS," 10.

94. *Przedświt*, 3 (May 1896): 19.

95. Kelles-Krauz, "Rachunek," 11.

96. On Luxemburg and the SDKP, see Blobaum, *Feliks Dzierżyński*; Nettl; Orzechowski, 21–161; Walicki, "Kwestia narodowa w polskiej myśli marksistowskiej przed 1914 r.," in *Polska, Rosja, Marksizm*, 184–235; and Walicki, "Rosa Luxemburg."

97. The first National League cell in Poznania was founded in 1899, and as late as 1903 there were only twenty members in the entire German partition. For several years the only National Democrats in Galicia were exiles from the Kingdom, and in 1903 the first meeting of the newly formed Galician branch of the Democratic-National Party attracted 80 participants. On the Endecja's membership in each partition, see Kozicki, *Historia*, 95–99. For more on the Endecja's development in the German Empire, see Marczewski.

98. On all these early organizations, see Kozicki, *Historia*, 95–97. On the *Collegium Secretum*, see the files of Father Bronisław Mariański and Father Kazimierz Merklejn (PANK, Teka Zielińskiego, sygn. 7785, vol. 4). On *Polak*, see Jakubowska, 28; Kmiecik, "Prasa polska," 57; Kozicki, 123; Myśliński, 41–42; Toporowski, 306–10; Wapiński, *Narodowa Demokracja*, 69; Wojnar, 379–457. On *Przegląd Wszechpolski*, see Dmowski, *Polityka polska*, 52; Dmowski, "Relacja," 427–28; Głąbiński, 29; Kmiecik, "Prasa polska," 56; Myśliński, 51; Wapiński, "'Przegląd Wszechpolski,'" in Henryk Zieliński, 84; Zygmunt Wasilewski, "Podróże Dmowskiego," in *Roman Dmowski: przyczynki*, 73–74.

99. Wojciechowski, 77.

100. Kieniewicz, "Polska kultura polityczna w XIX wieku," in Gierowski, 145–48.

101. Bogacz, 326–27; Koszutski, 78–79.

102. "Pierwszy a trzeci maja," *Przedświt*, 3 (April 1893): 1–3.

103. On the *Kilińszczyzna*, see Cywiński, *Rodowody*, 326–30, 350–51; Koszutski, 92–103; *Materyały do historyi PPS*, 134–36.

104. "Demonstracya Warszawska," *Przedświt*, 3 (April 1894): 1–2. For an example of how the PPS could appropriate the memory of Kiliński, see "Odezwa PPS," *Przedświt*, 3 (April 1894): 21–22; "Za naszą i waszą wolność!" *Przedświt*, 3 (May 1894): 1–2.

105. *Przedświt*, 3 (July 1894): 25–26.

106. *Przedświt*, 3 (July 1894): 26. All these arguments were rehearsed once again when *Przedświt* published a forum on relations between the PPS and the LN a year later. See M. Luśnia [Kelles-Krauz], "W kwestyi 'równoległości,'" *Przedświt*, 3 (July 1895): 19–22; S. Lasota, "O stosunku do patryotów; W kwestyi 'monopolu'"; Ignotus, "Kilka słów o patryotach (Z powodu 'W kwestyi równoległości')"; Michał Luśnia [Kelles-Krauz], "Państwo konspiracyjne i Skarb Narodowy," Luśnia [Kelles-Krauz], "Rachunek," *Przedświt*, 3 (October/November 1895): 1–12.

107. Malinowski, *Sześćdziesiąt lat nieprzerywalnej codziennej pracy* (Unpublished: AHRL, sygn. P. 52.; written in Warsaw, 1939), 59. On the blurred ideological lines in the countryside, see "Wyjaśnienie," *Przedświt*, 3 (December 1894): 21–22.

108. *Z dzisiejszej doby IX*, 6–7.

109. *Z dzisiejszej doby VI*, 4, 10–12.

110. [Dmowski], *Nasz patriotyzm*, 247, 261–63.

111. *Przedświt*, 3 (October 1893): 22–23.

112. Dmowski to Limanowski, 2 December 1895 (PANK, Teka Zielińskiego, sygn. 7808).

113. On the importance of this turning point, see Wojciechowski, 129–30.

114. "Do członków i sekcyi ZZSP," Centralny Komitet Robotniczy, Warsaw, 12 November 1899 (AAN PPS, sygn. mf. 2552).

115. Marx, *Capital*, 91–92. On Marx's initial reception in Russia, and his attitude toward the idea of a separate Russian path of development, see Kindersley; Mendel, 154–55; Offord, 116–60; Walicki, *The Controversy over Capitalism*, 132; Wortman, 146.

116. G. V. Plekhanov, "Our Differences," in Leatherbarrow and Offord, 294–96. On the reasons this sort of determinism might be appealing to a Russian revolutionary, see Mendel, 104–5.

117. V. P. Vorontsov, *Ot semidesyatykh godov k devyatisotym* (Petersburg, 1907), as cited in Mendel, 35.

118. Mikhailovsky, "Literatura i zhizn," *Russkaia mysl* (June 1892), as cited by Mendel, 97. For more on the debates in Russia about determinism and action, see Naimark, *Terrorists and Social Democrats*.

119. A. Więckowski, "Lud w programach demokratycznych," *Głos*, 5 (26 May/7 June 1890): 273–75.

120. A. Więckowski, "Lud w programach demokratycznych," *Głos*, 5 (2/14 June 1890): 288–89.

121. A. Więckowski, "Lud w programach demokratycznych," *Głos*, 5 (23 June/5 July 1890): 323.

122. A. Więckowski, "Lud w programach demokratycznych," *Głos*, 5 (11/23 September 1890): 409–11.

123. A. Więckowski, "Lud w programach demokratycznych," *Głos*, 5 (11/23 September 1890): 409–11.

124. A. Więckowski, "Lud w programach demokratycznych," *Głos*, 5 (7/19 July 1890): 347–48.

125. "Pokrewny prąd," *Głos*, 2 (18/30 April 1887): 257. Emphasis added.

126. "Polskie partje robotnicze i sprawa narodowa," *Przegląd Socjalistyczny*, 1 (October 1892): 1–7.

127. "Polskie partje robotnicze i sprawa narodowa," *Przegląd Socjalistyczny*, 1 (October 1892): 1–7. Even Miłkowski greeted this essay with approval, in "Bibliograficzne zapiski: Przegląd Socjalistyczny," *Wolne Polskie Słowo*, 6 (1 March 1892): 8.

128. B., "Kilka uwag o kwestyi polskiej w programie politycznym socyalistów," *Przegląd Socjalistyczny*, 4 (1893): 38.

Chapter Six

1. Józef Buszko, Ryszard Kołodziejczyk, and Stanisław Michalkiewicz, "Początki ruchu robotniczego na ziemiach polskich," in Kołodziejczyk, 215–20.

2. Józef Buszko, Stanisław Michalkiewicz, and Jerzy Myśliński, "Ruch robotniczy w zaborze pruskim i austriackim w latach osiemdziesiątych. Królestwo Polskie po upadku Proletariatu," in Kołodziejczyk, 387.

3. Kern, 152.

4. Blobaum, *Rewolucja*, 189.

5. Michel Foucault, "Two Lectures," in Dirks et al., 219.

6. Chatterjee, *Nationalist Thought*, 51; Mallon, *Peasant and Nation*, 19. In Polish, see Andrzej Biernat, "U progu umasowienia obiegu informacji," in Wolsza and Żarnowska, 185–88.

7. Rémond, 217. For a slightly different view, see Peck, vii–ix.

8. Volkov, 10.

9. See, for example, Sternhell, *Birth of Fascist Ideology*, 5.

10. Czarnecki, 9.

11. "Szkice programowe III: program ludowy," *Przegląd Społeczny*, 1 (May 1886): 330.

12. Popławski, "Nałóg kastowy," *Głos*, 6 (24 October 1891), in *Szkice*, 134. Hłasko incorrectly dated this article as 1890. See also Popławski's "Powieść szlachecka," *Głos*, 5 (22–29 November 1890), in *Szkice*, 114.

13. Balicki, "Demokratyzm i liberalizm," *Przegląd Społeczny*, 1 (August-October 1886).

14. "Genewa, 30 listopada 1892," *Wolne Polskie Słowo*, 6 (15 December 1892): 3–4.

15. Kazimierz Bystrzycki, "Trzy drogi," *Głos*, 2 (14/26 March 1887): 194. See the similar argument in Redakcja, "Polityka wahadłowa," *Głos*, 1 (17/29 November–24 November/6 December 1886): 161–62; 177–78; and "Pokrewny prąd," *Głos*, 2 (18/30 April 1887): 257.

16. On the Żyrardów strike, see Naimark, *History of the "Proletariat,"* 139–41.

17. Naimark, *History of the "Proletariat,"* 142–44.

18. Untitled, *Walka Klas*, 2 (June 1884), in Molska, 2:348.

19. "Słowo wstępne," *Walka Klas*, 1 (May 1884); in Molska, 2:25–61. See also Kancewicz, 4; Naimark, *History of the "Proletariat,"* 151.

20. sp., "Wspomnienia z dwóch lat (1892–1893)," in *Z pola walki*, 30. On the desire among socialist activists to oppose "spontaneity," see Żarnowska, "Rewolucja 1905–1907 a kultura polityczna robotników," in Wolsza and Żarnowska, 25.

21. Próchnik, "Ideologja 'Proletarjatu,'" 2.

22. Blobaum, *Rewolucja*, 51.

23. Piłsudski to M. Sokolnicki, as cited by Nałęcz, 72.

24. [W. Jodko-Narkiewicz], "Programowe żądanie niepodległości w stosunku do chwili dzisiejszej," *Robotnik*, 204 (1906): 1; in Nałęcz, 110.

25. Wasilewski, "Jan Ludwik Popławski. Szkic wizerunku," in Popławski, *Pisma*, xxxv.

26. "Świt," *Pochodnia*, 1 (March 1899): 1–2. For more on *Pochodnia*, see Jakubowska, 36–38; Piotr Panek, no title (1931) (Teka Stanisława Kozickiego; PANW, Sygn. 30, Jednostek 3), 121–26. Panek was the editor of *Pochodnia* until his arrest in 1901, when Dmowski took over.

27. "Adam Mickiewicz," *Polak*, 3 (May 1898): 67.

28. "Program stronnictwa demokratyczno-narodowego w zaborze rosyjskim," *Przegląd Wszechpolski*, 9 (October 1903): 721–57.

29. See the accompanying editor's note to B. L. (Bolesław Limanowski?), "Zurich, 5 listopada 1887," *Wolne Polskie Słowo*, 1 (15 November 1887): 3–4.

30. Dr. Feliks Górski, "Lagor, d. 5 kwietnia 1889," *Wolne Polskie Słowo*, 3 (1 May 1889): 4–5.

31. "Mowa Ob. St. Mickaniewskiego w Paryżu na obchodzie rocznicy 29 listopada 1888," *Wolne Polskie Słowo*, 3 (1 January 1889): 6.

32. "Jan Kasprowicz," *Wolne Polskie Słowo*, 2 (15 November 1888): 8.

33. "Socjalizm w obec sprawy polskiej," *Wolne Polskie Słowo*, 6 (15 November 1892): 1–2.

34. "Lud," *Wolne Polskie Słowo*, 8 (15 May 1894): 1–2.

35. Redakcja, "Nasz Program," *Wolne Polskie Słowo*, 1 (15 September 1887): 1–2.

36. W. F., "Lwów, październik 1887," *Wolne Polskie Słowo*, 1 (15 October 1887): 4.

37. "W. ks. Poznańskie, 24 października," *Wolne Polskie Słowo*, 1 (1 November 1887): 2. Guttry revealed himself to be the author of this letter in *Wolne Polskie Słowo*, 5 (15 February 1891): 2. For a similar argument, see "Młodzież polska w momencie obecnym," *Wolne Polskie Słowo*, 2 (1 April 1888): 1–2.

38. "Październik 1887," *Wolne Polskie Słowo*, 1 (15 November 1887): 2–3. Miłkowski added an editor's note to this letter: "Mr. W. F. considers himself a patriot. We have no right to accuse him of insincerity, particularly since socialism is not necessarily tied to cosmopolitanism."

39. "Zagrożenie narodowości naszej IV," *Wolne Polskie Słowo*, 3 (15 May 1889): 1.

40. "Zagrożenie narodowości naszej V," *Wolne Polskie Słowo*, 3 (1 June 1889): 1.

41. "Zagrożenie narodowości naszej IV," 2. The reference to Spencer is in the original.

42. "Zagrożenie narodowości naszej IV," 1–2.

43. "Odpowiedź redakcji," *Wolne Polskie Słowo*, 4 (15 April 1890): 4–5. The letter that inspired Miłkowski's response was "Z kraju, marzec 1890. Stara i młoda demokracja. Młodzież polska przed sądem Wolnego Polskiego Słowa," *Wolne Polskie Słowo*, 4 (15 April 1890): 2–4.

44. "Sofia, 25 grudnia 1890," *Wolne Polskie Słowo*, 5 (15 January 1891): 3.

45. "Paryż, 30 listopada 1895," *Wolne Polskie Słowo*, 9 (1 December 1895): 3.

46. Verax, "Paryż, 26 stycznia 1893," *Wolne Polskie Słowo*, 7 (1 February 1893): 4.

47. For an example of an essay equating socialism with loyalism, see "Genewa, 31 January 1892: po zjeździe w Genewie," *Wolne Polskie Słowo*, 105 (15 January 1892): 3. The few pro-socialist essays appearing during the 1890s include: "Przemówienie na dzień 23 stycznia 1892 roku Pułkownika Józefa Gałęzowskiego," *Wolne Polskie Słowo*, 6 (1 February 1892): 3–6; Eustachy Leszczyc, "Głos z kraju: posłanie do braci Polaków zgromadzonych na zjeździe Towarzystw Polskich w Szwajcarji," *Wolne Polskie Słowo*, 6 (1 March 1892): 5–6; "Nieco o organizacji emigracyjnej," *Wolne Polskie Słowo*, 7 (1 March 1893): 1–2; "Genewa, 1 grudnia," *Wolne Polskie Słowo*, 7 (15 December 1893): 3; "Odczyt ob. St. Kośmińskiego wypowiedziany na obchodzie rocznicy Powstania Listopadowego w Genewie," *Wolne Polskie Słowo*, 10 (1 January 1896): 6–7; "Paryż, 25 stycznia 1897," *Wolne Polskie Słowo*, 11 (1 February 1897): 5; "Rozmaitości," *Wolne Polskie Słowo*, 12 (25 July 1898): 8.

48. "Program stronnictwa demokratyczno-narodowego w zaborze rosyjskim," *Przegląd Wszechpolski*, 3 (1 June 1897): 243. A year later this same document was serialized in *Polak* as "Polityka polska pod panowaniem moskiewskiem (Program stronnictwa demokratyczno-narodowego)," *Polak*, 3 (February–July 1898).

49. [Popławski], "Interesy ludu i polityka narodowa," *Przegląd Wszechpolski*, 3 (15 July 1897), 310.

50. [Popławski], "Nasz Demokratyzm," *Przegląd Wszechpolski*, 6 (March 1900), in Popławski, *Pisma*, 1:104–5.

51. Balicki, *Metody*, 28–30.

52. B. Ostoja [Balicki], *Uwagi krytyczne*. This was originally published in the short-lived National Democratic quarterly, *Kwartalnik Naukowo-Polityczny i Społeczny*, 1 (1898): 60–91.

53. "Sprawozdanie Zygmunta Balickiego," *Niepodległość*, 7 (1933): 282–83.

54. [Popławski], "Program stronnictwa demokratyczno-narodowego" (1897): 243. Emphasis added.

55. "Komitet Centralny Liga Narodowej. Odezwa," *Teka*, 2 (January 1900): 18. This text simultaneously appeared as "Liga Narodowa," *Przegląd Wszechpolski*, 6 (January 1900): 7.

56. [Popławski], "Walka o lud," *Przegląd Wszechpolski*, 4 (1 September 1898): 260.

57. "Odezwa," Komitet Centralny Ligi Narodowej, Warsaw, 8 December 1899 (BN DŻS Teka IB13). This text is also preserved in PANK, Teka Józefa Zielińskiego, sygn. 7782, and was reprinted at the time in *Teka*, 2 (January 1900): 14. For a similar formulation of the Endecja's goals at the time, see "Liga Narodowa," *Przegląd Wszechpolski*, 6 (January 1900): 5.

58. "Program stronnictwa demokratyczno-narodowego," (1903): 726–27. Emphasis added.

59. Wojciech Grochowski, "O gospodarce narodowej," *Polak*, 1 (December 1896): 6.

60. [Dmowski], "Jawna i tajna polityka," *Przegląd Wszechpolski*, 8 (August 1902), in Dmowski, *Dziesięć lat walki*, 64, 71; [Popławski], "Nasz demokratyzm," 1:102–3.

61. [Popławski], "Program stronnictwa narodowo-demokratycznego," (1897): 243–45.

62. Władysław Jabłonowski, untitled memoir excerpts (PANK, Teka Zielińskiego, sygn. 7847), 3.

63. [Dmowski], "Nowe zadania," *Przegląd Wszechpolski*, 10 (March 1904), in Dmowski, *Dziesięć lat walki*, 352–53.

64. "Gawędy sąsiedzkie II," *Polak*, 2 (December 1897): 180–81. See also "Odezwa Ligi Narodowej," *Polak*, 4 (January 1900): 2–4; W. Z., "O różnych formach rządu," *Polak*, 3 (September 1898), 124–26. The conversations between Jan and Mateusz were reprinted in book form as *Gawędy sąsiedzkie*.

65. "Gawędy sąsiedzkie IV," *Polak*, 4 (December 1900): 153–55.

66. Balicki, *Parlamentaryzm*, 1:144, 2:104–5, 111–14.

67. Balicki, "Czynniki zachowawcze i postępowe w dobie ostatniej," *Przegląd Wszechpolski*, 11 (July 1905): 398.

68. "Pogrzeb ś.p. Jana Popławskiego," *Gazeta Codzienna*, 75 (1908). This clipping is preserved in Teka Zielińskiego, PANK, sygn. 7786.

69. Obywatel, "Nasze potrzeby a nasze stronnictwa. Głos z Galicyi," *Przegląd Wszechpolski*, 9 (December 1903): 913–26. See also "Doktryna i realizm w polityce," *Przegląd Wszechpolski*, 8 (8/1904): 561–67.

70. B. Ostoja [Balicki], "Powrotna fala kosmopolityzmu," *Przegląd Wszechpolski*, 2 (2/1903), 95.

71. "Program stronnictwa demokratyczno-narodowego," (1903): 745–48.

72. "Ostatnie bezrobocie," *Pochodnia*, 4 (October 1899): 2.

73. Bolesław Nidzicki, "Polityka ekonomiczna demokracyi narodowej," *Przegląd Wszechpolski*, 9 (February 1903): 107.

74. "Narodowy Związek Robotnicy. Regulamin narodowego Koła Robotniczego" (no date; BN DŻS, Teka IB).

75. Nidzicki, "Polityka ekonomiczna demokracyi IV," *Przegląd Wszechpolski*, 9 (May, 1903): 350.

76. "Walka o ziemie," *Polak*, 3 (October/November 1898): 137. See also Wojciech Grochowski, "O gospodarce narodowej," *Polak*, 1 (December 1896): 6; "W sprawie ludowej w zaborze rosyjskim," *Polak*, 2 (October 1897), 150; G. Topór [T. Grużewski], "Wczorajsze hasła," *Przegląd Wszechpolski*, 7 (July 1901): 394–400.

77. S. G., "Rozwój ekonomiczny i kultura narodowa," *Przegląd Wszechpolski*, 3 (1 April 1897): 148–51. See also S. G., "Samopomoc w polityce ekonomicznej III," *Przegląd Wszechpolski*, 3 (5 August 1897): 336.

78. S. G. "Narodowa polityka ekonomiczna," *Kwartalnik Naukowo-Polityczny i Społeczny*, 1 (1898): 31–59. Emphasis added.

79. Nidzicki, "Polityka ekonomiczna demokracyi I," *Przegląd Wszechpolski*, 9 (January 1903), 26–31.

80. S. G. "Narodowa polityka ekonomiczna," 31–59. Emphasis added.

81. Panek, 15.

82. "Liga Narodowa," *Pochodnia*, 2 (March 1900): 1.

83. Piltz, *Nasze stronnictwa skrajne*, 165.

84. B. Ostoja [Balicki], "Charakter demokracyi narodowej jako stronnictwa," *Przegląd Wszechpolski*, 9 (May 1903): 326–38.

85. Helena Ceysingerówna, "Liga Narodowa i Związek Unarodowienia Szkół w walce o szkolę polską," in Nawroczyński, 4. See also Stanisław Kozicki, *Pamiętniki, 1875–1914* (unpublished, AHRL, sygn. P-127), 132.

86. Balicki, *Metody nauk społecznych*, 56.

87. "Polskie odrodzenie polityczne," *Teka*, 2 (October 1900): 329–34. Emphasis in the original.

88. Włodzimierz Klawer, untitled memoir, Warsaw, 1930 (BNZR, akc. 9090).

89. *Pochodnia*, 4 (January 1902): 2; "Ustawa Ligi Narodowej," 1 April 1893 (PANK, Teka Zielińskiego, sygn. 7783), 43–45.

90. "Program stronnictwa demokratyczno-narodowego," (1903): 739.

91. "Protokół posiedzeń zjazdu lokalnego członków Rady Tajnej Ligi Narodowej w Genewie, dn. 10, 11, 12, 21, 27, 29 czerwca 1895" (PANK, Teka Zielińskiego, sygn. 7783).

92. Michał Terech, no title, no date (Teka Stanisława Kozickiego; PANW, Sygn. 30, Jednostek 3), 202. A copy of this text is also preserved in PANK, Teka Zielińskiego, sygn. 7785, vol. 7.

93. *Pochodnia*, 2 (May 1900): 1–2.

94. [Dmowski], "Organizacja opinji," *Przegląd Wszechpolski*, 10 (April 1904), in Dmowski, *Dziesięć lat walki*, 203–4.

95. "Sprawozdanie za rok 1901–1902. Komitet Centralny Ligi Narodowej do Komisji Nadzorczej Skarbu Narodowego Polskiego" (24 July 1902), in "Do historji Ligi Narodowej," *Niepodległość*, 9 (22) (1934): 294–95.

96. [Dmowski], "Walka o prawo i organizacja narodowa," *Przegląd Wszechpolski*, 9 (June 1903), in Dmowski, *Dziesięć lat walki*, 342–43.

97. "Nasze Drogi," *Teka*, 3 (January 1901): 2–3. For more military metaphors see "Genewa, 30 listopada 1892," *Wolne Polskie Słowo*, 6 (15 December 1892): 3.

98. "Na przyszłość," *Teka*, 2 (November 1900): 389.

99. "Polskość naszego programu," *Teka*, 3 (October 1901): 401–3.

100. "Stronnictwo demokratyczno-narodowe, jego zasady i działalność. Odczyt wygłoszony na zjeździe przedstawicieli stronnictwa w Warszawie i na szeregu zebrań w kraju," *Przegląd Wszechpolski*, 11 (July 1905): 483–84.

101. Untitled, undated one-page leaflet (BN DŻS, sygn. 2932, Teka IBM).

102. Stanisław Bukowiecki, "Wspomnienie Stanisława Bukowieckiego o Lidze Narodowej," 1931 (Teka Stanisława Kozickiego; PANW, Sygn. 30, Jednostek 3), 25. See also the account of Jozafat Bohuszewicz, "Wspomnienia z czasów przynależności do Ligi Narodowej," Wilno, 20 April 1932 (Teka Stanisława Kozickiego; PANW, sygn. 30, Jednostek 3), 8.

103. Dmowski to Miłkowski, 9 April 1906 (PANK, Teka Zielińskiego, sygn. 7808, no. 30).

104. Untitled one-page leaflet, Warsaw, 5 February 1905 (BN DŻS Teka IB13).

105. R. Dmowski, "Podstawy polityki polskiej," *Przegląd Wszechpolski*, 11 (July 1905): 343, 349, 358–59.

Chapter Seven

1. Malraux is cited in Eugene Weber, "The Right: An Introduction," in Weber and Rogger, 8.

2. [Dmowski], "Jedność narodowa, 1" *Przegląd Wszechpolski*, 1 (15 March 1895): 81–83.

3. Dmowski, *Myśli*, 87.

4. Ryszard Bender, "I wojna światowa i Polska niepodległa (1914–1939)," in Kłoczowski, 516–17. For a more balanced discussion of the role of the Jews as the Polish "other," see Cała, 175.

5. For examples of this view, see Peck, 88–97; Volkov, 221.

6. On positivism and the Jews, see Blejwas, "Polish Positivism and the Jews"; Blejwas, *Realism*, 100; Cała, 216–67; Rudzki, 156.

7. "Dwa głosy w kwestyi żydowskiej," *Przegląd Tygodniowy*, 18 (23 January/4 February 1883): 57–59. See also the ridicule directed toward the anti-Semitic press in W. Wścieklica, "Gniazdo paszkwilu," *Prawda*, 4 (1 November/20 October 1884–15/3 November 1884); and "Apostołowie kłamstwa," *Prawda*, 5 (4 July/22 June 1885): 314–13.

8. The dramatic decline in conversion is detailed in Endelman, 37. On *Izraelita*, see Fuks, 85–102.

9. "Wymowna przestroga," *Prawda*, 1 (7 May/25 April 1881): 217–19. For more on Świętochowski and the Jews, see Sandler's introduction to Świętochowski, *Wspomnienia*, xiii–xviii.

10. "Przypomniany obowiązek," *Prawda*, 1 (21/9 May 1881): 241–42. Note the distinction between "Jews" and "people." See also Świętochowski, "Zmienione pytanie," *Prawda*, 1 (28/16 May 1881): 253–55.

11. On the pogrom, see Cała, 268–78. For an anti-Semitic spin on the events, see Kościesza, 2.

12. A. Świętochowski, "Bez złudzeń," *Prawda*, 1 (31/19 December 1881): 625–27.

13. Orzeszkowa, *O żydach*, 5, 27–31.

14. Bolesław Prus, "Kronika tygodniowa," *Kurier Warszawski*, 280 (28 September/10 October 1886): 1. The article by Nusbaum that inspired this attack is cited and discussed below.

15. Świętochowski, "Walka o byt III (klasyfikacya wyznaniowa)," *Prawda*, 3 (27/15 January 1883): 37.

16. Orzeszkowa, *O żydach*, 88–89.

17. Cała, 167–71. See also Fuks, 41–124.

18. Orzeszkowa, *O żydach*, 72.

19. On Jeleński, see Cała, 279–94; Jaszczuk, 210–41; Kościesza, vii–xxix.

20. His two articles for *Przegląd Tygodniowy* were standard liberal fare. Jelemski, "Małómiasteczkowa inteligencya i jej działalność społeczne," *Przegląd Tygodniowy*, 7 (2/14

July 1872): 217–18; Jeleński, "Pomoc wzajemna i pomoc własna," *Przegląd Tygodniowy*, 7 (17/29 September 1872): 305–6.

21. Przyborowski, 174. Others charged that he was not as "self-made" as he seemed. Many believed that he was financed by the Russians, as is implied in "Antysemityzm polski w Ameryce," *Wolne Polskie Słowo*, 53 (15 November 1889): 1.

22. On the circulation of *Rola*, see Jaszczuk, 223. On the circulation of the other Warsaw papers, see Kmiecik, *Prasa warszawska*.

23. Kozicki, *Pamiętniki, 1875–1914* (unpublished: AHRL, sygn. P-127), 33.

24. Poseł Prawdy [Świętochowski], "Liberum veto," *Prawda*, 3 (5/13 September 1883): 441; W. Wścieklica, "Gniazdo paszkwilu I," *Prawda*, 4 (1 November/20 October 1884): 525–26. Wścieklica continued his assault on Jeleński in the next two issues of *Prawda*. Jeleński had a ready adjective for such liberal critics: they were simply "Jewish." See "Niesumienność literacka," *Rola*, 1 (23 April/5 May, 1883): 9.

25. The first advertisement for *Rola* can be found in *Kurier Warszawski*, 63 (1 January 1883): 15. The daily was already criticizing Jeleński in "Wiadomości bieżące," *Kurier Warszawski*, 63 (3/15 March 1883): 4. A few weeks later *Rola* printed a notice (on page 1) that *Kurier Warszawski* had refused to accept any more of *Rola*'s business: *Rola*, 1 (12/24 March 1883): 1.

26. Father A. Z. "W odpowiedzi 'Roli,'" *Przegląd Katolicki*, 34 (29 October 1896): 702–3. On Rola and the Catholic Church, see Jaszczuk, 123–25.

27. "Z zaboru rosyjskiego," *Przegląd Wszechpolski*, 4 (6/15/98): 183.

28. For an alternative interpretation of *Rola*'s audience, see Cała, 285. Jeleński's only prominent collaborators—the painter Jan Matejko and (more surprisingly) Zygmunt Miłkowski—were from outside the kingdom and (to be charitable) may not have fully understood the nature of his paper. T. T. Jeż, "O Bułgaryi i Bułgarach," *Rola*, 1 (24 December 1882/6 January 1883): 2–5; "List Matejki do Redakcyi 'Roli,'" *Rola*, 1 (29 January/10 February 1883): 1–2.

29. Jeleński, 5. Emphasis in the original.

30. Jeleński, 26.

31. Wzdulski, 40.

32. The expression "modern conservatism" can be found in Pancerny [Jeske-Choiński], "Na posterunku," *Rola*, 1 (17/28 April 1883): 8–9; Pancerny, "Na posterunku," *Rola*, 1 (15/26 May 1883): 7–8; Pancerny, "Na posterunku," 1 (18/30 June 1883): 7–8.

33. Pancerny [T. Jeske-Choiński], "Na posterunku," *Rola*, 1 (22 January/3 February 1883): 8. See also "Warszawa, d. 27 stycznia 1883," *Rola*, 1 (15/27 January 1883): 1–2; Kościesza, 90; and "Czego chcemy?" *Rola*, 1 (24 December/6 January 1882/3): 1–2. For a detailed itemization of *Rola*'s program, see J. J., "Co robić?" *Rola*, 1 (9/21 April 1883): 1–2.

34. C. Reklewski, "Z teki wieśniaka," *Rola*, 1 (22 January/3 February 1883): 3–5; "Czego chcemy? II," *Rola*, 1 (1/13 January 1883): 1.

35. Wzdulski, 16, 32, 37–38.

36. Pancerny [Jeske-Choiński], "Na posterunku," *Rola*, 1 (22 January/3 February 1883): 8–9.

37. On Jeleński's difficulties with the Church, see "Nieporozumienie," *Rola*, 1 (12/24 February 1883): 11; Z., "Przepraszam," *Rola*, 1 (5/17 March 1883): 1–3. Perhaps in response to *Przegląd Katolicki*'s complaints, Jeleński insisted that he was advocating only "defense," not a ruthless struggle to the death. J. J., "Ważna chwila," *Rola*, 1 (26 February/10 March 1883): 1–2. Contrast *Rola*'s deference toward *Przegląd Katolicki* with his attacks on the conservative paper, *Słowo*: Pancerny [Jeske-Choiński], "Na posterunku," *Rola*, 1 (17/28 April 1883): 8–9; "Raz na zawsze," *Rola*, 1 (30 April/12 May 1883): 1–2. For more on the ongoing debates on the right between *Słowo* and *Rola*, see Pąkciński, 129–47.

38. Gumplowicz, *System Socyologii*, 3. An American scholar has described Gumplowicz as "completely caught up in the . . . Germanic *Zeitgeist*," but a Polish biographer has disputed this claim. See Irving L. Horowitz, "Introduction: The Sociology of Ludwig Gumplowicz, 1838–1909," in Gumplowicz, *Outline*, 13; and Gella, "Introduction," in Gella, *The Ward-Gumplowicz Correspondence*, xvi–xvii. According to Gella, most of Gumplowicz's work was composed in Polish, published in Polish newspapers and journals, and only then recast in German.

39. The 1963 Horowitz edition cited here was based on F. W. Moore's 1899 translation of the German text. Gumplowicz also published a brief Polish summary of the *Grundriss* shortly after the book came out. Ludwik Gumplowicz, "Zarys socyologii," *Prawda*, 5 (4 July/ 22 June 1885): 318–20. The following citations from the *Grundriss* are based on Horowitz's translation, modified slightly for clarity.

40. Gumplowicz, *System socyologii*, 229. See also the comparable passage in Gumplowicz, "Zarys socyologii," 318–20. Here he describes "the struggle to the death with every foreigner" as a "basic instinct."

41. Gumplowicz, *Outline*, 208, 233–35. It is in this context that we must understand his use of the term "race." For Gumplowicz there was no such thing as a "genealogical unit in which a fixed anthropological type was transmitted from generation to generation." Nonetheless, he used the concept of "race" as a means of explaining the origins of the social struggle and for labeling the cohesive communities that engaged in this struggle. He explained his use of this term, in Gumplowicz, "Najnowszy stan kwestyi rasowej," *Prawda*, 4 (8 March/25 February–15/3 March 1884): 110–11; 122–23; and *Outline*, 163, 171, 227.

42. Gumplowicz, *Outline*, 199–200; and *System socyologii*, 237–38. See also "Prawidłowość w rozwoju państw," *Prawda*, 4 (23/11 February 1884): 88–89.

43. Gumplowicz, "Rodzina i naród," *Prawda*, 4 (19/7 January 1884): 26–27.

44. Gumplowicz, *Outline*, 207–8. See also 226–27.

45. Gumplowicz, "Rodzina i naród," *Prawda*, 4 (19/7 January 1884): 26.

46. Gumplowicz, "Istota własności," *Prawda*, 3 (15/3 December 1883): 591–93; and *System socyologii*, 250, 397, 415.

47. Gumplowicz, *System socyologii*, 230–31, 253.

48. Gumplowicz, *Outline*, 203, 229.

49. Gumplowicz, *Outline*, 164.

50. Gumplowicz, *Outline*, 231–32; 302–6; *System socyologii*, 464. See also Gella's discussion of this issue in *Ward-Gumplowicz*, xix.

51. Gumplowicz, *System socyologii*, 470.

52. Gumplowicz, *Outline*, 234. The Polish passage is even more specific, arguing that large nations should be satisfied with an "indemnity" instead of risking the dangers of excessive expansion. Gumplowicz, *System socyologii*, 329.

53. Gumplowicz, *Outline*, 235; *System socyologii*, 330.

54. Adolf J. Cohn, "Walka ras," *Prawda*, 3 (8 September/27 August–22/10 September 1883): 450. When the Polish edition of Gumplowicz's book appeared, *Prawda* gave it an unprecedented two-page advertisement, including citations of praise from reviewers in France, Germany, and Italy. *Prawda*, 8 (10 March/27 February 1888). The advertisement was included in this issue as an unpaginated insert.

55. The most extended example of this argument is in Balicki, *Metody*, 35.

56. Edward Przewóski, "Nasi prawnicy i ekonomiści," *Głos*, 3 (15/27 January 1888): 41–42.

57. Ludwik Krzywicki, "Socyologia Gumplowicza," *Prawda*, 8 (1 September/20 August 1888–15/3 September 1888): 413–14; 423–24; 438–39; Krzywicki, "Sprawozdania naukowe i literackie," *Głos*, 3 (15/28 October 1888): 513–14; Krzywicki, "Kwestyja jednopochodności i

wielopochodności rodu ludzkiego (Z powodu *Systemu Socyjologii* prof. Gumplowicza)," *Głos*, 3 (22 October/3 November 1888): 522–24; Krzywicki, "Prądy i kierunki w socyjologii (Z powodu *Systemu Socyjologii* prof. Gumplowicza)," *Głos*, 3 (29 October/10 November 1888): 535–37; and Krzywicki, "Rozwój umysłowy ludzkości (Z powodu *Systemu Socyjologii* prof. Gumplowicza)," *Głos*, 3 (12/24 November 1888): 561–63.

58. Krzywicki, "Socyologia Gumplowicza III," *Prawda*, 8 (15/3 September 1888): 439.

59. Krzywicki, "Sprawozdania naukowe i literackie," *Głos*, 3 (15/28 October 1888): 513–14.

60. J. K. Potocki, "Szkice socyjologiczne. Społeczna walka o byt," *Głos*, 7 (28 March/9 April 1892): 170–73; Maryan Bohusz [Potocki], "Bez obłudy," *Głos*, 4 (18/30 March 1889): 168; J. K. Potocki, *Współzawodnictwo*, 3–70.

61. A. D. "Cara Vendetta," *Głos*, 1 (4 October 1886), 46–47. On the French context to which the author refers, see Sternhell "Paul Déroulède."

62. Józef Hłasko, "W redakcji 'Głosu,'" *Gazeta Warszawska*, 273 (7 September 1932): 5. Unfortunately, Hłasko did not clarify what this "adventure" entailed.

63. J. L. P., "Posiew miłości," *Głos*, 3 (2/14 April 1888): 165.

64. Marian Bohusz [J. K. Potocki], "Bez obłudy," *Głos*, 3 (9/21 April 1888): 188.

65. *Prospekt Głosu* (n. p., n.d.): 5. He repeated this argument in Henryk Nusbaum, "Jestem Żydem—dlaczego?" *Głos*, 1 (4 October 1886), 35–36. Bolesław Prus's response to this essay is cited above.

66. Untitled Manifesto, PPS, 9 November 1894 (AAN, PPS, sygn. mf. 2552).

67. Heybowicz-Herburt, 445–47, 452.

68. Untitled Manifesto, PPS, Warsaw, 9 June 1903 (AAN, PPS, sygn. mf. 2552).

69. The term "Ukraine" was acquiring its modern definition only in the late 1880s and 1890s, and most Poles still used the label "Ruthenian." On the changing names of the Ruthenians/Ukrainians, see Wandycz, 256. One of the earliest uses in Polish of the term "Ukraine" in the modern sense seems to be by Tadeusz Rylski, "Z Ukrainy," *Głos*, 2 (21 February/5 March, 1887): 157–58. Rylski compared the *lud ukraiński* with the *lud polski*.

70. "Szkice programowe II: narodowość," *Przegląd Społeczny*, 1 (April 1886): 251–58. See also Bolesław Limanowski, "Ruch międzynarodowy," *Przegląd Społeczny*, 2 (April–May, 1887): 289–305; 377–97.

71. *Materyały do historyi PPS*, 217.

72. Popławski, "Haniebna solidarność," *Głos*, 2 (10/22 October 1887), 645.

73. J. L. Popławski, "Polityka pańska," *Głos*, 3 (1/13 October 1888): 481–82.

74. J. L. Popławski, "W dobrej wierze III," *Głos*, 3 (16/28 April 1888): 193–94.

75. [Potocki], "Partyje i programy: część krytyczna I," *Głos*, 2 (6/18 June 1887): 369.

76. Potocki, "Partyje i programy: część krytyczna II," *Głos*, 2 (11/23 July, 1887): 450.

77. [Potocki], "Partyje i programy I," 370.

78. Limanowski, "Dyskusje," *Przegląd Społeczny*, 1 (July 1886): 51–52.

79. H. Polanowski, "Polska historyczna i etnograficzna," *Pobudka*, 1 (June 1889): 1–6.

80. Redakcja, "Nasz program," *Wolne Polskie Słowo*, 1 (15 September 1887): 1–2.

81. "Głos z zaboru rossyjskiego," *Wolne Polskie Słowo*, 2 (15 February 1888): 5–6.

82. Dr. Feliks Górski, "Lagor, 23 kwietnia 1889," *Wolne Polskie Słowo*, 3 (1 June 1889): 3–4. The Union of Lublin joined Poland and Lithuania in 1569.

83. "Zurich, 28 stycznia 1889," *Wolne Polskie Słowo*, 3 (15 February 1889): 2–3.

84. "Lyon, 10 lutego 1889," *Wolne Polskie Słowo*, 3 (1 March 1889): 3–4. See also "Antysemityzm polski w Ameryce," *Wolne Polskie Słowa*, 3 (15 November 1889): 1–2; "Antysemityzm w Polsce," *Wolne Polskie Słowa*, 3 (1 December 1889): 1–2; L. C. "Zurych, 8 lipca 99," *Wolne Polskie Słowo*, 13 (20 July 1899): 4.

85. "Warszawa d. 26 lipca," *Przegląd Wszechpolski*, 1 (1 August 1895), 222–23.

86. Dmowski, "Liga Narodowa (1886–1903)" (PANW, Teka Kozickiego sygn. 30). This is a copy; the original is from Materiały K. Kaczmarczyka, Archiwum PAN w Poznaniu, P III-35.

87. Witold Ziemiński, "Czem jest Izrael?" *Głos*, 5 (22 September/4 October 1890): 484. See also J. K. P., "Wzrost antysemityzmu," *Głos*, 7 (5/17 December 1892): 599–600; J. P., "Antysemityzm w Niemczech," *Głos*, 8 (7/19 August 1893): 385–86.

88. Redakcja, "Antysemityzm i sprawa żydowska I," 1 (11 October 1886), 51–52. The Jewish assimilationist periodical, *Izraelita*, reacted to this article in *Głos* by agreeing that the Jews were, indeed, "different," but they were also every bit as much a part of Poland as anyone else, having lived there for so many centuries. See *Izraelita*, 42 (1886), in Żbikowski, 82.

89. Redakcja, "Antysemityzm i sprawa żydowska I," 1 (11 October 1886), 51–52.

90. "W dobrej wierze II," *Głos*, 3 (9/21 April 1888): 183.

91. J. H. Siemieniecki [Józef Hłasko], "Z obcego świata," *Głos*, 3 (26 November/8 December, 1888): 597–98.

92. A. P. Ordyński, "Żyd w wiosce," *Głos*, 4 (14/26 January–21 January/2 February 1889): 42–43, 54–55.

93. A. Wiśniewski, "Kilka słów o żydach," *Głos*, 4 (15/27 July 1889): 378–79; P., "'Nowa szlachta,'" *Głos*, 4 (2/14 September 1889): 461–62.

94. J. L. P., "Antysemityzm wśród inteligencyi," *Głos*, 4 (21 October/2 November 1889): 547–48.

95. "Z prasy," *Głos*, 5 (27 October/8 November 1890): 514–15.

96. Marian Bohusz, "Bez Obłudy," *Głos*, 4 (11/23 November 1889): 592–93. For an even more explicitly racial reading of anti-Semitism, see Z. J., "O antysemityzmie," *Głos*, 5 (24 March/5 April 1890): 165–67.

97. J. L. Popławski, "Liberalne wykręty," *Głos*, 5 (6/18 January 1890): 27.

98. J. K. Potocki, "Antysemityzm Głosu" *Głos*, 6 (12/24 January 1891): 38–39.

99. Witold Ziemiński, "Czem jest Izrael?" *Głos*, 5 (4/16 August–6/18 October 1890).

100. Witold Ziemiński, "Czem jest Izrael?" *Głos*, 5 (4/16 August 1890): 395.

101. Witold Ziemiński, "Czem jest Izrael?" *Głos*, 5 (18/30 August 1890): 422.

102. Witold Ziemiński, "Czem jest Izrael?" *Głos*, 5 (6/18 October 1890): 504.

103. Witold Ziemiński, "Czem jest Izrael?" *Głos*, 5 (1/13 September 1890): 445.

104. Witold Ziemiński, "Czem jest Izrael?" *Głos*, 5 (8/20 September 1890): 457.

105. Witold Ziemiński, "Czem jest Izrael?" *Głos*, 5 (15/27 September 1890): 469–70; and (6/18 October 1890): 504–7. A note a few weeks earlier had suggested that once settled in Palestine, the Jews would in fact change their nature, cultivate their "better characteristics, and bring something basically useful to the general treasury of humanity." "Z Prasy," *Głos*, 5 (18/30 August 1890): 423–24. This brief aside was not developed—nor could it be, without challenging the image of the Jew as racially immutable. Note the ambiguity in J. L. P., "Kolonizacyja żydowska," *Głos*, 5 (18/30 May 1891): 253–54.

106. Alfred Nossig, "Próba rozwiązania kwestji żydowskiej II," *Przegląd Społeczny*, 1 (September 1886): 231; "Próba rozwiązania kwestji żydowskiej III," *Przegląd Społeczny*, 1 (October 1886): 320; "Próba rozwiązania kwestji żydowskiej IV," *Przegląd Społeczny*, 1 (November 1886): 363. For more on Nossig, see Mendelsohn, "From Assimilation to Zionism." For another attempt at articulating a position for *Przegląd Społeczny* on the "Jewish question," see Iwan Franko, "Semityzm i antysemityzm w Galicji," *Przegląd Społeczny*, 2 (May 1887): 431–44.

107. J. L. Popławski, "Nowy zwrot w nauce prawa," *Głos*, 5 (8/20–15/27 December 1890): 616–17, 628–29.

108. A. P., "Walka o byt i moralność," *Głos*, 6 (29 June/11 July 1891): 330–31. This article was inspired by the work of the Russian sociologist S. Juzhakov.

109. Dmowski began contributing to *Głos* with a book review of Henryk Sienkiewicz's *Bez Dogmatu*. R. Skrzycki, "'Bez dogmatu.' Luźne notatki," *Głos*, 6 (24 August/5 September 1891): 428–29.

110. R. Skrzycki, "Z ekonomii interesów duchowych I," *Głos*, 7 (8/20 February 1892): 86–87.

111. R. Skrzycki, "Z ekonomii interesów duchowych II," *Głos*, 7 (15/27 February 1892): 98–100.

112. Świętochowski, "Liberalne bankructwa," *Prawda*, 3 (28/16 April 1883): 193–94.

113. "Geneva, 2 grudnia 1888," *Wolne Polskie Słowo*, 2 (15 December 1888): 4.

114. For more examples of this rhetoric, see "59ta rocznica," *Wolne Polskie Słowo*, 3 (15 December 1889): 1–2; "O powstaniach polskich z okazji tegorocznej rocznicy styczniowej," *Wolne Polskie Słowo*, 4 (1 February 1890): 1–2.

115. "Co robić?" *Wolne Polskie Słowo*, 4 (15 December 1890): 6–7. See also Dr. L. Górski, "Lagor, 30 lipca 1889," *Wolne Polskie Słowo*, 3 (15 August 1889): 3–4; Lynch, "Głos młodzieży z kraju. Polityka pokojowa a obrona czynna," *Wolne Polskie Słowo*, 3 (1 December 1889): 6–7; "Bern, 27 sierpnia 1892," *Wolne Polskie Słowo*, 6 (15 September 1892): 2–3; "Mowa Dra. Karola Lewakowskiego, członka izby deputowanych w Wiedniu na Kongresie Pokoju w Bernie, dnia 26 sierpnia 1892 roku." *Wolne Polskie Słowo*, 6 (15 September 1892): 4–5.

116. "Nasz z Moskwą rachunek," *Wolne Polskie Słowo*, 2 (15 May 1888): 1–2. See also "Polska wobec Europy," *Wolne Polskie Słowo*, 2 (1 September 1888): 1–2; "Petersburg, 10 października 1888," *Wolne Polskie Słowo*, 2 (1 November 1888): 3–4.

117. "Wyzwolenie narodu rosyjskiego," *Wolne Polskie Słowo*, 7 (1 September–15 October 1893). This last passage is from (1 October 1893): 2.

118. "Nasz z Moskwą rachunek," 2.

119. "Ruś a Polska," *Wolne Polskie Słowo*, 1 (15 September 1887): 2–3.

120. "Lwów, 20 czerwca 1890," *Wolne Polskie Słowo*, 4 (1 July 1890): 5.

121. "Głos z kraju. Przejawiające się obecnie śród nas dążności i kierunki," *Wolne Polskie Słowo*, 3 (1 November 1889), 4–5.

122. "Etnografja a polityka," *Wolne Polskie Słowo*, 4 (1 October 1890): 1–2.

123. "Dyplomacja rusińska," *Wolne Polskie Słowo*, 4 (1 September 1890): 1–2.

124. "Polska cała, wolna i niepodległa," *Wolne Polskie Słowo*, 4 (15 October 1890): 1–2.

125. "Z Rusi, październik 1896," *Wolne Polskie Słowo*, 10 (15 November 1896): 3.

126. "Lwów, w sierpniu 1890," *Wolne Polskie Słowo*, 4 (15 September 1890): 5.

127. "W obroży," *Wolne Polskie Słowo*, 5 (1 February 1891): 1–2.

128. "Z Porzecza Dnieprowego, wrzesień 1891," *Wolne Polskie Słowo*, 5 (1 October 1891): 2–3.

129. "Polska, Litwa i Ruś," *Wolne Polskie Słowo*, 9 (1 December 1895): 1–2.

130. Miłkowski, *Sprawa ruska*, 3–6, 62, 68, 86. Emphasis in the original. Miłkowski softened his tone a few years later when he finally broke with the National Democrats. See the 1910 re-edition of Miłkowski, *Rzecz*, 7. While this revision of Miłkowski's classic attracted little attention, *Sprawa ruska* did get reviewed in *Przegląd Wszechpolski*, 14 (January 1903): 67–70, where it was praised for demonstrating that the Ruthenians, not the Poles, started all the trouble.

Chapter Eight

1. Renan, 86.

2. Syzyf, "Z powodu pewnej broszury," *Przegląd Wszechpolski*, 4 (1 November 1898): 327.

3. Anderson; Hroch, 23.

4. The term *ethnie* is from Smith, 13.

5. Le Rider, particularly 294.

6. Pippin, 3.

7. Sternhell, *The Birth of Fascist Ideology*, 36–91.

8. Marinetti, 112–16.

9. Balicki, *Egoizm*, 58–60, 73.

10. Le Rider, 40.

11. Diego Iguenaza [Dmowski], "Listy do przyjaciela III," *Głos*, 9 (12/24 March 1894): 138–39.

12. Dmowski, "Podstawy polityki polskiej," *Przegląd Wszechpolski*, 11 (July 1905): 344.

13. Diego Iguenaza [Dmowski], "Listy do przyjaciela II," *Głos*, 9 (26 February/10 March 1894): 115–16.

14. R. Skrzycki [Dmowski], "Młodzież polska w zaborze rosyjskim VI," *Przegląd Wszechpolski*, 2 (15 March 1896): 124–25.

15. R. Skrzycki [Dmowski], "Młodzież polska w zaborze rosyjskim VIII," *Przegląd Wszechpolski*, 2 (15 April 1896): 173.

16. R. Skrzycki [Dmowski], "Młodzież polska w zaborze rosyjskim IX," *Przegląd Wszechpolski*, 2 (1 May 1896): 198–99. Dmowski's attitude toward women is only hinted at in the available documents. For some limited insight, see Wolikowska. See also the 1892 letter from Dmowski to Żeromski (PANK, Teka Zielińskiego, sygn. 7809), in which the former complains about his sex life while in Paris. For more on the linkage between nationalism and images of masculinity, see Mosse, *Confronting the Nation*, 46–47; Mosse, *Nationalism and Sexuality;* Parker et al., particularly 1–18.

17. Dmowski did not actually coin the term, although to my knowledge he was the first to use it in Polish. Paul Déroulède employed the same phrase as early as 1870, although its meaning in France was not quite as stark as it would become for the National Democrats. See Sternhell, "Paul Déroulède," 51.

18. R. Skrzycki [Dmowski], "Młodzież polska w zaborze rosyjskim IV," *Przegląd Wszechpolski*, 2 (15 February 1896): 77–80.

19. I. Za-wskiego, "Etyka i polityka," *Przegląd Wszechpolski*, 7 (January 1901): 19.

20. Dmowski, *Myśli*, 41, 75.

21. Balicki, *L'organisation*, 16–18. See also Balicki, *Hedonizm*, 2.

22. Balicki, *Hedonizm*, 24–27.

23. Balicki, *Hedonizm*, 30.

24. Balicki, *Hedonizm*, 31–32, 35–38.

25. Balicki, *Egoizm*, 37. See also 4–7, 29, 47–48, 75.

26. Balicki, *Egoizm*, 19, 37–38.

27. J. Elski, "O 'Egoizmie Narodowym' Zygmunta Balickiego," *Teka*, 4 (October 1902): 430–37.

28. Balicki, *Egoizm*, 58.

29. Balicki, *Egoizm*, 56–57.

30. I. Za-wskiego, "Etyka i polityka," *Przegląd Wszechpolski*, 7 (January 1901): 21–22.

31. For an attempt to credit the Endecja with an ethnic definition of the nation, see Kozicki, 456; Shelton, in Sugar, *Eastern European Nationalism*, 267; Tomasz Wituch, "Przedmowa do obecnego wydania," in Dmowski, *Polityka polska*, 17. For alternative views, see Toporowski, 385; Porter, "Who Is a Pole," 639–53; Wapiński, *Narodowa Demokracja*, 17; Wapiński, "Z dziejów tendencji nacjonalistycznych," 826; Zimand, "Uwagi," 9, 13.

32. Dmowski, "Szkice polityczne z zakresu kwestyi polskiej: ogólny rzut oka na sprawę polską w chwili obecnej," *Kwartalnik Naukowo-Polityczny i Społeczny*, 1 (1898): 23–43, in Dmowski, *Dziesięć lat walki*, 5.

33. The Rappersville collection eventually grew into an impressive archive on Polish history and was used as the repository for the documents of the Polish League and the National League. It was moved to Warsaw after 1918 and was burned during the Nazi invasion. Thus the largest source of documents related to the topics explored in this book was destroyed.

34. Zygmunt Wasilewski, *Życiorys, 1865–1939* (PANW, sygn. 127), 81. Excerpts of this text have been reprinted as "Życiorys," in Wasilewski, *Pokolenia*, 13–14, 68, 81.

35. Vistalanus, "Białoruś a Białolechia," *Przegląd Wszechpolski*, 1 (1 February 1895): 33–37. The term *lachy* was used by Ukrainians as a derogatory label for Poles, but some Poles took it as a reference to a prehistoric, proto-Polish tribe (linked to a foundation myth about the brothers Lech, Czech, and Ruś).

36. Victor [Popławski], "'Nasza sprawa,'" *Przegląd Wszechpolski*, 3 (15 May 1897), in Popławski, *Pisma*, 1:166. For a similar argument, see Sieciech, "Na manowcach wszechsłowiańskich," *Przegląd Wszechpolski*, 6 (September 1900): 529–40.

37. [Dmowski], "Jedność narodowa," *Przegląd Wszechpolski*, 1 (15 March 1895): 82. Emphasis in the original.

38. [Popławski], "Szkodliwe mrzonki," *Przegląd Wszechpolski*, 4 (1 July 1898), in Popławski, *Pisma*, 1:210; [Popławski], "Polityka słowiańska," *Przegląd Wszechpolski*, 3 (15 December 1897), in Popławski, *Pisma*, 1:203.

39. [Popławski], "Polityka autonomiczna w Austryi," *Kwartalnik Naukowo-Polityczny i Społeczny*, 1 (1898), in Popławski, *Pisma*, 2:164. Elsewhere an anonymous contributor wrote that "a nation can preserve its language and lose its nationality, and, inversely, lose its language and preserve a living national sentiment." Ligeza, "Listy z zaboru pruskiego," *Przegląd Wszechpolski*, 9 (September 1903), 708.

40. [Popławski], "Nasz demokratyzm," *Przegląd Wszechpolski*, 6 (March 1900), in Popławski, *Pisma*, 1:110–11.

41. In 1901 he argued that Gdańsk (Danzig), along with all of West Prussia, would eventually become Polish. This, he believed, was "beyond doubt." [Popławski], "Jubileusz Pruski," *Przegląd Wszechpolski*, 7 (January 1901), in Popławski, *Pisma*, 1:241.

42. [Popławski], "Żywioł polski w Galicyi Wschodniej," *Przegląd Wszechpolski*, 9 (April-May 1903), in Popławski, *Pisma*, 2:337.

43. [Dmowski], "Jedność narodowa," *Przegląd Wszechpolski*, 1 (15 March 1895): 82.

44. Dmowski, *Myśli*, 26.

45. Balicki, *Egoizm*, 56–57.

46. Wasilewski, "O kulturze duchowej," *Przegląd Wszechpolski*, 11 (July 1905): 431. See also Wasilewski, "Nowy Konrad," in Wasilewski, *Śladami Mickiewicza*, 233.

47. Dmowski, *Myśli*, 28, 36.

48. Dmowski, "Podstawy polityki polskiej," *Przegląd Wszechpolski*, 11 (July 1905): 334–60.

49. G. Topór [T. Grużewski], "Naród, tradycya i postęp cywilizacyjny," *Przegląd Wszechpolski*, 11 (July 1905): 410.

50. Dmowski, "Podstawy," 340–41. Dmowski had recently returned from a trip to the Far East, during which he became convinced of Japanese superiority over what he now called the "individualism" of England.

51. Andrzej Walicki suggested this distinction to me in a personal letter of 19 May 1997.

52. Kozicki, *Pamiętniki* (AHRL, sygn. P-127), 138–40.

53. Dmowski to Miłkowski, 23 January 1902 (PANK, Teka Zielińskiego, sygn. 7808, no. 13).

54. G. Topór [T. Grużewski], "Europejska opinia i polski humanitaryzm," *Przegląd Wszechpolski*, 7 (December 1901): 718–22.

55. This is from a review of Balicki's *Egoizm* by Topór [Grużewski] in *Przegląd Wszechpolski*, 8 (March 1902): 222.

56. "Ustawa Ligi Polskiej" (December, 1887), in Kozicki, 487, 489–90. Almost identical language can be seen in a declaration of cooperation between the Polish League and Limanowski's "National-Socialist Commune," signed in January, 1889. "Umowa Ligi Narodowej [sic—should be Polskiej] z Paryską Gminą Narodowo-Socjalistyczną," in Pobóg-Malinowski, "Do historii Ligi Narodowej III," *Niepodległość*, 7 (1933): 433.

57. Irena Koberdowa, "Materiały II Zjazdu Delegatów Ligi Polskiej w Ouarville w 1889 r.," *Z pola walki*, 3, no. 83 (1978): 215–23.

58. *Z dzisiejszej doby III*, 10.

59. "Lietuviai!" (Warsaw, 1894) (PANK, Teka Zielińskiego, sygn. 7783, no. 1). This is the Lithuanian original. A Polish translation appears in Pobóg-Malinowski, *Narodowa Demokracja*, 104.

60. "Do ludów podwładnych panowaniu rosyjskiemu," Komitet Centralny Ligi Narodowej, Warsaw 1894" (PANK, Teka Zielińskiego, sygn. 7783, no. 13). The same text is reprinted in Pobóg-Malinowski, *Narodowa Demokracja*, 99–100.

61. [Dmowski], "Słowo wstępne," *Przegląd Wszechpolski*, 1 (1 January 1895): 1–4.

62. Dmowski, *Polityka polska*, 59–61; and "Relacja," 420. The original copy of this document is in PANW, Teka Kozickiego, sygn. 30.

63. "Do narodów słowiańskich," Komitet Centralny Ligi Narodowej, Warsaw 1894 (PANK, Teka Zielińskiego, sygn. 7783, no. 14). This text is also reprinted in Pobóg-Malinowski, *Narodowa Demokracja*, 98.

64. "Russkomu obshchestvu," Warsaw, 1894 (PANK, Teka Zielińskiego, sygn. 7783, no. 1). For a Polish translation, see Pobóg-Malinowski, *Narodowa Demokracja*, 101–2.

65. No title, Warsaw, March 1895 (PANK, Teka Zielińskiego, sygn. 7783, no. 25). Emphasis added. A similar discussion of hatred can be found in *Z dzisiejszej doby X*, 38.

66. No title, January 1894, Warsaw (PANK, Teka Zielińskiego, sygn. 7783, no. 9).

67. *Z dzisiejszej doby X*, 10.

68. [Dmowski], *Z dzisiejszej doby XI*, 16.

69. They repeatedly used the term "realism" to describe themselves. See Dmowski, *Myśli*, 12, 14; [Dmowski], "Program 'Wszechpolski,'" *Przegląd Wszechpolski*, 8 (September 1902), in Dmowski, *Dziesięć lat walki*, 76; Kozicki, *Historia*, 452; Popławski, "Stosunek prawno-polityczny Królestwa Polskiego do Rosyi," *Przegląd Wszechpolski*, 11 (July 1905), in Popławski, *Pisma*, 406; Seyda, 15; Wasilewski, *Śladami Mickiewicza*, 211, 241, 264; Wasilewski, *Współcześni*, 67–69.

70. [Dmowski], "Ojczyzna i doktryny," *Przegląd Wszechpolski*, 8 (May 1902), in Dmowski, *Dziesięć lat walki*, 49. Emphasis in the original.

71. "Niepodległa Polska a polityka chwili bieżącej," *Przegląd Wszechpolski*, 3 (1 July 1897), 287. See also Popławski, "Polityka polska w zaborze pruskim," *Przegląd Wszechpolski*, 5 (January 1899), in Popławski, *Pisma*, 2:186; and "Manifest pokojowy cara," *Przegląd Wszechpolski*, 4 (15 September 1898): 276–77.

72. Balicki, *Niepodległość wewnętrzna*, 5. This was an offprint from *Kwartalnik Naukowo-Polityczny i Społeczny*, 1 (1898): 1–22.

73. Balicki, *Egoizm narodowy*, 66.

74. [Dmowski], "Istota walki narodowej," *Przegląd Wszechpolski*, 8 (February 1902), in Dmowski, *Dziesięć lat walki*, 102.

75. R. Skrzycki [Dmowski], "Szowinizm," *Przegląd Wszechpolski*, 9 (November 1903), in Dmowski, *Dziesięć lat walki*, 124.

76. Dmowski, *Myśli*, 64.

77. "Zamachy na patrjotyzm polski," *Wolne Polskie Słowo*, 10 (15 July 1896): 1–2.

78. Balicki, *Egoizm*, 42–43.

79. Balicki, *Hedonizm*, 39.

80. Ksiądz Polak, "Rząd i my," *Dla Swoich*, 57. This copy of *Dla Swoich*, the only one still existing (as far as I could determine), has lost its cover page, so more detailed publication data is unavailable. The article itself was dated 22 May 1903. The magazine is located in PANK, Teka Zielińskiego, sygn. 7784.

81. [Popławski], "Program Stronnictwa Demokratyczno-Narodowego w zaborze rosyjskim," *Przegląd Wszechpolski*, 3 (1 June 1897): 243.

82. "Nad grobem polityki ugodowej w zaborze pruskim," *Przegląd Wszechpolski*, 3 (1 March 1897): 99. The final words are in English in the original.

83. Civis, "Przeszacowanie wartości politycznych," *Przegląd Wszechpolski*, 7 (October 1901): 580.

84. [Popławski], "Nasz patryotyzm i nasza taktyka," *Przegląd Wszechpolski*, 5 (May 1899), in Popławski, *Pisma*, 1:66–68.

85. Dmowski, *Myśli*, 26.

86. Dmowski, *Myśli*, 14.

87. R. Skrzycki [Dmowski], "Szowinizm," *Przegląd Wszechpolski*, 9 (November 1903), in *Pisma*, 121. See also *Myśli*, 28.

88. Dmowski, *Myśli*, 14.

89. Studnicki, "Patryotyzm a antagonizmy narodowe," *Tydzień*, 22–24 (July 1902), in Studnicki, 360–62.

90. Dmowski to Miłkowski, 27 January 1903 (PANK, Teka Zielińskiego, sygn. 7808, no. 20). This letter is also reprinted in Kulakowski, 1:249–50.

91. Balicki, *Egoizm*, 58.

92. Balicki, *Egoizm*, 68, 72–73.

93. *Pochodnia*, 1 (May 1899): 3–4; "Z dzisiejszej doby," *Pochodnia*, 1 (June 1899): 3.

94. [Dmowski], *Z dzisiejszej doby II*, in Dmowski, *Dziesięć lat walki*, 257.

95. [Dmowski] *Z dzisiejszej doby XI*, 20–21.

96. Dmowski, "Relacja," 421.

97. Student, "Z zaboru rosyjskiego. Warszawa d. 10 października," *Przegląd Wszechpolski*, 1 (15 October 1895): 302. Emphasis in the original.

98. "Rosyanie w Polsce," *Przegląd Wszechpolski*, 1 (15 September 1895), 261–62.

99. Studnicki, "Patryotyzm," 374–75.

100. The text of this declaration is reprinted in full in Nawroczyński, 235–36.

101. "Z dzisiejszej doby," *Pochodnia*, 1 (May 1899): 2.

102. B. O., "Nasz 'szowinizm,'" *Przegląd Wszechpolski*, 2 (15 October 1896): 460–63. This attitude toward the Russians was not abandoned after 1905, even though Dmowski (against much opposition from within his own movement) adopted a policy of tactical cooperation with the Russian government. In his own mind, he was dealing with Petersburg politicians much as a diplomat might negotiate with an enemy. He never accepted the old argument that one should cooperate with "good Russians," and work with them to build a more democratic empire; there was always a clear distinction between Dmowski's form of

ugoda and more traditional approaches to Russo-Polish cooperation. For Dmowski's own account of that period, see *Polityka polska*, 108–32.

103. [Popławski], "Polityka polska w zaborze pruskim," 184.

104. [Popławski], "Polityka polska w zaborze pruskim," 179. See also [Popławski], "Podwójna polityka," *Przegląd Wszechpolski*, 6 (August 1900), in Popławski, *Pisma*, 1:98.

105. "Germanizacya," *Przegląd Wszechpolski*, 2 (15 May 1896): 217–20. See also "Wyzwalanie się ludu," *Przegląd Wszechpolski*, 2 (15 October 1896): 457–60.

106. Dmowski, "Ogólny rzut oka," 11, 20; [Dmowski], "Istota walki narodowej," *Przegląd Wszechpolski*, 8 (February 1902), in Dmowski, *Dziesięć lat walki*, 99. Popławski advanced similar ideas in "Bez złudzeń," *Przegląd Wszechpolski*, 4 (1 February 1898), in Popławski, *Pisma*, 2:96.

107. St. Komornicki, "Powracająca fala," *Przegląd Wszechpolski*, 1 (15 February 1895): 55.

108. Dmowski, *Myśli*, 88–89.

109. Studnicki, "Nowych ludzi plemię," *Tygodnik Polski*, (24 October 1903), in Studnicki, 377.

110. "Nowe zadania," *Przegląd Wszechpolski*, 3 (1 January 1897): 1.

111. Dmowski, *Myśli*, 29, 75.

112. Balicki, *Egoizm*, 80–90.

113. Dmowski, *Myśli*, 14.

114. G. Topór [T. Grużewski], "Odbudowania Polski III," *Przegląd Wszechpolski*, 9 (August 1903): 575–76. See also [Dmowski], "Państwa rozbiorcze jako teren polityki polskiej," *Przegląd Wszechpolski*, 10 (January 1904), in Dmowski, *Dziesięć lat walki*, 162–64.

115. Balicki, *Niepodległość wewnętrzna*, 16.

116. "Z zaboru rosyjskiego," *Przegląd Wszechpolski*, 4 (1 March 1898): 70.

117. "Polityka polska pod panowaniem moskiewskiem," *Polak*, 3 (January 1898): 5.

118. "Niepodległa Polska," 285.

119. [Popławski], "Realizm polityczny i przyszła Polska," *Przegląd Wszechpolski*, 5 (March 1899), in Popławski, *Pisma*, 1:88.

120. [Popławski], "Polityka autonomiczna," 164–65.

121. [Dmowski], "Nasze cele i nasze drogi," *Przegląd Wszechpolski*, 11 (January 1905), in Dmowski, *Dziesięć lat walki*, 372.

122. [Popławski], "Polityka autonomiczna," 164–65.

123. Dmowski, "Podstawy," 345–49.

124. [Popławski], "Realizm polityczny," 90.

125. Dmowski, *Myśli*, 74.

126. Popławski itemized these two types of "national expansion" in "Zadania polityki narodowej na kresach," *Przegląd Wszechpolski*, 9 (August–September 1903), in Popławski, *Pisma*, 366.

127. G. Topór [T. Grużewski], "Odbudowanie Polski IV," *Przegląd Wszechpolski*, 9 (September 1903), 661; Dmowski, "Polityka zagraniczna," *Przegląd Wszechpolski*, 8 (January 1902): 45, 49–51; Popławski, "Zadania polityki narodowej na kresach," 366.

128. "Ruszczenie i dyplomacya," *Przegląd Wszechpolski*, 1 (15 December 1895): 344.

129. Dmowski, *Myśli*, 32, 66.

130. Dmowski, *Myśli*, 69–71. The mention of colonies was not an idle suggestion. Dmowski traveled to a Polish colony in Paraná, Brazil, and the idea was raised several times on the pages of *Przegląd Wszechpolski*. Popławski, in an unusual moment of despair, suggested that a colony might be Poland's only hope for survival. [Popławski], "Kilka uwag w

sprawie kolonizacyi polskiej," *Przegląd Wszechpolski*, 5 (October 1899), in Popławski, *Pisma*, 2:203.

131. Panek, 11.

132. W. B., "Polityka i historya II," *Przegląd Wszechpolski*, 6 (March 1900): 151.

133. "Program Stronnictwa Demokratyczno-Narodowego w zaborze rosyjskim," *Przegląd Wszechpolski*, 9 (October 1903): 726.

134. [Dmowski], "Państwa rozbiorcze," 172.

135. J. L. Jastrzębiec, "Z całej Polski," *Przegląd Wszechpolski*, 8 (January 1902): 43.

136. Untitled. Wilno, September 1904 (BN DŻS Teka IB13).

137. Popławski, "Sprawa Ruska," in Popławski, *Pisma*, 299–300. No source is given for this essay.

138. "Nasze stanowisko na Litwie i Rusi," *Przegląd Wszechpolski*, 2 (15 April 1896): 169–72.

139. "Program Stronnictwa Demokratyczno-Narodowego," (1903): 732–33.

140. Dmowski, *Myśli*, 87.

141. Dębicki, 79–81.

142. R. Skrzycki [Dmowski], "Listy Warszawiaka z Galicyi VI," *Przegląd Wszechpolski*, 3 (1 April 1897): 152. Curiously, he never even considered the possibility that East Galicia might remain subject to Vienna.

143. See, for example, the selection of topics examined in Conolly, "The 'Nationalities Question' in the Last Phase of Tsardom," in Oberländer, 152–81; Kastelianskii; Sussex; Sugar, *Eastern European Nationalism.*

144. R. Skrzycki [Dmowski], "Listy Warszawiaka z Galicyi, VII," *Przegląd Wszechpolski*, 3 (15 April 1897): 173.

145. Dmowski, "Podstawy," 347.

146. A. P., "O potrzebie podniesienia ruchu umysłowego," *Teka*, 3 (March 1901): 103–10.

147. [Popławski], "Nasz demokratyzm," 109–10.

148. [Popławski], "Żywioł polski w Galicyi wschodniej," 352–53.

149. Popławski, "Sprawa Ruska," 299–300.

150. "Program Stronnictwa Demokratyczno-Narodowego w zaborze rosyjskim. Dodatek A: działalność stronnictwa w odrębnych warunkach Krajów Zabranych a w szczególności Litwy," *Przegląd Wszechpolski*, 9 (October 1903): 756.

151. Dmowski, "Podstawy," 347–48.

152. Popławski, "Pochodzenie i istota syonizmu," *Przegląd Wszechpolski*, 8 (November 1902), in Popławski, *Pisma*, 252–53, 257.

153. Stanisław Głąbiński, *Wspomnienia polityczne* (Pelplin: Sp. z O. ODP, n.d.), 50, 53.

154. R. Skrzycki [Dmowski], "Wymowne cyfry," *Przegląd Wszechpolski*, 1 (15 May 1895): 147.

155. [Dmowski], "Nasze dziesięciolecie," *Przegląd Wszechpolski*, 11 (July 1905), in Dmowski, *Dziesięć lat walki*, 242.

156. Popławski, "Pochodzenie i istota syonizmu," 248–49.

157. J. L. Jastrzębiec, "Z całej Polski," *Przegląd Wszechpolski*, 3 (1 March 1897): 104–5.

158. J. L. Jastrzębiec, "Z całej Polski," *Przegląd Wszechpolski*, 3 (1 March 1897): 104–5.

159. J. L. Jastrzębiec, "Z całej Polski," *Przegląd Wszechpolski*, 3 (15 August 1897), 363–64.

160. "Sprawozdanie za rok 1904–1905. Komitet Centralny Ligi Narodowej do Komisji Nadzorczej Skarbu Narodowego Polskiego," in Pobóg-Malinowski, ed. "Do historji Ligi

Narodowej," *Niepodległość*, 10 (1934): 288. This document was dated 4 August 1905. The original no longer exists, but copies can be found in PANK, Teka Zielińskiego, sygn. 7783.

161. "Kwestya robotnicza w programie demokratyczno-narodowym," *Przegląd Wszechpolski*, 9 (April 1903): 249.

162. [Dmowski], "Listy warszawskie," *Przegląd Wszechpolski*, 9 (June 1903): 617, 621.

163. R. Skrzycki [Dmowski], "Wymowne cyfry," 147. See also Popławski, "Pochodzenie i istota syonismu," 263.

164. [Dmowski], "Półpolacy," *Przegląd Wszechpolski*, 8 (November 1902), in Dmowski, *Dziesięć lat walki*, 103–8. One could also translate this sentence more strongly as "the race of 'half-Poles' must die." The key term here—*zginąć*—is defined by *Mały słownik języka polskiego*, 1002, as "to endure death, to lose life, to be killed, to fall," although an alternative second meaning, "to cease to exist, to vanish," could suggest a slightly less violent (although roughly equivalent) message.

Dmowski did not actually use the word "Jew" to identify the object of his attack, but his meaning was clear. Lest there be any doubt, he defined the "coalition of half-Poles" in another article as a "throng of young, shrill Israelites" along with all the political enemies of the Endecja (the *ugoda*, the socialists, and the positivists). Dmowski, "Dziwna koalicja," in Dmowski, *Dziesięć lat walki*, 110. The editors of *Dziesięć lat walki* state that this article appeared in the December 1902 issue of *Przegląd Wszechpolski*, but in fact it did not. Neither was it in any issue from 1903. It is apparent from the text that it was written shortly after the "Półpolacy" article of November 1902, so we can only assume either that it was not published or that it appeared in a different magazine.

165. J. L. Jastrzębiec, "Z całej Polski," *Przegląd Wszechpolski*, 3 (15 April 1897): 178. The article that inspired Popławski's response was "Po wyborach w Galicyi," *Przegląd Wszechpolski*, 3 (1 April 1897): 147.

166. J. L. Jastrzębiec, "Z całej Polski," *Przegląd Wszechpolski*, 4 (1 July 1898): 197.

167. The manifesto was cited by Ignotus [Dmowski], "Listy warszawskie," *Przegląd Wszechpolski*, 9 (June 1903): 460–61.

Conclusion

1. Zweig, 5.

2. As cited by Mendel, 112

3. Michnik, *Church*, 128. See also Isaiah Berlin, "Introduction," in Venturi, xxvi; Mendel, 115–16.

4. Kozicki, *Historia*, 452. For similar descriptions of National Democratic "realism," see Seyda, 15; and Wasilewski, *Współcześni*, 67–69.

5. [Dmowski], "Ojczyzna i doktryny," *Przegląd Wszechpolski*, 8 (May 1902), in Dmowski, *Dziesięć lat walki*, 55.

6. [Dmowski], "Polityczna konieczność," *Przegląd Wszechpolski*, 2 (February 1905), in Dmowski, *Dziesięć lat walki*, 380.

7. R. Dmowski, "Nowa powieść społeczna (uwagi o 'Ziemi Obiecanej' Wł. St. Reymonta)," *Przegląd Wszechpolski*, 2 (February 1899): 88–89.

8. Popławski, "O modernistach," *Melitele* (1899)," in Popławski, *Szkice*, 176. These last words were in English in the original. For similar descriptions of modern democracy, see [Dmowski], 'Wobec kryzysu rosyjskiego," *Przegląd Wszechpolski*, 6 (June 1904), in Dmowski, *Dziesięć lat walki*, 310–11; G. Topór [T. Grużewski], "Dawne i obecne pojęcia o Rosyi," *Przegląd*

Wszechpolski, 1 (January 1902): 14; Topór, "Istota państwowości rosyjskiej," *Przegląd Wszechpolski*, 7 (July 1902): 500–501.

9. Andrzej Bryk, "The Hidden Complex of the Polish Mind: Polish–Jewish Relations During the Holocaust," in Polonsky, *"My Brother's Keeper?"* 164. See also Walicki, "nacjonalizm liberalny," 32–50; and Gerö, 196.

Selected Bibliography

Archives

Archiwum Akt Nowych, Zbiór PPS (AAN PPS)
Archiwum Historii Ruchu Ludowego (AHRL)
Archiwum Polskiej Akademii Nauk w Krakowie (PANK)
Archiwum Polskiej Akademii Nauk w Warszawie (PANW)
Biblioteka Narodowa, Dokumenty Życia Społecznego (BN DŻS)
Biblioteka Narodowa, Zbiór Rękopisów (BNZR)

Periodicals

Ateneum, 1876–1888
Dla Swoich, 1903
Gazeta Narodowa, 1872
Głos, 1886–1894
Kurier Warszawski, 1883–1886
Kwartalnik Naukowo–Polityczny i Społeczny, 1898
Niwa, 1873–1874
Nowiny, 1883
Pobudka, 1889
Pochodnia, 1899–1902
Polak, 1896–1902
Prawda, 1881–1890
Przedświt, 1891–1896
Przegląd Katolicki, 1883–1905
Przegląd Powszechny, 1896–1905
Przegląd Socjalistyczny, 1892–1893
Przegląd Społeczny, 1886–1887

Przegląd Tygodniowy, 1866–1886
Przegląd Wszechpolski, 1895–1905
Teka, 1899–1904
Wolne Polskie Słowo, 1887–1899

Published Sources

Alter, Peter. *Nationalism*. Translated by Stuart McKinnon-Evans. London: Edward Arnold, 1985.

Anderson, Benedict. *Imagined Communities: Reflections of the Origin and Spread of Nationalism*. London: Verso, 1983.

Armstrong, John A. *Nations before Nationalism*. Chapel Hill: The University of North Carolina Press, 1982.

Askenazy, Szymon. *Uniwersytet Warszawski*. Warsaw: Gebethner i Wolff, 1905.

Baczko, Bronisław, ed. *Towarzystwo Demokratyczne Polskie: Dokumenty i pisma*. Warsaw: Książka i Wiedza, 1954.

Balicki, Zygmunt. *Egoizm narodowy wobec etyki*. 3rd ed. Lwów: Towarzystwo Wydawnicze, 1914.

———. *Hedonizm jako punkt wyjścia etyki*. Warsaw: Przegląd Filozoficzny, 1900.

———. *L'organisation spontanée de la société politique*. Paris: V. Giard & E. Briere, 1895.

———. *Metody nauk społecznych i ich rozwój w XIX stuleciu*. Warsaw: E. Wende, 1903.

———. *Niepodległość wewnętrzna*. Lwów: Przegląd Wszechpolski, 1898.

———. *Parlamentaryzm*. Lwów: H. Altenberg / Warsaw: E. Wende i Spółka, 1900.

———. *Uwagi krytyczne nad socyalizmem współczesnym*. Lwów: Przegląd Wszechpolski, 1898.

Bartoszewski, Władysław, and Antony Polonsky, eds. *The Jews in Warsaw: A History*. London: Basil Blackwell, 1991.

Battistelli, Fabrizio. "War and Militarism in the Thought of Herbert Spencer." *International Journal of Comparative Sociology*, 34 (1993): 192–209.

Baumgarten, Leon. *Dzieje Wielkiego Proletariatu*. Warsaw: Książka i Wiedza, 1966.

Ben-Ghiat, Ruth. "Fascism, Writing and Memory: The Realist Aesthetic in Italy, 1930–1950." *Journal of Modern History*, 67 (September 1995): 627–65.

Bhabha, Homi K., ed. *Nation and Narration*. New York: Routledge, 1990.

Błaszczyk, L. T., and J. Danielewicz. "Szkoła Główna Warszawska (1862–1869) i jej rola w kształtowaniu się ideologii pozytywistycznej." *Przegląd Nauk Historycznych i Społecznych*, 2 (1952): 159–84.

Blejwas, Stanislaus A. "Polish Positivism and the Jews." *Jewish Social Studies*, 46 (1984): 21–36.

———. *Realism in Polish Politics: Warsaw Positivism and National Survival in Nineteenth Century Poland*. New Haven: Yale Concilium on International and Area Studies, 1984.

———. "Warsaw Positivism: Patriotism Misunderstood." *The Polish Review*, 27 (1982): 47–54.

Blit, Lucjan. *The Origins of Polish Socialism: The History and Ideas of the First Polish Socialist Party, 1878–1886*. Cambridge, England: Cambridge University Press, 1971.

Blobaum, Robert. *Feliks Dzierżyński and the SDKPiL: A Study of the Origins of Polish Communism*. Boulder, Col.: East European Monographs, 1984.

———. *Rewolucja: Russian Poland, 1904–1907*. Ithaca, N.Y.: Cornell University Press, 1995.

Bobińska, Celina. "Spór o ujęcie pozytywizmu i historyków pozytywistów." *Kwartalnik Historyczny*, 61 (1954): 178–204.

Bobińska, Celina, and Jerzy Wyrozumski, eds. *Spór o historyczną szkolę krakowską*. Kraków: Wydawnictwo Literackie, 1969.

Bogacz, Marian. *Akademicy Warszawy: z dziejów organizacji studenckich w XIX wieku*. Warsaw: Iskra, 1960.

Boudou, Adrian T. J. *Stolica Święta a Rosja*. Translated by Zofia Skowrońska. Kraków: Wydawnictwo Księży Jezuitów, 1928.

Breton, Albert, Gianluigi Galeotti, Pierre Salmon, and Ronald Wintrobe, eds. *Nationalism and Rationality*. Cambridge, England: Cambridge University Press, 1995.

Breuilly, John. *Nationalism and the State*. New York: St. Martin's Press, 1982.

Bromke, Adam. *Poland's Politics: Idealism versus Realism*. Cambridge, Mass.: Harvard University Press, 1967.

Brubaker, Rogers. *Citizenship and Nationhood in France and Germany*. Cambridge, Mass.: Harvard University Press, 1992.

Brykalska, Maria. *Aleksander Świętochowski: biografia*. Warsaw: Państwowy Instytut Wydawniczy, 1987.

———. *Aleksander Świętochowski: redaktor Prawdy*. Wrocław: Ossolineum, 1974.

Brzeziński, Edmund. "Wspomnienia z mojego życia." *Niepodległość*, 4 (1931): 44–70.

Buckle, Henry Thomas. *Historja cywilizacji w Anglji*. Translated by Władysław Zawadzki. Lwów: Karol Wild, 1864–1868.

———. *History of Civilization in England*. 2nd ed. New York: D. Appleton, 1875.

Burke, Edmund. *Reflections on the Revolution in France*. Edited by J. G. A. Pocock. Indianapolis: Hackett Publishing Company, 1987.

———. *The Works of the Right Honorable Edmund Burke*. 4th ed. Boston: Little, Brown and Company, 1871.

Burrow, J. W. *Evolution and Society: A Study in Victorian Social Theory*. Cambridge, England: Cambridge University Press, 1966.

Cała, Alina. *Asymilacja Żydów w Królestwie Polskim, 1864–1897: postawy, konflikty, stereotypy*. Warsaw: Państwowy Instytut Wydawniczy, 1989.

Carlen, Claudia, ed. *The Papal Encyclicals, 1740–1878*. Raleigh, N.C.: McGrath, 1981.

Carr, Edward Hallett. *Nationalism and After*. New York: Macmillan, 1945.

Ceysingerówna, Helena. "Działalność okresu konspiracyjnego." *Bluszcz*, 58 (27 June 1925): 707–8.

Charlton, D. G. *Positivist Thought in France during the Second Empire, 1852–1870*. Oxford: Clarendon Press, 1959.

Chatterjee, Partha. *The Nation and Its Fragments: Colonial and Postcolonial Histories*. Princeton: Princeton University Press, 1993.

———. *Nationalist Thought and the Colonial World: A Derivative Discourse*. Minneapolis: University of Minnesota Press, 1986.

Chmielowski, Piotr. *Pisma krytycznoliterackie*. Edited by Henryk Markiewicz. Warsaw: Państwowy Instytut Wydawniczy, 1961.

Chrzanowski, Ignacy. *Optymizm i pesymizm polski: studia z historii kultury*. Warsaw: Państwowe Wydawnictwo Naukowe, 1971.

Cieszkowski, August. *Prolegomena do historiozofii, Bóg i palingeneza oraz mniejsze pisma filozoficzne z lat 1838–1842*. Edited by J. Garewicz and A. Walicki. Warsaw: Państwowe Wydawnictwo Naukowe, 1972.

Cole, Juan R. I. "Marking Boundaries, Marking Time: The Iranian Past and the Construction of the Self by Qajar Thinkers." *Iranian Studies*, 29 (Winter/Spring 1996): 35–56.

Cooper, Frederick. "Conflict and Connection: Rethinking Colonial African History." *American Historical Review*, 99 (December 1994): 1515–45.

Corrsin, Stephen D. *Warsaw before the First World War: Poles and Jews in the Third City of the Russian Empire 1880–1914*. Boulder, Col.: East European Monographs, 1989.

Cottam, Kazimiera Janina. *Bolesław Limanowski (1835–1935)*. Boulder: East European Quarterly, 1978.

Cywiński, Bohdan. *Ogniem próbowane: z dziejów najnowszych Kościoła katolickiego w Europie środkowo-wschodniej*. Rzym: Papieski Instytut Studiów Kościelnych, 1982.

———. *Rodowody niepokornych*. Warsaw: Biblioteka 'Więzi,' 1971.

Czarnecki, Paweł. *Młody Kasprowicz a grupa warszawskiego 'Głosu.'* Poznań: Fundusz Naukowy Senatu Uniwersytetu Poznańskiego, 1935.

Czepulis-Rastenis, Ryszarda, ed. *Inteligencja polska pod zaborami*. Warsaw: Państwowe Wydawnictwo Naukowe, 1978.

Dąbrowski, Józef [J. Grabiec]. *Czerwona Warszawa przed ćwierć wiekiem: moje wspomnienia*. Poznań: Karol Rzepecki, 1925.

Daszyński, Feliks [Ślaz]. *Pod pręgierz! Szopka wigilii bożego narodzenia*. Paris: Wydawnictwo Polskiej Partyi Socjalno-Rewolucyjnej, 1889.

Davies, Norman. *God's Playground*. New York: Columbia University Press, 1982.

Dębicki, Zdzisław. *Iskry w popiołach: wspomnienia lwowskie*. Poznań: Księgarnia Św. Wojciecha, n.d.

Deutsch, Karl W. *Nationalism and Social Communication*. 2nd ed. Cambridge, Mass.: MIT Press, 1966.

Dirks, Nicholas B., Geoff Eley, and Sherry B. Ortner, eds. *Culture/Power/History: A Reader in Contemporary Social Theory*. Princeton: Princeton University Press, 1994.

Djakow, W. A. "Polski ruch wyzwoleńczy w latach trzydziestych i czterdziestych XIX stulecia." *Kwartalnik Historyczny*, 84, no. 4 (1977): 977–88.

Dmowski, Roman. *Dziesięć lat walki: zbiór prac i artykułów publikowanych do 1905 roku*. Volume 3 of *Pisma*. Częstochowa: Antoni Gmachowski, 1938.

———. *Gawędy sąsiedzkie*. Kraków: Wydawnictwo Stronnictwa Demokratyczno–Narodowego, 1900.

———. *Myśli nowoczesnego Polaka*. 7th ed. London: Koło Młodych Stronnictwa Narodowego, 1953.

———. *Polityka polska i odbudowanie państwa*. Warsaw: Pax, 1988.

———. "Relacja Romana Dmowskiego o Lidze Narodowej." Edited by Andrzej Garlicki. *Przegląd Historyczny*, 57 (1966): 415–43.

———. *Z dzisiejszej doby II: nasz patriotyzm*. Kraków: Paweł Madejski, 1893.

Drozdowski, Marian Marek, and Andrzej Zahorski. *Historia Warszawy*. 3rd ed. Warsaw: Państwowe Wydawnictwo Naukowe, 1981.

Drozdowski, Marian Marek, Jerzy Myśliński, Janusz Sujecki, and Anna Żarnowska, eds. *Stulecie Polskiej Partii Socjalistycznej, 1892–1992*. Warsaw: Gryf, 1993.

Duara, Prasenjit. *Rescuing History from the Nation: Questioning Narratives of Modern China*. Chicago: University of Chicago Press, 1995.

Dylągowa, Hanna. *Duchowieństwo katolickie wobec sprawy narodowej, 1764–1864*. Lublin: Wydawnictwo Towarzystwa Naukowego KUL, 1983.

Dziamski, Seweryn, ed. *Myśl socjalistyczna i marksistowska w Polsce, 1878–1939*. Warsaw: Państwowy Wydawnictwo Naukowe, 1984.

Dziewanowski, M. K. *The Communist Party of Poland*. Cambridge, Mass.: Harvard University Press, 1959.

Edie, James M., James P. Scanlan, and Mary-Barbara Zeldin. *Russian Philosophy*. Knoxville: The University of Tennessee Press, 1976.

Eisenbach, Artur. *The Emancipation of the Jews in Poland, 1780–1870*. Edited by Antony Polonsky. Translated by Janina Dorosz. Oxford: Basil Blackwell, 1991.

———. *Wielka Emigracja wobec kwestii żydowskiej, 1832–1849*. Warsaw: Państwowe Wydawnictwo Naukowe, 1976.

Eisenbach, Artur, D. Fajnhauz, and A. Wein, eds. *Żydzi a powstanie styczniowe*. Warsaw: Państwowe Wydawnictwo Naukowe, 1963.

Eley, Geoff. *Reshaping the German Right: Radical Nationalism and Political Change after Bismarck*. New Haven: Yale University Press, 1980.

Eley, Geoff, and Ronald Grigor Suny, eds. *Becoming National: A Reader*. New York: Oxford University Press, 1996.

Endelman, Todd M. "Jewish Converts in Nineteenth-Century Warsaw: A Quantitative Analysis." *Jewish Social Studies*, 4 (Fall 1997): 28–59.

Engel, David. "Poles, Jews, and Historical Objectivity." *Slavic Review*, 46 (Fall/Winter 1987): 568–90.

Fischer, George. *Russian Liberalism: From Gentry to Intelligentsia*. Cambridge, Mass.: Harvard University Press, 1958.

Fountain, Alvin Marcus. *Roman Dmowski: Party, Tactics, Ideology*. Boulder, Col.: East European Monographs, 1980.

Fox, Richard G., ed. *Nationalist Ideologies and the Production of National Cultures*. Washington, D.C.: American Anthropological Association, 1990.

Fuks, Marian. *Prasa żydowska w Warszawie, 1823–1939*. Warsaw: Państwowe Wydawnictwo Naukowe, 1979.

Gella, Aleksander, ed. *The Ward-Gumplowicz Correspondence: 1897–1909*. New York: Essay Press, 1971.

Gellner, Ernest. *Nations and Nationalism*. Oxford: Basil Blackwell, 1983.

Gerö, András. *Modern Hungarian Society in the Making: The Unfinished Experience*. Translated by James Patterson and Enikö Koncz. Budapest: Central European University Press, 1995.

Giddens, Anthony. *The Consequences of Modernity*. Stanford, Cal.: Stanford University Press, 1990.

Gierowski, Józef Andrzej, ed. *Dzieje kultury politycznej w Polsce*. Warsaw: Państwowe Wydawnictwo Naukowe, 1977.

Gieysztor, Aleksander, et al., eds. *History of Poland*. Warsaw: Polskie Wydawnictwo Naukowe, 1968.

Głąbiński, Stanisław. *Wspomnienia polityczne*. Pelplin: Sp. z O. ODP, 1939.

Gockowski, Janusz, and Andrzej Walicki, eds. *Idee i koncepcje narodu w polskiej myśli politycznej czasów porozbiorowych*. Warsaw: Państwowe Wydawnictwo Naukowe, 1977.

Grabski, Andrzej Feliks. "Warszawscy entuzjaści H. T. Buckle'a: z dziejów warszawskiego pozytywizmu." *Kwartalnik Historyczny*, 76 (1969): 853–63.

Greenfeld, Liah. *Nationalism: Five Roads to Modernity*. Cambridge, Mass.: Harvard University Press, 1992.

Grzybowski, Konstanty. *Ojczyzna—Naród—Państwo*. Warsaw: Państwowy Instytut Wydawniczy, 1970.

Gumplowicz, Ludwik. *Outline of Sociology*. Translated from the German by Irving L. Horowitz. New York: Paine-Whitman, 1963.

———. *System Socyologii*. Warszawa: Spółka Nakładowa, 1887.

Hagen, William W. "Before the 'Final Solution': Toward a Comparative Analysis of Political Anti-Semitism in Interwar Germany and Poland." *The Journal of Modern History*, 68 (June 1996): 351–81.

————. *Germans, Poles and Jews: The Nationality Conflict in the Prussian East, 1772–1914*. Chicago: University of Chicago Press, 1980.

Halecki, Oskar. *A History of Poland*. New York: Roy Publishers, 1943.

Handelsman, Marceli. *Rozwój narodowości nowoczesnej*. Warsaw: Gebethner i Wolff, 1926.

Hass, Ludwik. "Pokolenia inteligencji Królestwa Polskiego." *Przegląd Historyczny*, 65 (1974): 285–313.

Hayek, F. A. *The Counter-Revolution of Science: Studies on the Abuse of Reason*. 2nd ed. Indianapolis: Liberty Press, 1979.

Hayes, Carlton J. H. *The Evolution of Modern Nationalism*. New York: The Macmillan Company, 1931.

Heck, Roman, ed. *Studia nad rozwojem narodowym Polaków, Czechów, i Słowaków*. Wrocław: Ossolineum, 1976.

Hertz, Friedrich. *Nationality in History and Politics: A Study of the Psychology and Sociology of National Sentiment and Character*. London: Kegan Paul, Trench, Trubner & Co., 1944.

Hertz, Aleksander. *The Jews in Polish Culture*. Translated by Richard Lourie. Edited by Lucjan Dobroszycki. Evanston: Northwestern University Press, 1988.

Heybowicz-Herburt, Stanisław [I. Snitko]. *Zarys pojęć o narodzie*. Lwów: n.p., 1901.

Hillebrandt, Bogdan. *Polskie organizacje młodzieżowe XIX i XX wieku*. Warsaw: Młodzieżowa Agencja Wydawnicza, 1986.

————, ed. *Postępowe organizacje młodzieżowe w Warszawie, 1864–1976*. Warsaw: Państwowe Wydawnictwo Naukowe, 1988.

Himmelfarb, Gertrude. *Darwin and the Darwinian Revolution*. 2nd ed. New York: Norton, 1962.

Hłasko, Józef. "W redakcji 'Głosu' (wspomnienia z r. 1887–1895)." *Gazeta Warszawska* 265–92 (1–23 September 1932).

Hobsbawm, E. J. *Nations and Nationalism since 1780: Programme, Myth, Reality*. Cambridge, England: Cambridge University Press, 1990.

Hochfeldowa, Anna, and Barbara Skarga, eds. *Filozofia i myśl społeczna w latach 1865–1895*. Warsaw: Państwowe Wydawnictwo Naukowe, 1980.

————, eds. *Z historii filozofii pozytywistycznej w Polsce. Ciągłość i przemiany*. Wrocław: Ossolineum, 1972.

Hroch, Miroslav. *Social Preconditions of National Revival in Europe: A Comparative Analysis of the Social Composition of Patriotic Groups among the Smaller European Nations*. Translated by Ben Fowkes. Cambridge, U.K.: Cambridge University Press, 1985.

Hundert, Gershon. *The Jews in a Polish Private Town: The Case of Opatów in the Eighteenth Century*. Baltimore: Johns Hopkins, 1992.

Huth, Alfred Henry. *The Life and Writings of Henry Thomas Buckle*. New York: D. Appleton, 1880.

Huxley, Thomas. *Evolution and Ethics and Other Essays*. New York: D. Appleton, 1896.

Ihnatowicz, Ireneusz, Antoni Mączak, and Benedykt Zientara. *Społeczeństwo polskie od X do XX wieku*. Warsaw: Książka i Wiedza, 1979.

Itenberg, Boris S. *P. L. Lavrov v russkom revoliutsionnom dvizhenii*. Moscow: Nauka, 1988.

Jabłonowski, Władisław. *Z biegiem lat (wspomnienia o Romanie Dmowskim)*. Częstochowa: A. Gmachowski, 1939.

Jabłoński, Henryk. *U źródeł teraźniejszości*. Warsaw: Wiedza, 1947.

Jakubowska, Urszula. *Prasa narodowej demokracji w dobie zaborów*. Warsaw: Państwowe Wydawnictwo Naukowe, 1988.

Jaszczuk, Andrzej. *Spór pozytywistów z konserwatystami o przyszłość Polski, 1870–1903.* Warsaw: Państwowe Wydawnictwo Naukowe, 1986.

Jedlicki, Jerzy. *Jakiej cywilizacji Polacy potrzebują: studia z dziejów idei i wyobraźni XIX wieku.* Warsaw: Panstwowe Wydawnictwo Naukowe, 1988.

Jeleński, Jan. *Żydzi, Niemcy i my.* Warsaw: Jan Noskowski, 1876.

Jeske-Choiński, Teodor. *Pozytywizm w nauce i literaturze.* Warsaw: Gebethner i Wolff, 1908.

———. *Na schyłku wieku.* Warsaw: Wiek, 1894.

Kaczyńska, Elżbieta. *Dzieje robotników przemysłowych w Polsce pod zaborami.* Warsaw: Państwowe Wydawnictwo Naukowe, 1970.

Kalabiński, Stanisław. *Antynarodowa polityka endecji w rewolucji 1905–1907.* Warsaw: Państwowe Wydawnictwo Naukowe, 1955.

Kalabiński, Stanisław, and Ryszard Kołodziejczyk, eds. *Warszawa Popowstaniowa, 1864–1918.* Warsaw: Państwowe Wydawnictwo Naukowe, 1968.

Kalembka, Sławomir, ed. *Powstanie Styczniowe 1863–1864: wrzenie, bój, Europa, wizje.* Warsaw: Państwowe Wydawnictwo Naukowe, 1990.

Kamenka, Eugene, ed. *Nationalism: The Nature and Evolution of an Idea.* Canberra: Australian National University Press, 1973.

Kancewicz, Jan. *Rozłam w polskim ruchu robotniczym na początku lat dziewięćdziesiątych XIX wieku.* Warsaw: Książka i Wiedza, 1961.

Kareev, Nikolai I. "Profesura w Warszawie." Translated by Irena Lewandowska and Witold Dąbrowski. *Przegląd Historyczny,* 69 (1978): 263–78.

Kastelianskii, A. I., ed. *Formy natsional'nago dvizheniia v sovremennykh gosudarstvakh: Avstro-Vengriia, Rossiia, Germaniia.* Petersburg: Obshchestvennaia pol'za, 1910.

Katz, Jacob. *From Prejudice to Destruction: Anti-Semitism, 1700–1933.* Cambridge, Mass.: Harvard University Press, 1980.

Kawyn, Stefan. *Ideologia stronnictw politycznych w Polsce wobec Mickiewicza, 1890–1899.* Lwów: Filomaty, 1937.

Kedourie, Elie. *Nationalism.* London: Hutchinson University Library, 1960.

Kelles-Krauz, Kazimierz. *Pisma wybrane.* Warsaw: Książka i Wiedza, 1962.

Kemilainen, Aira. *Nationalism: Problems Concerning the Word, the Concept and Classification.* Jyväskylä, Finland: Jyväskylän Kasvatusopillinen Korkeakoulu, 1964.

Kern, Stephen. *The Culture of Time and Space, 1880–1918.* Cambridge, Mass.: Harvard University Press, 1983.

Kieniewicz, Stefan. *Dramat trzeźwych entuzjastów: o ludziach pracy organicznej.* Warsaw: Wiedza Powszechna, 1964.

———. *The Emancipation of the Polish Peasantry.* Chicago: University of Chicago Press, 1969.

———. *Historia Polski 1795–1918.* Warsaw: Państwowe Wydawnictwo Naukowe, 1987.

———. "Uprisings and Organic Work in the Nineteenth Century." *East European Quarterly,* 19, no. 4 (January 1986): 395–401.

———, ed. *Dzieje Uniwersytetu Warszawskiego, 1807–1915.* Warsaw: Państwowe Wydawnictwo Naukowe, 1981.

Kieval, Hillel. *The Making of Czech Jewry: National Conflict and Jewish Society in Bohemia, 1870–1918.* New York: Oxford University Press, 1988.

Kindersley, Richard. *The First Russian Revisionists: A Study of 'Legal Marxism' in Russia.* Oxford: Clarendon Press, 1962.

Klier, John Doyle. *Imperial Russia's Jewish Question, 1855–1881.* Cambridge, England: Cambridge University Press, 1995.

Klimaszewski, Bolesław, ed. *An Outline History of Polish Culture*. Translated by Krystyna Mroczek. Warsaw: Interpress, 1984.

Kłoczowski, Jerzy, ed. *Chrześcijaństwo w Polsce: zarys przemian, 966–1979*. Lublin: Towarzystwo Naukowe Katolickiego Uniwersytetu Lubelskiego, 1992.

Kmiecik, Zenon. "Oblicze społeczno-polityczne 'Głosu' (1886–1899)," *Przegląd Humanistyczny*, 10–12 (1981): 39–51.

―――. *Prasa warszawska w latach 1886–1904*. Wrocław: Ossolineum, 1989.

Kohn, Hans. *The Idea of Nationalism: A Study in Its Origins and Background*. New York: The Macmillan Company, 1956.

―――. *Pan-Slavism: Its History and Ideology*. New York: Vintage Books, 1960.

―――. *Prelude to Nation-States: The French and German Experience, 1789–1815*. Princeton: D. Van Nostrand Company. 1967.

Kołakowski, Leszek. *Positivist Philosophy from Hume to the Vienna Circle*. Translated by Norbert Guterman. Harmondsworth, England: Penguin Books, 1972.

Kołodziejczyk, Ryszard, ed. *Historia polskiego ruchu robotniczego do 1890 roku*. Warsaw: Książka i Wiedza, 1985.

Kormanowa, Żanna, and Irena Pietrzak-Pawłowska, eds. *Historia Polski*. Volume III, Part 1 (1850/1864–1900). Warszawa: Państwowe Wydawnictwo Naukowe, 1963.

Konarski, Kazimierz. *Nasza szkoła: księga pamiątkowa warszawskiej szkoły realnej. Tom I: dzieje warszawskiej szkoły realnej*. Warsaw: Stowarzyszenia wychowawców b. gimnazjum i b. szkoły realnej w Warszawie, 1932.

Koprukowniak, Albin. *Program Brukselski*. Lublin: Wydawnictwo Lubelskie, 1978.

Kornilov, A. A. *Obshchestvennoe dvizhenie pri Aleksandr II*. Moscow: A. I. Mamontova, 1909.

Korotyński, Władysław. *Losy szkolnictwa w Królestwie Polskim*. Warszawa: E. Wende, 1906.

Kosmowska, I. W. *Związki młodzieży polskiej*. Warsaw: M. Ostaszewska, 1924.

Kościesza, Zbigniew. *Ćwierćwiecze walki. Księga pamiątkowa Roli*. Warsaw: n.p., 1910.

Koszutski, Stanisław. *Walka młodzieży polskiej o wielkie ideały: wspomnienia z czasów gimnazjalnych i uniwersyteckich: Siedlce, Kielce, Warszawa, Kijów, Berlin, Paryż (1881–1900)*. Warsaw: Dom Książki Polskiej, 1928.

Kozicki, Stanisław. *Historia Ligi Narodowej*. London: Myśl Polska, 1964.

Kozłowska-Sabatowska, Halina. *Ideologia pozytywizmu galicyjskiego, 1864–1881*. Wrocław: Ossolineum, 1978.

Kozłowski, Władysław. *Pisma filozoficznie-psychologicznie*. Lwów: Wydawnictwo Polskie, n.d.

Kramer, Lloyd. "Historical Narratives and the Meaning of Nationalism," *Journal of the History of Ideas*, 58 (July 1997): 525–45.

Kraushar, Aleksander [Alkar]. *Czasy szkolne za Apukhtina: kartka z pamiętnika (1879–1897)*. Warsaw: S. Orgelbrand, 1915.

Król, Marcin. *Konserwatyści a niepodległość: studia nad polską myślą konserwatywną XIX wieku*. Warsaw: Pax, 1985.

―――, ed. *Stańczycy: antologia myśli społecznej i politycznej konserwatystów krakowskich*. Wrocław: Pax, 1985.

Krusiński, Stanisław. *Pisma zebrane*. Warsaw: Książka i Wiedza, 1958.

Krzesławski, J. "Spoliczkowanie Apukhtina." *Kronika Ruchu Rewolucyjnego w Polsce*, 4 (July/August/September 1939): 129–64.

Krzywicki, Ludwik. *Wspomnienia*. Warsaw: Czytelnik, 1947–1959.

Kulak, Teresa. *Jan Ludwik Popławski, 1854–1908. Biografia polityczna*. Wrocław: Wydawnictwo Uniwersytetu Wrocławskiego, 1989.

Kulak, Teresa, and Krzysztof Kawalec. "The Attitude of the National Democracy to the Jewish Question (1893–1939)." *Polish Western Affairs*, 34 (January 1993): 67–89.

Kulakowski, Mariusz, ed. *Roman Dmowski w świetle listów i wspomnień*. London: Gryf, 1968.

Kulczycka-Saloni, Janina, ed. *Pozytywizm*. Warsaw: Państwowe Zakłady Wydawnictw Szkolnych, 1971.

———. *Pozytywizm i Żeromski*. Warsaw: Państwowe Wydawnictwo Naukowe, 1977.

———. *Życie literackie Warszawy w latach 1864–1892*. Warsaw: Państwowy Instytut Wydawniczy, 1970.

Kulczycki, Ludwik. *Narodowa Demokracja*. Warsaw: Przegląd Społeczny, 1907.

Kurczewska, Joanna. "Dwie postawy wobec kryzysu etosu demokratyczno-patriotycznego: Bolesław Limanowski (1835–1935) i Zygmunt Balicki (1858–1916)," *Archiwum Historii Filozofii i Myśli Społeczne*, 21 (1975): 202–9.

———. *Naród w socjologii i ideologii polskiej. Analiza porównawcza wybranych koncepcji z przełomu XIX i XX wieku*. Warsaw: Państwowe Wydawnictwo Naukowe, 1979.

Kurkiewicz, Władysław, et al., eds. *Tysiąc lat dziejów Polski: kalendarium*. 5th ed. Warsaw: Ludowa Spółdzielnia Wydawnicza, 1974.

Labuda, Aleksander Wit. "O pojęciu 'świadomość narodowa.'" In *Kultura średniowieczna i staropolska*. Edited by Danuta Gawinowa et al. Warsaw: Państwowe Wydawnictwo Naukowe, 1991.

Leatherbarrow, W. J., and D. C. Offord, eds. *A Documentary History of Russian Thought from the Enlightenment to Marxism*. Ann Arbor, Mich.: Ardis, 1987.

Łepkowski, Tadeusz. *Polska—narodziny nowoczesnego narodu, 1764–1870*. Warsaw: Państwowe Wydawnictwo Naukowe, 1967.

Leslie, R. F. *Reform and Insurrection in Russian Poland, 1856–1865*. London: Athlone Press, 1963.

Levine, Hillel. *Economic Origins of Anti-Semitism: Poland and Its Jews in the Early Modern Period*. New Haven: Yale University Press, 1991.

Lewis, Richard D. "Revolution in the Countryside: Russian Poland, 1905–1906." *The Carl Beck Papers in Russian and East European Studies*, 506 (December, 1986): 1–57.

Libelt, Karol. *O miłości ojczyzny*. n.p., 1909.

Liebich, André. *Between Ideology and Utopia: The Politics and Philosophy of August Cieszkowski*. Dordrecht, Holland: D. Reidel, 1979.

Limanowski, Bolesław. *Pamiętniki*. Warsaw: Książka i Wiedza, 1958.

———. *Patriotyzm i socjalizm*. Geneva: Drukarnia Polska, 1881.

———. *Socjologia Augusta Comte'a*. Lwów: n.p., 1875.

Llobera, Josep R. *The God of Modernity: The Development of Nationalism in Western Europe*. Providence, R.I.: Berg, 1994.

Łojek, Jerzy. *Prasa polska w latach 1864–1918*. Warsaw: Państwowe Wydawnictwo Naukowe, 1976.

Ludwikowski, Rett. *Continuity and Change in Poland: Conservatism in Polish Political Thought*. Washington, D.C.: Catholic University of America Press, 1991.

———. *Konserwatyzm Królestwa Polskiego w okresie międzypowstaniowym*. Kraków: Uniwersytet Jagielloński, 1976.

de Maistre, Joseph. *The Works of Joseph de Maistre*. Edited and translated by Jack Lively. New York: Macmillan, 1965.

Mallon, Florencia E. *Peasant and Nation: The Making of Postcolonial Mexico and Peru*. Berkeley: University of California Press, 1995.

———. "The Promise and Dilemma of Subaltern Studies: Perspectives from Latin American History." *American Historical Review*, 99 (December 1994): 1491–515.

Mannheim, Karl. *Conservatism: A Contribution to the Sociology of Knowledge.* Edited and translated by David Kettler, Volker Meja, and Nico Stehr. London: Routledge & Kegan Paul, 1986.

Marczewski, Jerzy. *Narodowa Demokracja w Poznańskiem, 1900–1914.* Warsaw: Państwowe Wydawnictwo Naukowe, 1967.

Marinetti, Filippo Tommaso. *Let's Murder the Moonshine: Selected Writings.* Edited and translated by R. W. Flint and Arthur Coppotelli. Los Angeles: Sun and Moon Classics, 1991.

Markiewicz, Henryk. *Idee patriotyzmu i demokracji w literaturze pozytywistycznej.* Kraków: Polska Akademia Nauk, 1969.

———. *Pozytywizm.* Warsaw: Państwowe Wydawnictwo Naukowe, 1978.

Marx, Karl. *Capital: A Critique of Political Economy.* Translated by Ben Fowkes. New York: Vintage Books, 1977.

———. "Communism, Revolution and a Free Poland." In *The Marx and Engels WWW Library* (http://csf.colorado.edu/cgi-cin/mfs/24/csf/web/psn/marx/Archive/1848–Pole/index.html).

Marx, Karl, and Frederick Engels. *Marks i Engels o Polsce.* Warsaw: Książka i Wiedza, 1971.

Maslowski, Ludwik. *Prawo Postępu. Studjum przyrodniczo-społeczne.* Kraków: Czcionkami 'Kraju,' 1872.

Materyały do historyi PPS i ruchu rewolucyjnego w zaborze rosyjskim od r. 1893–1904. Warsaw: Życie, 1907.

Mazgaj, Paul. "The Origins of the French Radical Right: A Historiographical Essay." *French Historical Studies*, 15 (Fall 1987): 287–315.

Meducka, Marta, and Regina Renz, eds. *Kultura żydów polskich XIX–XX wieku.* Kielce: Kieleckie Towarzystwo Naukowe, 1992.

Mendel, Arthur P. *Dilemmas of Progress in Tsarist Russia: Legal Marxism and Legal Populism.* Cambridge, Mass.: Harvard University Press, 1961.

Mendelsohn, Ezra. "From Assimilation to Zionism: The Case of Alfred Nossig." *Slavonic and East European Review*, 49 (October 1971): 521–34.

———. *The Jews of East Central Europe between the World Wars.* Bloomington: Indiana University Press, 1984.

Micewski, Andrzej. *Roman Dmowski.* Warsaw: Wydawnictwo Verum, 1971.

Michel, Patrick. *Politics and Religion in Eastern Europe: Catholicism in Hungary, Poland and Czechoslovakia.* Translated by Alan Braley. London: Polity Press, 1991.

Michnik, Adam. *The Church and the Left.* Translated by David Ost. Chicago: University of Chicago Press, 1993.

———. *Szanse polskiej demokracji: artykuły i eseje.* London: Aneks, 1984.

Mickiewicz, Adam. *Księgi narodu polskiego i pielgrzymstwa polskiego.* Warsaw: Czytelnik, 1986.

———. *Les Slaves: Cours professé au Collège de France. 1842–1844.* Paris: Musée Adam Mickiewicz, 1914.

Miłkowski, Zygmunt. *Odpowiedź na adresy młodzieży polskiej.* Kraków: Nowa Reforma, 1883.

———. *Rzecz o obronie czynnej i o skarbie narodowym.* Paris: Adolf Reiff, 1887.

———. *Rzecz o obronie czynnej i o skarbie narodowym: wydanie nowe, rozszerzone i do stosunków obecnych zastosowane.* Kraków: Drukarnia Literacka, 1910.

———. *Sprawa ruska w stosunku do sprawy polskiej.* Lwów: Związek Wydawniczy, 1902.

Mill, John Stuart. *Autobiografia.* Warsaw: Przegląd Tygodniowy, 1882.

———. *Essays on Politics and Culture.* Edited by Gertrude Himmelfarb. Gloucester, Mass: Peter Smith, 1973.

————. *Logika*. Translated and edited by Adolf Dygasiński. Warsaw: Przegląd Tygodniowy, 1879.

————. *O rządzie reprezentacyjnym*. Translated by Gustaw Czernicki. Kraków: Wydawnictwo Dzieł Tanich i Pożytecznych, 1866.

————. *O wolności*. Translated by Juliusz Starkel. Lwów: E. Winiarz, 1864.

————. *O zasadzie użyteczności (Utilitarianizm)*. Translated by Feliks Bogacki. Warsaw: Przegląd Tygodniowy, 1873.

————. *Poddaństwo kobiet*. Translated by F. T. Rakowicz. Toruń: J. Buszczyński, 1870.

————. *Utilitarianism, Liberty and Representative Government*. New York: E. P. Dutton, 1950.

————. *Zasady ekonomiji politycznej z niektóremi zastosowaniami do ekonomiji społecznej*. Translated by R. P. i B. Petersburg: J. Ohryzko, 1859–1860.

Miłosz, Czesław. *The History of Polish Literature*. 2nd ed. Berkeley: University of California Press, 1983.

Minogue, K. R. *Nationalism*. New York: Basic Books, 1967.

Mistewicz, Teodor. "Uwagi na marginesie nowej biografii Romana Dmowskiego." *Dzieje Najnowsze*, 4 (1980): 169–89.

Mochnacki, Maurycy. *Poezja i czyn: wybór pism*. Edited by Stanisław Pieróg. Warsaw: Ludowa Spółdzielnia Wydawnicza, 1987.

Modras, Ronald. *The Catholic Church and Antisemitism: Poland, 1933–1939*. Chur, Switzerland: Harwood Academic Publishers, 1994.

Modzelewski, Wojciech. *Naród i postęp: problematyka narodowa w ideologii i myśli społecznej pozytywistów warszawskich*. Warsaw: Państwowe Wydawnictwo Naukowe, 1977.

Molska, Alina, ed. *Pierwsze pokolenie marksistów polskich: wybór pism i materiałów źródłowych z lat 1878–1886*. Warsaw: Książka i Wiedza, 1962.

Mosse, George. *Confronting the Nation: Jewish and Western Nationalism*. Hanover, N.H.: University Press of New England, 1993.

————. *Nationalism and Sexuality: Respectability and Abnormal Sexuality in Modern Europe*. New York: H. Fertig, 1975.

————. *The Nationalization of the Masses: Political Symbolism and Mass Movements in Germany from the Napoleonic Wars through the Third Reich*. New York: H. Fertig, 1975.

Mosse, W. E. *Alexander II and the Modernization of Russia*. London: The English Universities Press, 1958.

Myśliński, Jerzy. "Prasa wydawana przez Ligę Narodową w Krakowie przed 1905 rokiem." *Rocznik Historii Czasopiśmiennictwa Polskiego*, 2 (1963): 32–56.

Naimark, Norman M. *The History of the "Proletariat": The Emergence of Marxism in the Kingdom of Poland, 1870–1887*. Boulder, Col.: East European Quarterly, 1979.

————. *Terrorists and Social Democrats: The Russian Revolutionary Movement under Alexander III*. Cambridge, Mass.: Harvard University Press, 1983.

Nałęcz, Tomasz. *Irredenta Polska*. Warsaw: Książka i Wiedza, 1992.

Narkiewicz, Olga A. *The Green Flag: Polish Populist Politics, 1867–1970*. Totowa, N.J.: Rowman and Littlefield, 1976.

Nawroczyński, Bogdan, ed. *Nasza walka o szkołę polską, 1901–1917*. Warsaw: Książnica-Atlas, 1932.

Nettl, J. P. *Rosa Luxemburg*. London: Oxford University Press, 1966.

Nowak, Andrzej. *Między carem a rewolucją: studium politycznej wyobraźni i postaw Wielkiej Emigracji wobec Rosji 1831–1849*. Warsaw: Gryf, 1993.

Oberländer, Erwin, et al., eds. *Russia Enters the Twentieth Century*. New York: Schocken Books, 1971.

Ochorowicz, Julian. *Wstęp i pogląd ogólny na filozofie pozytywna.* Warszawa: J. Noskowski, 1872.

Odpowiedź na broszurę: o obronie czynnej i o skarbie narodowym. Kraków: Anczyc i Spółka, 1889.

Offord, Derek. *The Russian Revolutionary Movement in the 1880s.* Cambridge, England: Cambridge University Press, 1986.

Ognisko: książka zbiorowa wydana dla uczczenia 25 letniej pracy T. T. Jeża. Warsaw: K. Kowalewski, 1882.

Olszer, Krystyna M., ed. *For Our Freedom and Yours: The Polish Progressive Spirit from the Fourteenth Century to the Present.* 2nd ed. New York: F. Ungar, 1981.

Opalski, Magdalena. "Polish-Jewish Relations and the January Uprising: The Polish Perspective." *Polin*, 1 (1986): 68–80.

Opalski, Magdalena, and Israel Bartal, *Poles and Jews: A Failed Brotherhood.* Hanover, N.H.: University Press of New England, 1992.

Orzeszkowa, Eliza. *O żydach i kwestyi żydowskiej.* Wilno: Wydawnictwo E. Orzeszkowej i Spółki, 1882.

———. *Patryotyzm i kosmopolityzm: studyum społeczne.* Wilno: Wydawnictwo E. Orzeszkowej i Spółki, 1880.

Orzechowski, Marian. *Rewolucja, socjalizm, tradycje: przeszłość narodowa i tradycje w myśli politycznej rewolucyjnego nurtu polskiego ruchu robotniczego.* 2nd ed. Warsaw: Książka i Wiedza, 1984.

Osvobozhdenie krest'ian. Moscow: Nauchnoe Slovo, 1911.

Pachoński, Jan. *Jeszcze polska nie zginęła. W 175-lecie powstania polskiego hymnu narodowego.* Wrocław: Ossolineum, 1972.

Pąkciński, Marek. *Konserwatyzm na rozdrożu: 'młodzi konserwatyści' warszawscy wobec ideowych dylematów schyłku XIX wieku.* Warsaw: Instytut Badań Literackich, 1994.

Pamiętnik zjazdu b. wychowawców Szkół Lubelskich. Lublin: Komisja Zjazdu, 1926.

Panek, Piotr. *Zasady gospodarki narodowej.* Lwów: Związek Wydawniczy, 1903.

Parker, Andrew, et al., eds. *Nationalisms and Sexualities.* New York: Routledge, 1992.

Paul, Ellen Frankel. "Herbert Spencer: The Historicist as a Failed Prophet." *Journal of the History of Ideas*, 44 (October 1983), 619–38.

Payne, Stanley. *Fascism: Comparison and Definition.* Madison: University of Wisconsin Press, 1980.

Peck, Abraham J. *Radicals and Reactionaries: The Crisis of Conservatism in Wilhelmine Germany.* Washington, D.C.: University Press of America, 1978.

Peel, D. Y. *Herbert Spencer: The Evolution of a Sociologist.* Brookfield, Vermont: Gregg Revivals, 1992.

Pepłowski, Franciszek. *Słownictwo i frazeologia polskiej publicystyki okresu oświecenia i romantyzmu.* Warsaw: Państwowy Instytut Wydawniczy, 1961.

Perl, Feliks [Res]. *Dzieje ruchu socjalistycznego w zaborze rosyjskim.* Warsaw: Wydawnictwo "Życie," 1910.

Petrusewicz, K., and A. Straszewicz, eds. *Materiały do dziejów myśli ewolucyjnej w Polsce.* Warsaw: Państwowe Wydawnictwo Naukowe, 1963.

Piątkowski, Wiesław. "Idee społeczno-polityczne 'Polaka' 1896–1906: Przyczynek do kształtowania się ideologii Narodowej Demokracji." *Rocznik Historii Czasopiśmiennictwa Polskiego*, 5, no. 2 (1966): 45–65.

Pick, Daniel. *War Machine: The Rationalization of Slaughter in the Modern Age.* New Haven: Yale University Press, 1993.

Pigoń, Stanisław. *Miłe życia drobiazgi.* Warsaw: Państwowy Instytut Wydawniczy, 1964.

Piltz, Erazm [Scriptor]. *Nasza Młodzież*. Kraków: W. L. Anczyc, 1903.

———. *Nasze stronnictwa skrajne*. Kraków: W. L. Anczyc, 1903.

Piotrowski, Mirosław, ed. *Na przełomie stuleci: naród-kościół-państwo w XIX i XX wieku*. Lublin: Klub Inteligencji Katolickiej, 1997.

Pippin, Robert B. *Modernism as a Philosophical Problem: On the Dissatisfactions of European High Culture*. Oxford: Blackwell, 1991.

Platz, Stephanie. "Pasts and Futures: Space, History and Armenian Identity, 1988–1994." Doctoral dissertation, University of Chicago, 1996.

Pobóg-Malinowski, Władysław. "Do historii Ligi Narodowej." *Niepodległość*, 7–10 (1933–34).

———. *Najnowsza historia polityczna Polski*. 2nd ed. London: B. Świderski, 1963.

———. *Narodowa Demokracja, 1887–1918: fakty i dokumenty*. Warsaw: Polska Zjednoczona, 1933.

Podgórski, Wojciech Jerzy. *Pieśń ojczyzny pełna: Mazurek Dąbrowskiego w dziejowych rolach*. Warsaw: Wydawnictwo Sejmowe, 1994.

Polonsky, Antony, ed. *From Shtetl to Socialism: Studies from Polin*. Washington, D.C.: The Littman Library of Jewish Civilization, 1993.

———, ed. *"My Brother's Keeper?" Recent Polish Debates on the Holocaust*. New York: Routledge, 1990.

Polonsky, Antony, Jakub Basista, and Andrzej Link-Lenczowski, eds. *The Jews in Old Poland 1000–1795*. New York: I. B. Tauris, 1993.

Pomper, Philip. *Peter Lavrov and the Russian Revolutionary Movement*. Chicago: University of Chicago Press, 1972.

Popławski, Jan Ludwik. *Pisma polityczne*. Edited by Zygmunt Wasilewski. Kraków and Warsaw: Gebethner i Wolff, 1910.

———. *Szkice literackie i naukowe*. Warsaw: Księgarnia E. Wende, 1910.

Porter, Brian. "The Construction and Deconstruction of Nineteenth-Century Polish Liberalism." In *Historical Reflections on Central Europe*. Edited by Stanislav J. Kirschbaum. New York: Macmillan, 1999.

———. "Konstrukcja i dekonstrukcja liberalizmu polskiego 19ego wieku," *Studia Polityczne*, 6 (1996): 81–102.

———. "The Social Nation and Its Futures: English Liberalism and Polish Nationalism in Late Nineteenth-Century Warsaw," *American Historical Review*, 101 (December 1996): 1470–92.

———. "Who Is a Pole and Where Is Poland? Territory and Nation in the Rhetoric of Polish National Democracy before 1905." *Slavic Review*, 51 (Winter 1992): 639–53.

Potocki, J. K. *Współzawodnictwo i współdziałanie*. Lwów: Towarzystwa Wydawnicze, 1900.

Prakash, Gyan. "Subaltern Studies as Postcolonial Criticism." *American Historical Review*, 99 (December 1994): 1475–90.

Procesy polityczne w Królestwie Polskim: materjały do historji ruchu rewolucyjnego w Królestwie Polskim: materjały z okresu 1878–1885: zeszyt 1, rok 1878–1879. Kraków: Wydawnictwo Materjałów do Historji Ruchu Rewolucyjnego w Królestwie Polskim, 1907.

Próchnik, Adam. "Budowa i odsłonięcie pomnika Mickiewicza w Warszawie." *Kronika Ruchu Rewolucyjnego w Polsce*, 3 (January/February/March 1937): 1–12.

———. "Ideologja 'Proletarjatu.'" *Kronika Ruchu Rewolucyjnego w Polsce*, 2 (January/February/March 1936): 1–17.

Prus, Bolesław. *Wybór kronik i pism publicystycznych*. Edited by Zygmunt Szweykowski. Warsaw: Spółdzielnia Wydawnicza 'Książka,' 1948.

Przyborowski, Walery. *Stara i młoda prasa. Przyczynek do historyi literatury ojczystej (1866–1872)*. Petersburg: K. Grendyszyński, 1897.

Pulzer, Peter. *The Rise of Political Anti-Semitism in Germany and Austria*. Rev. ed. London: Peter Halban, 1988.

Radlińska, Helena. "Wspomnienia uczennicy i nauczycielki," *Niepodległość*, 5 (1932): 321–42.

Reddaway, W. F., et al., eds. *The Cambridge History of Poland*. Cambridge, England: Cambridge University Press, 1951.

Reeves, Marjorie, and Warwick Gould, *Joachim of Fiore and the Myth of the Eternal Evangel in the Nineteenth Century*. Oxford: Clarendon Press, 1987.

Rémond, René. *The Right Wing in France: From 1815 to de Gaulle*. Translated by James M. Laux. Philadelphia: University of Pennsylvania Press, 1966.

Renan, Ernest. *Qu'est-ce qu'une Nation?* Paris: R. Helleu, 1934.

Riasanovsky, Nicholas V. *A History of Russia*. 4th ed. New York: Oxford University Press, 1984.

Richter, Melvin. *The Politics of Conscience: T. H. Green and His Age*. Cambridge, Mass.: Harvard University Press, 1964.

Le Rider, Jacques. *Modernity and Crisis of Identity: Culture and Society in Fin-de-Siècle Vienna*. Translated by Rosemary Morris. New York: Continuum, 1993.

Robertson, John M. *Buckle and His Critics: A Study in Sociology*. London: Swan Sonnenschein, 1895.

Roman Dmowski: przyczynki-przemówienia. Poznań: Głos, n.d.

Rudzki, Jerzy. *Aleksander Świętochowski i pozytywizm warszawski*. Warsaw: Państwowe Wydawnictwo Naukowe, 1968.

Rumney, Jay. *Herbert Spencer's Sociology*. New York: Atherton, 1966.

Ruskiewicz, Tomasz, ed. *Księga pamiątkowa Kielczan, 1856–1904*. Warsaw: Nakładem Uczestników Zjazdu, 1925.

———. *Tajny związek młodzieży polskiej w latach 1887–1893*. Warsaw: Drukarnia Przemysłowa, 1926.

Rzewuski, Henryk. *Listopad: romans historyczny z drugiej połowy wieku XVIII*. Kraków: Krakowska Spółka Wydawnicza, 1923.

———. *Pamiątki imci pana Seweryna Soplicy*. London: Veritas, 1955.

———. *Pamiętniki Bartłomeja Michałowskiego*. Petersburg: B. M. Wolff, 1856.

———. *Pisma*. Petersburg: B. M. Wolff, 1851.

Sadowski, Lesław. *Polska inteligencja prowincjonalna i jej ideowe dylematy na przełomie XIX i XX wieku*. Warsaw: Państwowe Wydawnictwo Naukowe, 1988.

Schieder, Theodor. *Nationalismus und Nationalstaat: Studien zum nationalen Problem im modernen Europa*. Göttingen: Vandenhoeck & Ruprecht, 1991.

Schmidt, Mieczysław. *Wspomnienia: młodzież z przed 50-ciu lat*. Warsaw: F. Hoesick, 1929.

Semmel, Bernard. "H. T. Buckle: The Liberal Faith and the Science of History." *British Journal of Sociology*, 17 (September 1976): 370–86.

———. *The Liberal Ideal and the Demons of Empire: Theories of Imperialism from Adam Smith to Lenin*. Baltimore: Johns Hopkins, 1993.

Seten-Watson, Hugh. *Nations and States*. Boulder, Col.: Westview Press, 1977.

Seyda, Marian. *Z zagadnień polityki demokratyczno-narodowej*. London: Richard Madley, Ltd., 1946.

Shafer, Boyd C. *Faces of Nationalism: New Realities and Old Myths*. New York: Harcourt Brace Jovanovich, 1972.

Simon, Walter M. *European Positivism in the Nineteenth Century: An Essay in Intellectual History*. Ithaca: Cornell University Press, 1962.

Singer, Brian C. J. "Cultural versus Contractual Nations: Rethinking Their Opposition." *History and Theory*, 35 (October 1996): 309–37.

Skurnowicz, Joan S. *Romantic Nationalism and Liberalism: Joachim Lelewel and the Polish National Idea*. Boulder, Col.: East European Monographs, 1981.

Słowiński, Lech. *Z myślą o Niepodległej: z dziejów edukacji narodowej okresu postyczniowego*. Poznań: Wydawnictwo ABOS, 1993.

Smith, Anthony D. *The Ethnic Origins of Nations*. New York: Basil Blackwell, 1986.

———. *National Identity*. Las Vegas: University of Nevada Press, 1991.

———. *Theories of Nationalism*. London: Duckworth, 1971.

Snyder, Timothy. *Nationalism, Marxism, and Modern Central Europe: A Biography of Kazimierz Kelles-Krauz (1872–1905)*. Cambridge, Mass.: Harvard Papers in Ukrainian Studies, 1997.

Soja, Edward. "History: Geography: Modernity." In *The Cultural Studies Reader*. Edited by Simon During. New York: Routledge, 1993.

Sorkin, David. *The Transformation of German Jewry, 1780–1840*. New York: Oxford, 1987.

Spencer, Herbert. *Herbert Spencer on Social Evolution: Selected Writings*. Edited by J. D. Y. Peel. Chicago: University of Chicago Press, 1972.

———. *Illustrations of Universal Progress: A Series of Discussions*. New York: D. Appleton and Company, 1865.

———. *Jednostka wobec państwa*. Warsaw: A. Gruszecki, 1886.

———. *Klassyfikacya wiedzy*. Translated by A. Nal. Warsaw: Przegląd Tygodniowy, 1873.

———. *O wychowaniu umysłowem, moralnem, i fizycznem*. Translated by Michał Siemiradzki. Warsaw: Gebethner i Wolff, 1879.

———. *Pierwsze zasady*. Translated by J. K. Potocki. Warsaw: Wydawnictwo Głosu, 1886.

———. *The Principles of Psychology*. New York: D. Appleton, 1920.

———. *The Principles of Sociology*. 3rd ed. New York: D. Appleton, 1897.

———. *Social Statics, or the Conditions Essential to Human Happiness Specified and the First of Them Developed*. London: John Chapman, 1851.

———. *The Study of Sociology*. Ann Arbor: University of Michigan Press, 1961.

———. *Szkice filozoficzne*. Warsaw: Wydawnictwo Imienia T. T. Jeża, 1883.

———. *Wstęp do socjologji*. Translated by Henryk Goldberg. Warsaw: Gebethner i Wolff, 1884.

———. *Zasady Etyki*. Translated by Jan Karłowicz. Warsaw: Spółka Nakładowa Warszawska, 1884.

———. *Zasady Socyologii*. Translated by J. K. Potocki. Warsaw: Wydawnictwo Głosu, 1889–90.

"Sprawozdanie Zygmunta Balickiego, złożone Centralizacji Związku Zagranicznego Socjalistów Polskich." *Niepodległość*, 7 (1933): 282–83.

St. Aubyn, Giles. *A Victorian Eminence: The Life and Works of H. T. Buckle*. London: Barrie Books, 1958.

Stefanowska, Zofia. *Swojskość i cudzoziemszczyzna w dziejach kultury polskiej*. Warsaw: Państwowe Wydawnictwo Naukowe, 1973.

Stephens, Sharon. "Children and Nationalism," *Childhood*, 4 (1997): 7.

Stern, Fritz. *The Politics of Cultural Despair*. Berkeley: University of California Press, 1961.

Sternhell, Zeev. *Neither Right nor Left: Fascist Ideology in France*. Translated by David Maisel. Princeton: Princeton University Press, 1986.

————. "Paul Déroulède and the Origins of Modern French Nationalism." *The Journal of Contemporary History*, 6, no. 4 (1971): 46–71.

Sternhell, Zeev, with Mario Sznajder and Maia Asheri. *The Birth of Fascist Ideology: From Cultural Rebellion to Political Revolution*. Translated by David Maisel. Princeton: Princeton University Press, 1994.

Strauss, Herbert A., ed. *Hostages of Modernization: Studies on Modern Antisemitism, 1870–1933/39*. Berlin and New York: Walter de Gruyter, 1993.

Studnicki, Władysław. *Od socyalizmu do nacyonalizmu*. Lwów: Towarzystwo Wydawnicze, 1904.

Sugar, Peter F., ed. *Eastern European Nationalism in the Twentieth Century*. Washington, D.C.: American University Press, 1995.

Sugar, Peter F., and Ivo Lederer, eds. *Nationalism in Eastern Europe*. Seattle: University of Washington Press, 1969.

Suleja, Włodzimierz. *Polska Partia Socjalistyczna, 1892–1948: zarys dziejów*. Warsaw: Wydawnictwo Szkolne i Pedagogiczne, 1988.

Sullivan, Eileen P. "Liberalism and Imperialism: J. S. Mill's Defense of the British Empire," *Journal of the History of Ideas*, 44 (October 1983): 599–617.

Supiński, Józef. *Pisma*. 3rd ed. Warsaw: Gebethner i Wolff, 1883.

Surzycki, Stefan. *Kartka z dziejów rosyjskiego wychowania państwowego w Polsce*. Warsaw: Myśl Narodowa, 1933.

————. *Z dziejów pamiętnego 'Zetu.'* Kraków: Myśl Narodowa, 1930.

Sussex, Roland, and J. C. Eade, eds. *Culture and Nationalism in Nineteenth-Century Eastern Europe*. Columbus, Ohio: Slavica, 1985.

Świętochowski, Aleksander. *Liberum veto*. Edited by Samuel Sandler. Warsaw: Państwowy Instytut Wydawniczy, 1976.

————. *Publicystyka społeczna i oświatowa*. Edited by Zenon Kmiecik. Warsaw: Ludowa Spółdzielnia Wydawnicza, 1987.

————. *Wspomnienia*. Edited by Samuel Sandler. Wrocław: Ossolineum, 1966.

Symmons-Symonolewicz, Konstantin. *National Consciousness in Poland: Origin and Evolution*. Meadville, Penn.: Maplewood Press, 1983.

Szacki, Jerzy. *Ojczyzna, naród, rewolucja: problematyka narodowa w polskiej myśli szlacheckorewolucyjnej*. Warsaw: Państwowy Instytut Wydawniczy, 1962.

Szujski, Józef. *Dzieła Józefa Szujskiego*. Kraków: Anczyc i Spółka, 1885.

Szwarc, Andrzej. *Od Wielopolskiego do Stronnictwa Polityki Realnej: zwolennicy ugody z Rosją, ich poglądy i próby działalności politycznej (1864–1905)*. Warsaw: Uniwersytet Warszawski, 1990.

Talmon, J. L. *The Myth of the Nation and the Vision of Revolution: The Origins of Ideological Polarization in the Twentieth Century*. Berkeley: University of California Press, 1980.

————. *Political Messianism: The Romantic Phase*. New York: Frederick A. Praeger, 1960.

Targalski, Jerzy. *Ludwik Waryński: próba życia*. Warsaw: Książka i Wiedza, 1976.

Taylor, M. W. *Men versus the State: Herbert Spencer and Late Victorian Individualism*. Oxford: Clarendon Press, 1992.

Tazbir, Janusz, ed. *Zarys historii Polski*. Warsaw: Państwowy Instytut Wydawniczy, 1980.

Thaden, Edward C. *Conservative Nationalism in Nineteenth-Century Russia*. Seattle: University of Washington Press, 1964.

Topolski, Jerzy. *An Outline History of Poland*. Translated by Olgierd Wojtasiewicz. Warsaw: Interpress, 1986.

Toporowski, Lorraine F. E. "The Origins of the National Democratic Party 1886–1903: A Study in Polish Nationalism." Doctoral dissertation, Columbia University, 1973.

Toruńczyk, Barbara. *Narodowa Demokracja: antologia myśli politycznej 'Przeglądu Wszech-polskiego,' 1895–1905.* London: Aneks, 1983.

Tradycje liberalne w Polsce. Warsaw: Wydawnictwo DiG, 1993.

Ujejski, Józef. *Dzieje polskiego mesjanizmu do powstania listopadowego włącznie.* Lwów: Ossolineum, 1931.

Ulam, Adam B. *In the Name of the People: Prophets and Conspirators in Prerevolutionary Russia.* New York: Viking Press, 1977.

Van der Veer, Peter, ed. *Conversion to Modernities: The Globalization of Christianity.* New York: Routledge, 1996.

Venturi, Franco. *Roots of Revolution: A History of the Populist and Socialist Movements in Nineteenth Century Russia.* Translated by Francis Haskell. New York: Grosset and Dunlap, 1960.

Verdery, Katherine. *National Ideology under Socialism: Identity and Cultural Politics in Ceauşescu's Romania.* Berkeley: University of California Press, 1991.

Volkov, Shulamit. *The Rise of Popular Antimodernism in Germany: The Urban Master Artisans, 1873–1896.* Princeton: Princeton University Press, 1978.

Walicki, Andrzej. *The Controversy over Capitalism: Studies in the Social Philosophy of the Russian Populists.* Oxford: Clarendon Press, 1969.

———. "Czy możliwy jest nacjonalizm liberalny?" *Znak,* 502 (March 1997): 32–50.

———. *The Enlightenment and the Birth of Modern Nationhood: Polish Political Thought from Noble Republicanism to Tadeusz Kościuszko.* Translated by Emma Harris. South Bend, Ind.: University of Notre Dame Press, 1989.

———. *A History of Russian Thought from the Enlightenment to Marxism.* Translated by Hilda Andrews-Rusiecka. Stanford, Cal.: Stanford University Press, 1973.

———. *Legal Philosophies of Russian Liberalism.* South Bend, Ind.: Notre Dame University Press, 1992.

———. *Między filozofią, religią, i polityką: studia o myśli polskiej epoki romantyzmu.* Warsaw: Państwowy Instytut Wydawniczy, 1983.

———. "Nikolai Chernyshevsky and the 'Enlighteners' of the Sixties." In *A History of Russian Thought from the Enlightenment to Marxism.* Translated by Hilda Andrews-Rusiecka. Stanford, Cal.: Stanford University Press, 1973.

———. *Philosophy and Romantic Nationalism: The Case of Poland.* Oxford: Clarendon Press, 1982.

———. *Poland between East and West: The Controversies over Self-Definition and Modernization in Partitioned Poland.* Cambridge, Mass.: Harvard Ukrainian Research Institute, 1994.

———. "Polish Romantic Messianism: Revolution, Hero-Worship and the 'New Revelation.'" Unpublished paper delivered in Tulsa, Oklahoma, April 1992.

———. *Polska, Rosja, Marksizm: studia z dziejów marksizmu i jego recepcji.* Warsaw: Książka i Wiedza, 1983.

———. "Rosa Luxemburg and the Question of Nationalism in Polish Marxism (1893–1914)." *Slavic and East European Review,* 61 (October 1983): 565–82.

———. *The Three Traditions in Polish Patriotism and Their Contemporary Relevance.* Bloomington, Ind.: The Polish Studies Center, 1988.

———, ed. *Filozofia i myśl społeczna w latach 1831–1864.* Warsaw: Państwowy Wydawnictwo Naukowe, 1977.

———, ed. *Polska myśl filozoficzna i społeczna, 1831–1863.* Warsaw: Książka i Wiedza, 1973.

———, ed. *Zarys dziejów filozofii polskiej, 1815–1918.* Warsaw: Państwowe Wydawnictwo Naukowe, 1986.

Wandycz, Piotr. *The Lands of Partitioned Poland, 1795–1918*. Seattle: University of Washington Press, 1974.

Wapiński, Roman. "Elita Endecka: przyczynek do dziejów kształtowania się grup przywódczych polskich partii politycznych." *Acta Universitatis Wratislaviensis*, 543 (1981): 441–52.

———. "Endecka koncepcja państwa." *Dzieje Najnowsze*, 1 (1969): 148–58.

———. *Narodowa Demokracja 1893–1939*. Wrocław: Ossolineum, 1980.

———. "Pokolenia Drugiej Rzeczypospolitej." *Kwartalnik Historyczny*, 3 (1983): 483–504.

———. *Pokolenia Drugiej Rzeczypospolitej*. Wrocław: Ossolineum, 1991.

———. *Roman Dmowski*. Lublin: Wydawnictwo Lubelskie, 1988.

———. "Z dziejów tendencji nacjonalistycznych: o stanowisku narodowej demokracji wobec kwestii narodowej w latach 1893–1939." *Kwartalnik Historyczny*, 80 (1973): 828–39.

Warzenica, Ewa. *Pozytywistyczny 'obóz młodych' wobec tradycji wielkiej polskiej poezji romantycznej (lata 1866–1881)*. Warsaw: Państwowe Wydawnictwo Naukowe, 1968.

Wasilewski, Zygmunt. *Pokolenia w służbie narodu*. London: Katolicki Ośrodek Wydawniczy, 1962.

———. *Pomnik Mickiewicza w Warszawie, 1897–1898*. Warsaw: Komitet Budowy Pomnika, 1899.

———. *Śladami Mickiewicza: szkice i przyczynki do dziejów romantyzmu*. Lwów: Towarzystwo Wydawnicze, 1905.

———. *Współcześni: charakterystyki pisarzy i dzieł*. Warsaw: Gebethner i Wolff, 1923.

Wasiutyński, Wojciech. *Czwarte pokolenie: szkice z dziejów nacjonalizmu polskiego*. London: Odnowa, 1982.

Weber, Eugene, and Hans Rogger, eds. *The European Right: A Historical Profile*. Berkeley: University of California Press, 1965.

Weeks, Theodore R. *Nation and State in Late Imperial Russia: Nationalism and Russification on the Western Frontier, 1863–1914*. Dekalb, Ill.: Northern Illinois University Press, 1996.

Weiler, Peter. *The New Liberalism: Liberal Social Theory in Great Britain, 1889–1914*. New York: Garland Publishing, 1982.

Weiss, Tomasz. *Romantyczna genealogia polskiego modernizmu: rekonesans*. Warsaw: Państwowy Instytut Wydawniczy, 1974.

Wiltshire, David. *The Social and Political Thought of Herbert Spencer*. Oxford: Oxford University Press, 1978.

Wojciechowski, Stanisław. *Moje wspomnienia*. Lwów and Warsaw: Książnica–Atlas, 1938.

Wojnar, K. "Ze wspomnień i przeżyć 1888–1908." *Niepodległość*, 18 (1938): 379–457.

Wolikowska, Izabela z Lutosławskich. *Roman Dmowski: człowiek, Polak, przyjaciel*. Chicago: Komitet Wydawniczego, 1961.

Wolsza, Tadeusz, and Anna Żarnowska, eds. *Społeczeństwo i polityka: dorastanie do demokracji: kultura polityczna w Królestwie Polskim na początku XX wieku*. Warsaw: Wydawnictwo DiG, 1993.

Wołyński, Jan. *Wspomnienia z czasów szkolnictwa rosyjskiego w b. Królestwie Polskiem, 1868–1915*. Warsaw: Published by the author, 1936.

Woodward, Susan L. *Balkan Tragedy: Chaos and Dissolution after the Cold War*. Washington, D.C.: The Brookings Institution, 1995.

Wortman, Richard. *The Crisis of Russian Populism*. Cambridge, England: Cambridge University Press, 1967.

Wroczyński, Ryszard. *Pozytywizm warszawski: zarys dziejów oraz wybór publicystyki i krytyki*. Warsaw: Państwowe Zakłady Wydawnictw Szkolnych, 1948.

Wroński, Andrzej. *Duchowieństwo i Kościół katolicki w Królestwie Polskim wobec sprawy narodowej w latach 1832–1860*. Warsaw: Wydawnictwo Neriton, 1994.

Wyka, Kazimierz. *Młoda Polska*. Kraków: Wydawnictwo Literackie, 1987.

———. *Teka Stańczyka na tle historii Galicji w latach 1849–1869*. Wrocław: Ossolineum, 1951.

Wzdulski, Konstanty. *Żydzi polscy w świetle prawdy*. Warsaw: Drukarnia Stanisława Niemiery, 1887.

Young, Robert M. "Herbert Spencer and 'Inevitable' Progress." *History Today*, 37 (August 1987): 18–22.

Z dzisiejszej doby III: z powodu artykułu p. Wsiewoloda Krestowskiego w Nrze. 221 'Warszawskiego Dniewnika.' Kraków: Paweł Madejski, 1893.

Z dzisiejszej doby IV: o święcie 'trzeciego maja' i o obchodach narodowych w ogóle. Kraków: Paweł Madejski, 1893.

Z dzisiejszej doby V: w trzydziestą rocznicę powstania styczniowego: kilka słów o polityce narodowej. Kraków: Paweł Madejski, 1893.

Z dzisiejszej doby VI: kilka słów o stanowisku rządu rosyjskiego wobec naszych ruchów robotniczych. Kraków: Paweł Madejski, 1893.

Z dzisiejszej doby VII: polityka rządu względem kościoła. Lwów: Edward Webersfeld, 1893.

Z dzisiejszej doby VIII: gorzka prawda. Lwów: Edward Webersfeld, 1893.

Z dzisiejszej doby IX: warszawska młodzież uniwersytecka. n.p.: 1894.

Z dzisiejszej doby X: po manifestacyi 17 kwietnia. Lwów: Wojciech Dąbrowski, 1894.

Z dzisiejszej doby XI: ugoda czy walka? Lwów: Wojciech Dąbrowski, 1895.

Z pola walki: zbiór materyałów tyczących się polskiego ruchu socyalistycznego. London: Wydawnictwo Polskiej Partyi Socyalistycznej, 1904.

Zaionchkovskii, Petr A. *The Abolition of Serfdom in Russia*. Edited and translated by Susan Wobst. Gulf Breeze, Fla.: Academic International Press, 1978.

Żarnowska, Anna. *Robotnicy Warszawy na przełomie XIX i XX wieku*. Warsaw: Państwowy Instytut Wydawniczy, 1985.

Żbikowski, Andrzej, ed. *Dzieje Żydów w Polsce: ideologia antysemicka, 1848–1914. Wybór tekstów źródłowych*. Warsaw: Żydowski Instytut Historyczny w Polsce, 1994.

Zeldin, Theodore. *France, 1848–1945*. Oxford: Clarendon Press, 1973.

Żeromski, Stefan. *Dzienniki (wybór)*. Edited by Jerzy Kądziela. Wrocław: Ossolineum, 1980.

Zieliński, Andrzej. *Naród i narodowość w polskiej literaturze i publicystyce lat 1815–1831*. Wrocław: Ossolineum, 1969.

Zieliński, Henryk. ed. *Na warsztatach historyków polskiej myśli politycznej*. Wrocław: Ossolineum, 1980.

Zimand, Roman. *Dekadentyzm warszawski*. Warsaw: Państwowy Instytut Wydawniczy, 1964.

———. "Uwagi o teorii narodu na marginesie analizy nacjonalistycznej teorii narodu." *Studia Filozoficzne*, 4 (1967): 3–39.

Żurawicka, Janina. "Lud w ideologii 'Głosu' (1886–1894)." *Kwartalnik Historyczny*, 4–5 (1956): 316–40.

———. "Zespół redakcji 'Głosu' (1886–1894)." *Rocznik Historii Czasopiśmiennictwa Polskiego*, 1 (1962): 155–83.

Zweig, Stefan. *The World of Yesterday*. New York: The Viking Press, 1943.

Żychowski, Marian. *Polska myśl socjalistyczna XIX i XX wieku (do 1918 roku)*. Warsaw: Państwowe Wydawnictwo Naukowe, 1976.

———, ed. *Studia z dziejów myśli społecznej i kwestii robotniczej w XIX wieku*. Warsaw: Państwowe Wydawnictwo Naukowe, 1964.

Index